Karnataka Government and Politics

ABOUT THE EDITORS

Dr. Harish Ramaswamy has over 19 years of experience in teaching and research in the Post-graduate Department of Political Science both at the University of Mysore, Mysore and at Karnataka University, Dharwad, Karnataka, India. Presently, he is a Senior Reader in the Department of Political Science.

He is the author of over 20 research publications and has reviewed several books. He has completed projects of University Grants Commission, Minor Projects funded by UGC and Projects of Government of Karnataka (through Institute of Social and Economic Change, Nagarabhavi, Bangalore) for pojects on Election Studies, 1996, 1998 and 1999, conducted through C.S.D.C., Delhi (with Lokanithi Group).

He has authored a concise but insightful book 'Distance Education', and is currently editing books on 'Human Rights in Karnataka, Diplomacy and Terrorism and their Interdependence' (with co-authors).

S.S. Patagundi (b. 1953) is a Professor of Political Science at the Karnataka University, Dharwad, India. Earlier, he was a faculty in Political Science at the Lingaraj College, Belgaum. He has worked as Chariman of the Post-graduate Department of Political Science, Karnataka University, Dharwad for two terms from 1998 to 2000 and 2004 to 2006. Also, he is the Secretary of the Indian Institute of Public Administration, Local Branch, Dharwad. Prof. Patagundi is the author of two books, *Political Parties, Party System and Foreign Policy of India* (1987), and *India's Foreign Policy: An Elitist Perception* (1995) and co-author of two books, *Outlines of Political Science Vol. II* (1988) and *Political Analysis* (1997). He has published 27 papers in various reputed journals. He has completed three research projects sponsored by the ICSSR, New Delhi (1993), Karnatak-University, Dharwad (1996) and Public Affairs Centre, Bangalore (2005). He participated in the 19th IPSA World Congress held in Durban (South Africa) in June 2003 and 20th IPSA World Congress held in Fukuoka (Japan) in July 2006.

Dr. S.H. Patil was formerly a Professor of Political Science at Karnataka University, Dharwad. He has many books to his credit including *The Congress Party and Princely States; Gandhi and Swaraj; A Text Book of Political Thought (Plato to Machievelli); Modern Western Political Thought (Hobbes to Laski); Central Grants and State Autonomy; Political Analysis (Co-author); Bharatadalli Dharmani-rapekshe (Secularism in India); Bharatad Swatantra Mattu Kranataka Ekikaran: Lingayatar Patra* (The Rule of the Lingayats in the Freedom Movement and Karnataka Ekikaran (Co-editor); and *Community Dominance and Political Modernsation: The Lingayats*. His lessons are published in the form of three books by the Bangalore University and changing bases of Federal Units in India. He has also published thrity papers in many journals of repute. His thirty-nine articles have been published in Kannada newspapers. His thirty-four discussions and talks have been broadcast from All India Radio, Dharwad, He has reviewed some books in journals and newspapers. He has participated in several regional and national conferences and seminars.

KARNATAKA
Government and Politics

Harish Ramaswamy
S.S. Patagundi
S.H. Patil

CONCEPT PUBLISHING COMPANY, NEW DELHI-110059

Cataloging in Publication Data—DK
Courtesy: D.K. Agencies (P) Ltd. <docinfo@dkagencies.com>

Karnataka government and politics / [edited by]
Harish Ramaswamy, S.S. Patagundi, S.H. Patil.
p. cm.
Includes bibliographical references.
Includes index.
ISBN 818069397X

1. Karnataka (India)—Politics and government. 2. Political participation—India—Karnataka. I. Harish, R. (Ramaswamy), 1960- II. Patagundi, S. S., 1953- III. Patil, S. H. (Shankaragouda Hanamantagouda), 1936-

DDC 320.954 87 22

ISBN 81-8069-397-X

First Published 2007

Published and Printed by
Ashok Kumar Mittal
Concept Publishing Company,
A/15-16, Commercial Block, Mohan Garden,
New Delhi-110059 (INDIA)

Phones : 25351460, 25351794
Fax : 091-11-25357103
Email : publishing@conceptpub.com

Dedicated to our teacher
Professor K. Raghavendara Rao

Preface

State politics constitute a major part of Government and Politics in general. The nature and problems of state politics are not homogenous. In view of this understanding of individual State Government and the politics becomes significant.

A survey of literature relating to State Government and politics indicates inadequacy of material required for its understanding. In the context of Karnataka, this is all the more true. For overcoming this inadequacy of literature, the Department of Political Science at Karnatak University, Dharwad, under the leadership of the Late Professor G. S. Halappa, brought out a book on *State Administration in Karnataka.* This is an important contribution. It contributed greatly to overcome the inadequacy of literature relating to Karnataka Government and politics. In spite of this the available literature is not enough. Keeping this in mind, the Department of Political Science has taken the initiative in collecting articles on various topics of contemporary relevance for better understanding of Karnataka Government and politics. However, this may not fulfil the entire lacunae found in this area of study; but, nevertheless, this volume makes a substantive contribution.

Perhaps, these various perspectives on different themes indicate the comprehensiveness of our study and our concern for getting these selected papers to provide a platform for understanding the subject both descriptively and analytically with the hope that it will fulfil the requirements of post-graduate students and researchers. Though the project was started years ago, the delay is primarily due to our preoccupation with various other academic activities. Though late, the volume is now in your hands for your review.

We express our sense of gratitude to all the contributors for their promptness in responding to our invitation. We thank our colleagues in the Department for encouraging us to complete this work. We are grateful to Prof. A.A. Mutalik-Desai, retired Professor of English, IIT, Mumbai, for his help in editing this work from the language view point.

We take this opportunity to thank the librarian and other staff members of the Karnatak University, Dharwad, for their kind support. We also thank the University authorities for encouraging us to undertake such academic work and complete it.

HARISH RAMASWAMY
S. S. PATAGUNDI
S. H. PATIL

Contents

Preface *vii*

Contributiors *xiii*

Introduction *xv*

1. Karnataka 1
K. Raghavendra Rao and *A.M. Rajasekharaiah*

2. Geography of Karnataka 22
Y.M. Madar and *B. Hyamavathi Reddy*

3. The Emergence of Modern Karnataka: History, Myth and Ideology 30
K. Raghavendra Rao

4. Karnataka's Political Culture: Reflections on a Soft State 43
R.L.M. Patil

5. Office of the Chief Minister 57
S.A. Palekar

6. Evolution of the Office of the Speaker in Karnataka 64
K.F. Pawar

7. Judiciary in Karnataka 94
I. Sharath Babu

8. The Leader of the Opposition in Karnataka Legislative Council, 1995-1998: A Functional Analysis 109
Vijayakumar N. Torgal

9. The Functions of Public Service Commission 119
Okaly B.B. Patil

10. The Karnataka Government Secretariat 146
Vijayakumar N. Torgal

11. Urban Government and Politics 161
S.A. Javeed

12. Panchayati Raj in Karnataka: An Empirical Evaluation 173
A.T. Kittur and *Harish Ramaswamy*

13. Representation of Women in Local Government with Special Reference to Karnataka 192
(Smt.) Malavika M. Deshpande and *S.S. Patagundi*

14. District Administration in Karnataka: Prospect and Retrospect 206
S.M. Jaamdar

15. Socio-Economic Bases of Karnataka Politics: A Historical Survey 228
S.H. Patil

16. Party System in Karnataka 245
S.S. Patagundi

17. Tenth Assembly Elections in Karnataka: An Analysis 259
H.M. Rajashekara

18. Citizens' Awareness of their Elected Representatives 269
Sandeep Shastri and *Harish Ramaswamy*

19. Change of Priorities in Planning: Karnataka 279
D.M. Nanjundappa

20. The Karnataka Right to Information Act, 2000 302
B.K. Chandrashekar

21. New Social Movements in Karnataka: History, Strategies and Discourses 312
Muzaffar Assadi

22. Impact of Language on Karnataka Politics 333
Midatala Rani

23. Communal Issues and Minorities 349
Mumtaz Ali Khan

24. Demand for Separate State—Issues and Problems: A Study of Hyderabad Karnataka 361
Chandrakant Yatanoor

25. Movement for Statehood in Kodagu 377
P.E. Somaiah

26. Backward Classes and Minorities in Karnataka Politics 397
V.K. Natraj

27. Karnataka Land Reforms: Political-Administrative Dynamics and Economic Change 414
S.V. Deshpande

28. The Press and State Politics 428
K.V. Nagaraj

Index 436

Contributors

Assadi, Muzaffar, Professor of Political Science, University of Mysore, Mysore.

Babu, I. Sharath, Professor of Law, Department of Law, Karnataka University, Dharwad.

Chandrashekar, B.K., Minister of State for Information and Publicity, Government of Karnataka, Bangalore.

Deshpande, (Smt.) Malavika M., Principal, SJMVS Arts and Commerce Pre-University College for Women, Hubli.

Deshpande, S.V., Population Study Centre, Bangalore.

Jaamdar, S.M., Commissioner (Resettlement and Land Acquisition) and Ex-officio Secretary to Karnataka Government, Revenue Department, Upper Krishna Project, Bagalkot.

Javeed, S.A., Reader, Department of Studies in Political Science, Kuvempu University, Shimoga.

Khan, Mumtaz Ali, 18, 1st C, Main Road, Behind HMT Bhavan, Gangenahalli Extension, Bangalore.

Kittur, A.T., Reader, Department of Political Science, Karnataka University, Dharwad.

Madar, Y.M., Professor of Geography, Karnataka University, Dharwad.

Nagaraj, K.V., Chairman, Department of Mass Communication and Journalism, Mangalore University, Mangalore.

Nanjundappa, D.M., Deputy Chairman, State Planning Board, Government of Karnataka, Bangalore.

Natraj, V.K., Currently Director, Madras Institute of Development Studies.

Palekar, S.A., Reader, Department of Political Science, Gulbarga University, Gulbarga.

Patagundi, S.S., Professor and Chairman, Department of Political Science, Karnataka University, Dharwad.

Patil, Okaly B.B., Member, Karnataka State Public Service Commission, Bangalore.

Patil, R.L.M., Professor and Head, Department of Political Science, Bangalore University, Bangalore.

Patil, S.H., Professor of Political Science (Retired), Karnataka University, Dharwad.

Pawar, K.F., Department of Political Science, G.I. Bagewadi Degree College, Nipani.

Rajasekharaiah, A.M., Professor of Political Science (Retd.), Karnatak University, Dharwad.

Rajashekara, H.M., Professor and Director, Academic Staff College, University of Mysore, Mysore.

Ramaswamy, Harish, Reader, Department of Political Science, Karnatak University, Dharwad.

Rani, Midatala, Reader in Political Science, University of Mysore, Mysore.

Rao, K. Raghavendra, Professor of Political Science (Retd.), Mangalore University, Mangalore.

Reddy, B. Hyamavathi, Reader (Retd.) Department of Geography, Karnataka University, Dharwad.

Shastri, Sandeep, Director, IACT, Hebbal, Bangalore.

Somaiah, P.E., Lecturer in Political Science, St. Joseph's College, Bangalore.

Torgal, Vijayakumar N., Private Secretary to the Hon'ble Minister for Major and Medium Irrigation, Government of Karnataka, Bangalore.

Yatanoor, Chandrakant, Reader in Political Science, Gulbarga University, Gulbarga.

Introduction

There was nothing like a united Karnataka and a united study of Karnataka Government and Politics before 1st November, 1956. The Kannada-speaking areas were divided into nineteen varied administrative units till then. These were: (I) Bombay Province, (II) Madras Province, (III) Princely State of Mysore, (IV) Princely State of Hyderabad, (V) Chief Commissioner Province of Coorg, (VI) Princely State of Kolhapur, (VII) Princely State of Sangli, (VIII) Princely State of Miraj (Senior), (IX) Princely State of Miraj (Junior), (X) Princely State of Kurandawad (Senior), (XI) Princely State of Kurandawad (Junior), (XII) Princely State of Jamakhandi, (XIII) Princely State of Mudhol, (XIV) Princely State of Ramadurg, (XV) Princely State of Jath, (XVI) Princely State of Akkalkot, (XVII) Princely State of Aundh, Princely State of Savanur and (XIX) Princely State of Sondur. To a great extent the Kannada speaking areas from these units were united into a single administrative unit (called New Mysore and later Karnataka) on 1st November, 1956, under the recommendation of the States Reorganisation Commission, by an Indian Parliamentary Act and as a result of a long struggle carried on by the Kannada speaking people in these nineteen units.

Kannada language received primacy; a uniform administrative system was set up and common political structure and political process came into existence in the united Karnataka. thus, in due course of forty eight years (1956-2004), united and uniform political structures like offices/institutions of Governor, chief minister, council of ministers, legislative assembly, legislative council, bureaucracy, political parties, urban and rural self-governing institutions, co-operative societies, etc., were established. Within this decorative institutional setup, political process in Karnataka is being influenced by socio-economic, cultural and educational associations and pressure groups, interest aggregation and interest articulation by these pressure groups, politics of regional imbalances, style of functioning of the chief ministers belonging to different caste and political parties, factional politics of various political parties, ambitions of dominant castes and communities, rising expectations of backward castes, scheduled castes, scheduled tribes and minorities in sharing the common cake, emergence of new leadership and new elite class at various levels from difference sections of the society, linguistic politics, border and inter-state water disputes, centre-state relations, socio-economic agendas of political parties, evolution of democratic culture of the masses and the mobilization of the masses for various purposes, etc. Thus, these socio-economic and political issues have been influencing the political process in Karnataka which is constantly in the process of change and evolution. In view of competitive and bargaining politics by various socio-economic and political groups, the politics of Karnataka is dynamic and never sterile and stereotype. It has set trends in radical land reforms, reservation for weaker sections and wider public space for them. Thus, Karnataka evolved its own identity not only on the basis of its dominant Kannada language but also by the various new trends of development, including information technology.

Though vast literature has come about Indian Government and politics, there are only a few works on state politics including Karnataka Government and politics. There is no comprehensive work on Karnataka. Though the late Prof. G. S. Halappa of the Department of Political Science, Karnatak University, Dharwad, had brought out an edited work, *Studies in State Administration,* in the early 1960s, it mainly dealt with administrative dimensions. There have been stray articles on Karnataka Government and politics by our own and foreign scholars. A few scholars have also done research on the political process and the institutions. However, there is a need for a comprehensive and unified work on Karnataka Government and politics. Though we made serious attempts to collect articles covering all the dimensions of the subject, we succeeded to a greater extent. However, we are happy that we are able to present at least glimpses if not the whole picture. In future editions we hope to do better.

Various articles show the dynamics of the functioning of political institutions and political processes going on in Karnataka within the theoretical framework of modernising and development oriented democratic political system.

Karnataka which is one of the units in the Indian federal system and is blessed with natural resources, vast land, sea coast, to ternate people, etc., has been making progress in all directions. Its leaders want it to be a model state.

The political process in Karnataka is influenced by the dominant castes and communities like the Lingayats and the Vokkaligas and a coalition of backward castes, scheduled castes, scheduled tribes and minorities. Political parties like the Indian National Congress, the Bharatiya Janata Party, the Janata Dal, etc., have been trying to penetrate into various caste constituencies by promising various facilities, perks and concessions. As a result of the increasing political socialization of various caste groups, the social composition of the political parties is heterogeneous to some extent. Various political institutions, at present, are controlled by the leaders belonging to the weaker sections of the society. Consequently, politics of these institutions are being increasingly formulated in favour of weaker sections. The dominant castes, have not taken such developments easily and have started voicing their grievances from public platforms. Thus, competition for public offices is on peacefully between dominant castes and the coalition of weaker sections within the democratic setup.

The purpose of this work is to provide a glimpse of the dynamics of the Karnataka Government and politics to the readers inside and outside out state.

The paper by K. Raghavendra Rao and A.M. Rajashekharaiah, on Karnataka discusses various institutions, namely, Chief Minister, Council of Members, State legislature, etc., thus introducing Karnataka in a nutshell from the historical perspective. The second paper by Y.M. Madar and Hymavathi Reddy on Geography of Karnataka gives a brief account of the geography of Karnataka. K. Raghavendra Rao's paper on Emergence of Modern Karnataka: History, Myth and Ideology examines the process by which modern Karnataka emerged.

R.L.M. Patil's paper on Karnataka's Political Culture: Reflections on a Soft State, presents a bird's eye-view of Karnataka's political culture. S.A. Palekar's paper outlines the position of the office of the Chief Minister. K.F. Pawar traces the origin and growth of office of the Speaker in Karnataka based on major events in the history of the state politics. I. Sharath Babhu's Judiciary in Karnataka examines the functional dimensions of the judiciary in Karnataka.

V.N. Torgal in his paper on the Lader of Opposition in Karnataka Legislative Council makes a functional analysis of the leader of the opposition and his role in state politics. Okaly B.B. Patil in his paper examines The Functions of Public Service Commission.

V.N. Torgal in his paper on Karnataka Government Secretariat discusses the structure and functioning of the secretariat in the state. S.A. Javeed's paper on Urban Government and Politics deals with urban government and politics with special reference to Mangalore Corporation.

The paper of M.M. Deshpande and S.S. Patagundi on Representation of Women in Local Government with Special Reference to Karnataka discusses the representation of women in local government.

Similarly A.T. Kittur and Harish Ramaswamy in their paper on Panchayati Raj in Karnataka throw light on the decentralized institutions in the state.

S.M. Jaamadar has contributed a scholarly paper on District Administration in Karnataka: Retrospect and Prospect. S.H. Patil's paper on Socio-Economic bases of Karnataka Politics: Historical Survey attempts to analyse the socio-economic bases of Karnataka Politics based on a historical survey. S.S. Patagundi's paper on Party System in Karnataka reviews the working of the party system. H.M. Rajashekara's paper analyses the Tenth Assembly Elections. Sandeep Shastri and Harish Ramaswamy in their paper empirically analyse the Citizen's Awareness about elected representatives.

D.M. Nanjundappa's paper on Change and Priorities in Planning in Karnataka evaluates the various dimensions of planning in the state. B.K. Chandrashekhar's The Karnataka Right to Information Act 2000 outlines the various provisions of Karnataka Right to Information Act, 2000.

Muzzafar Assadi, in his paper on New Social Movements in Karnataka History: Strategies and Discourses, attempts to analyse the social movements in Karnataka on the basis of history, strategies. Midatala Rani has written on the Impact of Language on Karnataka Politics. Mumtaz Ali Khan's article Communal Issues and Minorities contributes to an understanding of the implications of communal issues and minorities for Karnataka politics.

Chandrakant Yatnoor and P.V. Somaiah in their papers on Demand for Separate State Issues and Problems: A Study of

Hyderabad Karnataka and Movement for Statehood in Kodagu respectively attempt to understand the politics of separate statehood. V.K. Nataraj's paper on the Backward Classes and Minorities in Karnataka Politics make a critical survey of the movement. S.V. Deshpande in his paper on Karnataka Land Reforms: Political Administrative Dynamics and Economic Change makes an assessment of land reforms and their implementation in the context of political administrative process. K.V. Nagaraj's paper on Press and State Politics contributes to an understanding the role of the press Karnataka state politics.

1

Karnataka

K. RAGHAVENDRA RAO and A.M. RAJASEKHARAIAH

Modern Karnataka has a long and distinguished history. In the pre-colonial days and in the ancient or medieval times, it was known by various names such as Kannada, Kannadu, Kannadar, Karnate, Kuntala and Karnataka. There is no scholarly consensus on the exact connotation of the term, Karnataka. According to one group, it derives from *kar-nadu*, literally, black land and Karnataka is a Sanskritised form of this word. Others have held that it derives from *Karu-Nadu*, which means elevated land or country. Its boundaries also have been varying through its long evolution. According to one ancient text, the poetics entitled *Kavirajamarga*, which belongs to ninth century, that land of Karnataka stretched from Kaveri to Godavari.

Modern Karnataka, inhabited by the people who speak Kannada and are, therefore, known as Kannadigas, is situated between the latitude of 11° N and 19″ N, and longitudes of 74° E and 78° E, covering an area of some 6,500 sq. miles. Stretching for two hundred fifty miles from east to west and five hundred miles from north to south, it borders on Maharashtra on the north, Andhra and Tamil Nadu on the east and south, and Kerala and the Arabian Sea on the south-west.

The present territorial boundaries have crystallised through a long process of historical evolution. After the last Mysore War of 1799, resulting in territorial acquisitions, all south Indian provinces came to be reorganised. The districts were divided between the British and their allies. This process taking place from 1800 to 1840 distributed the Kannada speaking population into a multitude of politico-administrative jurisdictions. As a result, Kannadigas found themselves as minority pockets in non-Kannada areas. The Kannada districts of Bidar, Gulbarga and Raichur were ceded to the Nizam's territory, while the northern districts of Belguam, Bijapur, Dharwad and North Kanara were annexed to the Bombay presidency. The districts of Bellary and South Kanara were joined to the Madras presidency. The small native state of Coorg was made a centrally adMinistered unit, and Mysore was maintained as a separate unit, a princely state.

Karnataka played a glorious part in the anti-colonial struggle against the British. Some of the great figures in this freedom struggle merit mention here. Belavadi Mallamma fought the British until her death in 1678. The great Rani of Kittur, Channamma waged a keen war against the British when she was refused permission to adopt a son. During the 1857 war of liberation there were legendary heroes like Sangolli Rayanna who fought the government, and are today sung in ballads. Another such hero was Babasaheb of Naragund. There were also militant groups like the hunting community of Bedars, from Halagali who resisted the British authority.

After Pax Britanica was estabished in the later part of the nineteenth century, the people of Karnataka were involved in two large-scale political movements—one, regional and the other, national. On the one hand, they participated actively in the Congress movement, both pre-Gandhian and Gandhian, in driving the British out of the country. On the other hand, they also organised successfully the Karnataka Ekikarana Movement or the Movement for Karnataka Unification, demanding that all the territories inhabited by Kannadigas should be reconstituted into a single province based on the principle of one language-one province. The people of Karnataka had been living under five separate jurisdictions: the Bombay province, the Madras province, the Chief Commissioner of the province of Coorg, and the princely states of Mysore and Hyderabad. They were a minority everywhere excepting in the princely state of Mysore. The coming of freedom in 1947 did not bring the Kannadigas their long-cherished unified Karnataka. So, this movement was continued in free India, and it ceased only in 1956 when the Government of India under Prime Minister, Jawaharlal Nehru granted their demand as part of the reorganisation of the India. The unification movement stimulated much political activity and brought about a resurgence of Kannada literature and culture. The people of Karnataka remember Gandhiji with gratitude for the clear support he gave to the demand for unified Karnataka. Sardar Patel also conceded the justice of this demand at the Karnataka Unification Conference held in Bombay in 1946, which he inaugurated.

Under the States Reorganisation Act of 1956, the new state of Mysore was born on 1st November, 1956, with Bangalore as its capital. But while the unification leaders were anxious to have the new state named Karnataka, which had been an historical aspiration, the need for accommodating some separatist elements in old Mysore state resulted in a compromise on this point. The first Chief Minister of the new state was quite appropriately S. Nijalingappa, who had been a central figure in the unification movement. It took seventeen years for the renaming of the state as Karnataka, and this was done on 1st November, 1973 under the Chief Ministership of the late Devaraj Urs. The state as it now stands has an area of 1,91,791 square kilometres, which is roughly 5.85 per cent of the total territory of India. According to the 1981 census, the population of Karnataka is 3,70,43,451, of which the females are slightly fewer than the males. Both by area and population Karnataka ranks today eighth among the Indian states. More than 70 per cent of the people live in the villages. The literacy rate is 38.41 per cent.

The political process in Karnataka is strongly influenced by its social demography to a significant extent. While no single caste or community enjoys a clear numerical majority or even decisive dominance, Lingayats (about 21%), Vokkaligas (about 19%), Brahmins (4%), the loosely co-ordinated cluster of backward castes, sometimes known as intermediate castes (about 30%), the Harijans (about 14%), and minorities like the Muslims (about 10%), together make up the state's caste-community composition. Though Kannada is the majority language, the state has sizeable linguistic minorities concentrated in specific areas such as the Marathi-speakers in the north, Telugu and Tamil speakers in the south.[1]

Karnataka is richly endowed with natural resources. It has considerable mineral resources in iron and manganese ores, chromite, gold and bauxite. There are also limestone deposits which are used in the production of cement. It has a large forest area, around 18.5 per cent of the total area. The old princely state of Mysore, now the core of the present Karnataka state, has a long history of industrialisation under such distinguished Dewans as Sir M. Vishweshwaraiah. It has an impressive record of irrigation projects and hydro-electric projects, the most notable being the Tungabhadra and the Sharavati projects.

Chief Ministers and the Council of Ministers

The political executive of the state is based on the relevant provisions of the Indian Constitution—Article 163 and 164, in particular. The Council of Ministers headed by a Chief Minister, is assigned the task under the Constitution to "aid and advise the Governor". The Governor, who is expected to function as a nominal executive, though with some discretionary power, is himself appointed by the President of India, which means virtually by the Central Council of Ministers under the leadership of the Prime Minister. But the convention has grown up by which the Chief Ministers are consulted in the choice of the candidate for the Governor's position. Under Article 164, the Chief Minister is appointed by the Governor, and the other Ministers are also appointed by the Governor on the advice of the Chief Minister. But the Governor is bound by the rule of parliamentary executive in appointing the Chief Minister, since the person so chosen should be in a position to command a majority in the legislature. Normally the leader of the legislative party that has won a majority of seats in the assembly is invited to form a government. If no party commands a majority, then the leader of the party with the largest number of seats is invited to explore the possibility of forming a government. Secondly, it is a requirement that the Chief Minister and the Ministers must be members of legislature and, if they are not at the time of appointment, they should get elected within a period of six months. Thirdly, the Governor is expected to function as constitutional head, exercising advisory functions.

The Council of Ministers is responsible to the legislature as a parliamentary executive, and it is supposed to function on the basis of the principle of collective responsibility. Their responsibility to the legislature is both in respect of their specific departments or portfolios as well as the council as a whole. The normal tenure of office for a Chief Minister and his Ministers if five years, but the assembly may be dissolved on the advice of the Chief Minister, and in that case the period is cut short, or President's rule may be imposed by the Centre, in which case the Council of Ministers is dismissed. Of course, Ministers and the Chief Minister may resign for personal reasons or the Chief Minister may ask a ministrial colleague to resign. In short, the functioning of the council is essentially a political matter. Sometimes, public pressure may force a Minister to resign, as happened in the case of B. Basavalingappa, a Dalit member of the Urs cabinet. His public criticism of Kannada literature as "Bhoosa" (cattle-feed) was politically used to dislodge him. This was perhaps the first occasion in the whole country when a Minister was forced to quit by popular pressure.

The Chief Minister has a complex role to play, as a leader of the people of the state as a whole, as a leader of a party, as a person relating to national goals, and as an administrative holding the reins of the state's administrative machinery. To date Karnataka was has had the following Chief Ministers: S. Nijalingappa, B.D. Jatti, S.R. Kanthi, Veerendra Patil, Devaraj Urs, Gundu Rao and Ramkrishna Hegde. While the earlier Chief Ministers in the old Mysore state since it became a system of responsible government were all Vokkalingas—K.C. Reddy, K. Hanumanthiah and Kadidal Manjappa, the Chief Ministers under the old undivided Congress were all Lingayats—S. Nijalingappa, R.D. Kanthi and Veerendra Patil. After further split in her party, Indira Gandhi installed Gundu Rao as the first Brahmin Chief Minister of the state. When the Janata party came to power as a minority government supported by the BJP, the Communist parties and Independents, and a Brahmin, Ramakrishna Hegde, was installed as Chief Minister. The communal identity of the Chief Minister is a clue to the communal nature of the state politics. Of these Chief Ministers, it is difficult to state anything by way of an objective assessment, because we have none. Speaking impressionistically, while Nijalingappa earned the reputation as reasonably straightforward and clean (despite allegations of corruption). Chief Minister Jatti and Patil have been known for their efficiency in administrative management. Devaraj Urs, who had the longest stint as Chief Minister, can be regarded as the most successful since he could combine administrative skill and political management with some ideological commitment. The most controversial was Gundu Rao, whose government was perhaps a little too personalised and somewhat amenable to political corruption. But Gundu Rao's flamboyant public style also concealed some of his strong points such as administrative decisiveness, no doubt with the attendant risk of arbitrariness.

As regards the Council of Ministers as a whole, the main problem has been intra-party factionalism which has been a more genuine threat to government stability than the opposition parties. One thinks in this connection of the factional infighting between Nijalingappa and Joshi, Devaraj Urs and K.H. Patil or between Gundu Rao and his rivals. By and large there have been no glaring departures from the norms of collective responsibility except in the case of Bangarappa during the Gundu Rao ministry. Given the inherent insecurity of a minority government, the Hegde government has perhaps done as well as it could. While its solid policy achievements may be negligible, its symbolic achievements in the form of face-lifting the morale of the government have not been so. It has proved to be more accessible to the people, and its style of functioning so far has been closer to the life-styles of the people.

After a long period of comparative political stability, the state's politics turned complicated in 1969 when the Congress was historically split. Veerendra Patil's Congress (O) government was convulsed by large-scale political defections and he had to advise the Governor to dissolve the assembly. The state came for the first time under the President's rule. Again in 1977 and 1980, the state was under Governor's rule when the Urs ministry resigned. But these have been brief interludes.

The State Legislature

The princely state of Mysore was among the earliest of the native states to introduce representative institutions. As far back as in 1881, it had its first Representative Assembly. Later in 1939, the system was restructured to consist of two bodies—the old Representative Assembly and a second body called Legislative Council. While the assembly was essentially based on the notion of responsive government, the council was more like a democratically responsible institution. as a result, a limited, but still far from genuinely democratic, system of popular participation in the legislative process was initiated. With the coming of Indian independence and the integration of the native states, a struggle for responsible government was waged in old Mysore. After 1952 the present system as stipulated in the Indian Constitution, was installed. After the first General Elections, a Legislative Council came into existence. After the SR Act of 1956 and the consequent abolition of the Part A and B state distinction, the present system of legislature came into full operation. It is a bicameral legislature made up of legislative assembly and legislative council.

Under the constitutional provisions, the assembly with a total membership of two hundred twenty five is the more decisive body in relation to the council with a total strength of sixty three members. The fiscal bills cannot be initiated in the council. In essence, the council, which is a continuous body as only one-third of its members retire every two years, functions as check on the assembly, but this check is limited to delaying the process of legislation. The assembly is a more directly elected body, and, therefore, enjoys a higher status within our democratic political system. While the council has done well as a second chamber, it has also posed problems to the party system. As in the USA, sometimes the ruling party with a majority in the assembly has found itself facing a council controlled by the opposition parties, as is now the case with the Hegde government. But this is unavoidable, given the constitutional provisions. As a result, frictions between the two houses have surfaced frequently.

The Karnataka legislature, in tune with the spirit in the country as a whole, has also become a prey to considerable disorderly and unparliamentary conduct. But on the whole, such occurrences have been few. One reason for such developments could be that the nature and quality of the members have been undergoing changes. Not only younger persons but also persons from hitherto deprived groups and those belonging to the generation born after 1947 have contributed to qualitative changes in the membership. While they may be less order-oriented in a conventional sense, they are also more socially conscious and more acutely sensitive to public issues and problems. Part of the behavioural confusions in the legislature should be attributed to the transitional conditions due to a change of guards.

The Legislature is served by a Secretariat, whose origin goes back to 1881. This agency is common to both the houses. The recruitment and service conditions of its staff are governed by the Karnataka Legislature Secretariat (Recruitment and Conditions of

Service)—Rules of 1959, with subsequent amendments to it. Its staff is adMinistered and managed by a Board consisting of the Speaker of the assembly and the Chairman of the council. Its administrative head is the Legislature. The Secretary also has the responsibility of supervising the sessions of both the houses. The higher staff is made up of three Deputy Secretaries, one Registrar, eight Under Secretaries, one Estate Officer, one Editor, and one Assistant Editor.

There is a good library attached to the legislature. It is meant for use by the members, officers and the other staff of the legislature. It is particularly valuable for official reports and documents. It also has a small reference and research cell, which caters to the needs of the members.

The Secretariat Administration

Like most of the present administrative machinery of the present Government of Karnataka, the beginning of the Secretariat was a modest affair consisting of only four departmental Secretaries—the Chief Secretary to the government in general and revenue department, the Secretary to the government in the public works department, the Secretary to government in the education department, and the military Secretary to the Maharaja. Prior to 1956, this system was often reorganised. But in 1956, the present system was installed. Perhaps, the broad structure is not dissimilar to what is seen in other State Governments in the country.

The three components of the Secretariat structure are the Minister who decides policies, the Secretary who supplies the Minister with the inputs of information and advice necessary for the effective policy-making and the Executive Heads of the departments who have the responsibility for implementing the policies of the Minister. The administrative infrastructure supporting them is, in fact, the Secretariat organisation. It is devised into various administrative departments around specific subjects or tasks. While the hierarchical head of the Secretariat as a whole is the Chief Secretary, assisted by two senior officers, that is, the additional Chief Secretary and the Development Commissioner. Below them are a number of Secretaries, Additional Secretaries, Joint Secretaries, Deputy Secretaries, Under Secretaries and subordinate staff (non-gazetted), arranged in a hierarchical order. At present there are the following departments: (1) Cabinet Affairs and Administrative Reforms, (2) Additional Chief Secretary is associated with the Cabinet Affairs Department as well as with several subjects of which the most important is service matters, (3) the Development Commissioner dealing with the development matters, (4) Finance, (5) Revenue, (6) Home, (7) Planning, (8) Agriculture and Animal Husbandry, (9) Food and Forest, (10) Rural Development and Co-operation, (11) Public Works and Electricity, (12) Commerce and Industries, (13) Education and Youth Services, (14) Health and Family Welfare, (15) Law and Parliamentary Affairs, (16) Social Welfare and Labour, (17) Housing and Urban Development, (18) Ecology and Environment, and (19) Science and Technology. The Secretariat has its own library. It has a reference and general reading sections, which is under the control of the Department of Personnel and Administration. Hence it is under the direct control of the Chief Secretary.

The Chief Secretary's responsibility, besides providing overall leadership to the administrative system, extends to the following: matters relating to the Ministers and the Cabinet, Rules of Business, Public Service Commission, Vigilance Commission, Elections to the Legislature and the Parliament, State Bureau of Public Enterprises, All India Services, Karnataka Administrative Service Class I, Heads and Additional Heads of Departments. Class I posts/ officers of the Secretariat, Governor and the Raj Bhavan, Constitutional Questions, Law and Order, Minorities and so on. Even with the creation of the post of Additional Chief Secretary in October 1980, the Chief Secretary's list of responsibilities and functions looks very formidable.

In Karnataka, there is no Board of Revenue, but there is a Divisional Commissioner to mediate between the field administration and the Headquarters Secretariat. The state has been divided into four administrative divisions (or Revenue Divisions). They are: (1) the Bangalore Division, comprising the districts of Kolar, Tumkur, Shimoga, Chitradurga and Bangalore, (2) Mysore Division comprising the districts of Mandya, Kodagu (Coorg), Mysore, Dakshina Kannada, Chikamagalur and Hassan, (3) the Belgaum Division comprising the districts of Uttara Kannada, Belgaum, Dharwad and Bijapur and (4) the Gulbarga Division comprising the districts of Bellary, Raichur, Gulbarga and Bidar. It may be added that, in general, the size of the districts in Belgaum and Gulbarga Divisions are larger than those in the other two Divisions. The office of the Divisional Commissioner was first created in 1956 under Section 120 of the SR Act. His main function is to co-ordinate between the district and Secretariat levels, and between various departmental activities at the Divisional level. In certain revenue matters, the Divisional Commissioner also acts as an appellate authority. He is also heavily involved in co-ordinating developmental and planning activities at this level. He conducts quarterly co-ordination meetings, and is assisted by two gazetted assistants dealing respectively with revenue and development matters.

District Administration

There are nineteen districts in Karnataka, distributed in its four Revenue Divisions. Below the level of the Divisional Commissioner, there are Deputy Commissioners, one for each district. Below him are Assistant Commissioners, each in charge of a sub-division. Further, below in the line of command are Tahasildars, one for each taluka below his level are Hobli or revenue circles, which are groups of villages. Each Hobli or revenue circle is under the administrative charge of a Revenue Inspector.

The Deputy Commissioner is the administrative head of a district. He is usually a senior member of the IAS or the Karnataka Administrative Service (KAS). Since the district is a critical link in the administrative chain of the state, the functions of the Deputy Commissioner or the DC are varied and important. In his capacity as the revenue head of the district, his activities embrace the entire gamut of administrative functions in the district. Broadly, the DC's functions may be classified into three: (1) Revenue, (2) Law and Order, and (3) Development. Of these, the first two have been more or less traditional functions with which district administrative head has been associated in the colonial period. The developmental task, though it did devolve to a very limited extent on the colonial administrator, has become today a most crucial aspect of district administration. Additionally, he has to perform two more functions—the traditional one of co-ordination and the more recent one of welfare service. He is also regarded as the custodian of the whole district, including government property.

The DC is responsible for the determination, collection and accounting of land revenue. As the District Magistrate he is responsible for law and order. He is the head of all the Executive Magistrates located in the district, and hence exercises extensive power under the Criminal Procedure Code. He is in general charge of the police personnel in the district. As District Magistrate, he is the competent authority to issue licenses and permits under the Indian Arms Act and the Indian Explosive Act. As the head of the department in his own right, he is in charge of law and order, food distribution, excise, elections, municipal and developmental works and land reforms. Except in small districts such as Bidar, Kodagu, Chikkamagalur and Uttar Kannada, he is supported by a Special Deputy Commissioner. Attached to him in the district headquarters are two special Assistant Commissioners, one for headquarters and the other for food.

When there is a Special District Commissioner he looks after revenue matters, Land acquisition and Stamps and Registration in his capacity as District Registrar. All revenue matters regarding revenue are channelled through the DC and the Special Deputy Commissioner to the Divisional Commissioner. The DC is the Chairman of the District Rural Development Society which is responsible for Integrated Rural Development Programme, and in this function he is assisted by another Special Deputy Commissioner (Development), who also looks after other special programmes like the Special Component Plan for SCs and STs.

The DC has to co-ordinate the work of several departments at the district level and especially supervises the implementation of developmental programmes. He is in charge of all the development blocks in the district. He must acquire mastery over all departments so that he can effectively co-ordinate various developmental programmes. He is the *ex-officio* Chairman of the District Development Council, which is responsible for supervising and co-ordinating all development programmes in the district, including those of the Taluka Development Boards which implement community development schemes. Further, he is accountable for the successful execution of programmes under the Five Year Plan. Finally, he is also entrusted with the task of looking after social welfare in the district.

The Assistant Commissioner is allotted one sub-division of the district. Generally each district is divided into two or three sub-divisions, depending on its size. Usually each sub-division will cover up to five talukas. The Assistant Commissioner or AC is the administrative head of the sub-division, and he looks after revenue and developmental matters. His revenue functions are extensive. He also exercises magisterial powers within the sub-division. As the executive chief of the sub-division, the AC inspects and looks after the functionaries below him such as the Tahasildars, Revenue Inspectors and the Village Officers. He functions as an administrative link between the DC and the Tahasildars. By and large his functions are a replications of the functions of the DC but at the sub-division level. The AC is assisted by a supportive staff consisting of a Manager and others. He exercises control over all Revenue, Municipal, Taluka Development Board and developmental activities within the sub-division. Now there are Special Acs entrusted with the responsibility for implementing the Land Reforms Act and Land Acquisition for public purposes.

For Tahasildar, formerly known as Amaldar, Mamlatdar or Subedar in different regions, is head of the Taluka administration at the Taluka level. In his capacity as Taluka Magistrate, he is responsible for the maintenance of law and order within the Taluka. He is supported by a Shirastedar or Deputy Tahasildar. There are Special Tahasildars for special tasks such as the implementation of the Land Reforms Act. He is also expected to look after Muzari matters, elections and maintenance of revenue records.

Another officer operating at the Taluka level is the Block Development Officer or the BDO. For the purpose of his jurisdiction, each Taluka constitutes a Community Development Block. The BDO not only looks after the developmental activities at the Block level, he also functions as the Chief Executive Officer of the Taluka Development Board, and is its Secretary. He is in overall charge of supervising the work of extension personnel like the Agricultural Extension Officer, Co-operative Extension Officer, Fisheries Extension Officer, Extension Officer for Animal Husbandry, Mukhyasevikas, Gramsevakas and Gramasevikas.

At the lowest level of district administrative hierarchy are the Village Officers. A taluka is divided into Hoblis or revenue circles. Each revenue circle is under the administrative jurisdiction of a Revenue Inspector. He functions as the crucial field personnel directly executing the orders of the government in revenue matters. Below the Revenue Inspector and supervised by him are the Village Accountants who are in charge of villages. The Village Accountant (Talati) is responsible for village administration. He functions as the Secretary of smaller village panchayats. Technically he constitutes the lowest rung of the revenue hierarchy. Prior to the creation of the posts of Village Accountants, the village administration was carried on by a hereditary functionary known as the Shanbhog, who maintained land records, and, was assisted by another functionary, the Patel or Revenue Patel. Earlier the lowest village level officials used to be the Thoti and Talwar. Now these have been replaced by Gramasahayaks.

The Civil Service

As in the other states in general, the civil service personnel in Karnataka can be classified functionally and cadre-wise. Functionally they can be divided into: (1) Higher policy personnel (Secretary level), (2) Headquarter personnel (the Secretariat level) and (3) the field personnel (the district level and below). Cadre-wise they can be first divided into the Gazetted and Non-gazetted classes. Within the Gazetted, they are further divisible into the All-India cadres, the IAS and the IPS, and the state cadre, the KAS and KPS (or KSAS and KSPS). The state cadres are further hierarchically split into Class I and Class II. Below the Gazetted personnel, there are the non-gazetted personnel of the state cadre, classified into Office Superintendent level, Upper Division Clerk level, the Lower Division Clerk level and the manual level. The first three are referred to as Class III and the last group as Class IV. It is clear that, in Karnataka, as elsewhere in India, the spirit of hierarchy based on the principle of status, pervades the service personnel system, very strongly recalling the colonial days. However, the general democratic ethos mitigates this tendency towards status consciousness.

The recruitment to the All India cadre lies beyond the purview of the state administration, and belongs to the Union government. In a sense, the IAS personnel has an ambiguous role *vis-a-vis* the State Government. They function as the agents of the Union Government insofar as their recruitment, service rules and overall disciplinary control rests with the Union Government. Moreover, being outsiders, their involvement in, and commitment to, the state may not always be as deep as desirable. On the other hand, they are necessary to counter parochialism and local malfunctioning. However, they are regarded as superior and dominant group, for whom almost all key posts are earmarked. The IAS cadre also contains state members directly recruited and seconded from the KAS on a quota system.

All the other cadres are recruited through state agencies. The main recruiting machinery is, of course, the Karnataka Public Service Commission, which is a statutory body under the Indian Constitution. Prior to the setting up of the present KPSC in 1956, the old princely state of Mysore had established, as a Part B state then, the first Mysore Public Service Commission on 18 May, 1951 under the new Indian Constitution. It had a chairman and two members. After the creation of the present Karnataka state then known as Mysore state, in 1956, the MPSC was reorganised from time to time. Its strength was raised from two to four in 1962, and to six in 1973. The overall direction of the KPSC lies with the Secretary to the Commission. Half the members are statutorily required to be from the category of experienced civil servants, and the other half is to consist of distinguished non-official members. The Secretary is also the Controller of all the Examinations conducted by the Commission for the recruitment of state service cadres. The Secretary is supported by one Deputy Secretary and two Assistant Secretaries. The KPSC has, besides its function of recruitment, two other functions—that of tendering advice to the government on service matters referred to it, and the function of dealing with disciplinary and promotion issues pertaining to the state civil services. The Commission is not an appointing authority, and the government has the right to reject its recommendations. In that case, the government is required to explain its reasons for it and place it before the legislature in the annual reports of the Commission. The impartiality and independence of the Commission are ensured by the provisions of the Indian Constitution.

While the IAS personnel undergo general training at the Mussoorie Academy of Administration before being deployed in the state (the IPS cadre has a further training in the Police Academy now located in Hyderabad), they are required to undergo on-the-spot in-service training to get some grip on the nature of their tasks.

The state service personnel are put through systematic training in the various training institutions. A Secretariat Training Institute was set up in 1969 to raise the efficiency level of the Secretariat personnel. It also offers short-term training for the supervisory staff working as Heads of Department. In 1978 the Institute was reorganised and it works under the Department of Personnel and Administrative Reforms. It is managed by a Director, assisted by three Deputy Directors. These form the permanent teaching staff. It also draws on the expertise of outside experts who may work as special lecturers. The Administrative Research Institute, also located in Bangalore, was set up in 1982, with a special focus on the management input. It works under the direction of a Committee chaired by the Chief Secretary. The Administrative Training Institute, located in Mysore, (formerly called the Orientation and Study Centre), was actually set up by the Government of India in 1959, one of the eleven such centres throughout the country. At that time its task was envisaged as that of imparting training to district and block level personnel as well as non-officials involved in the Community Development Programme. In 1967, it was transferred to the state jurisdiction, and acquired the present name. It is now managed by a Director, two Joint Directors and eight Deputy Directors. It is now a residential institution under the control of the Department of Personnel and Administrative Reforms (since 1976). Now it offers training to direct recruits to the state cadre, orientation course to state personnel promoted to higher post under the state, and a variety of refresher and in-service sources to personnel. Even the IAS/IPS/IFS personnel allotted to the state are required to undergo a four-week orientation training at the institute. A District Training Institute system was set up under the Fifth Plan. Its function is to provide training in the districts to Ministerial staff and junior executive level personnel. Now the main job of these institutes is to offer job training to the new recruits and existing personnel at the level of first and second division clerks in all the departments. It also offers general courses, *ad hoc* short-term refresher courses and in-service programmes. They are headed by a Principal, one Instructor and other staff. Lastly, there are Village Training Institutes to train village level personnel including and Panchayat staff. There are four Village Accountant-cum-Panchayat Secretaries Training Centres at Kolar, Raichur, Sirsi and Shimoga. A BDO heads them as a Principal.

Public Enterprises in the State

The old princely state of Mysore was among the earliest in the country to have embarked on a state sponsored programme of industrialisation under the far-sighted leadership of Dewans like Sir M. Vishvesariah. The first government-controlled industrial unit, the Sandalwood Oil Factory, was established as far back as in 1917. Since then the State Government has been expanding its industrial involvement systematically. This led in the beginning to a division between public sector undertakings and the government managed undertakings. Subsequently, as a result of experience, a trichotomy was introduced by which we have now a public sector, a private sector and a joint sector. Further the public sector units are divisible into those under the management of the Central Government and those under the management of the State Government. The current situation with regard to the industrial structure in the state may be given as follows:

Table 1.1

Public sector	*No. of units*	*Investment (in lakhs)*
Central, excluding defence units	15	5,713
State undertakings	62	12,775
Corporations and Baords	87	484
Joint sector	03	6,907
Co-operatives	74	4,601
Private sector registered	4,945	56,291
Unregistered	589,792	11,853

Source: Karnataka State Gazetteer, Part I, 1982, p. 818.

The co-operatives can be included in the joint sector area since they imply a collaboration between the government and the private joint involvement. The total capital investment in public sector works out to Rs. 18,972 (in lakhs), and private sector investment to Rs. 68,114 (in lakhs). The joint sector has Rs. 11,508 (in lakhs) of capital investment. Therefore, it is clear that, in sheer size, the private sector exercises an overwhelming dominance in the industrial field. In terms of percentage, the public sector is 19.41, the joint 7.07 and the private 68.82. While the private sector is dominant the public sector is also significant.

The public sector has been a frequent target of public criticism on the grounds of inefficiency and unprofitability. While one may overdo this criticism, it must be admitted that things can be much better than what they are. The present Janata Government has promised to review the situation and take appropriate remedial measures. One of the crucial issues relates to managerial efficiency in relation to the employment of civil servants in industrial units. The issue may be posed as one of general administrator or technocrat. Then there is also the question of public accountability *versus* managerial efficiency. A third issue is public goals and profitability. A final issue is the glaring disparities in the remuneration of personnel as between the sectors. Generally speaking, private sector pays better, and within the public sector the Central units pay better. There is thus a serious need for a comprehensive survey of the whole public enterprise system in the state.

Planning

Planned development through the mediation of the state has become a necessity for most under-developed countries because they have not had the long historical tradition of private enterprise and capitalism which has charactersed the industrialisation of the Western countries. In Karnataka the concept of planning was mooted long before Independence in the politics pursued by Sir M. Vishveswariah, one of the architects of modern, industrial Karnataka. However, after Independence, Prime Minister Nehru embarked on a more ambitious and systematic programme of planned development through the Five Year Plans. Planning is nothing new to Karnataka, as Vishveswariah had produced the first over plan, a ten-year plan, as long ago as 1934.

The main objectives of planning in the state may be listed as (1) elimination of poverty and attainment of economic self-reliance, (2) raising the level of *per capita* income in both real and money terms, (3) tackling of unemployment problem by creating better employment opportunities, (4) optimal exploitation of natural resources like water, power, etc., (5) development of agricultural and industrial sectors, (6) control of inflation through increased production and distribution of essential commodities, (7) satisfying the minimum needs of the people, (8) improved social services,

(9) reduction of regional imbalances, (10) improvement of the conditions of the weaker sections and the poor, and (11) equitable distribution of income and wealth and attack on concentration of economic power. To date, the state has had six Plans. The outlay of the Plans has increased from 3.5 crores in the First Plan to 2,400 crores under the sixth Plan.

The emphasis under the Janata Party government today has shifted towards rural development. The state has a Department of Planning and a Bureau of Statistics, which are involved in the technical operations of preparing the details of the Plan. There is a Planning Board which is involved in an advisory capacity in the planning process. There is also a special planning cell known as the Council for Planning located in the Secretariat. During 1983-84, the system of District Plans was initiated to take the plans to the people. This has also meant more importantly a significant decentralisation of the planning process. District Planning Committees have come into existence, and they are to work in close association with District Development Councils. They are given substantial initiative and freedom to work out details within a given outlay framework.

There are also Tribal sub-plans to encourage the overall development of tribal populations in the state. This will benefit the tribal population concentrated in the districts of Mysore, Kodagu, Dakshina Kannada, and Chikkamagalur.

Union-State Relations

India is a federal polity or at least a quasi-federal polity. Therefore, the Union-State relations are very important from the perspective of the political functioning of the state and also the development of the state. Till 1969, the relations between the State Government and the Centre were relatively cordial because the same party ruled both the governments. In 1969, the Centre was under what was then known as Congress (R) while the State Government was under Congress (O). But even so, the relations between the two governments did not alter basically. After 1977, a similar situation arose when the Janata came to power in the Centre and the state was under Congress (I). This was understandably a period of political confrontation, which involved such dramatic events as the dismissal of Urs government and the election of Indira Gandhi in a by-election from Chikkamagalur to the Lok Sabha. Towards the very close of his Chief Ministership, Urs had to contend with the Centre ruled by a different party. But the most intense phase of confrontation seems to figure with the Janata Party coming to power in the state early in 1983. This political confrontation has taken the form of a demand for radical restructuring of Centre-State relations. In particular, the demand has focused on greater devolution of financial resources to the states and a significant weakening of the administrative hold of the Centre on the states. Early in August 1983, the Chief Minister R.K. Hegde organised a supposedly non-political seminar of experts on Centre-State relations at Bangalore, which turned out to be politically quite controversial. These are controversial political issues in the context of party politics, though they reflect the existence of genuine problems transcending partisan politics.

Apart from such developments, the relations between the Centre and state do not seem to be noticeably deteriorating. The Chief Minister is a seasoned politician and he is not anxious for needless confrontation with the Centre despite some employment of confrontation rhetoric in public. In any case, the issues here are all-India issues, and not narrowly related to Karnataka. There is every prospect of the ruling party keeping within realistic limits its efforts to put pressure on the Centre for greater advantages and benefits.

Citizen-Administration Relations

This is a theme on which we have no scientific data, and one can only go by impressionistic material. While there is a lot of loose widespread talk in the public against corruption and inefficiency of the administration, there is no effort on the part of either the citizenry or the government to get to grips with the problem. While there are government agencies like the Information Department or the Publicity wing to put across the governmental view point, there are no organised institutional channels to transmit to the government the pulse of the public in the state. There are very few or no agencies to do this. There are no opinion polls or other mechanisms to ascertain public reaction to administrative policies or their implementation. As a result the elections appear to be the only occasion, even if no more than a ritual occasion, in which public reactions are relayed to a limited extent. The proposed Lokayukta office should go some way in providing the public at least with one channel for representing its grievances. But this would be a negative, though necessary channel. We need more and better institutional infrastructure, at the public as well as government level to relate the citizens meaningfully to their administration.

NOTE

1. Demographic data for castes groups are not available as the census of India does not count the population on their basis, and hence the figures are very approximate, gathered from indirect sources such as the SRC Report.

REFERENCES

1. Bhashyam, K.T., *The Mysore Struggle*, Dharwad, 1940.
2. Freedom Movement in Karnataka: Who is Who, (i) Bangalore, 1969, (ii) Bangalore, 1971, (iii) Bangalore, 1972.
3. Gupta, S.V. and Bhashyam, K.T., *Mysore Congress: A Short History of the Mysore Congress,* with illustrations, Bangalore, 1942.
4. Havanur, I.G., *Specifying the Backward Classes without the Caste Basis,* Bangalore, 1942.
5. Kumaran, S.S., *The Mysore Congress that was…*, Swatantraya Thana, Smarana Sanchike, Bangalore, 1971.
6. Manor, James, *Political Change in an Indian State,* Mysore, 1917-1955, Pub. Manohar Book Service, New Delhi, 1977.
7. Manor, James., Hanumanthaiah, K., *In Mysore: The Style and Strategy of Individual Leadership in the Integration of Region's Politics,* South Asia IV, 1974, pp. 21-38.
8. Pattabhiraman, K., *Mysore Congress: Its First Year,* Bangalore, 1939.
9. Shama Rao, *Modern Mysore,* 2 Vols., Bangalore, 1936.
10. Halappa, G.S., *The History of the Freedom Movement in Karnataka,* 2 Vols., Bangalore, 1962 and 1964.
11. Ramaiah, P.R., *Mysore's Political Evolution,* Bangalore, n.d.
12. Weiner, M., *The Politics of Scarcity,* Chicago, 1962.
13. Chand, T., *History of the Freedom Movement in India,* Vol. III-IV, Government of India, New Delhi, 1972.
14. Divakar, R.R., *Union of Karnataka and Mysore,* Hubli, 1948.

15. Pushkin, L., *The Non-Brahmin Movement in Princely Mysore*, University of Pennsylavia,1974, (Unpublished Dissertation).
16. Gopal, M.H., *The Finances of the Mysore State 1799-1831*, Mysore, 1960.
17. Bjorn Hettne, *The Political Economy of Indirect Rules*, Mysore, *1881-1947*, Pub. Ambikar Publications, New Delhi, 1978.
18. Menon, A.G., *The Swadeshi Movement in India—The Mysore Review 1905*.
19. Puttaswamaiah, K., *Economic Development of Karnataka*, Vols. I and II, Pub., Oxford and IBH Publishing Co., New Delhi, 1980.

GOVERNMENT OF MYSORE—SERIALS

20. Reports on the Administration of Mysore, 1963-1881 and 1910-1947.
21. Reports on Public Instruction in Mysore, 1167-1881 and 1939-1952.
22. Proceedings of the Mysore Representative Assembly (PMRA) 1905-1947.
23. The Mysore Gazette 1908-1947.
24. Proceedings of the Mysore Legislature Council (PMCC) 1935-1947.
25. Mysore Information Bulletin, 1941-1946.
26. Report of the Committee for Revision of Land Revenue System, Bangalore, 1960.
27. Report of the Fact Finding Committee, (States Recognition), Bangalore, 1956.
28. Report of the Local Boards Enquiry Committee, Mysore State, 1954, Bangalore, 1954.
29. Interim Report, "Mysore Backward Class Commission", Bangalore, 1950.
30. Karnataka State Gazetteer, Part-I and II.
31. Report on Mysore Administration, A.D. Gorwala, Government of Mysore, 1957-58.
32. Report on Backward Classes, L.G. Havanur, Government of Karnataka, 1976.

UNPUBLISHED THESES

33. Raghavendra Rao, K., *Linguistic Politics and the Congress Party in Mysore (Karnataka)*, University of Toronto.
34. Raghavendra Rao, K., *Heart is Karnataka: Life and Thought of Alur Venkat Rao*, Alur Venkat Rao's Centenary Celebration Committee, Dharwad.
35. Patil, N.A., *Growth of Nationalism in Karnataka*, Karnataka University, Dharwad, 1968.
36. Avaragerimath, H.D., *Karnataka Ideology—A Study of the Political Idea of Karnataka Movement (1906-1956)*, Karnataka University, 1982.

2

Geography of Karnataka

Y.M. MADAR and B. HYAMAVATHI REDDY

India is known for "Unity in Diversity", the same is perhaps true with Karnataka which came into existence on the 1st of November, 1956, under the States Reorganization Act of 1956 by a merger of the Part B state of Mysore, Part C state of Coorg, parts of the presidencies of Bombay, Madras and Hyderabad, and the erstwhile princely state of more than a dozen princely states, the unifying factor being the Kannada language. The state which in 1956 was known as Mysore was ruled by various dynasties and kings before the advent of the British.

Karnataka, as it is known since 1973, has a varied topography—the magnificent Sahyadris, meandering rivers, golden beaches and also a monotonous undulating countryside. Climate varies from tropical wet to semiarid and the state abounds in natural vegetation; it is rich not only in sandalwood and spices but is also endowed with one of the world's richest bio-diversity. It has a variety of minerals and has made a unique contribution to the economy and wealth of India.

Locational Aspects

Karnataka state is situated in the west—central part of the Deccan peninsular India extending between 11°35″N and 18°30′N and 74°5′E and 78°35′W and covering an area of 1,91,791 sq. km. It is the eighth largest in terms of area and ninth largest in terms of population in India. It has a coast line of about 300 km. on the west bordering the Arabian sea. To the North-west and North are the states of Goa and Maharashtra, to the East is Andhra Pradesh and to the South and South-east are the states of Kerala and Tamil Nadu.

Brief History

Karnataka's location in peninsular India was responsible for its prominent role in the history of South India. It has had an eventful recorded history of more than 2,000 years and has been ruled by various dynasties—the Satavahanas, Kadambas, Chalukyas, Rashtrakutas, Yadavas, Hoysalas, the Vijayanagara to quote just a few; the Bahamani sultans, the Wodeyars, Hyder Ali and Tipu Sultan, Marathas also influenced the administration and policies of the state. From 1800 to 1947, a larger area of the state came under the British hegemony. The various dynasties have left an indelible mark on the land and its culture; the temples and carvings at Belur, Halebidu, Badami, Aihole, Pattadakal, Hampi and other places prompted Shivaram Karanth to call Karnataka "the cradle of temple architecture".

Karnataka is also a melting pot of various religions. The Vedic religion, Buddhism, Jainism, Islam, Christianity and the Lingayat cult and philosophies of Dvaita, Advaita and Vishistadvaita have existed harmoniously. It has a rich cultural heritage having given birth to many thinkers, writers, poets, exponents of music, Karnataka has also had its noteworthy share in the nationalist movement.

Geographical Environment

The geographical environment-physiography, climate, natural vegetation and other factors of the state have directly or indirectly influenced its strategic location, internal unity, relations with neighbours, economic viability and regional diversity.

The physiography of the state falls into three traditional divisions—the coastal lowland, malnad, i.e., the Sahyadris and the maidan, i.e., the eastern plateau. The coastal lowlands stretch from Uttara Kannada to the Dakshina Kannada district. They are narrow in the North (12 km) and are generally wider to the south near Mangalore and the Netravati valley (about 75 km). They are interspersed with hills ranging in elevation from the sea level to

150 m. and at places more than 300 m. It is composed of sandy beaches, coastal and dunes or mud flats, alluvial tracts along rivers or lagoons or estuaries and lateritic hills. These hills merge with the spurs of Sahyadris which runs almost continuously parallel to the coastline.

The Sahyadris or the Western Ghats, when viewed from the west coast look like a cliff rising almost perpendicularly from the coastal plain. In fact they form the edge of the upraised plateau and present youthful landscape composed of steep-sided valleys, narrow gorges and water falls of great magnitude. While the slope is steep to the west, it descends gently eastwards to below 400 m. to the "maidan", i.e., the plateau region.

The Ghats form the geographic barrier for peninsula India and act as a triggering mechanism for the condensation of water vapour into moist air, giving rise to an abundance of rain. It has rich water potential with many west flowing and east flowing rivers originating in the Ghats.

The "maidan" or the plateau is traversed by many north to south ridges which are eroded by rivers and now stand as interfluves. It also has isolated hills. The northern part of the country is a rolling land with open valleys and is largely drained by the Krishna and its tributaries. The southern maidan is higher and more rugged. It is largely drained by the Cauvery and its tributaries.

The entire state lies in the tropics and has mega thermal regime save for a small area in the Western Ghats section that has mesothermal climate due to its elevation. The Ghat section in the west is exposed to the full blast of south-west monsoon winds, while a few kilometers to the east is the rain shadow area of the plateau region. The influence of the sea is felt along the coast where it is hot and humid. Almost all over the state summers are warm and winters are cool. There is a continuous rise of temperature from January to April over most places and up to May elsewhere. North "maidan" records highest temperature in April, that is more than 40°C while Madikere on the Ghats in April records 27.9°C with the onset of monsoon temperatures are reduced all over the state. The annual rainfall in the state varies from less than 60 cms. over the north "maidan" to more than 300 cms. along the coast and "malanad". Four of the fourteen heavy rainfall sections of India receiving more than 500 cms. of annual rainfall, Agumbe,

Bhagamanala, Pullingoth and Makut, are located in the Ghat section of the state. Located on the leeward side of Western Ghats north "maidan" receives 60-70 cms. of annual rainfall and most of it form south-west monsoons while south "maidan" receives more than 100 cms. rain from both the south-west monsoon and retreating monsoon.

As the whole state lies in the tropics with an abundance of solar energy, luxuriance of vegetation is a result of the amount of rainfall received and its distribution through the seasons. The climax vegetation of the Western Ghats is the evergreen forest with a rich variety of species of trees, ferns, lianas and rattans. The trees are found in various tires with a variety of fauna at each level. Bordering the evergreen forests are the mixed deciduous forests with teak, sandal-wood and bamboo. These forests give way to tropical dry-deciduous and thorn forests over the maidan region. Along the coast coconut and palm trees are common while mangrove forests are seen in marshes, creek and estuaries. Scrub, poor grass and bamboo are found on the laterite hills where soils are leached due to heavy rainfall.

Though one-fifth of the area of the state is under the control of forest department, only eleven per cent is a well-wooded area and the remaining is in different stages of degradation.

There are five National parks and twenty one Wild life sanctuaries to preserve the rich bio-diversity of the state.

Resources and Economy

Karnataka has limited water resources, though it accounts for six per cent of the country's surface water, more than half the yield accounted for is from the west flowing rivers—Netravati, Sharavati, Gangavalli, Kali, Bedti-Aganasini and others. These have short swift courses and are harnessed for power generation. The Krishna river system drains more than half the state and the Cauvery, less than a fifth. Only small parts of the Godavari, the north Pennar, the south Pennar and Palar basins are in the state. The yield of the east flowing rivers is estimated at 56,600 mcum while that of the west flowing rivers 40,750 mcum at 50 per cent dependability. The total ground water resources are estimated at 2,70,000 mcum. Their recharge depends on the infiltration capacity of the soil and the rate of evapotranspiration.

There are 38,608 minor irrigation tanks in the state. In rural areas where tank irrigation is prevalent, "warabandi" system is still in practice. Some of the tanks are highly polluted and their storage capacities is reduced due to siltation. Many of the tanks in or near towns which were sources of water supply have been reclaimed for construction purposes.

The exploitation of water resources is not uniform in the state. Though large reservoirs are built on major rivers, no proper management by way of canals and field channels is made. Proper exploitation and management of water resources are particularly important when their availability for irrigation is crucial. The state, as a whole, has 25.9 per cent of cultivated area under irrigation. In general in North Karnataka percentage area irrigated is less except in the case of Belgaum and undivided Bellary districts. South Karnataka has a higher percentage of cultivated area under irrigation except in Kodagu and Chikkamagalore districts which receive very heavy rainfall.

Agriculture is the main stay of the state with nearly two-thirds of population depending on it. Khariff crops account for three-fourths of agricultural production and it is largely dependent on the vagaries of the monsoons. Cereals occupy more than half the cultivated area. Jowar, rice, maize, bajra and wheat are important cereals in the north, while rice, ragi and maize are important cereals in the south. Sugarcane is the major cash crop particularly in the irrigated areas with maximum concentration in Belgaum and Mandya districts. Oil seeds, pulses and cotton are other important corps. Karnataka is the largest producer of coffee in the country contributing to more than three-fourths of India's production; besides it is also known for spices, coconut and other horticultural crops. Floriculture is becoming increasingly important in the south. Large areas are brought under mulberry cultivation for rearing silk worms in the southern districts. Karnataka is the largest producer of silk with sixty five per cent of the country's total.

Infrastructure contributes a great deal to modern agriculture. Though rural electrification is given impetus there is no proper power supply. There is much to be done in providing proper roads, loans through financial institutions and regulated markets so that the agricultural populace is benefited. The state has 28.6 million livestock and it produces 5 million tones of milk besides various other dairy products and meat. It also has 18.8 million poultry.

Karnataka with about 7,000 sq. km. of continental shelf along its coast is a major fishing state of India, with five fishing harbours at Karwar, Honnavar, Tadri, Malpe and Mangalore and twenty five fish landing centres, the state contributes to seven per cent of India's fish production. Fishing is also important in various inland water spread areas of the state. There is immense scope for the development of fisheries and shrimp forming in brakish waters.

Karnataka lacks energy minerals. The State Government has recently awarded the continental shelf from Bhatkal to Mangalore for exploration of oil and gas. If the results are positive it will go a long way in the development of state's economy.

The state is fairly well-endowed with metallic and non-metallic minerals and building materials. The iron-ore of Bellary-Hospet region is considered to be one of the world's best. There are also iron ore deposits at Kemmanagundi, Kudremukh and others. The deposits are being exploited for export and for the iron and steel industries of the state. Karnataka is the leading producer of gold in the country. It is also rich in manganese, dolomite, limestone and granites including those of ornamental ores.

Karnataka was a pioneer state in the development of hydro-electric power and in fact till 1970s, there was sufficient power supply. Most of the hydro-power plants developed are on west-flowing rivers of Kali, Sharavati and Varahi. With the spurt in industrial development, rural electrification and urban expansion, the state now faces acute shortage even after the completion of Raichur and Yelahanka thermal power stations and the nuclear power plant at Kaiga. Impetus is also given to develop non-conventional energy sources. Yet the state is able to meet only seventy five per cent of the power required by various sectors.

Manufacturing accounts for nearly two-thirds of the income from the state's secondary sector. Traditional industries have been flourishing at various centres in the state since long. Towards the end of nineteenth century new industries and modern techniques were introduced in southern Karnataka. While Hyderabad Karnataka did not have much of industrial development under Nizam, textile mills and cement industries were developed in Bombay Karnataka. In old Mysore state under the vision of M. Vishwesharaiah, there was a spurt to industrial developments at various centres like Bangalore, Mysore, Davangere, Mandya, Shimoga, Bhadravati and others. Textiles, silk, sugar, iron and steel, paper, perfumes and various other industries were established. After independence, many new public sector undertakings of the Central Government including those of the defense department were established in and around Bangalore. Bangalore is known as the "electronic city". the information technology industry is the latest with ample scope for future growth. Software technology parks have vast potential for export. Other large industrial centres of the south are Mangalore and Mysore.

Though several industries like textile, sugar, paper, aluminum and iron and steel are established in North Karnataka, in general industrial development is much less compared to that of the south. Some weaving industries in Belgaum and textile industries at Gulbarga and Hubli are either closed or on the verge of closure as the State Government has not come to their rescue.

With the introduction of new industrial policy of 1996, there has been a considerable increase in the number of small scale industries. If sufficient incentives are given, small scale industrial sector can contribute substantially to the production and to the employment and reduce regional imbalance in the state.

For the development of any region, accessibility is very important. While the urban areas are fairly well connected either by national highways or state highways or district roads, there is lot to be done in the rural areas. At the time of the formation of the state, there was fairly good road development in the old Mysore state while North Karnataka, particularly Hyderabad Karnataka had no proper development of roads. Even now many of the villages are not even connected by surfaced roads or bus services. The same is true with regard to post, telegraph and telephone services.

All the districts except Kodagu have railway lines passing through them. In the recent budget announcement allocation has been made to connect Hassan to Mangalore by a broad gauge line. This is essential as all the commodities produced in the southern districts can be transported through Konkan railway to other destinations. Further, this will benefit the Konkan railway which is running at a loss in this section. Similarly, a railway line connecting Hubli to Ankola would have helped as this section has maximum revenue potential to the nation's exchequer by virtue of possible diversion of rich iron ore, granite and other commodities for export via Karwar, Belekeri and Marmagoa ports (KCCI, Hubli). Bangalore is well-connected to various parts of the country by

Indian airlines. An international airport is being built at Devanahalli nearby.

Water transport is important along the coast and in several west flowing rivers. So is ocean transport not only to export ores and other commodities but also to import various commodities. Mangalore is the only major port developed. Besides Karwar, Bhatkal, Honnavar, Ankola, Belekeri and the Mangalore old port are being developed.

Karnataka has the ninth largest population in India with 52,733,958 (2001) accounting for 5.13 per cent of India's total. The percentage decadal growth rate for (1991-2000) is 17.25 as against all India's 21.35 per cent. There has been a steady increase in the percentage of urban population in the state from 28.89 in 1981 to 30.92 in 1991 and 33.98 per cent in 2001. The national average of urban population is 27.78 per cent. The total urban population of the state is around 17,915 million and nearly a third of this live in Bangalore urban agglomeration alone. 66.02 of Karnataka's rural population, i.e., 34.82 million live in rural areas accounting for 5.69 per cent of country's rural population. While the sex ratio in the state is 963 females per thousand males, for urban and rural, they are 976 and 940 respectively. 4.32 per cent of the population is that of children in the age group of 0-6 years. As in the case of the whole country, the male child population out numbers the female child population. The literacy rate (7+years) in Karnataka is 67.04 per cent as against 65.2 per cent of India's. While there is discrepancy in the percentage of urban and rural literates, several districts of Hyderabad Karnataka have registered a lower percentage of literacy than that of the state's average.

The Human Development Report published by the State Government in 1999 finds Hyderabad Karnataka at the bottom of the scale of Human Development Index (HDI) while Uttara Kannada is well placed; Belguam and Dharwad districts are better placed than some of the southern districts like Mysore, Kolar and Mandya. The Gender Related Development Index (GRDI), in fact indicates that the whole of North Karnataka is at the bottom of the scale compared to the south, barring Mysore, Mandya and Kolar which are also at the bottom.

The quality of life which takes into consideration the state of primary education, public health and health care facilities and drinking water and sanitation facilities would have been a better indicator of development.

3

The Emergence of Modern Karnataka

History, Myth and Ideology

K. RAGHAVENDRA RAO

The central argument in this paper is that the process by which modern Karnataka came to be constituted involved the articulation of a particular ideological construction into which went both "history" and "myth". Before going into a detailed mapping and interpretation of the process in question, it seems necessary to indicate, in order not to get entangled in a futile definitional operation, the specific meaning attached to the three key terms—ideology, history and myth indicate and the theoretical relationship between them.

I

By ideology nothing more is meant than a system of proposition on the basis of which an organized group may formulate and implement a political programme of action. Such propositions may be normative or empirical, but in their totality they explain and legitimize the programme involved. It may contain references to goals, values and methods, underpinning the programme. It may contain metaphysical, psychological and historical propositions. For the purpose of this paper, history is simply a systematic account of what happened in a specific past confined to a specific place, time and human collectivity, claiming to base itself on empirical facts, retrieved from documents, oral evidence or monuments. In this sense, history is supposed to be sharply demarcated from myth. Both history and myth refer back to facts, but history regards itself chained to them in an allegedly subordinate relationship. Myth, on the contrary, uses facts imaginatively or symbolically or, to borrow a post-structural expression, topologically. A myth cannot be logically invalidated by "facts" but history can be so invalidated or undermined.

The theoretical framework of this paper may be briefly set forth as follows. A traditional society in the sense of one which does not assign a conscious role for individuals and groups to question on the grounds of rationality their political practices as embodied in institutional activities claims the right and the capacity to change them and was not allowed to continue to function within its traditional framework of low level of material productivity, non-competitive group hierarchies generating significantly less intra-group and inter-group conflicts, and institutional complexes embodying ideals or archaic harmony based on accepted hierarchy. But, it also experienced oppression or exploitation in ways and forms that tended to be constantly countervailed both by the oppressor's physical incapacity to oppress beyond a point and the traditional resources of the oppressed to contain the oppressor within a closed, localised political economy, whether in Asia, Africa or elsewhere, since the rise of modern Europe from its own medieval traditionalism from the fourteenth century onwards. This new Europe with its new ideology of what has been called "modernity" generated in the last five to six centuries tremendous historical energy and momentum, based on its new technologies of violence and its new institutional ideology of humanism based on a critical and ruthless abolition of all past in the name of the self-validating subjective rationality of human individuals. This process of world conquest by Europe based on its geographical and political expansion through trade and war and politics summarised by historians under the twin code words of industrialisation and capitalism within an overarching ideology of what is called modernity, whose best expression lies in the intellectual and ideational structures produced by the so-called European Enlightenment in the eighteenth century, imposed its local patterns of ideals, ideas, values and institutional practices as universal categories. What was European was claimed as a universally valid, rational and human package, and what seems now in retrospect astonishing, the rest of the world capitulated to this claim through physical force which certainly played a crucial role but also subsequently intellectually, culturally and morally. As Gandhiji rightly saw in his *Hind Swaraj*, the strength of the West rested most fundamentally on the internal weaknesses of the rest than on the abilities and virtues of the West itself. Western industrial capitalism accomplished its universal conquest and global control through a system of dominance that has been characterized variously as imperialism, colonialism and neo-colonialism. The hardware category of imperialism was legitimized subsequently by the ideological controls by the various new Western discourses which later transformed themselves into the modern social sciences in the nineteenth century. Within the Western framework, the only significant challenge to this was Marxism, though Marxism, at least as practised, also failed to generate genuine universalism out of its basically European entrails. This legitimation was done through a theory of modernisation, which functioned as a software equivalent to the hardware categories of imperialism and colonialism. While the theory of modernisation is valid as a descriptive term for what was happening under imperial-colonial dispensation and also valid as an ideology generated in, and imposed by, the Western civilization on the rest of the world, it, however, is not the whole story. The process of modernisation is never smooth, and it had thrown up situations of profound and almost unresolvable structural crises, and it has also produced countermanding processes of resistance. India, and the region now known as Karnataka, have been part of this global master-narrative. The emergence of modern Karnataka should be seen as part of this process of establishing and rooting the Western "modern" models of political organization and institutionalisation in that region.

The theoretical assumption underlying this paper is that the process of the emergence of modern Karnataka as a distinctive political sub-system within the process of the emergence of India as a political system under the auspices of colonialism was carried out by the agency of identifiable groups within the region—the linguistic group of Kannada-speakers, certain caste groups, and a group that can be loosely designated "class". In a very complex and intricately interlaced fashion, these groups employed ideology and historical identity, backed by a certain notion of collective material interest, to call into existence the contemporary Karnataka

State. This was, of course, not confined to one linguistic group, but involved virtually all language groups in India, though the commitment and activism varied, during the period beginning with the last decade of nineteenth century to around 1956 when the political map of the country was re-drawn along linguistic lines, though there were exceptions such as in the case of Punjabi-speakers or Marathi-speakers. But even those claims came to be subsequently accommodated.

II

In this section, I shall offer a brief account of the developments that led to the emergence of the political sub-system of modern Karnataka State.[1] Pre-colonial political life in India was organised around monarchical or imperial systems based on dynastic legitimacy and military conquest. Language and culture or ethnicity did not form the basis of these political units. This, however, should not be taken to mean that linguistic-cultural units or identities were absent. What is meant is that there was no institutional congruence between political structures and identities, on the one hand, and linguistic-cultural structures and identities on the other. In Kannada literature right from the very first well-known literary work, *Kavirajamarga* or the great poet Pampa's epic, *Bharatha,* one can already encounter articulations of linguistic-cultural or even territorial identities, but such articulations are invariably mixed up with dynastic or religious-sectarian identities. But we hardly see any evidence of political loyalties or allegiances cultivated around purely political or administrative identities. They cohere mostly around dynastic or religious or simple territorial entities. Even more importantly, they also cohere around a variety of administrative-political units below the larger kingdoms. Therefore, to claim, as the ideologues of the demand for a modern, politically-territorially unified Karnataka on historical grounds is not sustainable. This is because they claimed that it had existed in the past and that they were merely reviving it in demanding it. What they were trying to do was to transform a traditional identity into a politicised modern identity. In that sense, they were creating a myth of a united political past but investing it with an historical status as part of their modern ideology.

The process of the creation of modern Karnataka State took the historical configuration of a movement for unification of the Kannada-speaking people and areas into a single British Indian province prior to independence and the continuation of the same movement after independence but now for a united Karnataka state under the new Constitution of free India. Before independence, the Kannada-speaking people were scattered into several units within the two broad systems into which the British had divided India—the British Indian provinces and the native Indian states. On the eve of independence, besides a number of small Indian states such as Savanur or Jamkhandi, they were to be found in two major native states—Mysore and Hyderabad. Within British India, they were to be found in the major presidencies of Bombay and Madras, and also in one of the Chief Commissioner's provinces, Coorg. Exception in Mysore state and Coorg, the Kannada-speaking people constituted a minority in the other areas—the Bombay Presidency, the Madras Presidency and Hyderabad state. We may designate these five areas where Kannadigas lived as sub-regions—Bombay Karnataka, Madras Karnataka, Mysore Karnataka, Hyderabad Karnataka and Coorg. What triggered off the movement for a unified Karnataka state, first pertaining only to the British Indian territory, was the classical minority grievance. The Kannada people in Bombay Presidency—living in the districts of Belgaum, Dharwad, Bijapur and North Kanara—felt that they were neglected, educationally, politically and economically, due primarily to the dominance of the Marathi-speaking people who controlled the levers of power under the colonial dispensation. Similarly, in the two Kannada-speaking districts of Bellary and South Kanara in the Madras Presidency, the Kannada people felt that they were neglected due to the dominance of the Telugu-speaking people and Tamil-speaking people, who used the colonial state to promote their narrow interests. In the princely state of Mysore, there was no such grievance but here unification remained for long a merely sentimental and cultural aspiration, with very little political urgency. The main centre of the unification movement and aspirations was Bombay Karnataka which generated first, a small trickle towards the close of the nineteenth century, a loosely organised and elite-oriented attempt to protest against the neglect. It was basically confined to a small group of educated persons, who were interested in gaining government jobs and in establishing educational institutions which were the passport to government jobs under the colonial system. From here, it spread to the other Kannada sub-regions. In the first phase, the demand for a unified Karnataka came to be articulated in the mode of petitioning the colonial regime, an index to the political timidity of an as-yet small educated, urban middle class.

Thanks to the agitation for it within the Congress movement, the Indian National Congress conceded the demand, not only in principle, but also in practice by reorganising its own structure on linguistic lines in 1920 at its Nagpur session. In fact, as a consequence, the Kannada-speaking territory was separated from the Maharashtra Circle, and came to be constituted as an independent Karnataka Provincial Congress Committee. More importantly, the first Indian National Congress accepted the principle of linguistic provinces in its report of 1928. Subsequently, the All India Congress Committee endorsed the principle in its Calcutta session in 1937. The historical record leaves in no doubt about the commitment of the Congress to the policy of linguistic reorganization of Indian territory. In 1938, the highest policy-making body of the Congress, the Working Committee, accepted the principle.[2] After independence, a cleavage of views developed between the national level of the Congress party, along with its national government in Delhi, and its regional or provincial or state units over the question of linguistic provinces. The national Congress leadership, both at the party and the government levels, began to drag its feet over the issue. The regional leaders pressed for the inclusion of the linguistic states in the new constitution in 1946, then being deliberated. The Constitution Assembly appointed, as a result a joint sub-committee of the Provincial and Union Constitutions Committees of the Assembly, to deal with the question. In 1947, the sub-committee passed a resolution, demanding that "... immediately after independence the government should appoint a commission to consider the new provinces of Andhra, Karnataka, Maharashtra, Kerala, and possibly others..."[3] However, the voluminous reports of the Constituent Assembly make scanty references to this question, thus underscoring its low rating of the importance of the issue.[4] After independence, the Constituent Assembly appointed in 1948 the Dhar Commission, so named after its Chairman, S.K. Dhar. It appears that this appointment took place in the teeth of opposition from Nehru and Patel, but Rajendra Prasad persuaded them to do so as a politically expedient maneuver.[5] This committee's overall framework reflected the radical change in the thinking of the national political elite on the issue of linguistic division of the territory within a federal union. Now the concern for national unity came to dominate this thinking. It rejected the linguistic principle as the sole or the dominant principle of reorganisation, adding other modifying considerations such as geographical contiguity, financial self-sufficiency, administrative convenience and potential for economic development. It specifically regarded linguistic demand as a demand for "sub-nationalism" and hence a threat to national unit. It recommended postponement of any consideration of the issue in view of more pressing nation-building tasks. The report came out in December 1948, and it was greeted with hostility by the Jaipur Congress Session which followed its publication. The Indian National Congress was forced to appoint another Linguistic Provinces Committee, consisting of Nehru, Patel and Pattabhi Sitaramiah, popularly known as JVP committee. In its report, while the committee was alarmed by the depth of linguistic loyalties, it did recommend that only one linguistic province, Andhra, should be immediately taken up. It is almost certain that Pattabhi's Andhra partisan position was behind this unreasonable recommendation. If any linguistic group had a better claim for reorganisation, it was certainly Karnataka. Naturally, it led to deep dissatisfaction in Mysore Congress, and the Congress legislators from the region offered to resign, and some even went to the extent of threatening to quit the Congress itself. Nehru, instead of showing statesmanship, preferred to procrastinate and play divisive politics, by trying to capitalise on the internal differences within the Karnataka political elite, especially on party, sub-regional and caste grounds. Through the early fifties, the Karnataka Congress tried to press for the demand for a separate province. When the Andhra leader Potti Sriramulu died after fasting over the Madras city issue, Nehru hurriedly announced the formation of Andhra on 1 October, 1953 in the Lok Sabha.[6] The Karnataka leaders were understandably disappointed that only Andhra was conceded but calculated that once Andhra was given, their claim would become stronger. Eventually the Congress government at the Centre was forced to appoint the States Reorganisation

Commission (SRC) in 1953, which consisted of Justice Fazl Ali (Chairman), K.M. Pannikar and Pandit H. Kunzru, with authority to make interim recommendations.

The Commission's report came out at the end of 1955. Its perception was that the demand for linguistic states rested on a fusion of the notions of administrative rationality and linguistic-cultural identity. It recommended a multi-dimensional approach which language would be an important factor but not the sole factor in the re-constitution of the states. The other factors identified by it were financial viability, the needs of regional economic development, administrative rationality, geographical contiguity, local history and tradition, and local public opinion. But, in its actual recommendations, it tended to accord language an overriding role.

In the Karnataka region itself, the story of the linguistic movement was anything but straightforward and simple. First, the conflict between the Congress and the opposition parties created a complication, though both were agreed on the overall demand for Karnataka. The opposition groups felt that the local Congress was unable to put up an effective struggle because of its being part of a party whose national leadership was lukewarm towards the formation of Karnataka. Hence, they took a prominent part in setting up an all-party organisation, the "Akrani", the All Karnataka State Formation Conference ("Akhand Karnataka Rajya Nirman Parishat"). Secondly, there were complications arising out of a conflict of caste interests, basically between the Lingayats who saw in unification the opportunity to seize political power, and the Vokkaligas who saw in it, by the same logic, loss of power. Thirdly, this conflict was neatly reflected in two other contexts as an intra-Congress conflict and inter-sub-regional conflict. The Mysore state which had been given a separate Congress organisational identity in 1950 and the Karnataka Pradesh Congress Committee (KPCC) representing the rest of the Kannada areas, were divided over the issue—the former wanting two Kannada states based respectively on old Mysore and the rest of the Kannada areas. Fourthly, there was an inter-sub-regional conflict between old Mysore and the rest of Kannada areas as well as between Coorg and the other Kannada areas. Both old Mysore and Coorg were not prepared to commit political suicide by merging into a larger, unified Karnataka. The final emergence of

Karnataka state did not do away with these conflicts but merely accommodated them within a new framework. The story ended as it did because of an All India compulsion to create linguistic states and also because of an intangible but unifying class framework centred round the new, urban and educated middle class, committed to the democratic and populistic ideology of linguistic state.

III

In this final section, I shall analyse and interpret the historical record briefly set forth in the preceding section. This can be done at various levels and *also* in terms of opposed frameworks. At the level of *politics* what happened was that a group of people developed a common identity around language, but also managed to link the identity with common material interest, and fought for their fused goal, which was the establishment of a political-administrative unit within the larger unit of the nation-system of India. So far as the Karnataka demand for unification was concerned, the argument was not in terms of sub-nationalism or nationality but in terms of a federal unit within a union of other such units as envisioned and stipulated in the 1950 Indian Constitution. The demand, in essence, was for reconstituting the constituent units of the Indian Union on a linguistic basis as a more rational and legitimate basis than the one arbitrarily imposed by colonial history. But this political demand involved a very complex process of integrating a variety of interests and identities into a larger legitimate unit. There were different caste identities and community identities which were sought to be integrated during the unification or "Ekikarana" movement into a larger unit of Karnataka, based on a common language as a unifying focal point, the linguistic identity and interest, that is, language as an identifying group characteristic and the interest of the people speaking the same language as a common group interest. Language also served as a principle of integrating diverse sub-regional identities and interests. However, the key political and historical question is: Why and how did language become an integrative factor and force?

This question leads us to two further questions: What was the ideological basis for the demand for re-constituting the units of the federal or quasi-federal system enshrined in the Indian Constitution on a linguistic basis? Who were the historical agents who fashioned this ideology and fought for a united, single Kannada state on its basis? To take up first the issue of ideology, it was basically the Brahmin ideologues, with some reinforcement from the Lingayat ideologues, who developed the ideological foundations of a united Karnataka province/state, comprising all the Kannada-speaking people and the territory they inhabited, currently fragmented into countless major and minor jurisdictions. Though the ideology was a collective group construct, its best written articulation came from Alur Venkat Rao, a Brahmin intellectual leader hailing from the Bombay Karnataka sub-region. He was popularly called "Karnataka Kulapurohita", the High Priest of the Karnataka clan.[7] He gave currency to the concept of "Karnatakatva", the principle of Karnataka or the essence of being Karnataka, which became the key emotional term in the Karnataka ideology. The ideology claimed that a group of people speaking habitually a common language had a right to become a distinctive and separate political-administrative unit within the overall Indian nation-state system, they first reconciled Karnatakatva with Bharatatva, countering the possible charge of sub-nationalism or nationality status or separatist politics. Secondly, it assumed that people speaking a common language had a common identity and common interest, cutting across other divisions such as caste, sub-region or even class. The ideology did not deny the reality of these divisions but asserted that a community of language could and did contain them within a common framework of life and culture. The ideology as articulated had links with two theories appropriated from the Western modern political culture, tradition and thought—the theory of federalism and liberal democracy. It maintained that the linguistic group was a legitimate unit within a federal political arrangement, and also that linguistic homogeneity between the rulers and the ruled facilitated effective democratic government. It was this ideological structure which formed the basis of the political movement out of which eventually emerged modern Karnataka. The ideology contained an element of mythologised history because it advanced the *historical* claim that Karnataka had always been a single political system prior to its dislocation and fragmentation due to the colonial conquest. As we saw at the start, this claim rests on a half-truth at best. Karnataka had never before been a united territorial political-administrative system, though it must be conceded that it did enjoy a loose and vague reality as an apolitical and cultural category. Thus, history entered the ideology as a mythical element. But then all human action partakes to some extent the character of a myth, and indeed it is even arguable whether science can ever banish myth from history or life or even from science itself totally. Also one may consider the question whether such a banishment of myth is desirable, even if possible. Plato banished the poets as liars from his Republic but he himself invoked the help of myth in constructing his political theory in *The Republic*.[8] But a myth is not so much a lie as an imaginative and poetical re-capturing of reality and truth, and it dominated man's mode of reflective life prior to the rise of the modern Western civilization.

Who created this ideology and why? There is clear evidence that it was the handiwork of the new educated urban middle class called into existence by the exigencies of the colonial system and which was partly deliberately created by the system to serve its needs. Seeing in their political master the strength they thought that they lacked and also thought that it was the reason why they had been enslaved, they went about imitating the theories and practices of their rulers. They embarked on a process of Westernization without letting the Western culture confront their indigenous culture. They wrote off their past as the cause of their present woes, and tended to reject it uncritically and unconditionally. It is this class which had, under the impact of Western education and socialization into Western values, imbibed the modern political culture of the West as exemplified in their masters, the British. This class saw its interest bound up with the systematic implantation of the alien institutions and structures of thought into the Indian soil. The process of formation of Karnataka was a part of the larger process of political modernization involving the presence and operation of modern ideas and structure—the nation-state, parliamentary democracy, modern rule of law, modern classes and mondernised castes. It is the unity of this class, which was certainly not a class in the Marxist sense of being linked to a mode of production nor a class wholly in the Weberian sense of being united by life-style, which made possible the use of the resource of a common language to create a political structure that was part of a new modern political system—the federal, parliamentary democratic system sustained within a nation-state system. In particular, the history of the formation of modern Karnataka illustrates well the integrative as well as conflictual functions of a modern entity, the political party. Along with that other modern entity, the class, the political party played a key role in the historical emergence of present Karnataka state on 1 November, 1956.

I will conclude with a small list of critical issues worth debating by our academic community specialising in the theory and practice of modern political science. The first most broad issue is whether the modernisation process itself is morally or theoretically legitimate in relation to the traditional local modes of thinking, acting and evaluating. The second broad question is whether, even if accepted as valid and legitimate, it has been practised and implemented in the spirit, not just in the letter. The third issue for critical pondering will be whether the establishment of Karnataka state has provided an adequate framework for dealing with the problems which were supposed to be overcome by the constitution and functioning of a linguistic state. In answering this last question, one runs into a paradox. While the demand for a unified Karnataka state was based on the ground that Karnataka was in fact already a unified community of people prepared to owe allegiance to common linguistic identity and capable of generating a common/collective interest of the language group as a totality, it was also claimed that the creation of a Karnataka state would either create a common identity and collective interest or strengthen them if they are already there in some form. Also has the new state been successful in rallying round the people speaking one language into a single cultural, political and economic community, cutting across but not cutting out of existence the diversities of caste, class, party and sub-region? Also, as originally claimed, has the state of Karnataka been successful in balancing its regional interest and identity with its national Indian identity and interest? Arguably, the recent Cauvery issue seems to underscore the failure on both grounds. While Karnataka has made itself vulnerable to the charge of narrow linguistic chauvinism, it has also let itself be attacked on the ground of being incompetent in articulating and politically managing the genuine interest of the Kannada people. The fragmentation of political culture that existed prior to the formation of the state and which was also the ground for demanding the state has not been eliminated or at least controlled, resulting in a political leadership unable to generate and project a common political will. Has the formation of the linguistic state of Karnataka facilitated a better functioning of democracy at the regional level? A true criterion of democracy is not only its ability to provide opportunity for the expression of pluralism but also its capacity to contain that pluralism through political skill and statesmanship Democracy both releases and disciplines popular energy and will. As a nation, we have been lurching from crisis to crisis, with the current crisis being the most fundamental and challenging of them all. The entire past of our politics and public life, our institutions including the Constitution, are in need of a drastic re-examination and re-structuring. Do we have the will, even if not wisdom, to perform these tasks?

NOTES AND REFERENCES

1. This section draws heavily on my unpublished Ph.D., dissertation, Linguistic Politics and the Congress Party in Mysore State, 1947-1956, University of Toronto, 1974.
2. *The Future of Karnataka,* Samyukta Karnataka daily, 1 May 1940, p. 3.
3. Granville Austin, *The Indian Constitution—Cornerstone of a Nation,* Oxford University Press, Oxford, 1966, p. 241.
4. Of the few references, mention maybe made of the following: linking the linguistic movement to Muslim communalism by Jaipal Singh (Bihar), *Constituent Assembly Debates (CAD),* Vol. IV, p. 672; the plea of T. Prakasham (Andhra) for linguistic provinces, *CAD,* Vol. VII, No. 3, November 1948; R.R. Diwakar's forthright demand that the Constituent Assembly should not evade the issue of linguistic provinces, CAD, Vol. VII, No. 3, p. 292; and a strong plea for linguistic provinces by S.V. Krishnamurthy Rao, CAD, Vol. VII, No. 5, p. 382. It is worth noting that all these members belonged to the Congress Party. It is also interesting to note that Diwakar came from Bombay Karnataka while Rao hailed from old Mysore.
5. Austin, *Ibid.,* op. cit., p. 241.
6. *The Report of the Linguistic Provinces Committee,* AICC, New Delhi, n.d.
7. K. Raghavendra Rao, *Heart is Karnataka: Life and Work of Alur Venkat Rao,*Karnataka Kulapurohit Alur Venkat Rao Centenary Celebrations Committee, Dharwar, 1980.
8. Of course, one should not forget the specifically classical Greek context of Plato, especially the ritual and religious function of art.

4

Karnataka's Political Culture

Reflections on a Soft State

R.L.M. PATIL

In the socio-economic-political field, the achievements of the state of Karnataka border only on the national average. In the professional areas of science and technology, administration, militia, music, sports and banking, Kannadigas have registered individual distinctions much above the standards set by the nation. It is paradoxical but nonetheless true that the people of Karnataka give an average performance collectively but achieve extraordinary success individually. It should be interesting to know why this is so, and what would its implications be.

Only a guess, at this stage, be hazarded. It is well known that the glory and pride of Kannadigas as empire builders belong to a distant past. Owing to quirks of history they, in the later days, came to be splintered, separated and severed from one another and merged into different larger ethnic groupings. A kind of diaspora of the Kannadiga may be said to have lasted for about four hundred years from the downfall of the Vijayangar Empire in 1565 to the reincarnation of one state of Kannada-speaking people in 1956 as a part of the linguistic reorganisation of states in India. The chequered history of the Kannadigas in between the threshold years ought to have left a deep impress upon their traits and outlook. Being in the minority everywhere (excepting the Mysore princely state) they had to survive collectively and struggle to gain recognition individually. Neither political clout nor economic power they could command yet could they rise above the rest through individual efforts.

As an example, one might look at the four big districts of Bijapur, Dharwad, Belgaum and Karwar (now Uttara Kannada) in the old Bombay presidency. In this populous agricultural Kannada-speaking area there was hardly any investment in industry, education, health, roads and communications so long as it was a part of the Bombay state. Nonetheless, it did produce outstanding musicians, militiamen, poets and writers and saints. This kind of drag is seen replicated in other Kannada-speaking minority areas in the old Madras state and that of the Nizam of Hyderabad.

The national freedom movement from the times of Lokamanya Tilak subsumed the yearning of the Kannada minorities everywhere to regroup themselves after being freed from the domination of the stronger ethnic groups. Gandhiji understood intuitively these urges, and moved a resolution in the Congress party's meetings, as early as 1917, calling for the recognition of the principle that the language of the government and administration be the language of the people. Later on, this "linguistic dimension of freedom" provided a strong motive-force not only for the achievement of freedom of the country but also for the integration of Kannada-speaking areas into one state of Karnataka later on.

Once the emotional need for integration was fulfilled, the stark reality with regard to the economic and social conditions overwhelmed the people of Karnataka. There were five sets of people with a wide variation of economic, administrative and educational systems. Even linguistic undertones and dialects were different—at times even treated as funny by one another. Bombay, Madras, Hyderabad and Mysore cities were still regarded as the epicenters of higher culture. Bilinguism and biculturalism were generally prevalent in all those areas which were parts of British-India provinces of Bombay and Madras and that of Hyderabad under the Nizam.

Eventually, these Kannada-speaking areas were regrouped in 1956 along with the princely state of Mysore which was a unilingual Kannada-speaking and by far the largest unit. The group was named Mysore as though it was an enlargement of one unit rather than a amalgamation. This was obviously a ploy to win over the die-hard "Mysoreans" who might have been jealous about their own distinction which would have been lost if the new grouping was called Karnataka. Political unity among the Kannada-speaking population was thus achieved on November 1, 1956, but other diversities among them remained. The new state contained an unusually large number of linguistic minorities. The proportion of the minorities to the main—language—speakers in Karnataka is the highest in India barring the North-east states. They constitute about one-third of the state population and nearly two-third in the state's capital city of Bangalore! Fortunately, their presence has contributed to the development of cosmopolitan culture rather than fragmentation and internecine quarrels.

What is a surprising feature of Karnataka—a state born out of five sets of regions taken from different milieus—is the relative absence of sub-regional discontent. Though regional identities are not lost altogether, hardly is there any move for political recognition of regional groupings. North Karnataka with Hubli-Dharwad as the centre and Coorg/Kodagu districts have of late been agitated over the lack of developmental work, or "neglect" of these areas by the rulers who are all Bangalore-obsessed, the people as a whole seem to be using the agitations to draw attention of the government to their grievances rather than believe sincerely in the partitioning of the state. All political parties and almost all leaders have dismissed any question of separation of any region from the state. This wholesome trend can be attributed to two different reasons. One is the maturity and emotional satisfaction of the Kannadigas and their aversion for political adventurism. The second is the setting of the economic and social agenda before the people. Devaraj Urs as Chief Minister struck a blow for emotional integration when in 1974, he renamed the state as Karnataka. Again, it was Urs who sounded the bugle for the uplift of the socially and economically backward people of the state. To have intertwined the two emotions into a strong and irreversible strand was stroke of his political genius.

Unlike some other states in India, where electoral fortunes of parties fluctuate from one extreme to another, in Karnataka the Congress party is placed comfortably. It has been in power in the state continuously from the time of the creation of the state until now except for two brief spells—when the Janata party under Ramakrishna Hegde and S.R. Bommai and the Janata Dal under H.D. Deve Gowda and J.H. Patel ruled. Even as they did, there was hardly any difference between them and the Congress either on the ideological plane or in terms of caste-composition of their base. This flair for continuity and conservation is reflective of the Kannadigas' aversion to any form of political adventurism or ideological romance. The voter would prefer to refine the tools rather than go in for sensational change. The Aristotelian golden mean appears to be part of the mental make up of the people of the state.

It may also noted that unlike in Tamil Nadu there is neither politics of cult or sharp political radicalism in Karnataka, nor is there the ideological split as witnessed in Kerala, nor a strong regional bias as in Andhra Pradesh and Maharashtra though all these states surround Karnataka.

On another plane, Karnataka has displayed sobriety in its approach to inter-state as well as centre-state relations. In what might be termed as federal diplomacy, the state has evolved its typical broad-minded and nationalistic approach avoiding the path of confrontation. The stand the state has adopted *vis-a-vis* the border adjustment with Maharashtra and river-water with Tamil Nadu goes to show that the leadership (as well as the public) desired all the time to resolve the disputes through the method of dialogue and discussion rather than the path of confrontation, political pressure or litigation. Even with regard to the relationship with Central Government, the state-leadership has adopted co-operative and cordial approach as indeed displayed when an "opposite" party was controlling the state under the Chief Ministership of Urs (when Morarji Desai was the Prime Minter), of Ramakrishna Hegde (when Indira Gandhi and Rajiv Gandhi were Prime Ministers), of Veerendra Patil (when V.P. Singh was the Prime Minister), and J.H. Patel and S.M. Krishna (when A.B. Vajpayee was the Prime Minister).

What might be termed as the "Congress culture"—which is 'fighting within but putting up a united front against rivals"—is seen operating in Karnataka. There is an advantage in this style of operation: it helps to rule through consensus and adjustments. Yet, at the same time, it slows down political mobilisation and interest articulation. The social heterogeneity, moderate economic prosperity, intellectual smugness, culture catholicism, deep-rooted mystical heritage have all contributed to the political making of Karnataka—which can be described as accommodation, moderation and co-operation. If any proof for this be needed, the following random selection of issues of Karnataka's political canvas may be adduced.

Language Policy of Karnataka

Unlike many other states, Karnataka is facing a number of problems in enforcing the regional language in its administration and educational institutions. While the Kannada-speaking majority is pressing for the enforcement of its language in all walks of life, the minority groups which are numerically strong (in as much as they constitute 1/3rd of the state population and 2/3rd of the population of the capital of Bangalore, as mentioned earlier) are offering resistance to the imposition of the Kannada language to the detriment of their Constitutionally-guaranteed rights.

Technically, Kannada is declared the official language both through the legislature's resolutions and cabinet's decisions; and yet it is not implemented in full measure. Normally, the Head of the state is a non-Kannada-speaking person; additionally some of the ministers in the government, in recent times, have not been conversant with Kannada. Legislative bills and cabinet decisions are drafted in English. Kannada versions of the bills are provided when introduced in the legislative but in cases of discrepancy the English version prevails over the one in Kannada. The same is true with respect to official notifications as well.

In administration, English still continues to be the medium at the higher echelons even though the Chief Secretaries have, from time to time, asked officers to use Kannada, and even threatened to take disciplinary action against those who do not heed this advice. These threats appear to be way of appeasement of the Kannada protagonists. The lack of familiarity with Kannada as an administrative language as well as a genuine difficulty of getting hold of proper phrases and equivalents to well-known English usage employed in official communication are the chief hindrances in the implementation of Kannada as the administrative language.

In the courts, there is an additional dimension to the language controversy. Apart from the difficulty of arguing cases in Kannada when the laws, judgements and commentaries are all in English, it has been pointed out by respected professional, in the field that the moment a lawyer argues in Kannada the client ticks him off as incompetent, whatever the judge might think of him!

The slow and tardy implementation has prompted the government, over the past decade, to appoint a Kannada Watchdog Committee headed by a person with the rank of a Cabinet Minister. The Janata government of Ramakrishna Hegde started this practice which has since been continued by the Congress government. This experiment has not brought any significant changes.

The policy of introducing Kannada either as the medium of instruction or at least as a compulsory subject to be taught in the schools in Karnataka has run into rough weather. While the protagonists insist on making Kannada a compulsory subject not only in government-run schools but also in those managed by private bodies, a number of legal and practical problems have arisen. Three important questions need to be raised in this context: (i) whether the minority institutions can be forced to accom-modate Kannada in their educational programme; (ii) whether the parents of the children have the fundamental right to choose the language or the medium of instruction; and (iii) whether it is desirable and practicable to teach four languages to children (English, Hindi, the mother tongue Kannada)? The controversy has been rendered even more confusing by the contradictory demands of banning English medium schools by the well known educationists (H. Narsimhaiah, K.V. Puttappa and U.R. Anantha Murthy and the Kannada protagonists) as against the majority of the then ruling Congress (I) MLAs who asked, in 1990, the Education Minister to open new English medium schools in the rural areas so as to benefit the backward sections of the society. Leaders of minorities and the SC/ST sections also backed this request. The then Chief Minister, Veerendra Patil told the legislative assembly on 16 July, 1990, that "We cannot brush aside the fact that parents prefer to send their children to a convent rather than a government school where the standard of education is poor. ... It is important what parents feel, not what you and I do". This liberal view has come to prevail ultimately, though not without a torturous path taken by the language-policy evolution. To capture the enormously complex evolution in a capsule one might present it in a tabular form as below:

Table 4.1: Language Policy in Karnataka

Year	*Policy*
Till 1976	Sanskrit along with Kannada and other languages, included in the First Language in High Schools (leading to SSLC).
1976	The Kannada Sahitya Parishad urges the government to remove Sanskrit (which was viewed as a smooth pass-over and high-scorer to the detriment of Kannada at the SSLC examination).
1979	The Devaraj Urs government accepts the recommendation to do away with Sanskrit.
1980	Gundu Rao the new Chief Minister, promises to restore Sanskrit to its erstwhile place. Pro-Kannada agitation commences; A Committee of Seven headed by V.K. Gokak is appointed to recommend the relative position of Sanskrit and Kannada. Receives rebuff from Pro-Kannada agitators.
January 1981	The Gokak Committee report recommends primacy to Kannada and its compulsory teaching (with a graded mild form for minority children). Kannada agitators jubilant; demand its implementation in toto. Minorities unhappy; want its rejection or modification; counter agitation against it commences.
1982	Pro-Kannada agitation renewal ("Those minorities who do not want to learn Kannada should better go out"). Raj Kumar Fans Association launches an anti-minority protest movement.
19 April, 1982	Gundu Rao's cabinet after a round table meeting thrashes out a compromise solution; Kannada not the sole first language but compulsorily taught.
July and August 1982	Orders issued to make Kannada teaching compulsory in all primary schools; The order challenged; partial stay granted; partial implementation.
25 January, 1989	The High Court strikes down the order as unconstitutional (violation of minority rights of Article 14).
16 June, 1989	New language formula announced (during President's Rule): (a) Only one language as a compulsory subject and the mother-tongue to be the medium from Class I to Class IV. (b) Kannada for non-Kannadigas to be taught purely on a voluntary basis, with neither examination nor a pass required, from Class III to Class IV. (c) A third language along with the above second or Kannada introduced from Class V to Class VII, there being to be need to pass the examination in this third language. (d) All the three language to be studied and passes in examination from Class VIII to Class X (second and third languages however not reckoned for ranking).
11 December, 1993	The Supreme Court upholds the order.

The above formula seems to have gone well with a large section of the people even though the English medium school managements are utterly sore with it. The Supreme Court's decision upholding the language formula of June 1989, has not ended the controversy. The determination of the rights of minority institutions as well as those of the unaided privately-managed institutions, and those of institutions which are affiliated to Central Board of Secondary Education (CBSE) remains a vexed tangle. Further, the mushroom growth of professional colleges (Medical and Engineering) under private and minority managements has added a new-business-dimensions to the education-system in Karnataka. The picture, as of now, is far from clear.

The Issue of Reservation for Backward Classes

Almost coinciding with the starting of the anti-Brahmin movement in the Madras presidency, in the old Mysore princely state there was founded the Prajamitra Mandali, whose aim, too, was the displacement of Brahmins from power. C.R. Reddy, A. Banerji and Kantharaje Urs were some of the key supporters of the move which led ultimately to the resignation of Sir M. Vishveshwaraiah from the Dewanship of the state, and also resulted in the establishment of a Committee headed by Sir Leslie Miller (in 1918) to enquire into the grievances of the local backward communities about their inadequate representation in the services. The questions raised then in 1918—who are the backwards and what would be an adequate representation for them—continue to haunt the state even today. However, there is one very important difference between the reservation policy then and now. Earlier, the protection sought was against the Brahmin but now it is one against another backward community. The two politically dominant castes—Vokkaligas and Lingayats—are vying with the scheduled castes, scheduled tribes and other backward communities for a significant place in the reserved category. Between themselves the twin dominant communities command around 28 per cent of the population and nearly half the number of MLAs. Economic power, too, is held to a significant extent by them. Their capacity for mobilisation is also vast and effective. Hence, it has become virtually impossible for any politician to keep them both out of the pale of the reservations and yet survive in the electoral battle.

S. Nijalingappa kept both of them in, Devaraj Urs tried to keep the Lingayats out while keeping some Vokkalinga in. Ramakrishna Hegde accommodated both with a proviso for maximum annual income, and Veerappa Moily showed "large heartedness" to include both the communities with almost no bars, pushing up the total reservation to 73 per cent which was to go further up to 80 per cent ! However, this Act of the state was shot down when the Supreme Court pronounced its verdict in the Mandal case. It is interesting to note that in Karnataka, there are no two views, among the political parties, on providing a fairly high degree of reservation for the OBCs.

Table 4.2: Caste Profile of Karnataka

Caste	*Percentage of population*
OBCs	29.80
Lingayats	16.00
Vokkaligas	12.00
Muslims	11.20
Scheduled Castes	17.00
Scheduled Tribes	04.70
Christians	02.00
Brahmins	.03.18
Other (Jain, Vaishyas, etc.)	04.12
Total	100.00

Inter-state Dispute Resolution

Karnataka has two important disputes with its neighbouring states on account of its chequered history. Both of them—dispute with Maharashtra over Belgaum and the Cauvery Waters Dispute with Tamil Nadu—are quite old and have their origins in multiple factors.

Disputes between states within a federal system constitute a category of their own. They do not fit into the description of international disputes since the entities are not sovereign states. They do not have military forces at their disposal nor do they have access to international legal forums and the benefit of international law in resolving their differences. They do possess, nevertheless, what is vaguely connoted as "national interest" which are both vital and impersonal. No matter who or which party rules these states, there is hardly any scope for compromise on the interests of the state. At the same time, these inter-state disputes cannot be resolved like a municipal dispute within the state purview, especially when such disputes are many-dimensional. The Supreme Court does have some jurisdiction over inter-state disputes but the nature of the disputes most of the time are such that a strictly legal approach—Zero sum approach—is neither feasible nor desirable.

Karnataka's running battle with Maharashtra over the affinity of Belgaum whether that town belongs to Maharashtrians or Kannadigas—is as old as the hills.

Maharashtra's claim to Belgaum rests on the following grounds. Belgaum has been historically a part of Maharashtrian territory; and its elected representatives have been in favour of its merger with Maharashtra. On the other hand, Karnataka's claims are that Belgaum has historically been a town of the Kannadigas; a preponderant majority of the people of Belgaum taluk and district speak Kannada; the Marathi-speaking populace of Belguam town were the immigrants from the neighbouring Konkan and Poona regions from where the English educated bureaucratic and professional class came to work and eventually settled in Belgaum which had been seeing the expansion of commercial, administrative, military and railway activities and which intermittently, witnessed lakhs of local Kannada-speaking farming community perish in epidemics (1876, 1892, 1896 and 1900); and that there is no geographical contiguity between Maharashtra border and the town of Belgaum where the Marathi-speaking people constitute a simple majority.

Whatever the merits and demerits of their claims, the two sides have adopted two entirely different approaches in their efforts to resolve the dispute. While one has been brilliantly aggressive the other has been cleverly rational; while one has been a warrior-diplomat wanting all-or-nothing, the other has been like a merchant who has his interests incorporated in the preliminary terms of bargaining. The two tables below show that while Maharashtra is uncompromising on its claims to the town of Belgaum even to the extent of refusing attractive compensations, Karnataka is successful in putting across a rational argument as to why it is unsafe to go by a single consideration of linguistic majority in a village in deciding its affinity to a larger state.

Table 4.3: Border Dispute

State	*Claims advanced (1950-67)*	*Mahajan Award (1950-67)*	*Union Home Ministry Proposals*		
			Y.B. Chavan Home Minister	*Brahmananda Reddy Home Minister*	*H.M. Patel Home Minister*
			1970	1975	1979
Maharashtra	814-868 villages + Belgaum	264 villages without Belgaum	500 villages plus a division of Belgaum	In addition Supa petha forest area without Belgaum	617 villages 15.18 lakh population but without Belguam
Karnataka	528 villages (including the 246 offered voluntarily by Maharashtra)	248 villages	To lose (more)	To lose (even more)	To lose (much more)

Based on: (i) The Mahajan Commission Report, Vol. 1, pp. 21-22, 193-94.
(ii) Deccan Herald, 3 May, 1972.
(iii) The Hindu, 16 January, 1974.
(iv) The Statesman, 29 April, 1975.
(v) The Hindustan Times, 29 May, 1979.

Table 4.4: Fluctuation of Demographic and Linguistic Composition of Border Villages Between 1951 and 1961

Name of village	*Year of consensus*	*Marathi speaking*	*Kannada speaking*	*Total population*
Kurihal	1951	97%	0.0%	
(Belgaum Tlq)	1961	26%	73.7%	57(1961)
Bodkenhatti	1951	100%	0.0%	
(Belgaum Tlq)	1961	69%	30.2%	477(1961)
Bellanki	1951	98.3%	1.7%	
(Hukkeri Tlq. Belgaum dist.)	1961	0.0%		
Banjibasari	1951	41.7%	28.2%	
Katit (Khanapur Tlq. Belgaum dist)	1961	0.0%	74.1%	228(1961)

Source: The Mahajan Commission Report, 1967, Vol. I, p. 28.

The outcome of the Karnataka approach to this dispute-resolution can be summed up as a triumph of bargain-cum-flexibility-cum-rational negotiation over the method of sentimental, non-negotiable, one-point demand. As the years pass, the so-called "border dispute" between the two states is bound to recede from the public memory and national agenda which in a way suits Karnataka's interests eminently well.

The other historical dispute Karnataka has inherited relates to the sharing of waters of the Cauvery with Tamil Nadu. The dispute arose nearly a century ago between the then British ruled Madras presidency and the native princely state of Mysore. Guided by enlightened self-interests and sound principles of mutual accommodation, a political settlement between the two governments was arrived at in 1892. In it were enshrined the principles of equity and reasonableness much before one had over heard of the Harmon Doctrine (1885) or of the Helsinki Doctrine (1966). However, when the question of utilizing the "surplus waters" arose in 1906, when the Mysore government wished to construct a reservoir at Kannambadi (KRS) across the Cauvery near Mysore. The Madras government raised objections and demanded a re-examination of the agreement. As a result even as the Mysore government was in a disadvantageous position, on account of the superior power of the Madras presidency backed by the British government from London, another Agreement on Rules and Regulations was signed between the two in 1924. As per its own terms, it should have been reviewed and renegotiated after fifty years, that is in 1974. During the years in between, each state accused the other of violating, openly or surreptitiously, the various provisions of the Agreement. The main argument of the Mysore state was that the terms of the Agreement were unequal and weighed against the long-term interests of the state and that it was made to sign the Agreement on account of political pressure from outside.

Tamil Nadu dismisses the plea of the Mysore or Karnataka and insists that the latter conform strictly to the provisions and the share of waters as envisaged in the 1924 pact. Any review of it or even the suggestion that the pact is loaded against Karnataka is resented by Tamil Nadu. All the efforts to persuade the two parties to come to a negotiated settlement of their differences have proved fruitless—mainly on account of the fact that one of the two, viz.,

Tamil Nadu refuses to reopen the basic issue of equity and fairness in the allotment of the rights of riparian states but insists upon the implementation of the pact as concluded in 1924 and operated ever since. In all the 28 rounds of negotiations held so far, this party entered into the negotiation room with a declared lack of faith in negotiated settlement. It was forced into a charade of negotiation-rounds because of the pressure of the Central Government or public opinion from outside. And after the "failure" of a negotiated settlement process, it could justifiably knock on the doors of the Supreme Court.

Karnataka, on the other hand, has been insisting on negotiations on the basis of fairness, equity and practicability—the hall-mark of diplomacy. It also submitted that the very legal basis of the 1924 pact was untenable on many counts. The original pact (1924) was signed by the Mysore state under duress. Its terms were favourable to one and biased against another. The pact as reached then was between two state parties (the Madras state and the Mysore state) which are no more in existence after independence or at least after the commencement of the Constitution of India under which there are no sovereign entities to that pact. The then Madras state was split, and on other hand, the then Mysore state underwent fundamental changes after the 1956 reorganization of states and hence the original parties stood changed in law and geography. Apart from all these considerations, the Constitution of India bars the Supreme Court of India from entertaining any disputes arising out of the pacts or treaties or agreements reached or operated prior to the commencement of the Constitution (Art. 131). The Constitution also says specifically that "neither the Supreme Court nor any other court" has jurisdiction over the disputes arising out of a treaty or agreement reached during the British rule between any Princely state and the British Provincial or Dominion Government (Art 363). In the light of these arguments it was open to Karnataka to refuse to accept the jurisdiction of the Supreme Court or the Cauvery Water Tribunal. Yet it accepts. Further, the Supreme Court in its earlier stance, refused to entertain petitions in this regard which came from Tamil Nadu. But later on it changed its stand. This was regrettable because the Courts are not a proper forum to solve the multi-dimensional disputes like the river-waters, temples-masjid or social backwardness. They involve economics, sociology, technology, management, history, politics and law. Such multi-dimensional conflicts can be tackled satisfactorily only under the framework of a non-zero-sum games. The judicialization of such conflicts transforms the non-zero-game into a zero-sum-game and hence compounds the difficulties. Politics or diplomacy is the only approach available to solve such problems. Karnataka has stood for this line of conflict-resolution all the while.

It is needless to criticize the other state which has adopted the approach of speaking from the position of strength and holding out veiled threats of "do as I say or honour the pact, or else I'll take you the Court", but still it may be useful to point out that the approach of the Karnataka state has been reflective of the characteristics of its people, the political culture of the state, viz., moderation, accommodation and co-operation—be it the border or water dispute, be it with Maharashtra, Tamil Nadu, Andhra Pradesh or the Centre. This style or even philosophy of accommodation raises truly another important question in the context of federalism. What Karnataka has practised can be characterized as "federal diplomacy".

This essay was written before the kidnapping of Karnataka's movie icon Raj Kumar. The way the entire episode was handled by the Chief Minister S.M. Krishna affirms the view expressed in this essay, viz., about the people of Karnataka as well as their political culture, in an overall sense.

On the whole it may be concluded that the people of Karnataka with which the State Government is fully attuned, reflect the characteristics of a suave, reasonable, accommodative, moderate and co-operative culture. On the converse, it may also be said that frenzy, blood-letting, parochialism and stubbornness are out so far as Karnataka culture is concerned. Which one is better is a matter of individual taste. But certainly the people of Karnataka as a whole—there might be minor exceptions to it—have acted in conformity with the culture of Constitutionalism. Karnataka is, in other words, a soft state. If it is also a soft-ware state, it is a different matter.

5

Office of the Chief Minister

S.A. PALEKAR

The Indian constitution is federal in form, although Article 1 of the constitution describes it as a Union of States. In a federation, there are two sets of governments, the national and that of the constituent units. Both exercise powers granted to them by the constitution and both are supreme within the spheres assigned to them. The political and administrative organisation of the states is similar to the counterpart, the national government.

The Chief Minister of the state is the real executive head of the government although formally the executive authority is vested in the governor. The Chief Minister like the Prime Minister of India, is the key stone of the State Government. The unique position of authority enjoyed by him derives from his status as the leader of the majority party in the legislative assembly and from his power to recommend ministers for appointment to the governor and to obtain their resignation or dismissal individually.

The Chief Minister is appointed by the Governor. The constitution does not specify any qualifications for the Chief Minister. Under the constitution all that is needed is that the person be a citizen of India and possess such qualifications as required for becoming a member of the legislative assembly. There are no educational or other qualifications for his appointment. Such a person could be a member of either house of the legislature or even an outsider. Although constitutionally a non-legislator does not stand barred from becoming a minister or a Chief Minister, he must, however, become a member of the legislature within six months failing which he is liable to forfeit his office.

Usually, the leader of the majority party in the state legislative assembly is appointed as the Chief Minister. Under normal conditions when a single political party gets absolute majority, the governor has no difficulty in appointing the Chief Minister and he invites the leader of the majority party to assume the mantle. However, when no single political party enjoys a clear-cut majority in the assembly, the governor can use discretion in the appointment of the Chief Minister. If a number of political parties come to an understanding, elect a common leader and inform the governor of their decision, he failing which the governor has to use his discretion in the appointment of Chief Minister. But if the governor feels that the political composition of the state legislature is such that no stable government can be formed, he may recommend to the President of India that the state be placed under President's rule.

As a matter of convention, it is expected that the Chief Minister must be a member of the legislative assembly. However, there is no constitutional bar on the appointment of a member of legislative council. There are many instances to show that one who was a member of the upper house was appointed Chief Minister. In Karnataka D. Devaraj Urs was appointed as Chief Minister in 1972 without membership of the state legislature. Later he got elected to the legislative assembly in a by-election. In 1983 Ramakrishna Hegade was appointed as the Chief Minister of Karnataka without being member of the state legislature.

Thus the selection of the Chief Minister has always been a complex problem. It is a matter within the discretionary power of the governor. The Governor appoints the Chief Minister who is politically selected by the party as their leader. Now it has become common among all parties that Chief Ministers are nominees of the high command of the party. As a result, Chief Minister are now made in and exported from New Delhi.

The present Chief Minister of Karnataka, S.M. Krishna, is hand picked by the Congress high command especially the Congress President, Sonia Gandhi. However, the ready-made Chief Ministers are by no means non-entities. If any Chief Minister has shown signs of independence as a functionary, he has been immediately replaced under one pretext or the other. A.G. Noorani has rightly said, "The constitution established a parliamentary system at the centre and in the states in which the head of the government is responsible to the legislature and to no outside authority, that would be negation of the very basis of responsible government. It should be plain to all by now that the centralized authorization structure of the ruling party is incongruous in a democratic parliamentary system which is also a federation. Like governors, if the CMs are also to be nominated by the centre the federal principle is set at naught."[1]

The Chief Minister stays in office at the pleasure of the governor, but in reality he continues in office as long as he enjoys the support of the majority of the members of the house. The Governor cannot retain a person as Chief Minister who does not enjoy the majority support of the house. It has been rightly said, "The head of the state can neither withdraw his pleasure from a ministry, which enjoys the confidence of the house nor can be save a Ministry which has lost the confidence of the house by the continuance of his pleasure".[2]

The Chief Minister of a state enjoys a wide range of powers both in law as well as in practice. He has the power of forming a ministry of his choice. He can appoint any member or even a non-member as a minister and allocate him any portfolio. However, there are several practical limitations while selecting his ministers. There are considerations which weigh with him, for example, he has to give a fair representation to the different communities of the state. He cannot ignore the claims of prominent leaders of his party. The State Governor has little role to play in the ministry making. It is the prerogative of the Chief Minister. He decides who will be a cabinet minister or a minister of state or a deputy minister. While doing so he has to keep in mind the seniority and the political status of his ministers.

The Chief Minister has the privilege to reorganize the council of ministers if he so desires. He has the right to change the members of his ministry in the interest of the state's administration. He may ask any minister to resign. Moreover, he can get any minister dismissed by the governor. He is the real maker, modifier and destroyer of the council of ministers. He presides over the meetings of the cabinet. As chairman of the cabinet, he plays a key role in the deliberations held and the decisions taken. Every decision of the state cabinet bears the imprint of his ideas, views and perceptions. He can veto any decision by threatening to resign. Ministers are in fact never willing to displease him. The Chief

Minister acts as a link between the governor and the council of ministers. It is his duty to communicate to the governor the decisions of the council of ministers, relating to the administration of the state and proposals for legislation. He is also required to furnish such information about administration and legislative proposals, as the governor may call for. He also acts as a co-ordinator. As a co-ordinator he has to see that all the ministers work as a team and help each other. He resolves conflict and dead-locks between any two or more departments.

The Chief Minister is the leader not only of his party but also of the legislative assembly. He acts as the spokesman of the government and makes important announcements on behalf of the government. It is his duty to help the members of his cabinet on the floor of the house in case they are being cornered by the opposition. He defends the policies of the government. He has the right to advise the governor to dissolve the state legislative assembly. Normally he gives such advice on the basis of political considerations. The advice is binding upon the governor when the Chief Minister still has a majority support. As the real head of the government, it is his main responsibility to maintain good relations with the centre. It helps him for securing central grants and help, considered vital for carrying out the development work in the state. When the Chief Minister belongs to the same party which is in power at the centre, he has to use his influence for securing the interest of the state. In case, he belongs to a party other than the one which is in power at the centre he has to act as a good negotiator, as Karnataka Chief Minister, S.M. Krishna has been doing. All the major appointments and promotions are made by the governor on the advice of the Chief Minister.

A look at the powers of the Chief Minister enumerated above shows that he has really been vested with very extensive powers in the administration of the state. But the position of the Chief Minister of a state depends on his party affiliation and the majority support at his command. A Chief Minister belonging to a party which is in power at the centre and enjoying support of the party is in a very strong position. Such a Chief Minister enjoys the backing of the party high command and has hold over the party organization. Such Chief Ministers are even able to influence the governor of the state. His position belonging to a party which is not in power at the centre on the other hand cannot be as strong.

He may have a clear-cut majority in the state legislature, but he cannot expect a subservient governor, who is a nominee of the centre. Usually, in such states the Chief Minister has to be very tactful in handling his supporters so that they remain united, otherwise it may lead to dissentions in the party, which may be exploited by the opponents to bring about the fall of the government.

It can be said that the Chief Ministers of all the states do not possess an identical position. It varies a great deal and depends to a large extent on their personality, the party affiliation, and the amount of the party support they can muster. While generalizing about their position it may be said that usually the Chief Ministers belonging to the party which is in power at the centre and enjoying the support of the majority of the members of the state legislature and party high command, hold a much stronger position than the Chief Ministers of a party whose party is not in power at the centre or heading a coalition government. The strength of his office depends both on his personal qualities and the political environment prevailing in his state.

In Karnataka eminent personalities like K.C. Reddy, K. Hanumanthaiah, S. Nijalingappa, B.D. Jatti, Veerendra Patil, D. Devaraj Urs, Gundu Rao, Ramakrisha Hegade, Veerappa Moily, S. Basalingappa, J.H. Patel, S.R. Bommai occupied the office of the Chief Minister and played a significant role in state administration, state politics and also at the national politics.

K. Changalaraya Reddy, the first Chief Minister of the old Mysore state was a model Chief Minister. His patriotism, courage of conviction and honesty were worthy of emulation by today's politicians. Reddy, who ruled for over four years from October 1947, laid the foundation for the development of the new state. Though the construction of the Vidhana Soudha is attributed to Reddy's successor, Kengal Hanumanthaiah, hardly any mention is made of Reddy's role. The Vidhana Soudha project was planned and decided upon by the Reddy cabinet from which Hanumanthaiah had been left out. However, it had not been given the name Vidhana Soudha and was simply called "House of Legislature". It was the then Prime Minister, Jawaharlal Nehru, who laid the foundation stone of the House of Legislature project on July 13, 19...... and K.C. Reddy was the Chief Minister. The contribution of S. Nijalingappa, Kengal Hanumanthaiah,

Veerendra Patil, S.R. Bommai, D. Devaraj Urs was very significant towards the state administration.

Devaraj Urs as Chief Minister in 1974, renamed the state as Karnataka. Again it was Urs who called for the upliftment of the socially and economically backward people of the state. "To have intertwined the two emotions into a strong and irreversible strand was a stroke of political genius of Urs."[3]

In Karnataka the Congress party is placed comfortably and it has been in power in the state continuously from the time of the creation of the state up till now, except for two brief spells. When the Janata Party under Ramakrishna Hegade and S.R. Bommai and the Janata Dal under H.D. Deve Gowda and J.H. Patel ruled the state. Even as they did, there was hardly any difference between them and the Congress either on the ideological plane or in terms of caste composition of their base. The Chief Ministers of Karnataka have shown sobriety in their approach to inter-state as well as centre-state relations. They have adopted a broad-minded and nationalistic approach, avoiding the path of confrontation. The state leadership has always desired to resolve disputes through peaceful means rather than through the path of confrontation. Even with regard to its relationship with the Central Government, the state leadership has adopted a co-operative and cordial approach as indeed shown when another party controlled the state under the Chief Ministership of Devaraj Urs (when Morarji Desai was the Prime Minister), Ramakrishna Hegde (when Indira Gandhi and Rajiv Gandhi were Prime Minister), Veerendra Patil (when V.P. Singh was the Prime Minister), and J.H. Patel and S.M. Krishna (when A.B. Vajpayee is the Prime Minister).

It has become virtually impossible for any Chief Minister to keep two politically dominant communities—Vokkaligas and Lingayats out of the pale of reservation and yet survive in the electoral battle. S. Nijalingappa kept both of them in. On the other hand, Devaraj Urs tried to keep the Lingayats out while keeping some Vokkaligas in, whereas Ramakrishna Hegade accommodated both, and Veerappa Moily showed "large heartedness" to include both the communities. S.M. Krishna started functioning as Chief Minister in October 1999 with a distinct advantage. A clear majority for his government, the full backing of the party high command, his own long political and administrative experience coupled with his technocratic vision, provided him with a unique opportunity to chalk out the style and substance of his governance. A thinking politician that he is, together with his impressive educational background, Krishna has imparted a distinct developmental perspective to his government.

The position of Indian Prime Minister is unchallengeable which no other colleague of his can rival. But the Chief Ministers in majority of the states do not enjoy that unique position of exceptional authority. Members of the majority parties in the state legislature and ministers, clamour for office and seek favouritism casteism personal differences, intra-party conflicts, regionalism and communalism affect the functioning of the Chief Minister.

NOTES AND REFERENCES

1. A. G. Noorani, *Mr. Bhonsale and Congress I Culture*, Indian Express, February, 1982.
2. S. R. Maheshwari, *State Government of India*, ..., 1979.
3. Arun P. Bali (Ed.) *Refashioning the New Economic Order: Karnataka in Transition*, Jaipur, Rawat Publications, 2001, p. 47.

6

Evolution of the Office of the Speaker in Karnataka

K.F. PAWAR

The evolution of the office of the speaker in Karnataka legislature is closely connected with the history of democratic institutions in Karnataka. Therefore, this office may be understood by studying the origin and growth of legislative bodies in Karnataka state; this evolution is only a part of the Constitutional history of British rule.

The princely state of Mysore was perhaps the first in India to start the formation of a democratic institution with a view to associating representatives of the people in the administration of the state. This was known as Mysore Representative Assembly. The year 1881 is an epoch making year in the Constitutional history of Mysore. Chamarajendra Wodeyar ascended the throne of Mysore state on the 25th March, 1881. This put an end to fifty years of direct rule of the British. A new political arrangement was arrived at according to which the Maharaja was to administer the state with the assistance of a council of ministers consisting of the Dewan as *ex-officio* Prime Minister and two or more members.

The first meeting of the assembly was held on 7th October, 1881 under the presidentship of Dewan Rangacharlu. The official name of the assembly in the beginning was "The Assembly of Representative Ryats and Merchants from all the taluks of the province of Mysore". The first meeting was attended by one hundred forty four members. Rangacharlu, addressing the first meeting explained the object for bringing the assembly into existence in the following terms:

"We have met here today by the command of His Highness, the Maharaja and it is His Highness who wishes that I should place before you a report of the administration of the past year and the outline of the measures proposed to be carried into effect in the coming years. His Highness hopes that by this arrangement the action of the government will be brought into greater harmony with the wishes and the interests of the people. His Highness' government will be glad to receive any observations and suggestions which you may wish to make in the public interest and I need not assure you that they will be met with every consideration. I have only to express my hope that appreciating the spirit in which these arrangements have been initiated, your observations may be directed to matters of real public interest."[1]

Thus, the notification for establishing a representative body in Mysore state marked an important event in the Constitutional history of Mysore because the Maharaja and his Dewan began to take their subjects into their counsel for the first time.

Inaugurating the reformed Constitution in 1940, at a joint session of the two houses on 9th June, 1941, the Maharaja said, "Those who have watched the origin and growth of our political institutions have noted that Mysore has always been in the vanguard of progress. Our representative assembly was started sixty years ago when the principle of representative institutions was little known and practised in the continent, at any rate in India".[2]

The origin of the legislature may be traced to the days of Rendition. So, the credit for establishing the representative assembly should go to Dewan Rangacharlu. Hence, with the growth of political consciousness among the people, as a result of the agitation carried on in the rest of India for the establishment of responsible government, the government of Mysore appointed in 1938, a committee for the purpose of examining the working of the representative institutions in the state. Further, as this form of government and legislature was being tried, a continuous agitation for the setting up of responsible government under the aegis of the Maharaja developed.

Hence, taking note of the wishes of the people, the Maharaja took note of the proclamation issued on 29th October, 1947, and announced further reforms by expanding the ministry and making it responsible to the legislature and by setting up a Constituent

Assembly composed of elected representatives for the purpose of passing a Constitutional bill for the state of Mysore providing for responsible government. The Constituent Assembly of Mysore was constituted in the year 1947, for the purpose of drafting a Constitution of Mysore. But at the same time a Constituent Assembly of India drafted a Constitution for the whole of India. So, it was thought that there was no need to proceed with the work of the Constituent Assembly of Mysore.

Accordingly, the Maharaja by a proclamation issued on 25th November, 1949 ordered that the Constitution adopted by Constituent Assembly of India shall be the Constitution for the state of Mysore, and dissolved the two houses of legislature, namely, the Representative Assembly and the Legislative Council on the 15th December, 1949, and further ordered that until such time as the house or houses of legislature of Mysore has or have been duly constituted and summoned to meet for the first session under the provisions of the Constitution of India, there shall be only one House of the legislature to be known as the legislative assembly of Mysore, and the Constituent Assembly of Mysore would be converted as the said legislative assembly from 16th December, 1949. Consequently amendments were made to the Government of Mysore Act, 1940, and the members of the Constituent Assembly of Mysore became the members of the legislative assembly till 1952.[3]

With the adoption of the Constitution of India, a new era of legislative bodies started functioning from 1952, under its provisions. General elections by adult franchise were held in Mysore state along with the rest of India, and the two Houses of legislature, namely, the legislative assembly and the legislative council with 105 and 42 members respectively, were constituted. The first session of the legislative assembly was held on 18th June, 1952 and the legislative council met on 16th June, 1952.[4] With the reorganisation of the states in 1956, Kannada-speaking areas of Bombay, Madras, Hyderabad, the whole of Coorg (now Kodagu) and the whole of the erstwhile princely state of Mysore were brought together under a single state named New Mysore state. However, in response to persisting demand the state was renamed as Karnataka from 1st November, 1973.[5]

Both the political process and system, it can be stated, are evolutionary in nature rather than revolutionary. Evolution generates considerable experience. India has adopted this kind of evolutionary political system, i.e., parliamentary government. Hence, with this background it is essential to understand the evolution of the office of the speaker in Karnataka. As stated above, India has adopted the parliamentary system of government, which is essentially a method by which the government is run on the basis of the consent of citizens. The government, which is responsible to the elected legislative body and answerable to it, has to be watchful over the state administration. It also feel responsible to the society as it is, the aspirations of the promises made to the people by the elected government and it is its duty to get these promises fulfilled through the legislations.

Thus, the situation prevailing in a state or in a society is always reviewed now and then. When this power of review is vested in a parliament and in a state legislature, there can be no limitations of subjects on which deliberations take place in a parliament and in a state legislature. Therefore, no deliberative assembly can do without some officers who preside over its sitting and thus conducted the deliberations which may occasionally be heated and acrimonious, within bounds. Most of the offices of the legislature, therefore, must have existed in some form or other form the very beginnings of such institutions.[6]

Speaker and the Parliamentary Democracy

The essence of parliamentary democracy is an attempt to settle all differences by discussions. The main function of a presiding officer is to advance the cause of democracy by maintaining a balance between good government and maximum individual freedom. He serves not only the Constitutional needs but also, to a large extent, every phase of parliamentary life.[7] Articles 94 and 179 of the Constitution provide that the speaker will continue to be in the office even after the dissolution of the assembly till the next meeting of the assembly is held. This is to ensure that the head of the house is always in office. This is perhaps because the speaker is the symbol of democracy is intended to continue even after the dissolution of the House.[8] He is a link between one house and its successor, and as such he has to continue till the next sitting of the House.

Election of the Speaker

Legislature is a pivot of a democratic system of government and the presiding officer is the pivot of the parliamentary machinery. His office is one of such dignity, honour and power without which the house has no Constitutional existence. His office assumes great significance for which the Constitution provides an honourable position. He is the principal officer of the house. He is the most important among the several parliamentary functionaries, the others being the leader of the house, the leader of the opposition, party whips, etc.

In Karnataka his importance, has been recognised not only from the outset of the India's independence but even before. Speaking on 8th March, 1948, on the occasion of the unveiling of a portrait of Vithalbhai Patel, Pandit Nehru observed: "The speaker represents the house. He represents the dignity of the house, the freedom of the house and because the house represents the nation, in a particular way, the speaker becomes the symbol of the nation's freedom and liberty. Therefore, it is right that, that should be an honoured position, a free position and should be occupied always by men of outstanding ability and impartially".[9] The incumbent of this office, weak and strong alike, embodies in his own personality the dignity of the nations representative assembly, and hence, it is considered that to be elected to the chair is the greatest honour that can be conferred upon any one.

The governor of the state enjoys the right to summon the state legislature. The first business of the house, once the house is summoned, is to take and administer the oath or affirmation of allegiance.[10] Generally, a *pro tem* speaker is authorised to administer the oath of affirmation to members. After oath-taking by members, the first business of the house is to enter into the election of its speaker.[11]

Article 178 of the Indian Constitution gives the procedure to be followed in the legislative assembly: "Every legislative assembly of a state shall, as soon as may be, choose two members of the assembly, to be respectively speaker and deputy speaker thereof, and so often as the office of the speaker or deputy speaker becomes vacant, the assembly shall choose another member to be speaker or deputy speaker as the case may be". The practice followed in Karnataka is, "the governor shall fix a date for holding of the election and the secretary shall send to every member notice of the date so fixed".[12]

The tradition of electing a speaker to the assembly in the state of Karnataka originated with the first legislative assembly. The status of the speaker since then has been gradually evolving on democratic lines and conventions. The procedure for the nomination of the candidates for speakership in Karnataka is as per the provision in the Constitution of India. Rule 7 (2) of the Karnataka legislative assembly lays down the procedure of filing the nomination. It reads as follows: "At any time before noon on the day proceeding the date so fixed, any member may give notice in writing addressed to the secretary, of a motion that another member may be chosen as the speaker and the notice shall be seconded by a third member and shall be accompanied by a statement by the member whose name is proposed in the notice that he is willing to serve as speaker if elected; provided that a member shall not propose his own name or second a motion proposing his own name, or propose or second move than one motion".[13]

Provision is also made in the Karnataka Legislative Assembly Rules that, "all matters not specifically provided for in these rules (K.L.A. Rules) and all questions relating to the detailed working of these rules shall be regulated in such a manner as the speaker may, from time to time direct".[14] In exercise of these powers, the speaker has issued directions from time to time, which have been collected and issues as "Directions from the speaker". Further, the speaker gives rulings or decisions (on departmental files, etc.) on the specific matters or issues which arise and on which he is required to give decisions. Inside or outside the House, he enjoys wide powers regulated only by the "Rules of procedures and conduct of business" in the legislative assembly. He derives his power and owes his position partly to the Constitution, partly to the "Rules" and partly to his own personality and behaviour.[15]

Qualifications and Qualities of the Speaker

There are no legal qualifications required for speakership. Neither the Constitution nor the rules prescribe any for the office of the speakership. Generally speaking, it can be stated that the aspirant for the speakership must be a member of the house and he should have the support of the majority members of the respective house. But the incumbent of this office has to shoulder heavy responsibilities and, hence, the he should be a man of outstanding ability and impartiality.

The speaker must have first hand knowledge and experience of parliamentary life. Total impartiality is the basic requirement of good speakership. He must also be a man who can command authority with confidence. Hiren Mukerjee, a noted parliamentarian, aptly points out, "A good speaker requires to be very quick on the uptake and constantly alert. He has to have a plentiful reserve of good temper, of patience and tact. It is essential also to have genuine powers of judgement, both in respect of the mood of the house when, especially it comes suddenly (and even without sufficient provocation) to a bail, and of the requirements of adequate debate in the country's national forum. He must also have the invaluable capacity of offering, at the right moment, a spice of wit so that a tense situation can be dissolved in a burst of laughter. Having to tend his often unruly flock, the speaker needs also to possess a certain dignity in voice and bearing all this cumulatively amounting to specification that cannot be easy to satisfy".[16]

The creation of this image has rather naturally provoked iconoclastic tendencies on the part of some commentators on the subject and their desire to assess the speakership in a more realistic perspective manner. Sir Ivor Jennings has said: "The qualities required of a speaker are not really very high and so great is the prestige of the office, and so careful are all parties to maintain his independence and authority, that any reasonable man can make a success of the office".[17]

However, Herbert Morrison once described the essential qualities in a speaker as "Independence and impartiality. In the cut and thrust of parliamentary debate the treasury benches are fair game for attack but convention ordains that the speaker is always respected. It has been said that, 'the premier can do nothing right, whereas the speaker can do no wrong'. Smooth and successful running of parliamentary democracy in England owes not a little to the reverence and confidence built around the chair."[18] In order to attract a person with high qualities and also to enable him to discharge his Constitutional obligations impartially, certain safeguards have been provided. Further, it is in the exercise of control in the chamber that a speaker finds the opportunity to set certain principles of impartiality.

Nevertheless, it cannot be also said that only the foregoing are the qualifications and qualities required. The speaker or the candidate desiring to become one, should certainly know the history of the parliamentary democracy. He should get acquainted with the various traditions, conventions laid down by his predecessors. This can be said to be a requirement because like others speakers (who have left their own legacy on proceedings which they have presided), he is again called upon to continue and create his own legacy.

Powers and Functions of the Speaker

The duties he has to discharge and the responsibilities he has to shoulder are quite onerous. He enforces the rules of debate, and decides the admissibility of questions. In the words of Norman Wilding and Philip Lanudy, "The speakership is an ancient and hon'ble office and an essential feature of the parliamentary system.... An affront to the speaker is an affront to the house as a whole".[19] Though the Constitution terms him as an officer of the house, in actuality he is the servant of the house. The speaker should be capable of commanding authority with confidence.

In 1854, on the eve of the first legislature, Lord Dalhousie advised the council: "For controlling the order of those deliberations, authority be conferred upon their President by the Council itself. I apprehend the Council will feel no hesitation in conferring that authority and that they will at all time be prepared to uphold the legitimate exercise thereof".[20]

The speaker of the Karnataka legislative assembly has certain inherent and implied powers apart from those expressly conferred upon him by the Constitution and the rules of procedure. Accordingly, the speaker is responsible for regulating the proceedings of the House. Hence, he has to act within the framework of the Constitution and the rules of procedure of the legislature concerned. Within the walls of the house, his authority is supreme. No doubt this authority is based on the speaker's absolute and unvarying impartiality. The main feature of the office of speaker is the law of its life. This also tends to the respect for his authority.

In the whole set up of parliamentary democracy, the speaker is the only autocrat. He works like a link between the house on the one hand and the Governor and the government on the other. Usually, in an assembly consisting of members from various political parties, groups and factions, the speaker has to go through many difficulties and do multifarious duties. The speaker has two spheres of functions—first, as the presiding authority of the legislature and secondly, as the head of the legislature secretariat. These can be broadly be stated as follows:

1. To preside over the house whenever he is present in the house, excepting when a resolution for his removal from office is under consideration [Article 181(1)].
2. To adjourn the house when there is no quorum [Article 189(4)].
3. To permit a member who cannot adequately express himself in Hindi or English or the official language of the state, to address the house in his mother tongue [Article 20(10)].
4. To exercise a casting vote in case of an equality of votes [Article 189(1)].
5. To determine whether a Bill is a money bill and to certify a money bill [Article 199(3) and A].

Article 208 of the Indian Constitution states that the detailed duties and responsibilities of the speaker may be laid down by the respective house in its Rules of procedure. The fundamental principle is that the house is sovereign in the matter to frame its own rules of procedure and the conduct of business. Hence, whatever powers have been conferred on the speaker are intended to enable the house to function at all times in the interest of the country. It is also a paramount duty of the speaker to use the powers conferred upon him in the interest of the house. Though the rules of procedures vary from state to state, generally the rules of the assemblies are modelled on the Lok Sabha Rules. The speaker, in order to maintain a healthy atmosphere of democratic action, has been given procedural powers.[21] His position as the presiding officer of the house is one of great authority.

The speaker has a key role to play in the successful working of parliamentary democracy. The office of the speaker not only serves the Constitutional, and, to a large extent, legislative functions, but also influences almost every phase of parliamentary life. The main purpose of this paper is to trace the gradual evolution of parliamentary democracy in Karnataka which has flowed from the rulings and decisions of the various speakers from time to time. Every legislature has its own rules of procedure for the conduct of its business. Therefore, it has its office of the speaker with the power to interpret rules, apply decisions and pronounce rulings, whenever the situation demands.

Rulings and decisions of the speaker are based on the provisions of the Constitution, rules of procedure and the traditional practice. An effective speaker should always pronounce rulings in such a way, as it would reflect the will of the house, as embodied in its rules and precedents. Consequently, this will inspire confidence in his impartiality and obedience to his rulings. The speaker must maintain of balance between good government and maximum of individual freedom.

The speaker can play a decisive role for stabilising parliamentary democracy by adopting sound parliamentary traditions and by his impartial conduct. Different speakers have given rulings and decisions and these have become conventions and precedents. When we look into the history of the office of the speaker in the Karnataka legislative assembly, we see several eminent personalities like V. Venkatappa, H. Siddaiah, H.S. Rudrappa, S.R. Kanthi, B. Vaikunt Baliga, S.D. Kothavale, Mrs. K.S. Nagarathnamma, P. Venkataramanna, K.H. Ranghanath, D.B. Chandre Gowda, B.G. Banakar, S.M. Krishna, V.S. Koujalagi, S. Ramesh Kumar and the present speaker M.V. Vankatappa have occupied the post of the office speaker and have started important conventions and traditions in the deliberations of the house. Many of these have become trend-setting.

It is worthwhile in this connection to assess in brief the contribution of the various speakers of the Karnataka legislative assembly. Every speaker has his own approach and he leaves behind him events which are worth being recorded for the benefit of posterity. In the following pages the contribution made by the speakers to the development of parliamentary traditions and conventions in the Karnataka have been discussed.

Speakers and Their Rulings

Speakers of the Mysore/Karnataka legislative assembly have given important rulings. Some of them are explained in brief here. These only illustrative; they are not exhaustive.

I. V. Vankatappa (1949-1952)

Vankatappa was the first speaker of the princely Mysore state legislative assembly, unanimously elected. The first session of the legislative assembly sat on 12th January, 1950, under the Chairmanship of T. Siddalingaiah who had been appointed by His Highness the Maharaja of Mysore to preside over pending the election of the speaker. At the same session V. Vankatappa and L.H. Timma Bovi were unanimously elected speaker and deputy speaker.[22]

Conventions and traditions in pre-independence India prevalent at the time of this election were respected and followed, which was a healthy sign. He took over the office as the first speaker of the Mysore legislative assembly on 12th January 1950.

It is of course a well-known fact that democracy and free and fair elections go together. Such elections depend on the machinery which conducts them and it should be independent and under the law. On 29th August, 1950, when an MLA sought to move a motion of adjournment to discuss the exercise of official influence in the bye-elections to the legislature. Thereupon the speaker V. Vankatappa made the following observation regarding bye-election. "Bye-election to fill seats in the legislative assembly are now governed by the Constitution of India. I do not see how an adjournment motion of this kind will lie (sic) in a state legislature.... Further, I find from the Mysore legislative assembly election Rules that the several allegations contained in the adjournment motion may form the grounds for presenting election petitions. It is also difficult to hold that this matter is urgent within the meaning of our Rules. I therefore rule it out of order."[23]

Venkatappa contributed much to the laying down of conventions and traditions established by the past speaker like Vithalbhai Patel and also contributed towards establishing some new healthy conventions. He was impartial. He believed that he was the servant of the house and with that zeal presided over the debates.

II. H. Siddaiah (1952-1954)

When the first general elections were held in 1952 for the Lok Sabha and the state legislative assemblies, the Mysore legislative assembly met at Bangalore for its first session in the month of June 1952. Siddaiah was elected speaker. He defeated Gopala Gowda by 79 votes.[24]

Siddaiah was well aware of his duties. He has said: "To judge a man, there are so many factors. To make any remarks about an individual, his accomplishments and his weaknesses as well as virtues and vices should be taken into consideration. Taking these factors into consideration, it would naturally give me immense pleasure not now, but at the time I lay down my office, if through my conduct in this house, I have earned the esteem and affection of you all. During the period I hold this office and while we work together, I have every reason to expect and believe that you will extend your very effective, willing and ready co-operation".[25]

The legislative assemblies for the deliberations are related to the welfare of the public. Therefore, when the house starts its business, concerned ministers must be present in the house and promptly reply to the questions when the members are called by the speaker. On 22nd July, 1953, M. Lingappa raised a point of order whether one minister could answer to the question on behalf of another minister to whom the question pertained and both were present in the house. Thereupon. Siddaiah said: "It is usual for the concerned minister to answer such questions. But when the action of the concerned minister is questioned, I feel it is better, because it may be very delicate in some cases for the concerned minister to answer on such occasions, another minister may be allowed or permitted to answer on his behalf. Anyhow, I feel it is better for the concerned minister to answer as far as possible. But nothing prevents another minister whenever he knows more about a question to answer on behalf of the concerned minister".[26]

III. H.S. Rudrappa (1954-1956)

Rudrappa succeeded Siddaiah on his unanimous elected to the chair on 13th October, 1954. On his election he said: "As speaker, I know I must be fair and impartial to all the members of this house irrespective of their party affiliation, and hold the scales even. I must not only maintain a high traditions and prestige of the house, but also the dignity of the office I hold. More than all, I consider it as my sacred duty to safeguard the legitimate rights and privileges of the members of this house".[27]

In a parliamentary system, ministers are members of the legislature. They have to attend its sessions and reply to the questions put by the members who may ask regarding any act or omission of the administrative authorities from the highest to the lowest. Therefore, it is the duty of the ministers to prepare their answers and reply. On 17th October, 1955, in the course of a discussion on a resolution, minister was replying on behalf of the minister in charge. A member objected and submitted that the minister in charge should reply when he was present in the house. Thereupon the speaker said: "According to the Rules of Procedure, a minister means a member of the council of ministers and includes any member whom such minister may delegate .... under the rules. So he can delegate his powers to another minister to answer and that will be against the rules of procedure. But you say that if the minister is prepared to answer, it will be helpful to the members. That is our contention".[28]

IV. S.R. Kanthi (1956-1962)

Kanthi succeeded Rudrappa. He was the first speaker of the new legislative assembly ushered into being on 1st November, 1956. As a presiding officer, he played a very important part in conducting the business of the house. A Congressman, he was just to all the sections of the house. Not only did he try to see that the business of the house was conducted smoothly but on occasions he informed the government as well as the opposition about their responsibilities.

To change or amend the original questions comes under the powers of the speaker. On 5th November, 1958, when the Madras Commercial Crops Markets (Mysore Amendment and Validation of Levy of Cess) Bill, 1958 was under consideration, a point was raised by G. Vankatai Gowda whether the house was entitled to validate the collection of cess under a particular section of the Act which was validated by the High Court. Kanthi gave the following ruling regarding the power of the house: "The house is supreme and it can pass any law and repeal or amend any law within the rights given by the Constitution. It is for the High Court to say whether a law is valid or not. I am here just to see whether a bill or clauses of a Bill are on the face of it valid or invalid. Beyond that I cannot do anything. If the house feels that this Bill is beyond the scope of the original Act, it will not pass it".[29]

Admissibility of an amendment is to be decided by the chair only on the basis of the scope of the measures that is actually before the house and not on the basis of what might have happened between the members and the government on a previous occasion. Therefore, amendments, unless admitted by the speaker, do not appear on paper and are not circulated. The speaker allows postponement of an amendment the admissibility of which depends on his decision.[30]

Thus, in his tenure Kanthi could established healthy practices on which his successors have looked upon as guiding principles. He always treated himself as the servant of the house and with zeal presided over the debates. He was regarded as a friend, philosopher, and guide even by the opposition.

Kanthi was deputy speaker of Bombay legislative assembly in the year 1946. His success in that pre-eminent assembly made him a natural choice for the speakership of the New Mysore legislative assembly in 1956. Even there he had tried hard to maintain the dignity of the office and worked as the protector of liberties, rights and privileges of the members. Many rulings given him are "conventions" even today. In this way Kanthi took a leading part in laying a firm foundation for the new-born assembly of Mysore (Karnataka) state. Later on, he resigned the post of the speaker and became Chief Minister of the state.

V. B. Vaikunta Baliga (1962-1968)

Balaiga succeeded Kanthi, elected to the chair unanimously on 15th March, 1962.[31]

As far as the precincts of the house are concerned, no members can be arrested without obtaining the permission of the speaker. Rule 197(2) of the Karnataka legislative assembly Rules explains. A legal process, civil or criminal, shall not served within the precincts of the house without obtaining the permission of the speaker. It must, therefore, be remembered that the speaker is the supreme authority. On 21st December, 1963, Sri A. Krishna Shetty, a member of Karnataka legislative assembly, complained to the speaker that one or two police officers had accosted him even in the lounge thus causing embarrassment and inconvenience to him. Thereupon Baliga made the following observation regarding precincts of the houses: "The government should see that no member of the legislature is inconvenienced to the least extent by either the people in the regular force in regular dress or any other dress. I have issued instructions that on no condition should the police come to the lounge or any precincts of the house without my knowledge and without disclosing to me the purpose to see whether it is justifiable. I will adhere to the rule that no person of the police office, unless belonging to the watch and ward of the legislature secretariat, should come to the lounge".[32]

The question whether the authority of the speaker over the maintenance of order and security in the precincts of the house is absolute had become a subject of controversy between the speaker Vithalbhai Patel and the government. There were discussions between the him and the Viceroy, Lord Irwin. It took exactly a month to settle this matter, and arrive at an agreement. That agreement laid the foundation of the Watch and Ward staff of the parliament.[33]

This agreement has been recently extended in certain matters. At present all security arrangements are completely under the control of the speaker who exercises his power through subordinate officers directly appointed by him. This aspect points out that the speaker has his own absolute power not only within the four walls of the house, but also through the whole premises of the assembly. Another important observation made by Balaiga which is worth mention:

The house assembles for the deliberations on important matters directly or indirectly related to the welfare of the people. Ministers are responsible members because they are entrusted with responsibilities of some portfolios. Therefore, when the house begins its business, they must be present in the houses and be prompt when matters relating to their department are going on. On 6th December 1963, after the question hour S. Sivappa and several other members raised a point that the Chief Minister had decided to tour some districts with a view to influencing a bye-election to the legislative assembly precisely when the house was in session and wanted to know whether it was proper, and whether a copy of his tour programme was sent to speaker. Thereupon the speaker Baliga made the following observation regarding the ministers' presence in the house: "If a particular minister is not present, then he writes to me and sends his tour programme. The question arises whether I have jurisdiction, or right to compel and say he must not go out. It all depends upon the exigencies upon the demands, the imperative nature of the work or otherwise. It is agreed normally, when the assembly is in session, that every minister including the Chief Minister is expected to be attending to the work of the house ... But if there is some other urgent work which is equally important, he has to go ..."[34]

Even so the presence of a minister during the session helps greatly to come to a definite conclusion after the examination of the issue. Thus, the rules of procedure are the very foundation of parliamentary government and on their impartial enforcement by the speaker depends upon the efficient and smooth running of parliamentary democracy. Speaker B. Vaikunta Baliga worked as the speaker of the house during the period of 1962-68. Baliga created great confidence about him in the members. Probably because of this, he was re-elected to the chair for the fourth legislative assembly. This speaks for his impartiality and neutrality and the high status he had attained.

VI. S.D. Kothavale (1968-1972)

Kothavale, who succeeded speaker Baliga, was elected to the chair unanimously on 5th September, 1968.[35] During 1969, Kothavale, attended a parliamentary course conducted by the United Kingdom branch of the Commonwealth Parliamentary Association and later a conference held at Kaulalampur in 1971. Thus, because of his rich experience Kothavale guided the deliberations of the Karnataka legislative assembly with dignity, uprightness and impartiality.

It is a unique honour to preside over the deliberations of the house and on this matter the speaker has an absolute authority. Hence, it is the duty of each and every member to respect the chair, and his chamber. Kothavale, always a follower of good traditions, was not a blind follower of the British practice. On 4th September, 1969, S. Bangarappa, a member, raised a matter regarding the convention to meet the speaker in his chamber and stated that there is no rule framed for meeting the speaker in his chamber. On this point Kothavale made the following observation: "Now a very important question is raised that there is no provision in the rules to meet the speaker in his chamber. There cannot be a rule for all matters. There are many matters which go by conventions and for which there are no rules. For these matters the parliamentary practice ought to be followed. If the member does not know that, I suggest him to go through May's Parliamentary Practice and acquaint himself with the parliamentary practice".[36]

A legislature has the inalienable right to frame its own rules of procedure. But the interpretation and application of the rules so framed is the responsibility of the speaker. To put it in the legal parlance, the legislature is, as far as the rules of procedures are concerned, the legislative body and its speaker are the interpreting authorities. The speaker has to interpret a rule before he applies it. He proceeds to interpret *suo moto* when a situation in the house demands it, or he may interpret it on a point of order raised. His interpretation and the way the rules are applied become precedents. Therefore, the rules of procedures have to be interpreted in a dynamic manner so as to meet unforeseen and changing circumstances. Generally, the decision by the speaker cannot be questioned to avoid controversy. He is supposed to be above party politics and, hence, members should avoid attributing motives to him.

On 27th February, 1970, when Kothavale made an announcement about the allotment of seats to members, H.N. Nanje Gowda, a member, raised a point and on that the speaker gave a ruling. Nanje Gowda had submitted that the ruling was wrong. Supporting him K.H. Patil, another member, submitted that though the rulings of the speaker cannot be questioned, they can be condemned. Thereupon Kothavale made the following observation regarding the chair's ruling: "Rulings are to be obeyed without any comment. If any member were to feel that the chair's ruling on a particular matter is wrong, then the members should go the chamber of the speaker and point out that the ruling is wrong and if the chair is satisfied, the chair may revise its ruling. However, the chair's rulings cannot be commented upon in the house and they should be obeyed implicitly.[37]

As far as the observation of the speaker on the chair's rulings are concerned, once the decision has been given, it is supported to be final. This implies that no one enters into discussion about it. Members can question the ruling of the speaker on a substantial motion. Otherwise the speaker's decision is final whether it is given in the house or in the departmental files. Thus, the rules of procedure are the very foundation of parliamentary government and on their impartial enforcement by the speaker depends the efficient and smooth running of the parliamentary democracy.

VII. K.S. Nagaratnamma (1972-1978)

The fourth legislative assembly was dissolved on 14th April, 1971, and the fifth was constituted on 20th March, 1972. According to Article 179 of the Constitution the office of the speaker continues even after dissolution until immediately before the first meeting of the new assembly. The first meeting of the new assembly was held on 24th March, 1972, Kothavale who was the speaker during the life of the fourth assembly continued till 27th March, 1972. On 24th March, 1972,. K.S. Nagaratnamma was elected speaker of the legislative assembly.[38]

On her election to the chair Smt. Nagaratnamma assured that she would follow and maintain the precedents and traditions which had been followed by the past speakers.[39]

Call attention motion is the latest innovation in the parliamentary procedure and it serves a very useful purpose. It enables the member to highlight matters occurring from time to time and enables the Treasury Benches to place their point of view on important matters before the house and the public. It is these motions which have a great impact on public opinion. On 24th March, 1973, soon after the Calling Attention Notice, when the Kagodu Thimmappa and Vatal Nagaraj tried to raise a matter regarding police excess. Thereupon Nagaratnamma said regarding the Calling Attention Motion: "After the question hour and call attention notice, by precedent, an hour has developed which is called Zero Hour. There is nothing in the Constitution and the rules of procedure that "Zero Hour" should be allowed. But by precedent, something has developed like a zero hour. All sorts of things cannot be raised in that hour. But things like natural calamities, tragedies and acts of God, breach of peace, violence and fire can be raised so the government's attention can be immediately drawn to those matters and attended to. I do agree that other matters cannot be raised. Now, the matters raised by members, Vatal Nagaraj and Kagodu Thimmappa are grave one and I will request the government to make a statement on this Monday. Of course, Channabasappa, the minister may be in a position to make a statement. But, it should be in an effective manner".[40]

This is the first time in the history of our legislative assembly that a lady was elected speaker. During her tenure she created confidence about her in the members.

VIII. Venkataramana (1978-1980)

On 17th September, 1979, G.P. Vadeyaraj requested the chair to recognise his party as the main opposition party. Thereupon Venkataraman made the following observation regarding, recognition of a Parliamentary Legislature Party: "I am quoting a portion from Kaul and Shakdhar's book and it reads thus: As regards recognition of a parliamentary party or group formed as a result of a combination of different parties or groups with different ideologies and programmes, as happened recently in several states where different parties or groups joined to form United Front Government or United Opposition, the Page Committee observed: "If the constituent groups forming a party for the purpose of proper functioning of the house with a view to strengthen parliamentary democracy have a common programme of parliamentary work, a common organisation and have one leader and one whip to speak on their behalf inside the House, there is no objection to recognition being given to that party. This applies to both the government and opposition parties and no distinction can be made between a government party and an opposition party similarly formed."[41]

Thus, speaker Venkataraman was careful about the maintaining conventions. For the first time in the history of Karnataka legislative assembly a member of scheduled caste was elected as its speaker. In his brief tenure of speakership he contributed much.

IX. K.H. Ranganath (1981-1983)

Ranganath (also belonging to a scheduled caste) was unanimously elected as speaker on 30th January, 1981.[42]

The is like a judge. It is customary that any person speaking on any point should address the chair and not another member.

Lord Dalhousie advised the members of the legislative council to address "either to the President, as in the house of Commons, or to the Council collectively as in the house of Lords". The Council, however, adopted the house of Commons practice of addressing the chair. On 15th July, 1982, K. Bhaskar Naidu, a member, wanted to know as to how the chair should be addressed when a member from the panel of chairmen occupies and the deputy speaker occupies. Thereupon, Ranganath made the following observation: *"You are Correct. The Chair should be Addressed as Speaker or Chairman only."*[43]

Another important observation Ranganath which is worthy here is on the urgency of the matter. It is normally the practice of the house to transact the business mentioned in the list of business. Sometimes, an incident of urgent public importance happens and the members of the legislature are naturally anxious to bring it before the house. Such a matter of urgent public importance can be raised by interrupting the regular business of the house through what is known as "an adjournment motion", which may be made with the consent of the speaker. On 6th March 1981, the members of the opposition parties had given a notice of Adjournment Motion regarding the strike by the employees of public undertakings at Bangalore. After hearing the submissions of the embers and the government's reply, Ranganath made the following observation: "The things which are not under the control of the Government of Karnataka cannot form a part of an Adjournment Motion. The matter has been directly or indirectly discussed in the garb of seeking my consent. Members were allowed to make their submissions in view of its importance. However, as members know, strikes and lockouts are routine administration of law and order and not fit subjects for adjournment motions. I, therefore, withhold my consent to all the notices of adjournment motions connected with the strike and law and order situations".[44] Hence, while hearing the arguments of the members he should not lose his temper if any matter comes before the house in a particular form and if it cannot be admitted due to technical difficulties.

X. D.B. Chandre Gowda (1983-1985)

Chandre Gowda was elected as speaker on 24th January, 1983.

The Constitution provides for a parliamentary system of government in the states. The Governor is the nominal executive head of the state. But the real executive powers rest with the council of ministers chosen from and responsible to the legislature. In fact, the government of a state means the council of ministers headed by the Chief Minister. Under Article 164(2) of the Indian Constitution, the council of ministers is collectively responsible to the legislative assembly of the state. Hence, the ministry remains in office so long as it has the confidence of the house. In the light of this provision, on 12th August, 1983, the minister for Law and Parliamentary Affairs, A. Lakshmisagar moved a motion relating to the Karnataka Education Bill, 1983, to refer it to a joint select committee, on behalf of the education minister. On this M.S. Krishnan, a member, pointed out the absence of the concerned minister and also pointed out that no body was noting down the suggestions of the members. Thereupon Chandre Gowda made the following observation regarding, Collective Responsibility Towards the House: "I do concede that there is a point in the feeling of member M.S. Krishnan. I do share with his feelings. But we have to look to the situation also. The minister who is in charge of piloting the bill is not well and he has communicated well in advance. The Law Minister has just gone outside. It is the collective responsibility and there are other ministers. I hope that they would take care of all these things."[45]

This observation by Chandre Gowda clearly points out that as far as collective responsibility is concerned, in the absence of the particular minister another minister can move the motion relating to the particular matter on behalf of the absentee minister. They remain in the office so long as they retain the confidence of the legislative assembly. This is an example how under parliamentary system of government, collective responsibility plays a very significant role.

XI. B.G. Banakar (1985-1989)

Banakar was elected as speaker of the Karnataka legislative assembly on 18th March, 1985.[46]

In a parliamentary form of government such as we have in India, the party system dominates the activities of the government, as it is an integral part. A democratic government is said to be a government by political parties. The success of democracy depends on the existence of a well-organised party system. A parliamentary form of government draw its very sustenance from political parties. Thus, the opposition parties also play a vital role in democracies by providing alternative governments. In order to carry out the work of the house smoothly, it is necessary that there should be opposition, which can be consulted on all important matters in relation to the business before the house. Therefore, the recognition of a legislature party by the speaker is primarily intended to smoothen the transaction of parliamentary business of the house. Hence, a recognised opposition party always helps the proper functioning of the house.

On 16th February, 1989 the leader of the opposition K.S. Nagaratnamma, filed a petition under Rule 6 for the disqualification of 11 members of Janata Dal Legislature party for having signed an affidavit expressing their support to Janata Dal Party. Thereupon speaker Banakar made the following observation regarding the "Recognition of New Legislature party": "Janata Legislature Party consisting of 138 members of this house was recognised. S.R. Bommai, the leader of that party moved to recognise Janata Legislature Party consisting of 111 members. He furnished information in Form 1 prescribed by the Karnataka Legislative Assembly (Disqualification of Members on the Ground of Defection) Rules, 1986. In the light of the materials furnished to me and the well-established Parliamentary Practices and Conventions and the provisions of Tenth Schedule of the Constitution, I accorded recognition to the Janata Dal Legislature Party. All the members have been informed of it through a bulletin".[47] Thus, parliamentary democracy depends for its success on a stable party system which can make the federal structure work and take care of the stress and strain of social and political change in a developing country. By doing this, Banakar, with considerable foresight and tact, decided to recognise the opposition as the official opposition party, and took it into is confidence.

During his tenure of office as speaker lasting about four years and nine months, Banakar evinced an abiding and keen interest in the implementation of development works in the state, especially those about which the government had made a commitment on the floor of the assembly. He created a record of sorts by writing about 1,000 letters during his tenure to the Chief

Minister and different ministries on subjects concerning the development of the state. A new convention was established by him. According this, copies of the proceedings of the assembly were to be sent to local bodies and also reading rooms in villages so that the people could know about the happenings in the legislature.

XII. S.M. Krishna (1989-1993)

Krishna was elected as the 12th speaker to the ninth Karnataka legislative assembly on 18th December, 1989.[48]

Krishna during his brief tenure tried to set democratic conventions in Karnataka. Later, he resigned from the office of the speaker consequent on his appointment as Deputy Chief Minister of Karnataka in 1993.

XIII. V.S. Koujalagi (1993-1994)

Koujalagi succeeded Krishna. His tenure as speaker lasted for a brief period from 1993 to 1994. Even during his short period he conducted the business of the house impartially and satisfied all sections of the house.

XIV. Ramesh Kumar (1994-1999)

Ramesh Kumar was elected on 27th December, 1994 as the fourteenth speaker to the legislative assembly.[49]

Under the rules of procedure and conduct of business of Karnataka legislative assembly, it is the duty of the speaker to ensure that the house is properly constituted before it proceeds to take up its business. According to rules, to start the business of the house no fewer than one-tenth of the members must be present in the house. The speaker does not take the chair unless and until the required number of members are present. During a sitting, the speaker on his own attention or if any member draws the attention of the chair towards the need of a quorum, will direct the division bell to be rung. If the required number of members are not present in the house, the presiding officer will adjourn the house to the next sitting or suspend the meeting until there is quorum.

Taking a serious exception to the absence of ministers in the legislative assembly during a discussion when the leader of the opposition Mallikarjun Kharge was making submission on the no-confidence motion on 2nd November, 1998, Ramesh Kumar said that the ruling party's failure to ensure adequate representation of ministers in the treasury benches amounted to lowering the dignity of the house. Further, he said, "I cannot tolerate absenteeism by ministers when such an important issue is being discussed. It is insulting to the house. I may not hold proceedings if this continues".[50]

Another important caustic remark made by Ramesh Kumar against the government, which is worth mention here: The question hour is regarded as one of the processes through which the legislature puts the government to examination and reflects the public opinion. It is rightly observed: "the question hour is a great safety valve and a safeguard against abuses, and makes sure that government departments cannot get very far out of time with public opinion without being pulled up short". It enables the members to elicit information on the various problems of the state. At the same time it must be submitted that this hour is the most lively hour in the proceedings of the assembly. Public grievances are highlighted by means of questions. It is through the question hour that the government is able to feel the pulse of the people and try to adopt and attune policies and functions. Hence, it is the responsibility of every minister to be present in the house and prepare to reply.

On 24th March, 1999, Ramesh Kumar made caustic remarks against the government when none from the treasury benches was prepared to reply to a matter raised by K. Jayaram Shetty (BJP) during the zero hour. Alleging that many poor families have been deprived of ration cards in Mangalore, Shetty demanded a reply from the government. But neither the food and civil supplies minister nor the revenue minister was present to reply. None of the other ministers present were also prepared to reply. Realising this the speaker made the following observation regarding the absence of ministers: "Some of the ministers do not even inform me the reason for not coming to the House. It is better you (the government) make me P.A. to all ministers. You should try to understand my problem. Even the Chief Minister keeps me informed about his leave of absence. But, some ministers even do not to this. Even after sending notices pertaining to the matters to be raised by the members, the concerned ministers do not bother to be in the house. How do you expect me to work? I never thought you would treat me like this and go this far. I can pocket this insult only once but you want to repeat it".[51]

Thus, to maintain the decorum of the house it is always the duty of every member of the house to remain present in the house to enable the speaker to conduct the business of the house. It is, therefore, the work of the respective party and the whips to instruct the party members to attend the business of the house in time. If there is no quorum even after ringing the warning bell, the house is adjourned. During his tenure of speakership Ramesh Kumar tried to uphold the standards of this office. He conducted the business of the house effectively without any party considerations.

XV. M.V. Venkatappa (1999-present)

Mothakapalli Venkataramana Gowda Venkatappa was elected on 26th October, 1999, as the fifteenth speaker.[52]

Sometimes, members, in their enthusiasm to participate in debate, tend to forget the limitations of the debate. On such occasions the speaker can remind them and if necessary instruct them. If a member makes any remarks irrelevant to the subject under discussion or which affect the dignity and decorum of the house, the speaker can direct him to behave in a proper way or ask him to withdraw. On 22nd July, 2002 an issue was raised by the opposition regarding the controversy between the MLA S.R. Kashappanavar and the Urban Development Minister D.K. Shivakumar. Thereupon the speaker M.V. Venkatappa quoted a ruling given in 1963 and said: "Conversations held in the assembly lounge should not be discussed in the house. The lounge also comes under the purview of the legislature and the members should behave responsibly in the premises. Referring to MLA Kashappanavar's allegations the speaker questioned the propriety of filing a complaint by him after three days of incident and warned the member not to file false complaints and that he should act more responsibly in future keeping the decorum of the assembly in view".[53]

So far as the maintenance of the peace and order and discipline in the house is concerned, there are provisions in the Rules of

Procedures and the conduct of business which empower the speaker to take suitable disciplinary action. Karnataka Legislative Assembly Rules, Rule 355 says, "The speaker shall preserve order and have all powers necessary for the purpose of enforcing his decisions".

This is how some of the important landmarks, conventions and traditions have been set by well-known speakers in Karnataka. This assessment points out how these various speakers and contributed in their own way to enhance the prestige of the office of the speaker in Karnataka legislative assembly.

Conclusion

The institution of the office of the speaker in Karnataka, like the parliamentary system of democracy, is a legacy of British rule. Its evolution in the Lok Sabha as well as in Karnataka legislative assembly has been a dynamic and continuous process. The presiding officer has now acquired a decisive role to play in the successful working of parliamentary democracy. It can be stated in conclusion that the speaker's office has become the linchpin of the modern parliamentary democracy. His role and rulings have assumed great value in building sound democratic conventions, practice and procedures and thus moulding the development of parliamentary democracy in appropriate lines.

The successful working of the institution of the office of the speaker depends upon the independence and impartiality of the speaker: independent in the sense that he should not have any party affiliation. It is a well-established practice in England that a person elected to the chair severs his party affiliations as a mark of his independence and impartiality. Such dissociation upholds parliamentary democracy. Impartiality and independence of the office of the speaker depend upon the personality of the speaker. The British speaker became successful in establishing these traditions fully in the first half of the 19th century. Since the tenure of the speakership of Shaw Lefevre, this practice had been established due to full-fledged party system. But in the Lok Sabha as well as in Karnataka legislative assembly, we have yet to evolve political parties and healthy convention about speakership.

Generally, the speaker of the house of commons in England is elected from the back-benchers. But in Karnataka, this is not followed. we know that invariably the speaker is the handmaiden of the majority party. The candidate for the speakership is always decided by the majority party. In Karnataka usually a candidate for the speaker's post is chosen from the leading politicians of the majority party who works as senior member of the house. When we look into the history of speakers office in Karnataka, we can say that whoever adorns this post has been eminent like: V. Venkatappa, H. Siddaiah, H.S. Rudrappa, S.R. Kanthi, B. Vaikunta Baliga and even the present speaker M.V. Vankatappa who had taken active part either in the freedom struggle or state politics. The speakers in Karnataka as a rule do not sever party connections. Still they have played a great part in bringing about reconciliation between all elements and happier relations between various political groups in the legislature.

Hence, instead of following the British practice, our speakers have established their own system. This points out that the English practice is not a welcome idea in the Lok Sabha and in the Karnataka legislative assembly, considering the multi-party system. In that respect, the office of the speaker in Karnataka has worked in a better manner when compared to other state legislatures. Right from V. Vankatappa M.V. Venkatappa, all the speakers have been men of caliber. From this detailed study, it can be inferred that Karnataka legislature has always been successful in putting the right men in the chair.

But an unhealthy trend which is developing in Karnataka legislative assembly is that when they relinquish the office of the speakership, most of the speakers have become ministers or the chief minister or deputy chief minister. But the speakership of the House of Commons is no longer a stepping stone to some higher appointment. After retirement, a speaker does not re-enter the house as a member or as a minister. In the Karnataka legislative assembly, there have been some instances when members have questioned the impartiality of the speaker and complained against the speaker about his style of functioning. It is, indeed a bad precedent to complain against the speaker, who by all accounts is supreme and subordinate to none but the house.

In the cut and thrust of parliamentary debate, the treasury benches, are fair game for attack, and convention ordains that the speaker is always respected. It has been said that the premier can do nothing right, whereas the speaker can do no wrong. Smooth and successful running of parliamentary democracy in England owes not a little to the reverence and confidence built around the chair.

The ruling party and opposition have so far failed to come to an understanding on the establishment of this convention. Such a day seems far-away in the political system of Karnataka. At the time of elections the speaker has no alternative but to be a party candidate if at all he has a desire to get re-elected. As such they too can not be expected to divorce themselves from party loyalties. In the parliamentary history of Karnataka from 1949 to today there have been as many as fifteen speakers elected. One comes across only one incident of a continuance of sitting speaker in the assembly. In 1962 speaker Vaikunta Baliga was elected to the chair, and again in 1967.

From the above observation, it is evident that the presiding officers in Karnataka have yet to evolve sound convention for keeping the office of the speaker out of the dominance of party control. It can rightly be done if all the high traditions associated with British speakership, like securing unanimous choice of the speaker after consultation with the opposition, renouncing party membership by the speaker and assuring re-election as long as the speaker desires, and giving retirement benefits, etc., are followed in Karnataka and if all the members of the house obey the speaker. It would also help to increase the prestige and decorum of the house. This would be the sign of the faith of members in the speaker about his impartiality and independence. These would not only lend dignity to the chair by would also lay a firm foundation of parliament democracy in Karnataka.

NOTES AND REFERENCES

1. Dewan's Address to Representative Assembly on 7.10.1881, Bangalore, Government Press, 1914, Vol. I.
2. Venkatappa, M.V., *Origin and Growth of Legislature in Mysore State*, Journal of Parliamentary Affairs, Vol. 7, Issue—2, 5 June, 1988, pp. 17-23.
3. Proclamation dated 25.11.1949.
4. Journal of Parliamentary Affairs, *op. cit.*
5. The Mysore State (Alteration of Name) Act, 1973.
6. Mores, S.S., *Practice and Procedure of Indian Parliament*, Bombay: Thacker and Co. Ltd., 1960, p. 69.

7. D. Sundar Ram, *An Ideal Presiding Officer Sir, Vithalbhai Patel*, Journal of Parliamentary Affairs, Vol. 6, Issue A, December, 1987, p. 22.
8. Nagarathnam, K.S., *Role of Speaker*, Lectures on Parliamentary Practice and Procedure, December, Bangalore, K.L.A., 1972, p. 121.
9. Laundy, Philip, *The Office of the Speaker in the Parliament of the Commonwealth*, Macmillan India Ltd., 1984, p. 180.
10. Constitution of India, Articles 99, 104, 188, 193.
11. Constitution of India, Articles 93, 178, 182.
12. Karnataka Legislative Assembly Rules, 7(1).
13. *Ibid.*, Rules, 7(2).
14. *Ibid.*, Rules, 9 and 13.
15. Singh Yadav, J.N., *The Indian Speaker (Crisis of Identity)*, Haryana, The Academic Press, 1982, p. 187.
16. Mukerjee, Hirden, *Portrait of Parliament*, New Delhi, Vikas Publishers, 1978, p. 40.
17. Jennings Ivor, *Parliament*, London, Cambridge University Press, 1970, p. 65.
18. Indian Express, Daily, 18th April, 1991.
19. Norman Wilding and Laundy Philip, *An Encyclopaedia of Parliament*, London, Cassell and Co. Ltd., 1968, p. 688.
20. Quoted from Dube, Maya, *Speaker in India*,: New Delhi, S. Chand and Co. Pvt. Ltd., 1971, p. 84.
21. More, S.S., op. cit., pp. 11-13.
22. Report on the Administration of Mysore, 1949-50, p. 15.
23. Rulings and Observation by the Chair, K.L.A. from 1950-1989, p. 4.
24. Mysore Legislative Assembly Debates, Vol. VII, No. 1, 18.6.1952, p. 4.
25. *Ibid.*, pp. 18-19.
26. Rulings and Observations, op. cit., p. 225.
27. *Ibid.*, Vol. XI, 13th October, 1954, pp. 110-111.
28. Rulings and Observation, op. cit., p. 65.
29. *Ibid.*, Vol. V, 5th November, 1958, p. 330.
30. Dube, Maya, *Speaker in India*, New Delhi: S. Chand and Co. Pvt. Ltd., 1971, pp. 110-11.
31. Mysore Legislative Assembly Debates, Vol. XI, 15th March, 1962, pp. 6-7.
32. *Ibid.*, Vol. III, 21st December, 1963, pp. 6172-73.
33. Kaul, M.N., *Growth of the Position and Powers of Speaker*, Hindustan Times, 24th June, 1954.
34. Mysore Legislative Assembly Debates, Vol. III, 6th December, 1963, pp. 5378-81.
35. *Ibid.*, Vol. I, 5th September, 1968, p. 205.
36. *Ibid.*, Vol. XXI, 4th September, 1969, p. 204.
37. *Ibid.*, Vol. XXIV, 27th February, 1970, p. 335.
38. *Ibid.*, Vol. I, 24th March, 1972, pp. 15-16.

39. *Ibid.*, p. 31.
40. Rulings and Observations, op. cit., p. 73.
41. Karnataka Legislative Assembly Debates, Vol. XIX, 27th September, 1979, p. 739.
42. *Ibid.*, Vol. XXXII, 30th January, 1981, pp. 49-54.
43. Karnataka Legislative Assembly Debates, Vol. XXXXXIV, 15th July, 1982, p. 16.
44. *Ibid.*, Vol. XXXIV, 6th March, 1981, p. 85.
45. *Ibid.*, Vol. VI, 12th August, 1983, p. 338.
46. *Ibid.*, 18th March, 1985, pp. 10-11.
47. Rulings and Observation by the Chair, 1985-89, pp. 4-10.
48. Who's Who (Ninth K.L.A.) 1989, pp. 1-2.
49. Who's Who (Tenth K.L.A.) 1994, p. 1.
50. Deccan Herald Daily, 3rd November, 1998.
51. *Ibid.*, 24th March, 1999.
52. *Ibid.*, 27th October, 1999.
53. *Ibid.*, 23rd July, 2002.

7

Judiciary in Karnataka

I. SHARATH BABU

Hindu law recognizes the king as the fountain of justice and the Shastras require him to maintain permanent courts and to preside over them himself. The Dharmasutras and Arthasastra reveal to us a more or less full-fledged and well-developed judiciary.[1] The King was at its head and he was to attend the court daily to decide disputes. His time-table requires him to spend everyday about a couple of hours in adjudication. In theory the King could entertain any suit; but in actual practice he could have looked into only the important cases from the capital. He was often too busy to do even this and used to delegate the work to the Chief Justice or to some other royal officer. Pradnavaka or the Chief Justice was naturally a legal luminary of high reputation. He was to be well-versed in Substantive Law as well as in the Law of Procedure. He was to be a master in the Sacred as well as in the Customary Law. The interesting feature of the judicial administration was the system of jury. Even the King and the Chief Justice could not begin the trial of a case, if a panel of three, five or seven jurors did not assist them. The number of jurors was deliberately kept uneven to provide for the contingency of a difference of opinion; they were to be not only impartial, but also well grounded in the law. It was their duty to restrain a willful King going astray and giving a wrong decision. This was generally the view held by many historians—more especially the Western scholars—till recently about the administration of justice in our country. The Smritis are almost unanimous in stating that the Sabhyas or jurors should be Brahmanas, when knowledge of the sacred law was not necessary;

and when the dispute was among cultivators, merchants and foresters, Dharmasastra writers themselves recommended that the cases should be tried with the help of jurors selected from the castes or the professions of the parties themselves.[2]

When the kingdoms began to be fairly extensive ones after 600 BC, subordinate royal courts began to be constituted for important towns and cities. They were often located in the headquarters of territorial divisions, like Sthana (which included about 800 villages), Dronamukha (which comprised 400 villages) and Khurvatika (which was exactly half of the size of Dronamukha). These courts functioned under the authority of the royal seal and therefore called Mudrita in later times. There used to be also the Circuit Courts, which are referred to by Narada.[3] There were special royal courts of Criminal Jurisdiction known as Kantakasodhana Courts. According to Arthasastra (IV 1-2), these courts took cognizance not only of the serious crimes against the state but also of offences against society. Officers charged with misconduct, persons accused of theft, dacoity and sex offences had to appear before the same courts.[4]

In addition to these official courts, there were a number of popular courts in the ancient Indian polity known as Puga, Sreni and Kula. In the Vijayanagar administration these courts were called Anykya or secondary courts to distinguish them from the royal tribunals. The Puga courts consisted of members belonging to different castes and professions, but staying in the same village or town. Puga court later became known as Gota court in Maharashtra. In Karnataka it was known as Dharmasasana during the 17th century AD; the Mahajanas (elders) of the village and their twelve village sergeants were represented in it and it used to decide private disputes and its decisions were enforced by the state as a matter of course.[5]

After the fall of the Vijayanagar empire, the suzerainty over Mysore fell by degrees into the hands of small chieftains called Poligars who assumed independent power in the country round about them. Between 1568 and 1677 these Poligars carried on the administration of justice more ore less on the pattern of Vijayanagar, even though in important matters the Sultans of Bijapur did administer according to Islamic Law. From 1687 onwards, nearly a century Mysore changed hands among the various rulers and the pattern of administration of justice along with the political conditions appeared to be very uncertain and subject to frequent changes. But during the period of Hyder Ali and Tippu, the conditions were stabilized and the revenue officers were entrusted with judicial functions.[6] There was a "Sadar" Court at the capital city and *Kazis* in other places. Until the advent of the English the pattern of administration of justice in Karnataka was more or less the one that was prevailed during the days of Vijayanagar, in spite of the fact that it underwent many political changes and Muslims and Marathas held sway over some parts of this territory by turns.[7]

After the takeover of the administration of Mysore state by the British in 1831, the following courts were established: (1) The Amits, (2) Munsiffs, (3) Sadar Munsifs, (4) Principal Sadar Munsiffs and (5) The Court of European Superintendents. By 1862 the Huzur Adalat and the Munsiffs Courts were abolished and the judicial hierarchy consisted of the Judicial Commissioner, the Superintendents of Divisions, the Deputy Superintendents and Amildars of Taluks. As regards criminal justice, the Judicial Commissioner, the Superintendents and Admildars of taluks were entrusted with criminal jurisdiction also.[8] In the year 1881, the Court of the Judicial Commissioner, who was the head of the judicial administration in the territories of Mysore, was designated as the Chief Court of Mysore and by the Mysore Chief Court Regulation, 1884, its Constitution was statutorily amended with effect from May 28, 1884. The provisions of Mysore Act XII of 1930 designated this Chief Court as the High Court of Mysore. The jurisdiction of this High Court, which exercised jurisdiction over the territories of the former state of Mysore, was extended to the state of Coorg with effect from April 1, 1953, and to a part of the district of Bellary, which was until then in the state of Madras, with effect from October 1, 1953.[9]

In Mysore, the Revenue Officers used to exercise magisterial powers until 1927, when the Government of Mysore introduced a scheme, by which these Revenue Sub-Divisional Officers ceased trying the criminal cases. This task was entrusted to the Special Magistrates solely devoted for trial work. The High Court recruits mainly the members of the Bar as Munsiffs and posts them as the Magistrates. The positions of the Munsiffs and the Magistrates are interchangeable. The government has reserved a few places to which the Civil Service Officers are posted, so that they may get the magisterial training before they become the District Magistrates. The Revenue Officers are still ex-officio Magistrates, exercising the powers under the Criminal Procedure Code except those of actually trying the acccused.[10]

The Deputy Commissioner corresponding to the Collector in the Indian Union is the District Magistrate for each district. He is the chief revenue officer and also the head of police in his district. The Special Magistrates in each district, though recruited by the High Court, are placed under the District Magistrates. Later the system was changed.

The former state of Mysore, over which its High Court exercised jurisdiction until the first day of November, 1956, when there was reorganization of the states of the Union of India, became one of the Part B States specified in the First Schedule to the Constitution of India. By the States Reorganization Act, 1956, enacted by the Parliament a new state known as the State of Mysore was formed under the provisions of Section 7 of that Act comprising the territories specified in that Section. Those territories were the territories of the then existing state of Mysore, together with parts of the then existing states of Bombay, Hyderabad, Madras and the entire state of Coorg. As from the First day of November 1956, the High Court of the then existing Part B State of Mysore, which also exercised jurisdiction over the state of Coorg, was thus abolished and ceased to function and the new High Court was established for the new state of Mysore.

This High Court, therefore, which was established after the reorganization of the states, can by no means be said to be representative of the High Court of the former state of Mysore. This is not a case of extending the jurisdiction of an existing High Court but one case of abolishing the old High Court and establishing a new one, which has to exercise jurisdiction over the new state formed as a result of the reorganization.[11]

The Constitution of India provides a federal structure with a dual polity in which the legislative and executive powers are divided between the centre and the states, each being supreme within a Constitutionally assigned sphere, yet in the domain of administration of justice, the Constitution has adopted a unified system governed by a hierarchy of courts with the Supreme Court as its head, being the last court of appeal and invested with original jurisdiction in certain important matters. Next to it is the High

Court, with administrative control over all the subordinate courts subject to its appellate jurisdiction, and power of superintendence over all courts and tribunals throughout the territories in relation to which it exercises jurisdiction.

The present judicial system of India, created by the British, is founded mainly on the English Common Law, which has its own jurisprudence and judicial techniques, which were invented and developed in the course of 800 years by successive generations of English judges under changing social conditions in England. It is very largely a "judge-made" law. The whole process of trial, civil or criminal, has been moulded at all stages by the judiciary with the object of eliciting the truth in accordance with judicial conceptions of fair-play. Judges developed most of the principal rules of evidence including the exclusion of hearsay, and so is the rule of natural justice, which permeates the jurisprudence of British courts.[12]

High Court

The Constitution provides the establishment of a High Court for each state. Every High Court shall consist of a Chief Justice and other judges. The Constitution does not fix any maximum number of judges as may be deemed necessary by the President. But the President is under a Constitutional obligation to review the strength of each High Court basing on the arrears of cases pending.[13] The President shall appoint every Judge of a High Court after consultation with the Chief Justice of India, the governor of the state, and, in the case of appointment of a Judge other than the Chief Justice, the Chief Justice of High Court. The judge shall hold the office, until he attains the age of sixty-two but he can be removed by the President for proved misbehaviour or incapacity on an address to him by both houses of the Parliament supported by a majority of the total membership of that House and not less than two-thirds of the members of that House.

Every High Court is declared to be a court of record.[14] There are two characteristics of a court of record: (i) the records of such a court are admitted to be of evidentiary value and they cannot be questioned when produced in a court, and (ii) it has the power to punish for contempt of itself. The power to punish for contempt of court is a special power derived from Article 215 and not from the Contempt of Courts Act, 1971. No Act of legislature could take away that power and confer it afresh on the High Court by virtue of its own authority. The High Court's jurisdiction to try and punish for contempt of court includes all necessary and incidental powers to effectuate that jurisdiction.[15]

With the exception of summary cases (civil and criminal), all other cases will originate in the courts of the subordinate judges, and district and sessions judges, depending on the subject-matter. There will be one appeal to High Court as a matter of right, on question of law and facts. The Magistrates and Munsiffs are vested with criminal and civil jurisdiction in petty offences and small cause cases, which will be tried summarily and those decisions will be final and not appealable.

The jurisdiction and power of the High Courts is subject to the provisions of the Constitution and the provisions of any law of the appropriate legislature made by virtue of powers conferred on that legislature by the Constitution.[16]

Article 226(1) of the Constitution empowers every High Court to issue to any person of authority, including any government, within those territories directions, orders or writs in the nature *habeas corpus, mandamus, quo warranto,* prohibition and *certiorari* for the enforcement of fundamental rights guaranteed under Part III of the Constitution or for any other purpose.[17] The writ jurisdiction conferred on the High Court by Article 228 can be invoked to enforce not only a fundamental right but a legal right as well. The jurisdiction conferred on the High Courts under Article 226 is broader in range than that conferred on the Supreme Court under Article 32, for while the Supreme Court acts only when there is an infraction of a fundamental right, a High Court may act when a fundamental right or any other legal right is violated.[18]

Article 226 in terms does not describe classes of persons entitled to apply or seek remedy, but the existence of the right is the foundation of the exercise of jurisdiction by the High Court. The legal right that can be enforced must ordinarily be the personal right of the petitioner himself who complains of the infringement of such right and approaches the court for relief. This rule is subject to some exceptions in certain cases. But the petitioner need not wait till the actual infraction of his right. He can also approach the Court against imminent threat of such infraction.[19]

The writ of Habeas Corpus is a process by which a person who is confined without legal justification may secure a release from his confinement. The writ is, in form, an order issued by the High Court calling upon the person by who a person is alleged to be kept in confinement to bring such person before the court and to let the court know on what ground the person is confined. If there is no legal justification for the detention, the person who is so detained shall be released by the order of the court.[20] However, in cases of availability of alternative remedy, inordinate delay in seeking remedy under this Article or if the petition is frivolous, vexatious or *prima facie* unjust, the High Court may decline to entertain a writ petition under this Article. The writ of Mandamus is a judicial remedy which is in the form an order from the Court to any government, court, corporation or public authority to do or forbear from doing some specific act which that body is obliged under law to do or refrain from doing, as the case may be, and which is in the nature of a public duty and in certain cases of a statutory duty. No one can ask for a mandamus without a legal right.

There must be a judicially enforceable as well as legally protected right before one suffering a legal grievance can ask for a mandamus. A person can be said to be aggrieved only when he is denied a legal right by someone who has a legal duty to do something and abstains from doing it.

The object of the writ of Quo Warranto is to prevent a person who holds a public office wrongfully. The writ calls upon the holder of the public office to show to the court under what authority he holds the office. Before a citizen can claim a writ of quo warranto, he must satisfy the court that the office in question is a public office and is held by a person without legal authority. This necessarily leads to the enquiry by the court as to whether the appointment of the said person has been made in accordance with law or not. This writ will not lie in respect of an office which is of a private nature.

A writ of Prohibition is issued when the court or tribunal is exercising the wrongful jurisdiction. The writ prevents a court or tribunal exercising the judicial the judicial or quasi-judicial powers from assuming a jurisdiction which it does not possess. When an inferior court or tribunal takes up for hearing a matter over which it has no jurisdiction, the person against whom the proceedings are taken can move the court for a writ of prohibition and the court will issue an order forbidding the inferior court or tribunal from continuing the proceedings.

Finally, the writ of Certiorari means an order a High Court issued to inferior courts, tribunals or authorities to transmit to it the record of proceeding pending with them for scrutiny and, if necessary, for quashing the same.

Public Interest Litigation

The term "litigation" means a legal action including all proceedings therein, initiated in a Court of Law with the purpose of enforcing a right or seeking a remedy. Therefore, lexically the expression "Public Interest Litigation" means a legal action initiated in a Court of Law for the enforcement of public interest or general interest in which the public or a class of the community has pecuniary interest or some interest by which their legal rights or liabilities are affected.[21] There are a host of decisions explaining the expression "Public Interest Litigation" in its wider connotation in the present day context in modern society.[22]

The object of Public Interest Litigation is to see that provision of the Constitution or a person without any motivation or gain enforces the law for advancing the cause of the community or weaker section of the society or individual.[23] A person who professes to bring a litigation as public interest litigation should do so to achieve some public purpose and should not be motivated by some personal private interest. Further, such person should act *bona fide*. If, on the other hand, a petition is brought with *mala fide* intention in the name of public interest to achieve some private purpose, it does not deserve to be entertained as public interest litigation.[24]

The High Court has to innovate new methods and devise new strategies for the purpose of providing access to justice to large masses of people who are denied their basic human rights and to whom freedom and liberty have no meaning. The only way in which this can be done is by entertaining writ petitions and even letters from public spirited individuals seeking judicial redress for the benefit of persons who have suffered a legal wrong or a legal injury or whose Constitutional or legal rights have been violated but who by reason of their poverty or socially or economically disadvantaged position are unable to approach the court for relief.[25]

Any member of the public having sufficient interest can maintain an action for judicial redress for public injury arising from breach of public duty or from violation of some provisions of the Constitution or the law and seek enforcement of such public duty.[26]

Subordinate Courts of Civil in Nature

The state of Karnataka has enacted the Karnataka Civil Courts Act, 1964, to provide for a uniform law relating to the Constitution, powers and jurisdiction of the Civil Courts in the state of Karnataka subordinate to the High Court. This Act extends to the whole of the state of Karnataka except the city of Bangalore. It deals with the Constitution, powers and jurisdiction of the Civil Courts, which deal with civil matters exclusively. Under Karnataka Civil Courts Act, a Civil Court means a District Court, Court of a Civil Judge or a Munsiff's Court. As far as the criminal matters are concerned a separate hierarchy of judicial system is provided under the Criminal Procedure Code, 1973.

Class and Designation of Civil Courts

Section 3 of the Karnataka Civil Courts Act provides for three classes of Civil Courts to the High Court, namely:—

1. The District Court,
2. The Court of the Civil Judge, and
3. The Munsiff's Court.

The District Court is constituted for each district presided by a District Judge. The governor in consultation with the High Court will make the appointment, posting and promotion of District Judges. The exercise of the power of appointment by the governor is conditioned by his consultation with the High Court, which means that he could only appoint a person to the post of District Judge in consultation with the High Court.[27] The State Government on the recommendation of the High Court appoints one or more Additional District Judges to a District Court. The

District Court shall be the Principal Civil Court of Original Jurisdiction within the local limits of its jurisdiction. Subject to the provisions of the Code of Civil Procedure, 1908, the jurisdiction of a District Court shall extend to all original suits and proceedings of a civil nature. Appeals from the decrees and orders passed by a District Court in original suits and proceedings of a civil nature shall, when law allows such appeals, lie to the High Court. The District Court shall, subject to the general control of the High Court, have control over all other Civil Courts within the local limits of its jurisdiction.

The Court of a Civil Judge is established for each district in the state of Karnataka. The State Government in consultation with the High Court can also provide for a Court of a Civil Judge for a part of district or for more than one district, depending upon certain circumstances. Each Court of a Civil Judge is presided over by a Civil Judge. The jurisdiction of the Court of a Civil Judge is extended to all original suits and proceedings of a civil nature. Appeals from the decrees and orders passed by a Civil Judge in original suits and proceedings of a civil nature, when such appeals are allowed by law, shall lie:

1. to the District Court, when the amount or value of the subject-matter of the original suit or proceeding is less than twenty thousand rupees; and
2. to the High Court, in other cases.

The jurisdiction of the District Court and the Court of a Civil Judge in trying all original suits and proceedings, in fact, remain the same. But in respect of certain original suits, if the parties choose to file the suit in District Court in such cases, the appeals from the decrees and orders passed by the District Court, when such appeals are allowed by law, lie in the High Court. But if the parties choose to file such original suits in the Court of a Civil Judge, the next appellate court shall be the District Court.

The jurisdiction of a Munsiff's Court extends to all original suits and proceedings of a civil nature, if the amount or value of the subject-matter does not exceed ten thousand rupees. Appeals from the decrees and orders passed by a Munsiff in original suits and proceedings of a civil nature, when law allows such appeals, lie in the Court of the Civil Judge provided the amount or a value of the subject-matter of the original suit or proceedings is not more than five thousand rupees and in other cases to the District Court.

The High Court may, by notification, invest any Judge of the small Cause Courts Act, 1964, with powers to hear appeals from such decrees and orders of Munsiff's Court as may be referred to him by the District Judge.

The High Court may, by notification, invest any Civil Judge within such local limits and subject to such pecuniary limitation as may be specified in such notification, with all or any of the powers of a District Judge or a District Court, as the case may be under the following Acts, namely:—

(i) The Guardians and Wards Act, 1890.
(ii) The Indian Lunacy Act, 1912.
(iii) The Special Marriage Act, 1954.

Every order made by a Civil Judge in respect of the above matters, an appeal would lie before the District Court when the amount or value of the subject-matter is less than twenty thousand rupees and in other cases to the High Court.

Subordinate Courts of Criminal Nature

The Code of Criminal Procedure, 1973, provides the set up of Criminal Courts in every state. Under the Code of Criminal Procedure, 1973 in every state besides the High Court, the following classes of Criminal Courts are established. They are:

(i) Court of Sessions;
(ii) Judicial Magistrates of the first class;
(iii) Judicial Magistrates of the second class; and
(iv) Executive Magistrates.

The revised set up of Criminal Courts and allocation of magisterial functions between the Judicial Magistrates and the Executive Magistrates under the Criminal Procedure Code of 1973 are intended to bring about the separation of the judiciary from the executive. As a consequence of separation, there are now two categories of magistrates, namely, the judicial and the executive magistrates, the former being under the control of the High Court and the latter under the control of State Government. Broadly speaking, the functions that are essentially judicial in nature are the concern of the judicial magistrates, while functions which are of a police or administrative nature are legally qualified and experienced persons.

As far as the magistracy is concerned, for performance of magisterial functions on the judicial side or each district, there is a Chief Judicial Magistrate, Additional Chief Judicial Magistrate, Sub-Divisional Judicial Magistrates and other Judicial Magistrates. The High Court may, if requested by the State Government, appoint "Special Judicial Magistrates". In Presidency Towns to discharge the magisterial functions of judicial nature, the Code provides a special category of Magistrates called the Presidency Magistrates headed by a Chief Presidency Magistrate. In these areas the Commissioner of Police discharges some of the functions of the District Magistrate and the others by the chief presidency magistrate.

On the Executive side for each district, there is a District Magistrate, the Additional District Magistrates, the Sub-Divisional Magistrates and other Subordinate Executive Magistrates. The State Government may, if it things fit, appoint Special Executive Magistrates. The District Magistrate is primarily responsible for maintaining peace in the district. The District Magistrate exercises general control over the police force. The District Magistrate is the principal representative of the law for most purposes in the eyes of the people and occupies a position of great power and responsibility. A District Magistrate appointed under the Criminal Procedure Code of 1973, besides his powers under the code, also has other powers, which are not contemplated by the Code. He is the Collector of the District and is also the District Officer. In those capacities he has to perform many functions which are not covered by the Criminal Procedure Code.

Court of Sessions

The State Government shall establish a Court of Session for every district. Every Court of Session shall be presided over by a judge appointed by the High Court. The High Court may also appoint Additional Sessions Judges and Assistant Sessions Judges to exercise jurisdiction in a Court of Session. All the Assistant Sessions

Judges shall be subordinate to the Sessions Judge. The Sessions Judge distributes the business among the Assistant Sessions Judges.

Judicial Magistrate Courts

In every district (other than the Metropolitan area) there shall be a court of Judicial Magistrate first class and second class. The presiding officers of such magistrate courts shall be appointed by the High Court. The Judicial Magistrate of the first class shall be appointed by the High Court as the Chief Judicial Magistrate of the district. The Chief Judicial Magistrate defines the local limits of the areas within which the Magistrates are to exercise the powers vested in them under the Code of Criminal Procedure. Every Chief Magistrate shall be subordinate to the Sessions Judge and every other Judicial Magistrates, subject to the general control of the Sessions Judge, is subordinate to the Chief Judicial Magistrate. The Chief Judicial Magistrate distributes from time to time business among the judicial magistrates subordinate to him.

Powers of the Criminal Courts

The jurisdiction of every Criminal Court to try a particular offence is derived either from the statute, which creates the Court or from the statute, which defines the offence.

Every offence defined under the Indian Penal Code can be tried by the High Court or the Court of Session or any other Court having jurisdiction to try them as shown in the Schedule of the Criminal Procedure Code of 1973.

A High Court can pass any sentence authorized by law. A Sessions Judge or Additional Sessions Judge may pass any sentence authorized by law. But any sentence of death passed by any such judge shall be subject to confirmation by the High Court. An Assistant Sessions Judge may pass any sentence authorized by law except a sentence of death or of imprisonment for life or of imprisonment for a term exceeding ten years. Punishment by imprisonment under the Indian Penal Code means that the offender shall go to jail.

The Chief Judicial Magistrate can award any sentence authorized by law except sentence of death or life imprisonment or imprisonment exceeding seven years. A Magistrate of the first class will have powers to award sentence of imprisonment for a term which may extend to three years and fine up to Rs. 5000. A Magistrate of the second class will have powers to award sentences of imprisonment for a term which may extend to one year and a fine up to Rs.1000.

Thus the system of administration of justice has undergone a process of gradual change. What was considered once upon a time, to be the exclusive dominion of the king, changed in later times? The governing power in society at any given period has made, or accepted, rules of law which forbid a man to bring about certain specified acts through his conduct in order to protect the rights and freedom of another person even in the absence of well defined systematic legal norms. Later it can be seen that the concept of socialization of rime has assumed greater importance wherein the state is vested with the complete task of administering justice to its subjects concerning all matters of litigation under a codified legal system. The institutions established under various legislations has assumed greater importance in solving effectively the problems which press upon us from every side, and most importantly, the human problems of men and women living together in society.

NOTES AND REFERENCES

1. Kane, P.V., *History of Dharmasastra,* Vol. III, Poona, Bhandarkar Oriental Research Institute, p. 242.
2. Altekar, A.S., *State and Government an Ancient India,* Delhi, Motilal Banarsidas, 1958, pp. 23-24.
3. *Ibid.,* p. 28.
4. *Ibid.,* p. 28.
5. *Ibid.,* p. 28.
6. Chennabasappa, K., *Administration of Justice in Vijayanagar Times,* Bangalore, Mysore Law Journal, 1969, p. 15.
7. *Ibid.*
8. *A Hand Book of Karnataka 2001,* Bangalore, Karnataka Gazetteer Department, pp. 183-184.
9. *Basappa* v. *State,* Mysore Law Journal, 1958, pp. 580-583.
10. Narayana Rao, H.V., *Separation of the Judiciary from the Executive in Mysore,* Bangalore, Mysore Law Journal, 1950, p. 31.
11. In *Basappa* v. *State,* 1958 Mysore Law Journal, it was held that the new High Court came into existence after the States Reorganization

Act, 1956 is not bound by the decisions of the Chief Court of Mysore or the High Court of Mysore delivered prior to 1.11.1956.

12. Rajivee Dhavan, Precedent in India, New Delhi, Eastern Book House Publication, 1968, p. 158.
13. This issue has been settled by the Supreme Court in *S.P. Gupta* v. *Union of India,* 1981 Supreme Court Cases, Vol. 87, and *Subhash Sharma* v. *Union of India,* All India Reporter, 1991, SC 631.
14. Article 215 of the Constitution.
15. This was held by the Supreme Court in *R.L. Kapur* v. *State of Tamil Nadu,* All India Reporter 1972, SC 858.
16. *Vide* Article 225 of the Constitution.
17. The power conferred on the High Court under Article 226 shall not act in derogation of the power conferred on the Supreme Court under Article 32.
18. *Janata Dal* v. *H.S. Chowdhary,* All India Reporter, 1993, SC 892 at 906-907.
19. *Bokara & Rampur Ltd.* v. *State of Bihar,* All India Reporter, 1963 SC 518.
20. *Sunil Batra* v. *Delhi Administration,* All India Reporter, 1980 SC 1579.
21. While the expression "public interest litigation" has its origin in the United States, the expression "Social Action Litigation" seems to have been expressed by Professor U. Baxi in his paper, *Taking Suffering Seriously: Social Action Litigation in the Supreme Court of India,* 8-9 Delhi Law Review, Vol. 91, 1979-80. The paper also gives a very comprehensive account of the scope and development of such litigation in India.
22. *Dillip Karamnelkar* v. *Vishnu Bhagwat,* All India Reporter, 1997, Bom. 131, p. 279.
23. *Prayag Vyapar Mandal* v. *State of U.P.,* All India Reporter, 1997, All, p. 7.
24. *S.P. Gupta* v. *Union of India,* All India Reporter, 1982, SC 149, p. 189.
25. *D.S. Nakara* v. *Union of India,* 1983, Supreme Court Cases, Vol. 305, p. 344
26. *Bandhua Mukti Morcha* v. *Union of India,* All India Reporter, 1984, SC 802.
27. Under Article 233 of the Constitution.

8

The Leader of the Opposition in Karnataka Legislative Council, 1995-1998

A Functional Analysis

VIJAYAKUMAR N. TORGAL*

A democratic government presupposes the rule of the majority and the role of the minority. Majority governs and minority offers the check the tendencies of oppression and misrule. The opposition being in minority performs the role of speed breakers on the path of governance. The Leader of the Opposition is an official spokesman of the minority.[1] In performing his role he forms the "Shadow Cabinet". This shadow cabinet performs two functions. first, each minister's policies and actions are keenly observed by members of the shadow cabinet. Secondly, the shadow cabinet will be on alternate government in case the government falls. That is why in England the opposition is called Her Majesty's Opposition. In essence, the opposition has prominence and status in relation to that of Her Majesty's government.

The institution of opposition with the leader of the opposition facilitates in enhancing the effectiveness, responsiveness and efficiency of the government. This is done by the opposition by selling rival policies and plans of action. It also draws the government's attention to immediate necessities and priorities. In essence, it aids the government in fixing priorities for governance. Thus, the opposition is necessary to oppose the government's acts of omissions and commissions resulting in lapses and failures. It is a major check on corruption and defective administration.[2] It is also required for supporting the government through constructive criticism. Hence, it is not to be construed that the opposition parties oppose all the times. During emergency and national crisis both ruling and opposition parties act in unison in the national interest. In order to forge a common policy or action to safeguard the interests of the nation the opposition joins hands with the ruling party.

The institution of the opposition evolved in England. In 1844 Benjamin Disraeli said that "no government can be long secure without a formidable opposition". In India the institution appeared on the national political scene with the recognition of the Leader of Opposition in the Lok Sabha in December 1969. However, it was short lived. In 1977 the Congress became the opposition party and its leader was recognised as Leader of Opposition. Sine then the institution is growing and gaining importance in parliamentary exercises.

In this essay, a modest effort has been made to analyze the institution of the leader of the opposition in the Karnataka legislative council. The period 1995-1998 is chosen for functional analysis. The structural-functional framework is adopted for analysis. The analysis is primarily based on practical observations devoid of theoretical underpinnings.

Recognition

The party in opposition elects its leader or sometimes a group of parties elect a leader of the opposition. The leader of largest opposition party or group of parties is formally recognised by the presiding officer of the House. The process of recognition by the presiding officer is obligatory. The decision of the presiding officer is final and it will not be questioned in the court of law. H.K. Patil was chosen as the leader of the Congress party in Karnataka Legislative council in December 1994.

The Congress Party was the single largest opposition party in the Karnataka Legislative Council. The Chairman of the Karnataka Legislative Council recognised H.K. Patil as the Leader of the Opposition in the Legislative Council on 28.12.1994. After his re-election as MLC in June 1996, he was again recognised as the Leader of the Opposition in the Council on 1.7.1996 by the Chairman of the Karnataka Legislative Council.

The Leader of the Opposition is equated with the rank of a cabinet minister (*vide* G.O. No. DPAR 2 HWP 91 *DATED* 11.11.93) and as such all facilities provided to cabinet ministers are provided to him. His salary and other perks are governed by the Karnataka Legislative Salaries, Pensions and Allowances Act, 1956, as amended from time to time. He enjoys more privileges than a Cabinet Minister.[3] He enjoys certain privileges on ceremonial occasions.

He initiates discussions on the Governor's address and the Budget. On all important occasions he is asked to participate. "The Leader of the Opposition is by custom accorded certain peculiar rights in asking questions to the Ministers and has precedence in debates."[4] He can intervene in discussion on any issue. The Page Committee recommended that "The leader of the largest recognised Opposition Party (whether a regular party or a party composed of different parties or groups) should be recognised as the Leader of the Opposition. According to the Committee, it would be a healthy parliamentary convention if the Leader of the Opposition is invited by the Chief Minister before the latter makes any policy statement in the House and is given a copy of the statement in advance, and his suggestions for fixing any particular business on a particular day are, as far as possible, accepted by the Speaker and the Leader of the House. The Committee further suggested that the Leader of the Opposition should be paid a salary and provided with an office as well as residential accommodation and some secretarial staff".[5]

Sources of Information

In order to criticise, the Leader of the Opposition needs information. In the absence of information he cannot perform his role effectively. Apart from the library, government orders, circulars, cabinet decisions, statements of ministers, government publications are some of the sources. The Governor's address, budget speeches and documents, the replies by the government on the floor of House are the other primary sources which form the basis for the leader of the opposition to react and criticise. The lapses of the government are pinpointed on the basis of the information. However, he also can elicit information on specific-issues and subjects by writing to the government. The government does not all the time provide information. He travels throughout the state, and while on tour he gets information on government actions, failures and lapses. In the same manner the affected persons bring to him information on problems arising out of government policies and actions. Whenever the government takes a decision, the teaching community, students, unemployed bodies, merchant community, weaver association and the like bring the defects and failures of government's decisions to the leader of the opposition. This is another way the leader of the opposition receives information on government's operations and performance. One of the most important sources of information drawn on by the opposition is simply the experience of their own supporters gathered in party forums or a meeting over a cup of tea.[6]

Methods of Opposition

The Leader of the Opposition has been provided with a number of forums for highlighting the government's lapses and failures.

On the Floor of the House

The House provides ample opportunities for opposing government policies and actions. The legislative devices like, question hour, call attention notices, half-an-hour discussion, short notice discussion, adjournment motions and zero hour are important instruments through which the Leader of the Opposition offers criticism as well as suggestions. He draws attention of the government to its failure and lapses through the legislative devices. The legislative business such as passage of bills provides another opportunity to the Leader of the Opposition to speak and enlighten the government of its weaknesses and failures on a particular subject or department. The discussion on budget demands is one more occasion in which each department's performance is examined and suggestions for improvements are offered. The government's policies and actions are scrutinised and assessed while discussing the Governor's address to the legislature. Whenever the House takes up the passage of resolutions and motions the Leader of the Opposition speaks on it.

During the legislative session important and sensitive issues crop up. Such issues are discussed and resolved in the chambers of the presiding officers. This is called "behind the Speaker's or Chairman's chair".

The Leader of the Opposition had sent 110 Call Attention notices concerning public issues. Most of these concerned students, teachers, workers and farmers. The following table gives a picture of the number of issues raised under various instruments of legislature during 1995-1998.

Number of Issues Raised

Year	Zero hour	Adjournment motion	Matters under Rule 330
1995	22	07	07
1996	37	13	16
1997	21	05	13
1998	30	07	04
Total	**100**	**32**	**40**

Source: The debates of Karnataka Legislative Council, 1995-98.

Outside the House

Nowadays the number of days of legislative session are few. For instance, in 1973 the Council assembled for 93 days. Likewise, in 1972 it met for 79 days. Over the years the number of days stand reduced. For instance, in 1995 the Council met for 47 days, while in 1996 it met for 46 days, in 1997 it met for 52 days, in 1998 it met for 44 days. This requires the Leader of the Opposition to raise government's lapses outside the House too. This is done in the party forum, Legislative Party forums, public meetings and programmes. The press conferences and "Meet the Press" provide an opportunity to the Leader of the Opposition to criticise the governments actions and policies. In government meetings like KDP/20-Point Programme meetings the government's acts are criticised and performance is evaluated on important public matters and serious lapses of the government are represented to the Governor.

Important Issues Raised During 1995-1998

The government's failures, lapses, misdeeds, mismanagement and acts of omissions and commissions are raised. Along with this suggestions are offered to the government for improving its performance.

During 1995-1998 two issues figured prominently. The issue of Cauvery Water Dispute, on which the governments decision to release 6 TMC water, the five rounds of dialogue with the Tamil Nadu and ultimately the acceptance for Authority to implement the interim Award of Cauvery Tribunal were severely criticised by the Leader of the Opposition. The government's volte face in accepting the constitution of Authority to implement the Interim Award was brought to the public notice.

The status of Krishna basin project works and the need to give fillip to these works was brought to the public notice through the publication of *Keli Krishneya Koogu*. The handling of the Krishna water issue leading to the creation of the Inter-state Water Dispute was criticised by the Leader of the Opposition. The governments decision to allow an unofficial committee to visit the site of the Upper Krishna Project and subsequently muddling on dam height controversy was opposed and public awareness was created.

The circular issued by the Director of Mines and Geology stating "not to obey oral instructions of the Minister for Mines and Geology" is raised on the floor of the House. By this the issue of fake permits for quarrying, misdeeds of a few officials of the Forest Department and the very procedure of licensing of mining came to public light. The events culminated in the Constitution of the Joint Committee of Legislature to probe into the issues concerning mines' administration in the state.

The Vasudevan's case in which the governments actions leading to the contempt of the Supreme Court was debated. The inaction of the bureaucracy was criticised. The election malpractice in Bidar resulting in violation of election rules was raised and memorandum to this effect was submitted to the Governor. Ultimately this lead to the resignation of the Minister of State for Municipal Administration.

The criticism of the alleged role of the son of the Minister of State for Kannada and Culture in the desecration of Dr. Ambedkar's statue led to the resignation of the Minister. Further, a judicial enquiry was ordered. The land grabbing in and round Bangalore by influential people was raised and debated on the floor of the Council. The power tariff hike was fiercely criticised and an unprecedented night long dharna during the legislative session resulted in the Constitution of the Joint Committee of Legislature. Later, on the recommendations of this Committee power tariff was reduced marginally.

The continuation of agreement with the TAPCO for power generation at UKP was questioned. The agreement period was over but the company did not commence the work. The project cost of

TAPCO Rs. 617 crore while the state-owned public company KPCL had estimated it at Rs.554 crore. In view of its non-commissioning and project cost variations the Leader of the Opposition demanded scrapping of the contract and giving the same to KPCL.

The framing of Karnataka Excise Rules, 1997 in contravention of the 1989 rules and squashing of the same by the Karnataka High Court in W.P. No. 987/97 was raised. The 1997 Excise Rules aimed at allowing private distilleries in the supply of liquor. This denied the monopoly of state owned public undertaking MSIL in the supply of liquor, thereby the huge loss to the company and the state exchequer was allowed. This aspect was raised and demanded for the implementation of the High Court order. Further, an investigation into the framing of the 1997 rules and the alleged corruption in the said process the role of officer involved in framing rules and the intention of government was questioned. Memorandum to this effect was given to the Governor.

The deferment of the tax payment to MICO and Paper Mills, Dandeli resulting in Rs. 300 crore loss to the state exchequer was raised and demanded for squashing of G.O. No. FD 67 CSL/98(1) dated 30.5.1998 and FD 124 CSL 96(1) dated 15.12.1997. Further, a CBI enquiry to investigate into the persons involved in this exercise was demanded.

A number of farmers committed suicide on account of crop failure in North Karnataka. The Leader of the Opposition visited the areas of crop failures consoled the bereaved families and appealed to the government for compensation. The issue was taken to the National Human Rights Commission too. With the result, the government was forced to pay compensation of Rs. 500 per acre. The police atrocities on striking farmers of Bagur-Navile were raised. The Leader of the Opposition visited those villages to study police excesses. The opposition party's criticism forced the government to respond to their needs. The police surveillance of activities of people visiting these villages came to the notice of the Leader of the Opposition. This act of the police was brought to the notice of the Chairman of Karnataka Legislative Council and later it was referred to the Privileges Committee to examine the breach of privilege by the government.

The unprecedented rain caused havoc and more than two lakh of people were rendered homeless. Crops worth Rs. 31,745.86 lakh were lost. Public property like roads, culverts, bridges, buildings (worth Rs. 453.25 crore) were severely damaged. The Leader of the Opposition visited the rain affected areas before the minister or government secretaries did. The calamity relief works were examined, the inadequate and untimely government action was raised and debated thoroughly on the floor of the Council. The government was made to act positively in arranging the calamity relief and restoring public communication.

The Leader of the Opposition is consulted on important issues confronting the state such as Cauvery Water Dispute, Krishna Water Dispute and Border disputes. Likewise as a statutory requirement, while appointing Lokayukta and Upa-Lokayukta he is consulted.

Private Member Bill

The Leader of the Opposition initiated a Private Member Bill on the prevention of AIDS. AIDS is spreading like a wild fire. The Bill aims at preventing the spread of this deadly disease. The HIV Prevention Bill, 1998 has made provision for the establishing of HIV Prevention Board and curbing the spread of the virus, protecting the HIV affected persons from social disabilities. It also prescribes rights and obligations for health professionals. Further it provides for declaring certain areas a "high risk areas".

The Bill was introduced in October-November 1998 Session of the Legislative Council and referred to the Private Member Bill Committee.

The government should have come forward in bringing this Bill since in Western countries already enactments have been made to combat this deadly disease. Hence, this Bill has been initiated.

New Methods

Since 1994 the Leader of the Opposition has authored three booklets. The first one, *Keli Krishneya Koogu,* highlighted the government's failure in completing the Krishna Basin projects and the need to adhere to Bachwat Award. This effort boosted the government initiative in earmarking more funds thereby giving fillip to irrigation works. The *Chaluva Kannada Naadu Nanasagada Kanasu* is the second book which systematically and scientifically enumerates the regional disparities in various spheres. The injustice and discrimination meted out to North Karnataka were statistically documented. This resulted in state vide debate on balanced development and the constitution of a committee under Chief Secretary's Chairmanship.

The third book titled, *Heliddenu Madiddenu* brings out the unfulfilled promises made by the government. The promises made in Governor's address and Budget speeches are recorded and listed with reference to their non-fulfillment. The publication of these books have evoked good response among the public. A new method of presenting the government's failures, lapses and misdeeds was thus evolved by way of documentation. The government's attention was drawn to immediate issues of the state and the public. Prioritisation of government policies and plans was made possible by these documents.

Concluding Observations

The earlier Leaders of the Opposition, apart from recording the failures and lapses of government, unearthed scandals and acts of misappropriation. The Rolex Watch affair, telephone tapping, bottling issue, Rewajith Scandal and the like still haunt the public memory. But since 1994 a new trend is set in. Drawing the government's attention on substantive issues and subjects has gained momentum. The hitherto neglected areas, the social issues and alternate development models are brought to the government's notice as well as to the public for lively debate and awareness. The Krishna Basin works were neglected, thus the government's attention was drawn to this resulting in expediting the works. The Ghataprabha Right Bank Canal work was almost forgotten. This was brought to the government's notice. The regional imbalance and disparities were made the core issues for governance.

Public awareness was created by raising social issues like banning of Gutka and the prevention of AIDS. The banning of Gutka was debated on the floor of the Council. While initiating discussion on Governor's address and the Budget speech the Leader of the Opposition suggested some alternate models of developments like *Swadhyaya Movements* of Gujarat and so on. On one such occasion he demanded for the constitution of an administrative reforms commission to suggest improvements in government bureaucracy. Similarly, he even requested the

Governor to present "action-taken report" on Governor's assurances while addressing the Legislature. This will ensure the Governor's assurances will be fulfilled.

Lastly, the allegations made by the Leader of the Opposition on government's actions are invariably supported by documentary evidence. Each allegation is substantiated and given statistical support. Therefore, allegations made by the Leader of the Opposition are not emphatically denied by the government except on the political level.

The position of the Leader of the Opposition is a difficult one. He has to criticise the government and at the same time offer suggestions. In essence, constructive criticism is required. In the words of Harold MacMillan, "There is, I suppose, no position more difficult and in some ways more unrewarding than that of a Leader of the Opposition to criticise to find fault, and at the same time, of course, to develop his own proposals and policies without the power to implement them. It is in a sense, unrewarding, because any man who is conscious of and has capacity and the desire to operate his own plans must feel all the time a sense of frustration".[7]

NOTES AND REFERENCES

1. M. N. Kaul and S.L.Shakadhar, *Practice and Procedure of Parliament*, New Delhi, Metropolitan, 1995, p. 131.
2. Ivor Jennins, *Cabinet Government*, Cambridge, Cambridge University Press, 1980, pp. 499-502.
3. *Leader of the Opposition in Lok Sabha*, a paper prepared by Library and Reference, Research Documentation and Information Service (LARRDIS).
4. Erskine May, *Parliamentary Practice*, London, Butterworths, 1989, p. 200.
5. Quoted in Kaul and Shakdhar, *Practice and Procedure of Parliament*, op. cit., p. 132.
6. J.A.G. Griffith and Michael Ryle, *Parliament Functions, Practice and Procedure*, London, Sweet and Maxwell, 1989, pp. 338-363.
7. Quoted in Kaul and Shakdhar, *Practice and Procedure of Parliament*, op. cit., p. 131.

9

The Functions of Public Service Commission

OKALY B.B. PATIL

I joined the Karnataka Public Service Commission as a member on March 25, 1991. Whatever all I have heard, observed, studied and experienced during these four years makes me feel strongly that the functions of the Public Service Commission, as envisaged in the Constitution, need to be thoroughly examined. Certain actions of the government in recent year (withdrawal of the requisition for 600 and odd posts of degree college lecturers at a time when the recruitment process was at an advanced stages, withdrawal of the requisition (and later withdrawal of the posts of high school head masters from the recruitment purview of the Commission) for 507, etc., have made the task all the more important and urgent. It may be noted here that the government claims to have, so far, withdrawn forty six categories of posts from the recruitment purview of the Commission. The functions of the Commission are being examined from July, 1992, when the government cancelled the ongoing interviews for the posts of high school head masters abruptly. The Commission has already obtained the opinion of some eminent lawers and retired judges on the issues concerned and the Commission's stand that *Recruitment to the services of the state shall have to be made only by the Commission and none else* has been communicated to the government several times.

I desire to accelerate this process of examination and this paper intends to provide a basis for thoughtful interaction. I seek your considered and valuable views and comments on the issues involved.

Checks on the Executive

Experience has shown that those exercising executive authority have innumerable opportunities generating irresistible temptation for misuse of power for their personal advantage or for the advantage of relatives and friends. If the executive is not subjected to various checks, power will be misused on a very large scale leading to dangerous consequences. Therefore, in all democracies, the executive is subjected to legislative and judicial controls. In addition to these, there are three other important aspects of public life where democratic constitutions seek to control the executive by means of constitutionally-created independent and autonomous bodies. These bodies are the *Comptroller & Auditor General of India, the Election Commission and the Public Service Commission.*

Public money should be spent for the purpose of promoting public interest and not for any other purpose

Those exercising executive authority (both the officials and the non-officials), if not subjected to checks, are likely to misuse public money for their personal gain or for the gain of those in whom they are interested. Therefore, it is necessary that the authorities empowered to authorise expenditure follow rules and procedures. The Comptroller & Auditor General of India must be vigilant. Lapses must be punished.

It is unfortunate that the so-called audit objections are, in most cases, not taken seriously and officials responsible for the lapses are hardly punished. In short, *the Comptroller & Auditor General of India has not made the existence of the institution felt by the authorities and the general public, which is very badly needed.*

Free and Fair Elections

Politicians and political parties seek to acquire and retain political power *by whatever means and at whatever cost*. If they are allowed to do so the very existence of democracy will be seriously threatened. Proper working of democracy demands that periodic elections—the essence of democracy—are free and fair. The Election Commission—a constitutionally created independent body—is expected to work for the attainment of these objectives. Till recently the existence of the Election Commission was not known to many people and the general impression was that elections were conducted by the government. It is T. Sheshan introduced some discipline in the electoral process.

Free and Fair Selections

Persons exercising executive authority (both the officials and the non-officials) will have irresistible temptations to seize as many posts as possible in the services of the state for the benefit of their relatives, friends and others in whom they are specially interested. They were successful in their efforts for quite some time. The result was an inefficient machinery loaded with incompetent persons at important administrative positions. Nepotism and favoritism became rampant and merit played no significant role in recruitment of personnel for the services of the state. As a result, the quality of administration suffered greatly. After several years of experience, it was realised that the quality of public life depends upon the quality of administration and the quality of administration depends upon the persons constituting the administration. If the administrative machinery is not efficient progress cannot be achieved and problems cannot be solved in spite of earnestness of the men at the helm of affairs. Undoubtedly, the permanent services play a very important role in maintaining stability and in achieving higher and higher stages of progress. Therefore, the democratic countries in the world have Public Service Commissions for recruiting personnel for the services of the state on the basis of merit. The framers of our Constitution have made the Public Service Commission a constitutionally created independent body and have assigned the function of making recruitment to services of the state exclusively to the Commissions. Another important function of the Com-mission is to advise the government on important service matters.

Objectives of the Commission

(i) To ensure free and fair selections from the best available candidates for the services of the state. This objective cannot be realised if the recruitment work is entrusted to a body which is subordinate to the government.

(ii) To make the personnel of the services of the state feel assured that they would be treated fairly and impartially during the period of their service with reference to important service matters. This objective cannot be realised if the government is not advised, without fear or favour, on service matters and such advice cannot be expected from an authority or body which is subordinate to the government.

Recruitment Function

Articles 320 and 321 of the Constitution deal with functions of the Public Service Commission. Clauses (1) and (2) of Article 320 deal with recruitment functions. Article 321 pertains to additional functions that can be assigned to the Commission by an Act of the Legislature. It deals with consultative functions with respect to the services of the state on matters not covered by Clause (3) of Article 320 and both recruitment and consultative functions with respect to the services of local Authorities, Body corporates and Public institutions.

The text of Clause (1) makes it clear that the duty of the UPSC is the to conduct examinations and on that basis recruit personnel for appointment to the services of the Union. The duty of the Public Service Commission of a state is to conduct such examinations and on that basis recruit personnel for the services of that state. Examination may be only oral, only written or both. Examination may be competitive or selective. Neither the UPSC nor the Commission of a state can recruit personnel for the services of an organization in which two or more states have joint interest. The framers of the Constitution seem to have desired that the UPSC should confine itself only to framing and operating schemes of recruitment for the services of the Union and the Public Service Commission of a state should confine itself only framing and operating schemes of recruitment for the services of that state.

Clause (2) of Article 320, in this way, becomes relevant only under peculiar circumstances. When two or more states create a common organization (say, a River Valley Project) and desire to recruit personnel possessing special qualifications for appointment to the services of that organization, the states concerned may seek the assistance of the UPSC in making and operating joint schemes of recruitment. On request being made by the states concerned, the UPSC, a body with considerable expertise on recruitment matters and techniques, is duty bound to assist the states in making and operating joint schemes of recruitment.

In this way the Constitution has assigned the function of recruiting personnel to the services of the Union to the UPSC exclusively. Similarly, the Constitution has assigned the function of recruiting personnel to the services of a state to the Public Service Commission of that state exclusively. *The recruitment function of the Commission can only be extended* by an Act of the Parliament or the State Legislature to include recruitment and consultative functions with respect to the services of local authorities, Body Corporates and Public Institutions and consultative functions with respect to the services of the state on matters not covered by Clause (3) of Article 320 as Additional Functions (Article 321). It may be noted that the *Recruitment functions of the Commission can only be extended and cannot be abridged or altered in any way by any authority except the authority which has assigned the function—the Constitution.*

Recruitment Process

The recruitment process is initiated by the government by means of what has come to be known as the Requisition. Requisition is a communication from the government to the Commission asking the latter to recruit personnel for the number of posts and the name of the posts indicated in the requisition. The appropriate authority in a department examines the proposal in all respects and sends the requisition, complete in all respects, to the Commission. The Commission, after the receipt of the requisition, issues a notification in the official gazette and also in some leading newspapers. The candidates submit applications in response to the notification. The Commission thereafter examines the required number of candidates and on that basis recruits the candidates.

The requisition is a commitment of the government to the Commission that the candidates recruited by the Commission for the posts requisitioned will be appointed to those posts within a reasonable time. The notification of the Commission is a communication of this commitment of the government to the applicants and to the general public.

It is, therefore, necessary that the authority concerned should, before sending the requisition to the Commission, be fully satisfied that no developments, which could be foreseen by any reasonably good and efficient officer, are likely in the near future (say for a year) which could compel the government to postpone the appointments of the candidates recruited by the Commission, beyond a reasonable time limit. Because no good government would prefer to go back on their commitment unless there are very strong reasons—reasons which can stand the test of judicial scrutiny.

Recruitment of the personnel by the Commission is communicated to the government in the form of a list (which includes the main list and the additional list) of selected candidates. The list of the candidates selected by the Commission consists of two parts, namely, the main list and the additional list. The Commission selects candidates to include in the additional list if there is a special request by the government or if there is provision in the appropriate Recruitment Rules.

Recruitment to services of the state is the constitutional obligation of the Commission. Appointment of the candidates recruited by the Commission (in the main list in the first instance and in the additional list thereafter) is the constitutional obligation of the government. Neither the Commission nor the government can escape from these obligations.

No person, who has not been examined and recruited by the Commission, can be appointed to or can hold a post in the services of the state. Such appointments, if any, constitute irregular appointments and the expenditure constitutes irregular appointments and the expenditure incurred on their payments constitutes unauthorised expenditure recoverable from the authorities responsible for such irregular appointments.

Suitability of Candidates for Selection and Suitability of Candidates for Appointment

It is the prerogative of the Commission to decide about the suitability of a candidate for selection on the basis of the rules and regulations made by the Commission for the purpose. The government determines the suitability of a candidate for appointment on the basis of rules made for the purpose in consultation with the Commission under sub-clause (b) of Clause (3) of Article 320. Generally speaking, the candidates who are not medically fit or whose past records contain highly objectionable matters or who are found to be members of a banned organization are considered not suitable. The government is free not to issue appointment orders to such candidates even though their names are in the list of candidates selected by the Commission.

Withdrawal of the Requisition

Now and then we come across instances when the government sends a requisition to the Commission and thereafter withdraws before or after the vacancies are notified and sometimes the commencement of the interviews. The important question is whether the government have the power to withdraw a requisition? If the government have that power, whether such power can be exercised arbitrarily and with *mala fied* intention?

Exercise of power by any authority arbitrarily and with *mala fied* intention is not permissible. The government may be justified if the proposal to withdraw the requisition, before notification, is because of certain unexpected developments which could not be foreseen. But, proposals of withdrawal of requisition after notification for reasons of non-application of mind by the authority concerned should be considered seriously as it amounts to disrespect not only to the constitutional body, the Commission, but also to the applicants and the general public. Such situations arise for the simple reason that the authority did not examine the requisition seriously with due care and attention and failed to foresee the likely developments in the near future. Proposals of withdrawal of a requisition in order to regularise some *ad hoc* appointments should be outrightly rejected by the Commission because of the constitutional requirement that no person, who has not been examined and recruited by the Commission, can be appointed to or can hold a post in the services of the state.

A proposal of withdrawal a requisition should invariably contain reasons for which it is sought to be withdrawn. If the proposal does not contain the reasons the Commission should ask for them. If the Commission is satisfied that the reasons stated, the proposal of withdrawal may be allowed. The Commission will be fully justified in challenging the proposal of withdrawal if the reasons are not given or if the reasons given do not satisfy them because the government are not expected to act arbitrarily or with *mala fide* intention in any case and more so when it is a question of the credibility of the government and the Commission.

Consultative Functions

Clause (3) of Article 320 deals with the consultative functions of the Commission. As per this Clause the government are constitutionally obliged to consult the Commission on matters specified from Sub-clause (a) to Sub-clause (3). The Commission is duty bound to advise the government on the matters referred for consultation. The Commission is also duty bound to advise on any other matter referred to the Commission for consultation by the Governor.

As per the provision to Clause (3), the Governor may make regulations specifying the matters in which either generally, or in any particular class of case or in any particular circumstances, it shall not be necessary for the Commission to be consulted.

All regulations so made shall be, for not less than fourteen days, laid before each House of the Legislature, as soon as possible after they are made and shall be subject to such modifications, whether by way of repeal or amendment, as both Houses of the Legislature may make during the session in which they are so laid.

Consultation with the Commission on matters specified from Sub-clause (a) to Sub-clause (e) of Clause 3 of Article 320 excepting the matters specified in the regulations made under the proviso to Clause (3) by the Governor is *mandatory and failure to consult may nullify the action.*

The Commission is duty bound (Article 323) to present annually to the Governor a report about the work done by the Commission and non-receipt of such report the Governor shall cause a copy thereof together with a memorandum explaining, with respect to the cases, *if any*, where the advice of the Commission was not accepted, the reasons for such non-acceptance to be laid before each House of the Legislature.

Article 323 makes it clear that a government have power not to accept the advice of the Commission if there are good reasons for such non-acceptance. The government are answerable to the Legislature for non-acceptance of the advice of the Commission on matters referred for consultation.

It is expected that the government consult the Commission, generally speaking, on all matters specified from Sub-clause (a) to

Sub-clause (e) of Clause (3) of Article 320. It is also expected that the regulations made by the Governor under the proviso to Clause (3) specify only a few matters and only such matters on which consultation with the Commission would not be necessary or would not be possible for some special reasons. Specifying more than necessary matters and matters of general nature in the regulations made by the Governor would defeat the very purpose for which provision has been made for consultation with the Commission. The expression *if any* used in Article 323 makes it clear that non-acceptance of the advice of the Commission should be rare and the advice of the Commission should be accepted generally and in largest possible number of cases. Consultation with the Commission, on matters not specified in the regulations made by the Governor, is *mandatory* whereas the advice of the Commission on matters referred for consultation is directory. All references of consultation with the Commission have to be made under Clause (3) of Article 320.

The Commission is being Crippled by Wrong Interpretations

No power to reject the list of candidates selected by the Commission

The government approaches (has to approach) the Commission *under Clause (1) of Article 320 for recruitment and under Clause (3) of the same Article for consultation.* It is most unfortunate that for a large number of people, Clause (1) of Article 320 simply does not exist. For them Clause (3) is the one which in all cases matters. They think that the government approaches the Commission only under Clause (3) for recruitment and for consultation. In fact, Clause (1) of Article 320 sustains the existence of the Commission because consultative functions can shrink and, hypothetically speaking, can shrink to nothing, whereas recruitment functions can only expand and extend.

Requisition is not Consultation

It is argued that requisition is consultation regarding the suitability of candidates for appointment which the government sends to the Commission. Such an argument is based upon wrong understanding of the provisions of the clause in question. This sub-clause covers methods of recruitment and the decision on methods of recruitment always precedes actual recruitment. Requisition is nothing but a communication from the government to the Commission. Requisition is not a communication seeking the advice of the Commission on methods of recruitment. Requisition is sent to the Commission to comply with the constitutional obligation cast on the government. Based on such wrong understanding it is argued that the list of candidates selected by the Commission is advice (recommendation) to the government and the government is free not to accept the advice. The quintessence of consultation is deliberation. The two parties must exchange their views and examine the merits of the proposals and counter proposals upon the identical matters. Nothing of the kind can happen or expected to happen when the Commission makes recruitment. If the requisition were only consultation, the list of candidates selected by the Commission crystalising as an end product of requisition could have been considered as an advice of the Commission, and the government, would have been free not to accept the advice because the role of the Commission on matters specified from Sub-clause (a) to (e) is advisory.

Recruitment of personnel by the Commission, under Clause (1) of Article 320, is for appointment to the services of the state. The text of this clause makes it abundantly clear. The government cannot reject the list arbitrarily and with mala fide intention. Rejection of the list is a very serious matter because it not only affects the career of many young persons but also amounts to dilution of the credibility of the Commission. No constitutional body is permitted or expected to do this. However, it does not mean that the government cannot reject the list, if there are serious allegations of irregularities in the selections and if such allegations are proved after an enquiry by an acceptable authority. Such a situation may arise only rarely because no Commission will ignore the serious allegations of irregularities whenever they come to its notice. The Commission, in all such situations, scrutinises the allegations and rectifies errors, if any, at different stages of recruitment. Therefore, the list of the candidates selected by the Commission, will not, generally speaking, provide any reasonable ground for the rejection of the list, and it is wrong to hold that the list is recommendatory or directory. The list is mandatory because the government cannot reject the list on frivolous grounds and the action of the government can be challenged by the Commission and/or by the candidates if the government acts in that manner.

No Power to Withdraw the Posts from the Recruitment Purview of the Commission

On the basis of wrong understanding of the proviso to Clause (3) of Article 320, some people contend that the government have the power to withdraw one or more categories of posts from the recruitment purview of the Commission. The Governor, with respect to the other services and posts in connection with the affairs of the state, may make regulations specifying the "matters" in which either generally or in any particular class of case or in any particular circumstances, *it shall not be necessary for the Commission to be consulted*. The words underlined are understood to empower the government to withdraw posts from the recruitment purview of the Commission. They fail to understand that "matters" refers to matters specified from Sub-clause (a) to Sub-clause (e) of Clause (3) of Article 320. "Matters" means matters with respect to posts. It simply means, to use the expression in practice, *that one or more matters* from the matters specified from Sub-clause (a) to Sub-clause (e) can be withdrawn *from the consultative purview of the Commission* by means of regulations made by the Governor under proviso to Clause (3). Whereas matters can be withdrawn from the consultative purview, the contenders have conveniently converted the expression to mean that posts can be withdrawn from the recruitment purview of the Commission by substituting posts for matters and recruitment for consultation.

It should be noted that the proviso to Clause (3) does not start with the expression "Notwithstanding anything in this Article". The focus of the proviso is on 'matters' with reference to the other services and posts and not on category or categories of posts. The expressions "services and posts" are only incidental. Therefore, wrong interpretation of the proviso is not at all justified.

Clause (1) of Article 320 deals with recruitment, and whatever is done by the Commission under that clause constitutes recruitment purview. And Clause (3) deals with consultation and whatever is done by the Commission under that clause constitute consultative purview. These are themes which are altogether different from one another. The proviso is to Clause (3) and it does not start with expression like 'Notwithstanding anything in this Article'. Therefore, any and all Acts of the state which seek to interfere in the recruitment purview of the Commission by invoking the proviso to Clause (3) would be unconstitutional beyond doubt.

Any one, who has read a few constitutions and legislative enactments, knows as to how articles and clauses of an Article are drafted and sequenced. An Article deals with one theme and the Clauses of an Article deal with sub-themes of the main theme. Therefore, the theme of Clause (1) of Article 320 is recruitment which is entirely different from the theme of consultation of Clause (3). If Clause (1) and Clause (3) of Article 320 were to deal with the same theme, there would not have been two clauses but only one. Even if there were to be two clauses on the same theme (which might happen sometimes because of bad and defective drafting). Clause (3) would have followed Clause (1) and would have been numbered as Clause (2) instead of Clause (3). Therefore, the proviso to Clause (3), which is meant for the theme of consultation, cannot be invoked to interfere in Clause (1) the theme of which is recruitment.

Further, a proviso [here proviso to Clause (2)] cannot ravel beyond the main enactment [here Clause (3)] upwards or downwards. And a proviso can be used only as an exception and not to totally or substantially alter the main enactment [Clause (3)]. Please note a comparable proviso to Clause (2) of Article 83 for more clarification, if necessary.

It is wrongly claimed that more than forty categories of posts have been withdrawn from the recruitment purview of the Commission. The regulations meet the constitutional requirement perfectly. A careful reading of the Regulations makes it clear that *not a single category of posts stands withdrawn from the recruitment purview* of the Commission. What has been done is, matters from Sub-clause (a) to Sub-clause (e) of Article 320, with respect to the services and posts specified in Annexure-1 and 2 to the Regulations have been withdrawn from the consultative purview of the Commission. As a consequence of the regulations, the government need not consult the Commission on matters specified in the regulations with respect to the services and posts listed. The regulations do not affect the recruitment purview of the Commission in any way.

But, recruitments to the posts listed in regulations are not being done by the Commission. Recruitments of such posts are being done by other bodies called Recruitment Committees, and the candidates recruited by such committees have been appointed. All such appointments are irregular appointments and the expenditure incurred on their payments is unauthorised expenditure recoverable from the officers responsible for such irregular appointments.

No Power to Create Recruitment Bodies

There is also another serious misunderstanding that Article 309 empowers the government to create Recruitment Bodies and also to regulate recruitment. Article 309 confers only rule making power to regulate recruitment and conditions of service. The government is expected to make rules, in consultation with the Commission, to regulate recruitment in terms of quantity (determination of number of posts to be filled in), quality (determination of age, qualification, experience, etc.) and composition (determination of reservation of posts for different categories of candidates). Article 309 empowers the government to make rules to determine the "basis of recruitment" and not to create *Recruitment Bodies*, because such a Body—the Commission—has already been created by the Constitution. It should be noted that the Article 309 starts with the expression "subject to the provisions of this Constitution" which means that the Article is controlled by the various provisions of the Constitution including the Article 320 which is not controlled similarly by any other provision excepting those which expressly make provision for recruitment and appointment of certain services. (Article 234 makes provision for the recruitment and appointment of persons other than district judges to the judicial services).

It should be noted that the framers of the Constitution have not made any provision for the creation of a Body for recruitment and also have not made any provision to empower the government to withdraw posts from the recruitment purview of the Commission. These powers have been usurped by the executive unconstitutionally. It seems that the practice of withdrawing the posts from the recruitment purview of the Commission and creation of Recruitment Bodies for the recruitment of personnel for the posts withdrawn is an old practice started by some governments in some states and adopted enthusiastically by the governments in other states.

The enthusiasm of the governments in adopting this unconstitutional practice is understandable because such a practice enables them to load the recruitment bodies with their faithful subordinates for an unspecified term for the purpose of influencing the recruitments for their own advantage. This is the lobby which will not miss any opportunity to blame the Commission for delay and thereby demand for the withdrawal of more and more category of posts from the recruitment purview of the Commission. But the truth is that delay in recruitment, in almost all the cases, is caused by lack of planned actions on the part of the government. In some cases, the delay may be due to litigations. The Commission would rarely be responsible for delay in any case. This precisely was what was sought to be prevented by the framers of the Constitution because the practice negates the very objective for the realisation of which only one recruitment body for the Union and one recruitment body for every state were constitutionally created. But, the irony is that such an unconstitutional practice was started early and is being perpetually practised everywhere without being questioned by any one.

The appropriate body which could have rightfully questioned the practice is the Public Service Commission. Why no Public Service Commission has questioned the practice so far? Whether the constitutional deviation has not been noticed by any member of any Commission for so many years ?

The members of the Commission, generally speaking, are either retired persons or persons who are to retire shortly with very little fighting spirit left in them. Most of them do not prefer confrontation with the government even though very few governments may refuse to be persuaded to accept the correct constitutional position. The Secretary of the Commission will be an officer of the state on deputation who, being a subordinate officer, may not fully support a course of action which, he thinks, will displease his superiors. These appear to be the reasons for inaction on the part of the Commission with respect to the prevalent unconstitutional practice even after the constitutional deviation became known.

Duty is Right

It is wrongly argued that the Constitution has conferred only the duty and no right on the Commission. It is true that the Commission can perform the duty of conducting examinations and on that basis recruiting personnel for the services of the state only at the instance of the government, generally speaking, because the recruitment process commences after the receipt of the requisition by the Commission. (Some Public Service Commissions recruit personnel without any requisition from the government. In that case, it may be argued that there is no commitment on the part of the government that the persons recruited will be appointed. If the government desires to appoint certain number of persons for a particular category of posts and if the Commission has a list of selected candidates for those posts the government has to operate the list of the Commission. But, if the government decides to postpone appointments for a few years, the list may become out of date). If the government imposes ban on recruitments for a period (say, three years) the Commission will have no recruitment work during that period. In such a situation, *Duty cannot become a Right* in the sense that the Commission cannot force the government, by means of a petition, to ensure regular flow of requisition so that the Commission is reasonably engaged with recruitment work. But, when some authority attempts to take away a part of this Duty from the Commission to entrust the same to some other body, the *Duty becomes Right*. It is the Right of the Commission to perform the duty assigned by the Constitution without any kind of interference from any authority. If any authority attempts to interfere, the authority concerned may be restrained by a petition.

Duty cannot be Delegated or Divided

The Commission is not free to delegate any part of its Duty of conducting examinations to any existing or newly created body even if the Commission wills to do so. Similarly, the Commission is not free to divide or alienate a part of the Duty to any existing or newly created body. Therefore, the acts of setting up of the Staff Selection Board with the consent of the UPSC and service Boards in Tamil Nadu with the consent of the Commission are not constitutionally valid. But the Commission can have the assistance of individuals and organizations.

Limitations on the Powers of the Governor and the Legislature

The Governor and the Commission

The Governor exercises certain powers in relation to the Public Service Commission. It is he who appoints the Chairman and other members of the Commission (Article 316). He appoints one of the members of the Commission to perform the duties of the Chairman when the office of the Chairman becomes vacant or if he cannot perform his duties for any reason (Clause 1 A of Article 316). The Governor may suspend from office him or any other member about whom a reference has been made to the Supreme Court under Clause (1) of Article 317 [Clause (2) of Article 317]. He may make regulations and their conditions of service [Clause (a) of Article 318] and may make provision with respect to the number of members of the staff of the Commission and their conditions of service [Clause (B) of Article 318]. He may make regulations specifying the matters in which it shall not be necessary for the Public Service Commission to be consulted under Clause (3) of Article 320 [proviso to Clause (3) of Article 320]. It is the duty of the Commission to present annually a report as to the work done by the Commission to the Governor [Clause (2) of Article 323].

The Legislature and the Commission

The power of the Legislature in relation to the Commission is to provide for the exercise of additional functions about the services of the state and also about the services of any local authority or other body corporate constituted by law or of any public institution by means of an Act of the Legislature. The legislators can influence the working of the Commission indirectly by their critical comments and views and constructive suggestions when the report of the Commission is taken up for discussion. It is not proper on the part of the legislators to ask questions about the working of the Commission at any other time and it is desirable that the Speaker and the Chairman of the Council discourage legislators from doing so.

Temporary Appointments

I have not come across any provision which expressly empowers the government to make temporary appointments. Such a power seems to have been inferred from the executive powers of the government. There may be extraordinary situations when the government have to accomplish a task urgently and the task to be accomplished cannot be handled by or assigned to the existing staff. In such situations the government would be left with no alternative but to make temporary appointments because the Public Service Commission will not be in a position to recruit the personnel required at a short notice. The government will be fully justified in making temporary appointments in such and similar situations. Employment exchanges provide personnel, at short notice, for temporary appointments and (2) indicate the extent of unemployment from time to time.

Whenever temporary appointments are to be made the government have to get the personnel required from only the employment exchanges. If the employment exchanges are not in a position to make available the personnel with required qualifications, etc., the government may prefer persons, who have not registered with employment exchanges, for temporary appointments. The rules should clearly specify the authorities who can make temporary appointments and under what circumstances. If there are vacancies of posts for which temporary appointments are going to be made and if the government has no objection for filling up those vacancies a requisition should be sent to the Commission simultaneously. Under no circumstances, the services of the temporary employees should be continued beyond the specified period. Nothing should be done to create and sustain an impression that the temporary employees will one day become regular employees. If such an impression is created, most of the appointing authorities will be under pressure to make temporary appointments even when there is no extraordinary situation to justify temporary appointments.

Regularisation

Regularisation of the services of a person, appointed temporarily, is not permissible under the Constitution, because *no person, who has not been examined and recruited by the Commission, can be appointed to or can hold a post in the services of the state.* But the spate of temporary appointments and regularisation of the services of the persons appointed temporarily continues unabated because no one has preferred to challenge such actions. This has further reinforced the widespread belief that a person who somehow becomes a temporary employee will one day become a regular employee. This is a dangerous trend and cuts at the very roots of the Public Service Commission.

Judiciary and the Commission

Unfair Judicial Interpretation

According to Article 124(2), every judge of the Supreme Court shall be appointed by the Supreme Court and of the High Courts in the states as the President may deem necessary for the purpose. Consultation is a mandatory condition precedent. It should be "effective", which means—

(a) The President must disclose all the facts which are necessary for due deliberation by the Chief Justice of India.
(b) The Chief Justice must express his opinion, after full consideration of the matter, on which he is consulted and upon the relevant facts.
(c) The quintessence of consultation is deliberation. The two parties must exchange their views and examine the merits of the proposals and counter proposals upon identical matters.

According to Article 217 (1), every judge of a High Court shall be appointed by the President, after consultation with the Chief Justice of India, the Governor of the state, and, in the case of appointment of a judge other than the Chief Justice, the Chief Justice of the High Court. There has been a controversy as to the precise implication of the expression "*After consultation with*".

1. There is agreement on the proposition that failure to consult the specified dignitaries at all may nullify the appointment.

2. There is also fair consensus on the proposition that such consultation must be "effective" and not formal or nominal.
3. In order to ensure a proper selection, as well as to ensure the independence of the judiciary, the views of the Chief Justice of India should have a "Primacy" in the matter of appointment of a High Court judge.

According to Clause (3) of Article 320, the Public Service Commission *shall be consulted* on matters specified from Sub-clause (a) to Sub-clause (e) of Article 320.

The law laid down by the judiciary on the provision that Commission shall be consulted is:

1. Article 320 (3) does not confer any right.
2. The consultation prescribed is only to afford proper assistance to the government.
3. Omission of or irregularity in such consultation, the aggrieved has no remedy in the Court of Law nor any relief under Articles 32 and 226.

The expression used in Article 124 (2) and Article 217 (1) is *after consultation with* whereas the expression used in Article 320 (3) is *the Commission shall be consulted.* Consultation in case of appointment of judges is with *individual dignitaries,* whereas consultation in case of Article 320 (3) is with the Commission—a *Constitutional Body*. That being so, one fails to understand why the expression consultation has been studied so seriously and deeply when it is applied to the judiciary and indifferently when it is applied to the Commission. Consultation, as applied to the judiciary, is held to be mandatory and failure to consult leads to the nullification of the appointment. "The proposition that the views of the Chief Justice of India should have Primacy in the matter of appointment of a High Court judge" virtually makes not only consultation but also the advice of the Chief Justice mandatory. The same expression, *consultation*, as applied to the Commission is only to afford proper assistance to the government, and failure to consult does not nullify the action in spite of the fact that the word *shall* used in Clause (3) of Article 320 does not appear either in Clause (2) of Article 124 or in Clause (1) of Article 217.

Consultation with the Commission, on matters not excluded by the regulations made by the Governor is and should be mandatory but the advice of the Commission on the matter consulted is directory. When any of the matter can be excluded from the consultative purview of the Commission by means of regulations made by the Governor and when the advice of the Commission is directory, there is no reason why consultation on matters not excluded should not be mandatory. Clause (3) of Article 320 has lost much of its importance, since the decision of the Supreme Court that non-consultation shall not nullify the action. There may have been any number of cases when the Commission was not consulted even though the Commission had to be consulted. This particular decision of the Supreme Court will only strengthen that tendency. All those employees who are capable of manipulating will get their promotions bypassing the Commission because the promotion so obtained, they know, will be irreversible. The responsibility of the Supreme Court is to preserve the importance and independence of not only the judiciary but of other constitutional bodies as well. It is possible that the attention of the judiciary was not brought to the harmful implications the judgement would have on another Constitutional Body—the Commission.

Again, the matters excluded from the consultative purview of the Commission by means of the regulations made by the Governor need not remain excluded for a long time. Inclusion and exclusion of matters should be a continuous process depending upon the circumstances. The provision is meant for meeting the demands of extraordinary circumstances and extraordinary circumstances shall be there for a short period only, as otherwise they cannot be extraordinary circumstances.

Further, the matters excluded should be reasonably small in number, otherwise the subject of the very enactment will be changed substantially which is not permissible. Blanket Regulations such as "*it shall not be necessary for the Commission to be consulted on all matters covered by Sub-clause (a) to Sub-clause (e) of Clause (3) of Article 320 with respect to all the posts in the services of state*" will not be constitutionally valid and can be challenged.

Consequences of Confusion

Clause (1) of Article 320 is mandatory in the sense that the Commission is the only body which has been assigned constitutionally the duty of conducting examinations and on that basis recruiting personnel for appointment to the services of the state. Recruitment is for appointment and not for keeping the Commission engaged in futile exercises. The candidates who submit applications in response to the notification by the Commission acquire a right to be considered for selection. The list of candidates selected by the Commission is not an advice or recommendation because the Commission acts under Clause (1) and not under Clause (3) when it recruits personnel for the services of the state. The government is under constitutional obligation to appoint all the candidates (in the main as well as the additional lists) within a reasonable time.

The candidates included in the list of candidates selected by the Commission acquire a right to be appointed (particularly when selections are made by the Commission at the instance of the government). The government will be under the constitutional obligation to appoint all the candidates in the list within a reasonable time, subject to the circumstances explained earlier in this paper. (Those who are not suitable for appointment may be excluded and the list can be rejected if irregularities in the selection are proved.)

What, then, are the reasons because of which the judiciary has held that the list of candidates selected by the Commission is a recommendation (advice) of the Commission to the government and a candidate in the list selected candidates does not acquire any right to be appointed. At this juncture, it is significant to note that there is not a single case law on Clause (1) of Article 320. There may have been innumerable occasions when the Commission would have preferred to petition before the judiciary. Such occasions also may have been utilised for public interest litigations. Unfortunately nothing of the kind has happened. Aggrieved litigants may not have any *locus standi* to make the contentions of Clause (1) an issue before the judiciary. The contentions of Clause (1) of Article 320 have never been an issue before the judiciary and there has never been an occasion for the judiciary to focus its attention totally on the contentions of that clause. The observations of the judiciary related to some matters in Clause (1) are only incidental. The attention of the judiciary has been drawn, in almost all the cases, only to Clause (3) of Article 320 and the role of the Commission will be advisory when it acts under Clause (3). This confusion has lead to the consequences which will, if not attended to urgently, have ripple effects on the Commission even though, as it appears, the judiciary has not intended that eventuality.

To sum up, the Public Service Commission is basically *an expert recruiting body* and *not an advisory body* as is generally made out to be as more than eighty per cent of the time of the Commission is spent on work related to recruitment which is mandatory and non-shrinkable and hardly twenty per cent on work related to consultation, which is advisory and shrinkable. The main task of the Commission is to recruit personnel for the services of the state. The Commission advises the government on specified service matters. The Commission has the right to perform its constitutionally assigned duty of conducting examination and on that basis recruit personnel for the services of the state without any kind of interference from any authority once the posts are notified. It is the constitutional obligation of the government to appoint the candidates selected for appointment by the Commission. Non-consultation with the Commission on matters not excluded from the consultative purview of the Commission should be viewed seriously to erase the impression that consultation with the Commission is a mere formality to be complied with according to the convenience and discretion of the consultant.

Wrong opinion		*Correct constitutional position*
Proviso to Clause (3) of Article 320 empowers the government to withdraw various categories of posts from the recruitment purview of the Commission.	(1)	Recruitment functions are assigned *exclusively to the Commission* by Clause (1) of Article 320 which is beyond the operational limits of the proviso.
Article 309 empowers the government to constitute Recruitment Committees and Bodies.	(2)	(1) Article 309 empowers the government to make rules to regulate Recruitment and not to create Recruitment bodies. (2) Constitution has made the *Commission the sole Recruiting* body for the services of the state.
Government have powers to fill various categories of posts directly without an examination by the Commission.	(3)	(1) Examination and selection by the Commission is a *mandatory condition precedent* to appointment to all the posts in the services of the states. (2) No person, who has not been examined and selected by the Commission, can be appointed to a post on a regular basis.

Wrong opinion		*Correct constitutional position*
Government have powers to make appointments on temporary basis and also to regularise the services of persons so appointed.	(4)	(1) Government have powers to make appointment on temporary basis under special circumstances and for specified periods only by tapping the sources of employment exchanges first and the other sources thereafter. (2) Regularisation of the temporary employees without an examination by the Commission is unconstitutional. (3) Temporary employees also have to appear for examination and compete with others and only those selected by the Commission can be appointed on regular basis because examination and selection by the Commission is a mandatory condition precedent for appointment.
Government have powers to entrust the Recruitment work to the existing or created Recruitment bodies.	(5)	The government is under the Constitutional obligation to send the Requisition to the *Commission only* whenever appointments are to be made to the posts in the services of the state.
Government have powers to withdraw the Requisition from the Commission at any time.	(6)	Requisition, once sent to the Commission, cannot be withdrawn, in part or in full, particularly after the notification by the Commission.
A candidate, who submits application in response to the notification acquires no right.	(7)	The candidate acquires the right to be called for examination/interview.
A candidate, who is called for interview, acquires no right.	(8)	The candidate acquires the right to be considered for selection.
The list of candidates, selected by the Commission, is recommendation (advice) to the government and the government have powers to reject the list.	(9)	The government are under the constitutional obligation to issue appointment orders to all the candidates in the list within a reasonable time.
The government are answerable to the Legislature for rejecting the list.	(10)	(1) The government are answerable to the Legislature not for rejecting the list but for not accepting the advice of the Commission, if any, on service matters referred for consultation. (2) The government have no powers to reject the list and if at all the list is rejected at any time the reasons for doing so shall have to stand the test of judicial scrutiny.

Wrong opinion		*Correct constitutional position*
A candidate, whose name is in the list of candidates selected, acquires no right to be appointed.	(11)	The candidate acquires the right to be appointed within a reasonable time.
Consultation with the Commission on matters specified under Clause (3) is only a technical requirement.	(12)	Consultation on service matters, not withdrawn from the consultative purview of the Commission, is mandatory.
Non-consultation amounts only to a technical error which will not nullify the action.	(13)	Non-consultation will nullify the action.
Article 320 is directory.	(14)	It is mandatory. But the advice of the Commission, on service matters referred for consultation, is directory.

ARTICLES

83. Duration of the Houses of Parliament.—(1) The Council of states shall not be subject to dissolution, but as nearly as possible one-third of the members thereof shall retire as soon as may be the expiration of every second year in accordance with the provisions made in that behalf by the Parliament by law.

(2) The House of the People, unless sooner dissolved, shall continue for (six years) from the date appointed for its first meeting and no longer and the expiration of the said period of (six years) shall operate as dissolution of the House:

Provided that the said period may; while a Proclamation of Emergency is in operation, be extended by Parliament by law for a period not exceeding one year at a time and not extending in any case beyond a period of six months after the Proclamation has ceased to operate.

124 (2). Establishment and constitution.—(2) Every Judge of the Supreme Court shall be appointed by the President by warrant under his hand and seal after consultation with such of the Judges of the Supreme Court and of the High Courts in the states as the President may deem necessary for the purpose and shall hold office until he attains the age of sixty five years:

Provided that in the case of appointment of a Judge other than the Chief Justice, the Chief Justice of India shall always be consulted:

Provided further that (a) a Judge may, by writing under his hand addressed to the President, resign his office; (b) a Judge may be removed from his office in the manner provided in Clause (4).

146. Officers and servants and the expenses of the Supreme Court.—(1) Appointments of officers and servants of the Supreme Court shall be made by the Chief Justice of India such other Judge or officer of the Court as he may direct:

Provided that the President may by rule require that in such cases as may be specified in the rule, no person not already attached to the Court shall be appointed to any office connected with the Court, save after consultation with the Union Public Service Commission.

217. Appointment and conditions of the office of a Judge of a High Court.—(1) Every Judge of a High Court shall be appointed by the President by warrant under his hand and seal after consultation with the Chief Justice of India, the Governor of the State, and, in the case of appointment of a Judge other than the Chief Justice, the Chief Justice of the High Court, and shall hold office, in the case of an additional or acting Judge, as provided in Article 224, and in any other case, until he attains the age of sixty two years.

Provided that:

(a) a Judge may, by writing under his hand addressed to the President, resign his office;

(b) a Judge may be removed from his office by the President in the manner provided in Clause (4) of Article 124 for the removal of a Judge of the Supreme Court;

(c) the office of a Judge shall be vacated by his being appointed by the President to be a Judge of the Supreme Court or by his being transferred by the President to any other High Court within the territory of India.

229. Officers and servants and the expenses of High Courts.—(1) Appointments of officers and servants of a High Court shall be made by the Chief Justice of India of the Court or such other Judge or officer of the Court as he may direct:

Provided that the Governor of the state may by rule require that in such cases as may be specified in the rule no person not already attached to the Court shall be appointed to any office connected with the Court save after consultation with the state Public Service Commission.

234. Recruitment of persons other than district judges to the judicial service.—Appointments of persons other than district judges to the judicial service of a state shall be made by the Governor of the state in accordance with the rules made by him in that behalf after consultation with the state Public Service Commission and with the High Court exercising jurisdiction in relation to such state.

309. Recruitment and condition of service of persons serving the Union or a state.—Subject to the provisions of this Constitution, Acts of the appropriate Legislature may regulate the recruitment, and conditions of service of persons appointed, to public service and posts in connection with the Union or of any state:

Provided that it shall be competent for the President or such person as he may direct in the case of services and posts in connection with the affairs of the Union, and for the Governor of a state or such person as he may direct in the case of services and posts in connection with the affairs of the state, to make rules regulating the recruitment, and the conditions of services of persons appointed, to such services and posts until provision in that behalf is made by or under an Act of the appropriate Legislature under this Article, and any rules so made shall have effect subject to the provisions of any such Act.

320. Functions of the Public Service Commission.—(1) It shall be the duty of the Union and the state Public Service Commissions to conduct examinations for appointments to the services of the Union and the services of the state respectively.

(2) It shall also be the duty of the Union Public Service Commission, if requested by any two or more states so to do, to assist those states in framing and operating schemes of joint recruitment for any services for which candidates possessing special qualifications are required.

(3) The Union Public Service Commission or the state Public Service Commission, as the case may be, shall be consulted:

(a) on all matters relating to methods of recruitment to civil services and for civil posts;
(b) on the principles to be followed in making appointments

to civil services and posts and in making appointments to civil services and posts and in making promotions and transfers from one service to another and on the suitability of candidates for such appointments, promotions or transfers.

321. Power to extend functions of Public Service Commission.—An Act made by Parliament or, as the case may be, the Legislature of a state may provide for the exercise of additional functions by the Union Public Service Commission or the state Public Service Commission as respects the services of the Union or the state and also as respects the services of any local authority or other body corporate constituted by law or of any public institution.

323. Reports of Public Service Commission.—(1) It shall be the duty of the Union Commission to present annually to the President a report as to the work done by the Commission and on receipt of such report the President shall cause a copy thereof together with a memorandum explaining, as respects the cases, if any, where the advice of the Commission was not accepted, the reasons for such non-acceptance to be laid before each House of Parliament.

10

The Karnataka Government Secretariat

VIJAYAKUMAR N. TORGAL

Public administration in the words of L.D. Wight Waldo, "joins two forces, government and administrative technology ..."[1] The secretariat organisation a vital unit in public administration being a ling pin between political executive and the field level administrative units. The secretariat organisation is an important unit in the entire government bureaucracy. It aids and advises the political executive in initiating new policy. The execution of government policy is the primary responsibility of the secretariat. This is done by way of direction, control and supervision of the field level administrative units. The governmental policy, plan and programmes are all operationalised through the instrumentality of secretariat. The ministers' orders, directions and suggestions are realised by the secretariat. In the absence of secretariat the government cannot function, and the very existence if perceived through the secretariat. One cannot imagine a government without secretariat.

Organisation

The Constitution of India *vide* Article 166(3) provides allocation and transaction of government business. The government of the state frames rules in this regard.

The government business is divided and allocated into a number of departments. There are 31 departments at secretariat level (Annexure-1). Each department is headed by secretary to government. The chief secretary is the head of the secretariat organisation apart from heading the Department of Personnel of Administrative Reforms along with cabinet section. The departments below the secretary will have secretary-II, additional secretaries (in some cases), joint secretaries, deputy secretaries and under secretaries. The department is divided into sections headed by a section officer. The under secretary heads one or two sections. The deputy secretary controls two-three under secretaries depending upon the nature and magnitude of the department work.

Each section will have senior assistants, assistants and junior assistants and their number depends upon the work. There are case-workers looking after one or more subjects. They initiate the files based on the minutes/letters/notes/reports and petitions received in the section. Each section will have stenographers/ typists who provide typing assistance.

"The chief secretary has the overall responsibility for efficient functioning of the secretariat and for making continual effort for administrative improvement in the executive machinery of government."[2] He is also the cabinet secretary. There are a few additional chief secretaries who are senior most IAS officers. Most of the times they will be acting as Finance Commissioners and Development Commissioners. One will attach to the chief secretary looking after Administrative Reforms Division in DPAR. He supervises the disposal of pending files at the secretariat and subordinate offices.

The secretary is official head of his department.[3] The minister in charge of a department will be above the secretary. He is secretary to government not a secretary to the minister in charge. He is fully responsible for disposal of all business pertaining to his department.[4] The additional secretaries in a department are independent officers in charge of specific block of work in a department and they discharge all functions of secretary to government with regard to that block of work. The joint secretaries assist the secretaries in disposal of department business. The deputy secretary discharges such functions as are delegated to him by the secretary. The under secretary is a junior most officer in the first round of secretariat hierarchy. He exercises control over the sections under him and is authorised to issue orders in the name of the governor. The section officer is in charge of a section and is responsible for the disposal of files/papers in his section. The senior assistant/assistant and case workers work under the supervision and control of section officer. They initiate files. The junior assistant is entrusted with routine work of maintaining register and dispatching apart from assisting the senior assistant/assistant. The long hierarchy of secretariat organisation is stumbling block in the smooth and efficient administration. The chain beginning from assistant section officer - under secretary - deputy secretary (sometimes joint/additional secretary) - ends with secretary. The file has to pass through the multiplicity of officers for a final decision. This not only delays the disposal of cases but lowers the sense of responsibility at junior levels.[5] To overcome this system of "Desk officer" with "level jumping" should be provided. In Karnataka government secretariat, it is adopted in a limited scale, hence there is a need to adopt the same in a large scale to avoid delay in disposal of files/cases.

Staffing

The staff of secretariat is drawn from the following sources:

(a) Indian Administrative Service, (IAS),
(b) Karnataka Administrative Service, (KAS),
(c) The Karnataka Government Secretariat Service, (KGSS), and
(d) Other Departments/Services.

The top echelons like secretary, additional secretary and joint secretary are manned by IAS except a few technical departments like public works, irrigation, minor irrigation, law, and parliamentary affairs. The posts of deputy secretary and under secretary are drawn from KAS and KGSS. Majority of under secretaries belongs to KGSS. The section officers and ministerial staff of section primarily belong to KGSS. A few officers of other departments like police, forest, co-operative, judicial and state accounts also work in secretariat in different posts such as secretary II, internal financial adviser, deputy secretary, officer on special duty, and low officers.

The strength of the secretariat over the years has increased enormously. In 1956 the strength of the secretariat was 1,306. It rose to 2,258 in 1966 and now it is 4,276. In the staff strength the increase is noticeable in the posts of secretaries to government. In 1956 and 1966 there were 11 secretaries to government, now there are 44 secretaries. Of this 12 are principal secretaries, 12 are secretaries to government, 6 are technical secretaries to government, 12 are secretaries II to government and 2 are special secretaries. The increase is of per cent. Earlier the posts of joint and deputy secretaries were very few whereas presently there are 8 joint secretaries and 32 deputy secretaries in the secretariat. Likewise there are 10 IFAs which were non-existent earlier. There is corresponding increase in the strength of ministerial cadre.

Table 10.1: Strength of the Secretariat

Group	*1956*	*1966*	*1998*
Group A	37	128	256
Group B	80	145	365
Group C	844	1250	2589
Group D	345	735	1066
Total	**1306**	**2258**	**4276**

Source: (a) Report of the Mysore Pay Commission 1966-68, Vol. III, Government of Mysore, Bangalore,1968, pp. 885-886.
(b) Debates of Karnataka Legislative Council dated 5.11.1998.

The recruitment to the KGSS is made by the KPSC. The section officers are directly recruited who climb the hierarchy up to additional secretary. The assistants and junior assistants are directly recruited by KPSC through competitive examinations. There is a separate recruitment for KAS and other services.

The secretariat organisation is a hierarchial-vertical organisation with centralised system. The roles of officers are like watertight compartments. The organisation exhibits multiple units in the form of different departments. These variables necessarily bring the popular bureaucratic maladies such as red-tapism and delay. In this information age, to overcome this the secretariat organisation must be designed into horizontal plateau with matrixed units.[6] The roles of incumbents must be flexible.

The communication system in this kind of hierarchical organisation is obviously downward flow with monopolistic hold on information. Information is considered as symbol of authority with little cross communication. This is not conducive for new age of openness and liberalisation. It demands two way communications with information sharing.[7]

Procedure

The secretariat manual[8] prescribes the procedure for routing the papers/files in the secretariat. The incoming papers whether it is a dak or tapal is recorded in the central registry. These papers are stamped and sorted out section-wise. Some papers are diarised in the central registry. Rest of other papers are transmitted to the sections concerned and the same is acknowledged. The papers so received are perused by the under secretary and sent to the sections concerned with instructions/suggestions. The papers are marked to assistant concerned. The assistant often is called as the case-worker who receives the papers and registers the same in his diary. This is the stage the dak/tapal reaches the destination for initiating action. The action on paper commences from this stage.

The dak/tapal received by the assistant is filed in existing or new file. He summaries the contents of the paper and suggests probable action referring to provisions of relevant rules and laws. He submits the file to the section officer, the same is forwarded to the under secretary with his remarks/opinions. The file is considered by the under secretary if it is within his delegation of powers and he passed orders, if not he passes it to immediate higher officer. The officer authorised will pass orders or transmits it to his immediate officer.

After orders are passed the file is returned to section for issue of orders. The assistant/section officer submits drafts of order to under secretary or higher officer for approval. The approved draft order along with file is sent to section for issue of fair copy of orders. Fair copies are typed, compared and submitted to under secretary for signature. The officer authorised to sign orders of the signing the fair copy sends the file to section for issue of fair copy of orders.

The signed fair copies of orders are sent to central registry for dispatch. The file is returned to the assistant concerned along with office copy of the order issued. The pages in the file are serially numbered and docketed. The file is either marked for 'Record' or 'suspense' as the case may be. The 'suspense' file is placed in suspense rack by noting the same in the Desk Diary.

The 'Record' file classified and forwarded to the General Record Section with list of papers. The same is received in the General Record Section and deposited in the appropriate record rack.

The procedure involved in the passage of papers/file is a long one. It passes through many stages and officers. The secretariat hierarchy from assistant to secretary to the government comprises minimum of these stages and officers. In a simple case the file moves up and down twice. On most of the occasions, several times the file moves up and down. If the subject involves referring the file to finance or law department it is further delayed on account of the similar procedure followed in their departments. This obviously results in delay and the purpose of the paper/file is often missed. It also paves the way for corruption. The Administrative Reforms division of DPAR striving to minimise the stages in the hierarchy and reduce delay.

Procedure for Submitting Files to the Cabinet

The Chief Secretary is also the cabinet secretary. The list of subjects requiring cabinet approval are listed in the First Schedule of Karnataka Government Transaction of Business Rules, 1977. It includes proposals of legislation, ordinances, elections, taxation, budget, reduction in any revenue and administrative approval of works over Rs.100 lakh. The proposals relating to creation of new public corporations and dismissal of government employees, appointment of Chief Secretary and Advocate General are also brought before the cabinet. The cabinet also discusses and approves the government policies on any subject. The Reports of Inquiry Commission are discussed in cabinet.

The Draft Cabinet Note (DCN) is prepared by the secretary concerned and will be sent to the department minister through Chief Secretary. The memorandum of the proposal should state the case in brief and precisely and in the end of the memorandum the points/ questions are listed on which the cabinet decision is sought. If the proposal involves legislative matters the opinion of law department is noted in the cabinet note. When the proposals involve finance, taxation, revenue, the finance department's opinion will be invaluable and is recorded in the cabinet note.

The cabinet note will be circulated among all the cabinet

ministers. If the proposal relates to the department of minister of state, he will be asked to attend the cabinet meeting. The agenda for cabinet meeting is prepared by chief secretary in consultation with the Chief Minister. The Chief Minister presides over the cabinet meeting and in his absence the minister nominated by Chief Minister will preside over the cabinet meeting. The cabinet secretary prepares records of the decisions and copies of the same are forwarded to governor, Chief Minister and cabinet ministers and minister of state concerned. The secretary of the department will be consulted during the cabinet meeting. The extract of the decision is sent to the secretary of the department concerned for execution and necessary action.

Consultation with Other Departments

Whenever it is necessary to consult other departments a formal request is made to other department either by sending the file unofficially, or by means of a self-contained unofficial note or unofficial memorandum. The other department is asked to opine on specific points within the specified time limit.

In case of difference of opinion between two or more departments the case will be taken up at higher level involving secretaries. If difference still persists the issue will be taken up by arranging inter-departmental ministers' meeting. In case the differences are not resolved the issue will be decided either by the Chief Minister or in the cabinet. The finality is arrived here.

Consultation with Finance and Law Department

The cases involving release of funds and incurring extra expenditure are brought to the finance department for approval. The opinion of finance is invariably sought while initiating a new programme, scheme and project in any department. Now each department has internal financial advisor (IFA) who acts as the custodian of finance department and his views are invariably sought while releasing funds.

In the same manner any case involves interpretation of rules, statute and low, the law department is consulted and its opinion is recorded in the file. The decisions are taken on the basis of remarks/views of law department. The litigation cases in each department are pursued with the suggestion of law department. While framing new rules/laws or orders involving rules, legislation consultation with law department is must. With the famous case of contempt of Supreme Court in *Vasudevan case,* major departments have law officers to guide the departments in pursuing court cases.

Correspondence between Officers and Ministers

The secretariat manual prohibits officers writing DO letters to minister. All communications to ministers are sent through private secretary to minister. All instructions of ministers to officers are conveyed through secretary of the department. The instructions/ orders of ministers are sent to the secretary in the form of a "Note" signed by the minister. In certain cases the private secretary of the minister can convey the information/order of the minister to the officer concerned through a "Note". Such "Note" should clearly indicate that the private secretary is conveying the said instruction/ order as desired by the minister.

Checks on Delays

In order to check the delay in disposing of files/cases the secretariat manual prescribes various measures. The weekly arrears statement and monthly statement of pendency are basic instruments through which delay is checked. The monthly statement gives details of pendency of number of cases ranging from 1 month old to 2 years old. The secretary of the department sends the pending statement to chief secretary who receives it and suggest course of action. The private secretaries to minister also prepare list of the pending of files with minister and submit it to chief secretary, Chief Minister and the cabinet.

Inspections are made to review the working of organisation. The purpose of inspections is:

(a) To verify whether the prescribed procedure is followed/ observed.
(b) To give suitable guidance to raise the level of performance (see secretariat manual para 217). The inspection chart is as follows:

Section Officer—during April, July and October.
Under Secretary—July 2nd week and January 1st week.
Deputy Secretary—Annual inspection during 2nd week of January.

The inspection reports are sent to the office concerned and to DPAR. In order to remove difficulties in the working of secretariat department a periodical meeting of officers of each secretariat department is held every quarter.

State Archives

The archives is the repository of all government records classified as A, B, and certain C class files. The file registers are also sent to archives. In every year June to September the records are deposited with the archives. Wherever the government requests the director of state archives spares them for reference.

Functions of the Secretariat

The secretariat performs a number of functions.

Assisting the Council of Ministers in taking Decisions

The secretary of the department submits files for orders of minister. The minister may also ask secretary to submit a particular file/ paper for taking decisions.

Some decisions are taken at minister's level while some others at Chief Minister's level and at the cabinet. All these cases are routed through the ministers. The secretary of the department collects the information and works out alternatives along with relevant provisions of the rules/laws and submits the files to the minister. In the absence of secretariat the ministers, Chief Minister and cabinet cannot take any meaningful administrative decisions. This is because policy decisions require lot of inputs. These inputs are provided by the secretariat.

The legislative matters are pooled and collected by the secretariat. The necessity of new laws/rules is identified by the secretariat. Such new rules/laws are drafted by collecting various information from different sources.

2. *Delegated Legislation:* The cabinet and ministers give policy decisions in the skeleton form. The necessary flesh in the form of rules/conditions, etc., are filled by the secretariat to give life to government decisions. In the absence of this, the government decisions will become abstract statements without touching ground. To cite an example some provisions of the Karnataka Education Act of 1983, are not fully operative because necessary rules are yet to be framed. The secretariat in the form of delegated legislation frames concomitant rules/conditions, etc.
3. The important function of secretariat is the monitoring of execution of government decisions/policies. The ministers and cabinet can only take policy decisions. Ultimately it is the secretariat which sets in motion the decisions and policies of the government by sending them to the executive departments. In the absence of the secretariat, the government's decisions remain in paper and the very legitimacy of government is at stake. Thus the monitoring of execution of government decisions is the basic function of the secretariat. It forwards the government decisions to subordinate offices with necessary instructions, directions and time specifications.
4. The above functions involve administrative directions, control and supervision. In order to implement the government decisions the secretariat directs the subordinate organisations and supervises the implementation process. It also controls them. The chief secretary as the head of the entire government bureaucracy has over all responsibility for efficient functioning of the administration. The group A and B officers are directly under the control of each secretariat department. Their personnel matters are dealt here. The secretariat frames service and other concomitant rules for the conduct and control of civil service.
5. *Financial Control:* The finance department controls the finances of the state. The receipts and expenditures are daily watched by the finance department. On the basis of this, out flow of government funds are checked and controlled. In case of necessity it invokes economy measures to arrest the deterioration of state finance.

Therefore, all cases involving huge finance are brought to the notice of the finance department for its opinion and approval. The finance department is also responsible for framing rules/manuals regarding finance matters.

6. The government process is an ongoing process. In order to make it efficient and effective the secretariat is engaged in administrative reforms. The administrative reforms are necessary to cope up with new situations and new tasks. The Administrative Reforms division of the DPAR conducts studies in this regard. It undertakes training programmes for bureaucrats through various training institutes.

Secretariat—A Shadow of Executive Department

The secretariat process and procedure being cumbersome and slow often acts as stumbling block in the work of executive department. The field offices often complain that the secretariat instead of encouraging them frustrates them by queries and negativising their proposals and sometimes harasses and humiliates their positive action.

This is because of excessive paper work carried on with sole reliance on observance of rules and procedure without linking them to the goals. According to P.C. Alexandar the secretariat work is nothing but unproductive file work with repetition.[9] The secretariat system is essentially clerical in nature, hence there is very little that such a clerical organisation can contribute to the substantial issues.[10] As early as in 1945 the R. Tottenham Committee observed that too many clerks of the wrong and increase in quantity but deteriorating in quality in the central secretariat.[11] This is evident in every file of the secretariat. Whatever issue/question/case comes to secretariat that will be either based on the executive department's report or reference to the executive department for their report/situation. Nothing original is initiated in a secretariat. For all the work/case, it has to heavily depend upon the executive department. That is why this is an instrument of delay inconsistent with the demands of modern government. In the words of L.K. Jha, "the aim should be to do away, as far as possible, with a regime of controls applied on case by case, each being examined by an array of administrators, and to replace them by more sophisticated instrument of influencing economic activities and performance".[12]

Summing Up

The secretariat is an organic link between the ruler and the ruled. The inputs coming from ruled are processed and metamorphosed into outputs of government decisions. Further, these are delivered to the public in the form of government orders and so on. The secretariat works like a CPU of computer, of course, not with the same efficiency. In the absence of secretariat the positive perception of government is missed. In essence the secretariat gives necessary shape to the government proper.

The secretariat is growing in size every year. The growth is due to fattening and proliferation of departments. The over centralisation is also one of the reasons for bulging of secretariat. The secretariat should be compact unit. The larger the secretariat more the problem of coordinating and direction. Also it results in the rise of revenue expenditure. Best way to reduce the size of secretariat is the administrative decentralisation. The divisional and district officers should be strengthened with adequate power and finance. All the divisional level officers should be upgraded to directorates with additional director's post. These should be given all the powers and finance of directorate and in their division they are directorate for all purposes. The burden on secretariat will reduce and people will get the administration at their doorsteps.

In secretariat the emphasis is rather high on procedures. The excess observations of procedure rather terminate the ends and means takes over prominence. The long channel of hierarchy along with excess adherence to rules puts brake on the efficiency. In the words of Robert K. Merton, "Adherence to rule originally conceived as a means becomes transformed into an end in itself and whereby instrumental value becomes a terminal value".[13]

The staff in the secretariat is rather unaware of ground realities. The secretariat staff except IAS/KAS who have field experience have no or very little knowledge of field. They even lack sufficient knowledge of state history, geography and culture. Majority of secretariat staff (except IAS/KAS) are ignorant of basic ground realities. This is evident from their noting in files. In order to overcome this the secretariat staff should be made to serve 1/3 of their service in the field particularly at taluka office. In order to operationalise this, their service should be organised as follow:

I. 5 years—secretariat
II. 5 years—Taluk level office
III. 5 years—secretariat
IV. 5 years—District level offices
V. Remainder service: Secretariat: While transferring the secretariat staff the division-wise transfers should be effected. A person from Bangalore division to Gulbarga and Belgaum division to Mysore and *vice versa* should be accommodated.

The liberalisation and open economy has made dent in the working of government. The use of information technology is inevitable in the functioning of government. In this age of openness and deregulation policy there should be transparency in the working of secretariat. This will, to a certain extent, arrests the phenomena of corruption. The liberalisation coupled with information boom is pressing for transformation in public administration at all levels and the secretariat organisation should take lead in this. The new public administration is apparently moving from rule to result orientation, from systems to enterprises, obedience to reward, inaction to action, centralisation to decentralisation and from duties of administrators to the rights of citizen.[14] The Government of India has initiated measures in this regard. An "Action plan for an effective responsive government" has been prepared and state has been asked to implement the action plan. The Action Plan aims at[15]

(a) Making administration accountable and citizen-friendly,
(b) Ensuring transparency and the right to information and lastly,
(c) Taking measures to cleanse and motivate civil service.

APPENDIX
Departments of Government of Karnataka

1. Chief Minister's Secretariat
2. Department of Personnel and Administrative Reforms
3. Home and Transport
4. Department of Infrastructure Development
5. Finance Department
6. Rural Development and Panchayat Raj Department
7. Revenue Department
8. Education Department
9. Commerce and Industries Department
10. Urban Development Department
11. Housing Department
12. Public Works Department
13. Irrigation Department
14. Law Department
15. Parliamentary Affairs and Legislation Department
16. Agriculture and Horticulture Department
17. Health and Family Welfare Department
18. Animal Husbandry and Fisheries Department
19. Forest and Ecology Department
20. Information, Tourism and Youth Services Department
21. Food and Civil Supplies Department
22. Co-operation Department
23. Social Welfare Department
24. Women and Children Welfare Department
25. Labour Department
26. Energy Department
27. Kannada and Culture Department
28. Planning, Institutional Finance Department
29. Statistical, Science and Technology Department
30. Karnataka Legislative Assembly Secretariat
31. Karnataka Legislative Council Secretariat
32. Department of Information and Technology

NOTES AND REFERENCES

1. L.D. Wright Waldo, *The Enterprise of Public Administration*, (California, Chandler and Sharp Publication), 1988, p. 188.
2. The Karnataka Government (Transaction Business) Rules, 1977, p. 4.
3. *Ibid.*, p. 5.
4. *Ibid.*, (Section 7 and 30), pp. 4 and 14.
5. Committee to investigate into the question of personnel shortages, better utilisation of the manpower and improvement in methods of work, (Chairman: Girija Shankar Bajpai), Government of India, July 1947, p. 10.
6. Bata, K. Dey, *Liberalisation and Human Management Concerns*, Indian Journal of Public Administration, Vol. XLII, No. 3, July September, 1996, pp. 421-33.
7. *Ibid.*
8. For details see, *Revised Secretarial Manual of Office*, Government of Karnataka, DPAR, 1985.
9. P.C.Alexandar, Speech Delivered at IIPA, as quoted in P.R.Dubhashi, *Administrative Reforms*, (Delhi, B.R.Publishing House, 1986), p. 52.
10. *Ibid.*, pp. 52-53.
11. Sir Richard Tottenham, *Reports on the Reorganisation of the Central Government*, 1945-46, New Delhi, 1946.
12. L.K. Jha, *Towards More Efficient Economic Administration*, Sardar Patel Memorial Lectures, (New Delhi, October 30, 1984).
13. Robert, K. Merton, *Social Theory and Social Structure*, (New York, The Free Press, 1968), p. 253.
14. O. P. Minocha, *Good Governance: New Public Management Perspective*, Indian Journal of Public Administration, Special Number on Towards Good Governance, Vol. XLIV, No. 3, July-September 1998, pp. 271-280.
15. "Action Plan for an Effective and Responsive Government", Indian Journal of Puhlic Administration, *Ibid.*, pp. 626-660.

11

Urban Government and Politics

S.A. JAVEED*

Levels of government may be classified into national, provincial or state and local. The administration of a locality or a small community such as a village, town or a city, "by a body representing the local inhabitants possessing a fairly large amount of autonomy, raising a part at least of its revenue through local taxation and spending the proceeds on services which are regarded as local and as distinct from state and central governments—'is' local self-government. Decentralization of powers, functions and responsibilities is an integral part of democratic process. The local bodies adequately meet the requirements of democracy from this point of view. They also provide training in the art of self-government, which can be utilized for the wider affairs of the governments at other levels. Besides they are "the best school of political training for the masses living in cities and it is also to be cherished as a school of social service and a most efficient factor of social progress". The first Municipal Corporation was set up in Madras in 1688 followed by similar corporations in Bombay and Calcutta in 1726. The number of municipal bodies has increased manifold over the years. Their problems have become more complex. But the structure of these bodies has basically remained unchanged. The leadership of our freedom movement was in many ways nurtured in these civic bodies. Stalwarts like Dadabhoy Nauroji, Ferozeshah Mehta, Tilak, Gokhale, C.R. Das, Subhas Bose and Pt. Jawaharlal Nehru played a significant role in municipal administration. Though many of our leaders started their political careers in municipalities, the role of latter in the development of the country was limited at that time.

As far as the evolution of urban local self-government in Karnataka is concerned, it has a deep-rooted history. Among the princely states of India, Mysore was one and Travancore-Cochin the other: only the states where municipal government had made great stride with liberal enactment of legislation. Municipal committees were first experimented in Mysore state as early as 1862 for the cities of Bangalore and Mysore on the pattern of the Government of India Act, XXVI of 1850. Encouraged by the success of the experiment, the state came to have a municipal committee for each of the districts headquarters by 1864-65. The chief objective was to enlist the co-operation of local residents in local affairs. There were regularly organised boards for them consisting of influential residents. In small towns they were managed through the revenue officers. With the reorganisation of states on linguistic basis in1956 the present Karnataka state came into being. A state born out of five sets of regions: Bijapur, Dharwad, Belgaum and Karwar of the old Bombay presidency, Dakshina Kannada, Bellary and Kollegal taluk were subject to the former Madras presidency, districts of Bidar, Gulbarga and Raichur were parts of the Hyderabad state; the Coorg area and the princely Mysore state completed the formation. Each region has a history of its own municipal governments.

Princely Mysore State

The Mysore Town Municipalities Act, 1833 and the Mysore Minor Municipalities Act, 1933 (repealed by the Mysore Town Municipalities Act, 1951), and the City Municipalities Act, 1933, were the main enactments governing urban bodies, which introduced adult suffrage and increased the elected element in municipal councils.

Bombay Karnataka Area

In the erstwhile Bombay presidency, for the first time local bodies were created under the East India Company. Subsequently, municipalities were constituted under the Bombay District municipalities Act (III of 1901). Under this act the State

Government had power to declare, by a notification, any local area as Municipal District in which municipality has to be constituted. The term of office of a municipality was three years with a provision to extend for one more year. Control over the municipal bodies was exercised by the District Collector, the Director of Local Authorities and the State Government depending on the issues related.

In this area, according to the Bombay Districts Municipal Act, 1901, some municipalities were upgraded into Borough Municipalities, for which standing committees with wider powers were constituted. The urban local governments in the erstwhile Bombay state functioned under the Bombay Municipal Boroughs Act, 1929, at the time of the states' reorganisation.

Madras Presidency

The urban local governments in this area came into being with the passing of the Madras Town Improvement act X of 1865. As per the recommendations of a committee, the Madras government passed a new Act called Madras District Municipalities Act IV of 1884 superceding the Towns Improvement Act, 1871, and for the first time introduced the Town Municipality replacing the above Act. In 1920, on the recommendations of the Royal Commission, the Madras District Municipalities Act, 1920, was passed.

Hyderabad Areas

The introduction of Local Cess in 1887-88 marked the beginning of local self-government in the erstwhile Hyderabad state consisting of Bidar, Gulbarga and Raichur districts. In the same year the local fund department was constituted. During the year 1888-89 a Dastur-ul-amal (Regulation) was passed for control and administration of local funds. Further, the Local Cess Act enacted in 1900, authorised the municipalities to levy municipal and special taxes. The Act was subsequently amended in 1908, 1910, 1933-34 to suit the changing conditions of growing towns. Only during 1934, the State Government sanctioned the Constitution of municipal committees with a non-official majority. Rules were also framed for constituting town committees for small towns.

Kodagu Area

This area which was under the administration of commissioners had local self-government institutions inaugurated in the year 1870, when for the first time municipal committees were established to govern important towns like Madikere and Virajpet. Subsequently, other smaller towns were brought under the purview of the Municipal Act. Besides, the Municipal Council in Madikere and Virajpet, there were Notified Area Committees in the smaller towns until the common Municipalities Act of 1964 became applicable to Kodagu.

In 1956 the present Karnataka state was created. With the intention of having uniform type of local governments, Karnataka state enacted new laws for instituting urban local self-government bodies. The Karnataka Municipal Corporation Act of 1976, The Karnataka Municipalities Act of 1964, replaced all earlier Acts governing urban local bodies. As such five categories of urban local governments came into being.

1. The City Municipal Coporations
2. The City Municipal Councils
3. The Town Municipal Councils
4. The Notified Area Committees
5. The Sanitary Boards

In the year 1976 in the state during the year 1981-82, there were six City Municipal Corporations, twelve City Municipal Councils, two hundred sixteen Town Municipal Councils, nine Notified Area Committees and two Sanitary Boards in addition to one hundred twenty nine Town Panchayats. There were also certain special purpose urban bodies and agencies. The two major criterions for declaring a city municipal corporation is population of not less than two lakhs and revenue of not less than one crore per annum. The Act envisages a council for each corporation with a minimum of fifty and maximum of one hundred councilors directly elected for five years. A Mayor and Deputy Mayor are to be elected from among the members for a period of one year. There was provision for standing committees. Each committee elects a chairman. The Mayors and Deputy Mayors are ex-officio members. A Commissioner for each corporation appointed by the State Government will be the administrative officer.

Similarly the criterion for a City Municipal Council is a city having a population fifty thousand or more, a Town Municipal Council for a town with a population of more than ten thousand and less than fifty thousand. The Karnataka Municipalities Act, 1964 provided for constituting a Notified Areas Committee by a government notification to provide for civic facilities in area which cannot be constituted into municipalities. In order to cope with the increasing demands of urban life in respect of housing, water supply, sewerage management, pollution and slums, a number of special agencies and boards have been set up under the category special-purpose urban bodies. For example, City Improvement Boards, Town Planning Authorities, The Karnataka Water Supply and Sewerage Board, the Karnataka Slum Clearance Board, The Karnataka State Housing Board and so on.

The Constitution of India has (in parliament and in the state legislatures) made detailed provisions for ensuring protection of democracy. Hence, democracy in these institutions has survived and flourished. Unfortunately, the Constitution did not make local self-government in urban areas a clear-cut Constitutional obligation. While the Directive Principles of State Policy refer to village Panchayats, there was no specific reference to municipalities except implicitly in Entry five of the state list which places the subject of urban local-government as a responsibility of the states.

Entry five of the state list in the Constitution of India specifies local government that is to say, the Constitution and powers of Municipal Corporation, Improvement Trusts, District Boards, Mining Settlement Authorities and other local authorities for the purpose of local self-government. As a consequence of inadequate Constitutional provision for urban local self-government, democracy in municipal government had not been stable. Though the respective municipal Acts of states provide for regular elections to municipal bodies, they were frequently suspended and superseded for indefinite periods of time. In some cases, these had stretched to periods exceeding a decade. These steps erode the very basis of local self-government and have a deleterious effect on democracy at the grass-roots level.

The general position with regard to the financial resources of the municipal bodies was very unsatisfactory. Over the years, there has been a steady encroachment on the assigned functions and revenues of the urban local bodies by creation of specialized agencies by the State Governments. As a result, many urban local bodies have become weak and are not able to perform effectively.

The weakened status of urban local bodies crystallized public opinion in favour of the need for a Constitutional guarantee to safeguard the interests of the urban local governments in order to provide for:

(a) regular and fair conduct of elections to these bodies,
(b) holding of elections within a specified time-limit in case of supersession,
(c) adequate representation of SC/ST and women,
(d) placing on a firm footing the relationship between the State Governments and the urban local bodies with respect to:
   (i) function and taxation powers of the urban local bodies,
   ii) arrangement for revenue sharing between the State Government and urban local bodies, and
(e) involvement of elected representatives at the grass-roots level in planning at the district and urban local bodies.

In view of effecting these reformations in urban local governments the first ever initiative was taken in 1989 by the then Prime Minister, Rajiv Gandhi, who was committed to "vest power in the only place where power rightfully belongs in a democracy, in the hands of the people". He held wide-ranging consultations with the elected representatives of municipal bodies.

Three regional Sammelans were organised at Bangalore, Cuttack and Delhi in 1989. These were preceded by a seminar of municipal officers from all over the country held in the first week of June 1989 in Delhi. In all, 4,500 delegates attended these deliberations. Discussions were also held with the chief secretaries in a conference held on 27th June, 1989, and with ministers for local self-government at a conference held on 30th June, 1989, both at Delhi. A conference of Chief Ministers was held on 7th July, 1989 where the issues relating to strengthening and proper functioning of urban local government were taken up. Two meetings of the Consultative Committee of the parliament relating to the Ministry of Urban Development also attended to the subject-matter involved.

On the basis of these wide-ranging consultations, the then government introduced the Constitution (65th Amendment) Bill in the parliament in August 1989. The Lok Sabha passed the Bill.

Unfortunately, this Bill was not passed by the Rajya Sabha at that time.

Later on, with the assumption of power by the National Front Government in December 1989, the provisions of the Constitution (65th Amendment) Bill, 1990, incorporating the provisions relating to Panchayats as well as municipalities was introduced in the Lok Sabha in September 1990. This Bill lapsed on account of the dissolution of the then Lok Sabha.

When the Congress Government took charge in 1991, it was committed to the introduction of the requisite bill on Nagarpalika within the first hundred days of the government. It fulfilled that commitment and the Constitution (73rd Amendment) Bill 1991, pertaining to municipalities was introduced in the Lok Sabha on 16th September, 1991. This Bill was essentially based on the Constitution (65th Amendment) Bill, 1989. However, some of the provisions were deleted or modified taking into account the sentiments expressed by the members of the parliament during the parliamentary debate in 1989.

Certain apprehensions were expressed from time to time that this Bill would encroach upon the powers of the state. So utmost care was taken to preserve the basic framework of the Constitution in relation to centre-state relationships. Entry five of the State List remains untouched. Important matters have been left to be decided by the State Legislatures or the State Governments.

The Constitution (73rd Amendment) Bill, 1991 was referred to a Joint Parliamentary Committee with members drawn from both Lok Sabha and Rajya Sabha with K.P. Singh Deo as the Chairman. The Committee held several sittings and also took oral evidence and written comments from seventy six organisations and individuals. The Committee also had the opportunity of visiting various municipalities and held detailed discussions with their officers and elected representatives as well as with several State Governments. This was probably the first time that a parliamentary committee had deliberated so extensively on a legislation concerning urban management and local self-government. The Committee finalised its report and submitted it to the parliament in July 1992.

The Bill as reported by the Joint Parliamentary Committee was taken up for consideration in the Lok Sabha in its Winter Session of 1992. The Bill was passed in the Lok Sabha on 22nd

December, 1992 and in the Rajya Sabha on 23rd December, 1992. The Bill has since been ratified by a resolution of at least half the number of state legislatures. It received the assent of the President on 20th April, 1993. It was published in the Gazette of 20th April, 1993 as the Constitution (74th Amendment) Act, 1992.

Provision has also been made for seats to be reserved in the Council. Section 11, sub-section (2) of the Act specifies that seats shall be reserved in a Municipal Council for scheduled castes and scheduled tribes in the same proportion to the total number of seats to be filled by direct election in the Municipal Council as the population of SC/ST in the municipal area bears to the total population of the municipal area. As nearly as may be one-third of the total number of seats to be filled by direct election shall be reserved for backward classes. With respect to women it says, not less than one-third of the seats in reserved category, i.e., SC/ST and backward classes, and those of non-reserved seats in a Municipal Council shall be reserved for women, these four reserved categories can also contest from non-reserved seats.

The term of the elected Municipal Council will be of five years. Each Municipal Council will have a President and Vice-president elected from amongst the elected councilors in its first meeting. The term of President and Vice-president will be thirty months. The posts of the President and Vice-president are also reserved on the same formula adopted for reserving the council seats. The reservation will be done by the State Government taking into consideration the total number of offices in the state. The State Government also appoints a Municipal Commissioner or Chief Officer to each municipal area who is subject to transfer by the government. Provision has also been made for constituting Standing Committees of the Municipal Council.

Chapter V, Section 87 of the Act specifies the obligatory functions of Municipal Councils. It says it shall be incumbent on every Municipal Council to make adequate provision by any means or resources which it may lawfully use or take for each of the matters specified within the municipal area. The Act provides for a list of twenty five obligatory functions ranging from the lighting of public streets, places and buildings, protecting public life and property from fire, health, education, and so on.

The Municipal Council also has the power to carry certain functions at its own discretion. Section 91 specifies that every Municipal Council may, at its discretion provide either wholly or in part of the items mentioned. Section 91 provides a list of thirty eight discretionary functions.

As for the finances concerned, Chapter VI, Section 94 deals with the taxes of a Municipal Council can impose. A Municipal Council before imposing a tax on any item mentioned in Section 94, shall by a resolution passed at a general meeting select for the purpose of imposing a tax, one or other of the taxes. When such a resolution has been passed, the Municipal Council shall publish in the prescribed manner a notice of such resolution in the prescribed form calling for objections from the residents. After following this procedure and getting sanction of the State Government, the Municipal Council can impose tax on buildings or lands in the municipal area, vehicles, water, additional stamp duty on transfer of immovable property, advertisements and so on.

Thus, it may be said, urban governments in Karnataka have evolved over the past, one and a half century. Despite such a long history of urban local governments they have not been effective in the light of the philosophy governing the setting up of these institutions. Even now one may witness deteriorating urban environment giving rise to shanty towns and slums, unauthorised constructions, inadequate urban services such as water supply, sewerage, transport, education, recreational, health and welfare facilities. A micro level analysis of the urban local governments provides the answers for such a unsatisfactory output of these municipal governments. Sometime ago a case study of the Mangalore City Corporation was undertaken by this author. The empirical findings throw substantive light to justify the maladies of urban administration.

For instance, the mayoral office which symbolises the democratic supremacy in urban governance has been caught in the vortex of party politics and conflict. According to the Act governing Municipal Corporations in Karnataka, the mayor is elected from among the members of the Corporation Council. In actual practice, it is not the councillors who elect the Mayor of their choice. Rather it is the party high command which selects the Mayor and the councillors accept him. This was admitted by almost all the councillors interviewed. Also the Mayor's office has at times been used to appease the electorate on caste/communal lines. But if communal/caste viability is a major consideration and qualification for public office, the future of integrity, stability and character in politics does not appear hopeful, and the office is most likely to lose its dignity and functionality in course of time. But it appears, given the nature/type of plural society in Karnataka, that this convention cannot be avoided.

If the Mayor is the head of the deliberative wing, the Commissioner is the head of the executive wing. Provision has been made in the Act governing Municipal Corporations in Karnataka for the appointment of Municipal Commissioner. Section 14(1) says, the Municipal Commissioner will be appointed by the State Government in consultation with the Mayor of the concerned Municipal Corporation. But on certain occasions the State Government has violated this provision, resulting in strained relations between the Mayor and the Commissioner. A good relationship between these two heads is very necessary because they meet day-in and day-out, go around the wards, receive representations, hear complaints, inspect works in progress and take on-the-spot decisions, keeping in view the public interest. As such, in the good interest of urban administration, Section 14(1) has to be considered by the State Government.

In the deliberative wing another important cog is the elected corporator, the representative of city electorate. Each city is divided into many wards (Corporation Constituency). From each ward a corporator will be elected. The corporator plays many roles like as a mediator, he is a link between the citizen and the administrator. He interprets the problems of his constituency and asks the officers to attend to them. Sometimes, of course, the corporator is disliked and dubbed as an unwanted interloper. This was admitted by 80 per cent of the officers working in the corporation when they were interviewed. Besides, there is the political role he plays which is all pervasive. In normal times, he nurses the constituency, and at the time of elections he works explicitly for his own as well as his party's interests. The councillors take a great deal of interest in spending the money properly that will be allotted to their wards. Besides, the ward is the central focus of attention of the councillor and he nurses it carefully to ensure citizen satisfaction and his own political future. At the same time he does not allow any other councillor to interfere in the business of his ward. For instance, once, the trespass by some corporators into the wards of their fellow corporators, led to a commotion at one of the meetings of the Mangalore Corporation Council. Mr. X of the Congress (I), sought to move a resolution that the road in front of the pourakarmikas colony in Ballal Bagh be broadened to thirty feet and extended to meet the Kavoor cross-Bijai Road by the side of the KSRTC compound. Mr. Y of the BJP objected to the resolution as the proposed work was in his ward. He said, Mr. X's move amounted to interference with his work and he himself would move a resolution at the next meeting. Such instance are many which are not indicators of good urban governance.

The functions of urban governments are divided into two categories, obligatory and discretionary in which a long list is incorporated into the Act. The distrust of local government on the part of the State Government has brought about a gradual proliferation of competitive special authorities in urban administration. Mohit Bhattacharya argues that this administration fragmentation poses serious problems for effective co-ordination. But its effects on the citizens are far more harmful. He further observes that it is small wonder that people in general have little attachment to weak municipal government. Citizens' awareness of civic problems cannot be generated in a vacuum. It is through available opportunities that consciousness grows.

Urban governments in Karnataka are empowered by the Act to frame building bye-laws. According to the building bye-laws framed by Mangalore City Corporation, a new building or any housing or commercial construction, while being constructed, should leave a space of twenty feet, called the set-back space from the main road in its front or any side facing the road. Violation of this bye-law empowers the corporation to withhold the building licence and demolish that much of the structure which has been constructed twenty feet from the main road. In many cases the Corporation withdrew the building construction licence and issued demolition notice. The violators of the bye-law appealed to the State Government which is, of course, a superior authority to the Corporation. To protect the personal interests of the bye-law violators and to pose themselves as protectors of the common people, the State Government issued directions to the Corporation to relax the building bye-laws for those who had already commenced the construction work and were in an advanced stage of construction. Since the urban governments are the creation of the State Government, the Mangalore City Corporation had to accept the directions. As a result, the set back space of twenty feet was relaxed to ten feet in some cases and eight feet in some other cases resulting in narrow streets, narrow footpaths and congested traffic. There are many cases to prove this fact.

These are just some of the many areas which highlight the realities of urban politics. Improper planning, dearth of finances, the petty politics in which the councillors get involved, lack of co-ordination among the multiple agencies involved in the urban administration and development, uncalled for interference by the State Government in urban governance, and so on, efficient urban governance is a hope in the light of 74th Constitutional Amendment Act.

NOTES AND REFERENCES

1. Power to the people the Nagarpalika Act, booklet published by Ministry of Urban Development, Government of India, New Delhi, 1993.
2. Singh, U.B., *Revitalized Urban Administration in India,* Delhi, Kalpaz Publications, 2002.
3. Maheshwari, S.R., *Local Government in India,* New Delhi, Orient Longman Ltd., 1971.
4. Centenary Celebration Souvenir, Mangalore Municipality, 1966.
5. Simha, R.N., *The Karnataka Municipalities Act, 1964 with Latest Amendments 2001,* Bangalore, Aayana Publications, 2001.
6. Rajashekharaiah, A.M., Article on *Local self-government,* Karnataka State Gazetteer, Part II, Bangalore, Government of Karnataka, 1983.
7. Mohit Bhattacharya, *Civil Consciousness and Citizens Participation,* New Delhi, 1979.

12

Panchayati Raj in Karnataka

An Empirical Evaluation

A.T. KITTUR AND HARISH RAMASWAMY

Introduction

Politics could be broadly defined as a study of an interdependent relationship of those institutions and process by which authoritative decisions are made and enforced in order to bring about development of a society. In a democratic context as in the case of India, where people do not come forward to participate in the decision-making process, the governments will have to reach them and transform them into "Participants". Therefore, the institution of Panchayat Raj has been established at the rural level. It is charged with the task of developing the rural areas. In achieving this task several experiments have been made at the institutional level and in the strategies designed for development. The fact that no socio-economic change is possible without a suitable political structure; the need of the rural and urban local governments as extensions to discharge the innumerable responsibilities of the government; the physical impossibility for the government to reach each district, taluka or village within their jurisdiction while embarking upon development programmes; the impersonal nature of administration, etc., have all given greater prominence to the Panchayat Raj institutions linking with them the programmes of development. The institutions established to mobilize "Participants" have today become the focal points of any general study on Local Government in India, from their different working facets political, social, cultural, economic and developmental, rendering them indispensable in matters of national development in general and rural development in particular.

Development as the Task: A Continuity

After independence, plan documents of both Central and State governments and various study committees emphasized the importance of Panchayat Raj in rural and urban development. As the Chairman of the Study Committee on the welfare of the weaker sections Sri Jayaprakash Narayan had observed that the Panchayat Raj Institutions (PRIs) have been charged with the responsibility of planning and development. During the Second Five Year Plan special emphasis was laid on the importance of Panchayat Raj in the rural and urban development and plan documents envisaged the Panchayat as responsible for development, aiming at the transformation of socio-economic life of the people. It had further stressed that rural development depended entirely on the existence of an active organisation in the local area that could bring all with common need under one common programme to be carried out with the assistance of administration. Subsequent plans and policy pronouncements of national leaders further emphasized the role of PRIs in development.

The 73rd Amendment to the Constitution of India has envisaged the PRIs to become vehicles of development. Some other notable features of this law are conducting elections every five years, reservation of seats for SCs/STs according to population, and reservation of 33 per cent seats for women in all the positions from district to village. By this amendment powers are to be given at village level, middle level block or taluka and district Zilla Panchayat level for preparing plans and to implement them for economic development and social justice.

The major structural and functional aspects of the new system are that the Gram Sabha has now a legal status as per Article 243-A in the 73rd Amendment Act. It is considered as the only means of "direct democracy" where all important decisions have to be arrived at. But the lacunae in terms of a very small percentage of village population constituting Gram Sabha is major. It may serve the purpose of training ground for all people, especially the younger generation. Now, every Village Panchayat has a Gram Sabha and it will consist of persons registered in the electoral roll relating to the Village Panchayat. The Gram Sabha shall approve the village budget for the year and review the progress of the implementation of all schemes entrusted to the Village Panchayat. In addition, the State Government may entrust to the Gram Sabha such other functions as may be specified. Today, it may have to be decided as to whether the role of the Gram Sabha is mere advisory or executive or deliberative-cum-executive. There are also thus, convening and conduct of the Gram Sabhas and without the active support of the higher level bureaucratic apparatus may make it a remain a meaningless formality. On the other hand, the position of the Village Panchayat, the Panchayat Samiti, and the Zilla Panchayat in terms of their organisation has not undergone substantial changes in the new system. Although, there is provision for reservation of seats for scheduled castes, scheduled tribes and women, it has not resulted in their active involvement and today Village Panchayats have enough grants to manage (nearly 2.9 crore in Karnataka).

Although, there is no specific mention in the 73rd Amendment Act about the functions to be performed by different institutions at different levels of the Panchayati Raj system, a schedule entitled "Eleventh Schedule" has been appended as per Article 243-G, wherein 29 functions have been brought under the Panchayati Raj system and it was left to the respective State Government to specifically allot powers and functions in this respect out of their own jurisdiction under the State List.

Karnataka has been a pioneer even in this area. Taking into consideration the structural and functional aspects of change recently carried out in the states in the spirit of the 73rd Constitutional Amendment Act, a new approach in terms of establishing old organic linkage in one form or the other amongst the three tiers and substantial delegation of powers towards these institutions is the need of the hour to enhance adequately the status of PRIs as institutions of self-government.

The New Realities

Despite all this, fifty years of democratic governance have resulted in a paradoxical situation in the development process of our country. On the one hand, our achievements are worth appreciation where our macro realities give a progressive picture of India, while, on the other, the problems of rural poverty and unemployment are causing concern for policy-makers as our micro realities are shaking the very foundations of our democratic polity. Consequently, our rulers face a dilemma in regard to the adoption of a fruitful strategy to deliver the goods. Among different measures of ameliorating rural poverty and accentuating all round development, it is now being realized increasingly that people's active participation in grassroots politics and development activities alone can bring about sustainable development without which the present socio-economic problems cannot be faced.

The 73rd Constitution Amendment Act, bearing the basic proposition of "empowering people for development" has sought to bring about a significant change in the attitude, behaviour and performance of the Panchayati Raj system in India. But, mere passing of amendments and legislations cannot alter the existing situation. Everybody thinks that after enacting the 73rd Amendment Act and the subsequent State Panchayati Raj Acts, the system should have worked effectively with vibrancy. In reality it has not been so. This, however, calls for systemic overhaul and attitudinal change which can be brought about only through sustained involvement and participation of the people. The 73rd Constitutional Amendment was only a grand step in the direction which should be followed by a series of multi-pronged efforts to sustain the tempo for development.

Therefore, one must know that the corner stone of any system of decentralized governance is people's participation. And yet, this is probably the most difficult aspect of quality in governance to achieve. In the context of the Panchayati Raj system, the institutional framework for guided participation has been in existence since long. The Constitution of India in Article 243-A makes the Gram Sabha an integral part of the Panchayati Raj system and provides for assigning functions to it and empowering it to perform such functions. However, the Gram Sabhas are the most neglected institutions of the PRIs. Therefore, this attempt is made to assess the Panchayati Raj system in Karnataka through an empirical evaluation taking into account the working of the Zilla Panchayat at the top and the Gram Sabha at the bottom.

Decentralisation and Participation: Conception and Realities

Decentralisation has been a panacea to the many ills of maladministration, corruption, redundancy, etc. Visualising this in a true democracy, decentralization was seen as a book to raise the levels of democratic participation and to ensure that the people in a given geographical area are left to mange their own affairs. India having had the experience of republic since the Vedic period, of course, was not new to decentralized administration (Chandrashekhar 1984). The history of decentralization, democratization and Panchayat Raj in India thus is a pathfinder to many of the neo-colonial and post-colonial states around the world. Since the Balvantrai Mehta committee report in India, democratic decentralization has been quite successfully functioning with enough autonomy given to each state to design its own three tier, two tier or a single tier system in view of their socio-political, economic and cultural needs. One thing, however, that is common in all these exercises is the attempt made by subsequent governments to take administration near to the people. Gram Sabha thus formed the closest unit of administration in this system. These Gram Sabhas structurally are the smallest units of administration with a restricted area, minimum population and the philosophy of direct democracy of the Athenian kind. The difference that one finds when one speaks about Gram Sabhas is the state of Karnataka is that the state of Karnataka has not merely established Gram Sabhas to delegate the powers, but has clearly charged the Gram Sabha with the important task of development.

Development is a desired goal for the benefit of the people given to the local context and needs cannot hope to be shaped well by the people other than by those who desire it (Gandhi 1960). This truly is an innovative concept of designing development with full control over the process by the local people themselves, involving in full the members of the community itself; this perhaps in the reason why Gram Sabhas have today attracted academicians across the world. Panchayat Raj system, therefore, is seen as a unit which effectively helps the designated purpose of development by involving the people at the targeted level through organically linking the different levels of decentralized units from Gram Sabha to the state.

People everywhere want to determine their own destiny. decentralizing governance from the centre to the state, towns and villages can be one of the best means of promoting people's participation and efficiency in working. Democracy can be merely an empty ritual of periodic elections unless people actively participate and are aware and empowered in all the institutions of civil society. People's participation has to go hand in hand with human development. UNDP in its Human Development Report of 1998 has ranked Indian HRI (Human Development Index) at 139th position (UNDP, 1988), the index based on education, longevity and per capita income taken together. There is not doubt that without a large measure of decentralization and people's participation the primary economic, administrative and educational and health related problems facing India cannot be efficiently tackled. Participation in this sense acts like a highway of human development. The people must be seen as the greatest asset of the country and the true development must centre around them. It is required to be well understood that the people cannot be developed, but on the contrary, people have to develop themselves by participating in activities that affect their lives. The schemes and programmes, which are financially dependent on the government assistance invariably, have a shorter life unless the people, for whom they are meant, participate in them actively and continuously. In a way participation is a process wherein people are closely involved in economic, social, cultural and political affairs which affect their lives.

It has been long argued that people's participation is essential for the success of local government. Participation cannot be imposed, but it should be voluntary. It is not a process of involving everyone and reducing all to a common denominator. Rather it consists in evolving institutional structures from which diverse individuals with sense of dignity and self-respect are to determine their own destinies (Seth S.C., 1988). In a democratic country like ours compulsory participation is not desirable. Between spontaneous and sponsored, the former is most suitable. This will sustain for longer period (Behra 1988). The essence of the approach of people's participation is, it has the dual goal of promoting growth and equity while also ensuring the development of democratic processes at the grassroots (Tudor and Athkorala, 1996). SAARC (1992) specified that where the poor participate as subjects and not as objects of the development process, it is possible to generate growth, human development and equity (SAARC, 1992). The building of a nation cannot or will not be achieved by the elite alone nor can development activities be carried out exclusively by administrators or technocrats. Effective people's participation in the given programmes with opportunities is a development priority (Reddy and Others, 1999). It goes without saying that local involvement or people's participation also opens up the opportunities for people to add voluntary contributions to amplify a programme or project. In Kenya, high level of local participation in the rural access roads programme encouraged people to donate land to the project and permitted the construction of 150 extra kilometers of road (Bhatnagar, 2000).

Gram Sabha in Karnataka: An Empirical Evaluation

Thus in every Panchayat Raj, law gives a prominent legal position to the institution of the Gram Sabha, to ensure both decentralization and participation, but in practice, this remains only formal. A well functioning institution of Gram Sabha could in fact work wonders as an instrument of people's empowerment. The effort towards effective democratic decentralization would be futile without making the Gram Sabha truly representative of the people, their aspirations and their management skills. The Gram Sabha is a statutory body and considered the lifeline or the soul of the PRIs. It needs to reflect the voice of the local population in identifying the local needs, prioritizing the needs, identifying beneficiaries and planning local, specific programmes for the community. The Gram Sabhas are the effective agents creating awareness, facilitating people's participations, promoting transparency and accountability in the decision-making process. It serves as an assembly of the village and acts as a watchdog of the Gram Panchayat. In the state of Karnataka Gram Sabhas are not merely established to delegate the powers, but has clearly charged the Gram Sabha with the important task of development. This research work in fact deals with the working of Gram Sabhas in Karnataka by undertaking two Gram Sabhas in a newly-formed Haveri district for a micro study. This empirical study further identifies certain tools for strengthening this grassroots institution.

Choice of the Study Area

The choice of the area for this study was made in Haveri taluk which is one of the newly formed districts in Northern Karnataka. The villages chosen for the study are Kurubagonda and Kallapur. This choice is based on the method of understanding the impact of proximity or distance of a village to a district place and its effects on the working of Gram Sabhas. Given the context are the diverse variables that operate at different levels and in different forms at the rural local level. These, in fact, have an influence over the working of political institutions such as Gram Sabhas in a given geographical area. It is important to discuss here as to how the structure of the village societies, the many variables within the society such as education, economy, land holding, etc., influence the political process of the smallest unit of administration, viz., Gram Sabha. Gram Sabha given its context of a community life, where the people are dependent largely on the state, where people interact face to face on a daily basis, faces a number of problems in its functioning. Kondajji Basappa Committee Report, in Karnataka, in fact in 1962, observed that the Gram Panchayat itself was as a small unit of administration and as such it was not viable in terms of its economy. The report further observed that the co-existing communities that interact on a daily basis do not work to promote the efficiency of Gram Panchayats in matters connected with mobilizing finance for developmental purposes. Such criticism was later reiterated by the formation of Mandal Panchayats by the 1983 Act. However, in 1993 and subsequently by the Congress Government, even smaller units such as Gram Sabhas in Karnataka were favoured. In the light of these issues the survey was conducted in the study areas through the participant observation method having an unstructured questionnaire, which involved basic questions that related to the question of cognizance, evaluation and the development orientation of these institutions.

Brief Profile of the Villages

Kurubagonda and Kallapur are the study areas chosen for in depth analysis to understand the working of Gram Sabhas in detail. Kurubagonda is at a distance of eight kilometers from the district place, viz., Haveri. The village has about one kilometer radius with a population of around 15,000 with an average literacy rate of 40 per cent with primary school as minimum education and roughly 8 per cent have higher education starting from the bachelor's degree and more. The population of women to the total population is less than half, with literacy rate falling below 3 per cent. In spite of these social factors, the village seems to be economically quite well off over the years and there is also a chance to see more of its improvement in the light of Haveri being converted into a district. The total landholding varies somewhere between two to hundred acres representing the landholding pattern as found elsewhere in the Northern Karnataka, which is varied.

There are also irrigated and unirrigated lands with the pattern of landholding varying from 100 acres to 200 acres. This great divide is quite apparent to those who visit this village. The major crops are Jawar and Maize. Recently after Haveri's formation as a district, diversification of the agricultural produce and growing of day-to-day vegetables, etc., as noticed, is on an increase; this in fact is empowering the small land-holders.

In comparison, Kallapur, which is about 12 kilometers from Haveri with a half a kilometer radius and 100 families, which is about 2,000 population, is not really a very big village. In Kallapur land distribution is not very encouraging and the facilities for irrigation are comparatively fewer. Economically and educationally it is rather backward compared with the average scale for a district. However, it is noticed that some of the educated from this village have migrated for good and have not come back to the village. Keeping these comparative perspectives in mind, it is for researcher to assess legitimately the work of the Gram Sabhas in these villages.

Having given the profile of these study areas let us now turn to analyse the data collected as samples to understand the work of the Gram Sabhas. The size of the respondents chosen was on the basis of the total population of which only 0.01 per cent was taken up. This clearly gave us 150 respondents in Kurubagonda village alone which has a population of nearly 15,000. In Kallapur the choice of respondents was only 20, since the population here is only 2,000. The unstructured questionnaire was aimed primarily at assessing the awareness factor to evaluate the effectiveness of the working of Gram Sabhas. (See Table 12.1).

Table 12.1: Are you aware of your Gram Sabha?

(Yes/No)

Total Number of respondents	Yes	No	No answer	Total
170	69	81	20	170
Total %	40.6	47.64	11.76	100.00

Table 12.1 indicates that the majority of them (47.64%) were not aware of the Gram Sabhas and their functioning. While 40.6 per cent were aware and nearly 11.76 per cent did not have an answer. Then it was further investigated to learn why their villagers did not know Gram Sabhas. The results especially from Kallapur indicated that the Gram Sabhas were not functioning regularly and this irregularity has been almost so redundant that the Gram Sabhas in their village has failed to meet even after a year and half. This apart, lack of publicity, lack of availability of literature, lack of initiative from the leadership and lack of spare time to learn about these institutions by the labour class which invariably migrates to district places are also some of the reasons for this lack of awareness. Many of the earlier studies conducted similarly elsewhere in Karnataka have also discussed these problems (Bhargava and Raphel, 1994). Therefore, it is pertinent here to recapitulate that the success of any institution demands primarily proper socialization of the information about these institutions.

A second question was addressed to these respondents who were carefully selected on a random method through the voters list. After giving them a brief about Gram Sabhas, its functioning, its statutory position, thereby creating awareness about Gram Sabha, the question relating to its performance was asked as to how they evaluated Gram Sabhas including the past experiences they have had.

Table 12.2: How do you evaluate the performance of your Gram Sabha?

Total Number of respondents	Satis-factory	Not satis-factory	No answer	Total
170	84	85	01	170
Total %	49.4	60.0	0.58	99.98

Table 12.2, though slightly confusing, indicates that the performance of the Gram Sabhas in these villages to be promising (49.4%) with a thin margin of variation of those who believe that the Gram Sabhas are not performing satisfactorily (50.0%). In a logical sequence of the earlier question, the people of Kallapur who did not really have the experience of Gram Sabha functioning for the past one and a half year and had no occasion to evaluate performance felt that in the light of their past experience the Gram Sabha performed satisfactorily. However, four reasons were detected to verify the non-performance or unsatisfactory performance of the Gram Sabhas.

Table 12.2 (a): How do you evaluate the performance of your Gram Sabha?

A	*B*	*C*	*D*	*E*	*Total*
25 14.70%	30 17.64%	25 14.70%	50 29.41%	40 23.52%	170 99.97%

(A) Information about Gram Sabha is not available.
(B) Gram Sabha meetings are irregularly held.
(C) The meetings of Gram Sabha are not published in advance.
(D) All the above.
(E) Do not know.

Table 12.2(a) indicates that most of the respondents seem to believe (29.41%) that all the reasons mentioned above are the reasons for the dissatisfactory functioning of the Gram Sabhas, while nearly 23.52 per cent did not answer the question. Another 14.70 per cent believed that the information about Gram Sabhas is not available and, according them, it is this lack of information that fails to attract the Gram Sabha members for the meeting. Similarly, the another 14.70 per cent believe that the Gram Sabha meetings are not published in advance which amounts to a similar answer as seen above. Though redundant, it confirms the fact that the notification about a forthcoming meeting of the Gram Sabha is invariably concealed and this causes a drop in attendance. About 17.64 per cent of people believe that the Gram Sabha meetings are held irregularly and that causes the dissatisfactory performance of the Gram Sabha. The overall assessment of this reasoning is indicative of the fact that, despite the attempts to mobilize people's participation and to provide them a forum, the Gram Sabhas have not been successful due to the callousness of the lower ranking bureaucratic. A remedy for this must be found.

In order to understand the impact of the working of Gram Sabhas on the socio-political life of the village a direct question was asked to the respondents requesting them to identify the impact of Gram Sabhas have made on their lives.

Table 12.3: Is there a positive impact of the Gram Sabhas?

(Yes/No)

Yes	*No*	*Total*
88	82	170
51.74%	48.23%	99.97%

Table 12.3 indicates that about 51.76 per cent believe that there has been an impact on their lives, while 48.23 per cent see none. An investigation made further revealed that the question regarding those who preferred to say that Gram Sabhas made an impact on their lives, replied in fact to a subsidiary question. The responses were primarily taken note of as narrated by the respondents and were regrouped for the purposes of research findings. These groupings were given sub-headings such as Democratisation, Political Emancipation and Social Consciousness. As a result, we found that nearly 30 per cent answers could be grouped under all the 3 sub-headings identified above. About 11 per cent of them favoured democratization and social emancipation and nearly the same per cent (10.76) identified political emancipation as an identifiable effect that they have had on their lives. Further, in order to verify the effectiveness of the Gram Sabhas, a question was constructed differently as detailed below:

Table 12.4: Do you endorse the successful working of Gram Sabha?

A	*B*	*C*	*D*	*Total*
45	49	39	37	170
26.47%	28.82%	22.94%	21.77%	100.00%

Note: (a) Successful
(b) Partially successful
(c) Not successful
(d) Do not know

Table 12.4 is indicative of the fact that the working of the Gram Sabhas has been partially successful (28.82%). If one observes the logical development of Tables 12.1, 12.2, 12.3 and 12.4, one would find that there has been consistency in emphasizing the fact that the working of the Gram Sabhas has been a success and not a "pomp" filled success. Although much of literature produced by the government helps to strengthen the fact that the Gram Sabhas are a great success, this study substantiates it. This thin line of success is wrapped up with the silent revolution at the ground level to support the socially emerging classes, thus bringing about the needed and intended change in the social fabric of rural Karnataka that is dominated by a feudal system. On the other hand, there is a marginal difference of those who have been consistently arguing that there is a complete success story of the Gram Sabhas. This 26.47 per cent believes that the Gram Sabha, as discussed earlier, has been able to democratize and emancipate socially and politically the lives of the people in the village. As against those who argue of the partial success of Gram Sabha, while not disagreeing, group trends to argue that the Gram Sabhas were intended not only to emancipate but to develop the village as a self-sufficient unit. It is at this point that they believe that, the Gram Sabha has failed. They also argue that the Gram Sabhas have not been able to ameliorate the total interest of the village involving the infrastructure development, the minimum needs, the sanitary conditions and the like which are the minimal development activities essentially dependent on the functioning of the Gram Sabhas. They firmly and forcefully put forth their argument that the Gram Sabhas have also been victimized by the politics of the caste-ridden society and also the middle level ego politics, resulting in asphyxiating this delivery system. If this is one side of the story, on the other side the functionaries of Gram Sabha who have a fair knowledge of the politico-administrative dynamics of PRIs believe that the poor economic conditions are responsible for the partial success of the Gram Sabha. Nearly 22.94 per cent believe that the Gram Sabhas are not successful. Incidentally most of the respondents who favoured this category are members of the upper caste who have no direct benefit of the presence of the Gram Sabha. It is understandable that they would carry such an opinion about Gram Sabhas given their social disposition. It is also understandable that these people would criticize the very existence of the Gram Sabha. Nearly 21.77 per cent have responded as "do not know" to this question and it is difficult to assess as to why this neutral category does not want to respond to the question. Having assessed the question of the working of the Gram Sabhas, a leading question was asked regarding any proposals for changing the Gram Sabhas including its structure and functioning. The response given is assed in Table 12.5.

Table 12.5: Do you think there is need for change in the working of Gram Sabhas?

Yes	*No*	*Total*
34	136	170
20%	80%	100%

Table 12.5 indicates that an overwhelming 80 per cent did not favour any type of change (structural or functional in the Gram Sabhas) and only 20 per cent wanted certain changes in Gram Sabhas. The arguments of those who wanted changes were clearly motivated by the fact that they wanted to hold on to power as against the idea behind the participative decision-making. They also wanted to control the activities of the Gram Panchayats through the Gram Sabhas. So, too, they wanted the ward level Sabhas, below the Gram Sabha, to be removed and such argument of 20 per cent respondents only represented anti-decentralisation. (Annual Progress Report, 2001). The majority, however, despite their differences favoured the current disposition of the Gram Sabhas. In order to evaluate the response of Gram Sabhas as an institution contributing to the development of the villages, to a straight question as to how they assess their contribution was asked.

Table 12.6: How do you assess Gram Sabhas and their contribution to the development of villages?

Yes	*No*	*Total*
100	70	170
58.82%	41.17%	99.99%

Table 12.6 indicates that 58.82 per cent of the respondents agreed that there is some development in the village through Gram Sabhas. Many of them pointed out that Gram Sabha meetings were few. But still schemes including IRDP had contributed to development. Further, they argued that the presence of the Gram Sabha, despite its limitations, has positively contributed to bringing into focus many of the local problems to the attention of authorities of the Panchayat level. In this way the activisation of the Gram Sabhas has been able to deliver minimum services to the cause of the communities. However, the strain that the Gram Sabhas experience is more political in nature. If policy-makers can concentrate on avoiding the political and the ego clashes at the local level or if experiences can be teachers, Gram Sabhas can learn better and manage its affairs on its own.

Therefore, the key to Gram Sabhas success in Karnataka is mainly dependent on participation of the community while benefits for the community may be derived if Gram Sabhas function effectively. In both these cases inadequate participation affects the process of development. In the case of the chosen areas for the study this is true.

Zilla Panchayats in Karnataka: An Empirical Evaluation

On the other hand, if you look at the data obtained through empirical survey at the Zilla Panchayat level in Dharwad, where most of the representatives who had worked on various standing committees in Zilla Panahayat were identified as respondents depending on their availability, the picture is much more bright. For about 890 seats in the Zilla Panchayat and for about 325 seats in the Taluk Panchayats elections are due in December, 2005. The most important aspect of this timing is that in all early elections, the party in power at the state was the party that caught on to power at Zilla Panchayats. But for the first time in Karnataka the situation at the state level is one of coalition and there are chances that this might reflect as the Zilla Panchayats too, since they are seen as measuring scales to speak of the future of the Congress/JD(S) coalition in the state. Thus, the empirical survey of the Gram Sabhas at one extreme and of the Zilla Panchayats on the other presents a balanced picture of the Karnataka Panchayati Raj system, which is the key to the successful functioning of democracy in India.

For a question on the status and working of the Zilla Panchayati, the response as seen in (Table 12.7) is self-explanatory. In order to measure further the comprehension of the respondents, who have worked on various committees, were asked to name the committees active at the Zilla Panchayats. All the respondents were very correct in their answers. (See Table 12.7).

Table 12.7: Are you aware of the status and working of Zilla Panchayat?

Sl. No.	*No. of respondents*	*Yes*	*%*	*No*	*%*
1	14	14	100	0	0

Since some of them had already worked on these committees, they were asked to explain how they felt about their working. Most of them agreed that their experiences were rather complimentary to their chosen profession. However, some of them wanted representation of citizens and lower level representatives too to work with them, to establish organic linkage (See Table 12.8).

Table 12.8: Can you name some committees that are active at Zilla Panchayat?

Sl. No.	*No. of respondents*	*Yes*	*%*	*No*	*%*
1	14	14	100	0	0

It was because of this they believed, that Zilla Panchayat and whatever was under it, was the actual democracy at work. As a result they agreed to a proposition that in a democracy Zilla Panchayat, despite being the first stage of decentralization, symbolizes decentralized power (See Table 12.9) and they felt that it contributed to proper-sharing in a democracy.

Table 12.9: In a democracy Zilla Panchayat speaks of symbolizing decentralizing power. Do you agree?

Sl. No.	*No. of respondents*	*Yes*	*%*	*No*	*%*
1	14	14	100	0	0

Most of the respondents at the Zilla Panchayat seemed to be thoroughly trained as grassroot leaders and as such when enquired as to whether they were happy with the working of the Zilla Panchayat, they said they were happy. (See Table 12.10).

Table 12.10: Are you happy with the working of Zilla Panchayat?

Sl. No.	*No. of respondents*	*Yes*	*%*	*No*	*%*
1	14	14	100	0	0

This they felt because it was serving them as a truly a democratic space, which provided them the avenue to express themselves and to have a say in the democratic functioning of a state especially in a country where 76 per cent of population resided. (See Table 12.11 and 12.12).

Table 12.11: Do you think Zilla Panchayat provides enough democracy space?

Sl. No.	*No. of respondents*	*Yes*	*%*	*No*	*%*
1	14	14	100	0	0

Table 12.12: Do you think that working in the Zilla Panchayats has enlarged democratic participation in rural Karnataka?

Sl. No.	*No. of respondents*	*Yes*	*%*	*No*	*%*
1	14	14	100	0	0

What is more important at this stage was the response of these representatives to a question regarding the need for change in the composition of the Zilla Panchayat and its working. Nearly 60 per cent of them agreed that it was all right. Those who, in fact, disagreed said that the representatives at the state level must be given only an opportunity to be a part of the system, but they were unwilling to accept the current position given to the MLAs and MLCs to be a part of decision-making at this level also. (See Table 12.13).

Table 12.13: Do you think there is need to change the composition and working of the Zilla Panchayat?

Sl. No.	*No. of respondents*	*Yes*	*%*	*No*	*%*
1	14	10	60	04	40

Similar was the opinion to the next question which was divided evenly between those who favoured Zilla Panchayat as truly contributing to democratic functioning at rural local level. Those who agreed felt that since the land reforms had not completed its agenda in full, there was still a part of semi-decentralisation or quasi-decentralisation at the Zilla Panchayat due to factors like the presence of bureaucrats and MLAs. (See Table 12.14).

Table 12.14 :Do you think Zilla Panchayats have truly contributed to democratic functioning at the rural local level?

Sl. No.	*No. of respondents*	*Yes*	*%*	*No*	*%*
1	14	07	50	07	50

Thus, at the level of Gram Sabha the democratic process is maturing and at the Zilla Panchayat level, there is evidence of its maturity calling for greater freedom, independence and increased role for elected representatives within the given jurisdiction.

Thus, the empirical evaluation of the Panchayati Raj in Karnataka, apart from its theoretical perspective, presents a hopeful picture filled with aspirations and hopes for a stronger democratic state. In the state of Karnataka with its democracy firmly rooted in the decentralized institutions, it is all the more important for it to blossom for a better tomorrow.

Conclusion

Karnataka seems to be a fertile land for experimenting the successes and the failures of the Panchayati Raj in India. In the national context it is often seen that our state has representative character of Indianness. To some, this fertile land for experiments is also a torch-bearer, while Kannadigas often experience the distress and pains of Panchayat Raj experiments. However, nothing of this distress or pain seems to bother the rural elite in Karnataka at least since the period of the Maharajas. So long as the ruling elites do not wish to stop experimenting the Panchayat Raj mechanism with a hidden agenda to weaken it due to the vested interests and the ill will to share the power, it is for certain that the experiments at Panchayat Raj will never be complete. However, despite the glory of the Panchayati Raj under the Act of 1993 in Karnataka, the success of the 1983 Act is something very special to recall. However, in Karnataka it is sad to note that even on the verge of 2005 the amendment of the Panchayat Raj Act including the Gram Sabhas is still failing to gain a concrete shape and is being subjected to more experiments. Having said so much about experimentation, it is but essential to discuss research in the area of Panchayat Raj too. Since the beginning of the princely state of Mysore and its attempts to demonstrate adequately to the British that it was in tune with the British administration, the experiments in the area of the Panchayat Raj through subsequent governments have in fact over-exposed Panchayat Raj to the researcher. There is hardly anything that the researcher has left unturned thereby contributing greatly to the richness of literature on the subject. Yet the current study in its own form represents on little area of Panchayat Raj, which has been the dream of many to realize the Republic kind of units of administration seem to elude the attention of many. Karnataka can without doubt stand as torch-bearer in this to contribute to the efforts of governments both central and state to build a strong and vibrant democratic state which in the era of globalisation can be a model in managing its local affairs without seeking help from the Central or State Governments. Our efforts, therefore, should be to strengthen these grassroots democratic institutions to deal with a globalised world of tomorrow and get noticed by the world market directly. This then will be the uniqueness of the Karnataka state.

13

Representation of Women in Local Government with Special Reference to Karnataka

(SMT.) MALAVIKA M. DESHPANDE and S.S. PATAGUNDI

Introduction

The purpose of this paper is to examine the representation of women in local government with special reference to Karnataka. In this regard an attempt is made to understand the representation of women in urban as well as rural government. This paper is based on primary sources.

Democracy is considered as one of the best forms of government. In it the government runs the administration with four pillars like justice, liberty, equality and fraternity. The participation of people in the governance of the country is of the essence. Such participation by people will be meaningful when the powers are decentralized from the top to the grassroots level.

Democratic politics is not meaningful unless women participate in the decision-making process since they constitute half of the population of as per the 2001 census in Karnataka. Though Indian the Constitution provides many measures to involve them in the decision-making process at different levels, they lag. Therefore, empowerment of women plays a vital role from the perspective of making politics democratic.

Decentralization is important in democratic politics. It helps to take the administration closer to the common people and involve them. This also enables to mobilize the local resources for the well-being of the people with effective planning and implementation. This tends to the development of grassroots level. Obviously, it is empowering the local people through the system of Panchayat Raj institutions. As a result, the community takes part in decision-making to a considerable extent.

The study of Panchayat Raj in India is traced to the ancient vedic era. The establishment of village Panchayat was an ideology of the Indian National Movement and Gandhiji's idea of "Gram Swarajya". After independence, for the implementation of the Panchayat Raj various committees were appointed by the Government of India like Balwant Rai Mehta Committee (1957), Ashok Mehta Committee (1977), C.H. Hanumanth Rao Committee (1982), G.V.K. Rao Committee (1985), Laxmi Mal Singhvi Committee (1986), P.K. Thungan Committee (1989) and Harial Singh Kharra Committee (1990).[1]

Many committees were appointed in different states to recommend an organizational pattern, resources of Panchyat Raj institutions, administrative powers, personnel system and other matters.[2]

As a result of the recommendations made by various committees the Central Government decided to give a Constitutional status to Panchyat Raj institutions and passed the 73rd Constitutional Amendment Bill in December 1992 during the Narasimha Rao regime, which came into force on April 24, 1993.[3] The 1993 Act on Panchyat Raj provides uniformity to Panchyat Raj system throughout India. The main feature of the Act provides a three-tier system for all states having a population of over twenty lakh and regular Panchayat elections at the end of every year. At the same time reservation for SC/ST and women were also guaranteed by this Constitutional provision.

In view of the increasing importance of the Panchyat Raj, the state-wise Panchyat Raj Acts were passed in conformity with the constitutional 73rd Amendment Act is as under:

1. The Andhra Pradesh Panchyat Raj Act, 1993.
2. The Bihar Panchyat Raj Act, 1993.
3. The Gujarat Panchyat Raj Act, 1993.
4. The Karnataka Panchyat Raj Act, 1993.

5. The Tripura Panchyat Raj Act, 1993.
6. The Orissa Gram Panchayats, Taluka Panchayats, Zilla Parishads (Amendment) Act, 1993.
7. The Himachal Pradesh Panchyat Raj Act, 1994.
8. The Kerala Panchyat Raj Act, 1994.
9. The Madhya Pradesh Panchyat Raj Act, 1994.
10. The Bombay Village Panchayats and the Maharashtra Zilla Parishad and Panchayat Samiti (Amendment) Act, 1994.
11. The Assam Panchyat Raj Act, 1994.
12. The Manipur Panchyat Raj Act, 1994.
13. The Arunachal Pradesh Panchyat Raj Ordinance, 1994.
14. The Punjab Panchyat Raj Act, 1994.
15. The Rajasthan Panchyat Raj Act, 1994.
16. The Tamil Nadu Panchyat Raj Act, 1994.
17. The Uttar Pradesh Panchayat (Amendment) Act, 1994.
18. The West Bengal Panchayat (Amendment) Act, 1994.[4]

The credit goes to Karnataka as a state where decentralization of power among people was achieved much before the introduction of the 73rd and the 74th Amendment of the Constitution. It has also given more powers in terms of functions, functionaries and funds to the three-tier of Panchyat Raj than any other state in India.[5]

Women in Panchyat Raj

The Panchyat Raj (Constitutional 73rd Amendment) Act that came into effect on April 24, 1993, generated much discussion and debate.

The reason behind this was for the first time since independence women were represented at all levels of Panchayats in large numbers. There are two types of changes regarding women's participation in politics. One is the realisation and acceptance of having considerable women in the formal political system and the second is adopting of the reservation policy for increasing women's representation in all elected bodies—government as well local self-government institutions.

As a result of this, there are about one million women members along with women members of urban local bodies like the municipal councils and corporations. There are 2.25 lakh village Panchayats in India consisting of 7.5 lakh women members and 40,000 women chairpersons.[6] Table 13.1 shows the number of women representatives and details of the Panchayat Raj system.

As a result of this, women are able to get an opportunity to participate in the functioning of local governing institutions as the local political elites. This certainly contributes to the strengthening of the democratic process at the local level.

Table 13.1: Number of Women Representatives and Details of Panchayat Raj System in India

	Particulars	*Numbers*
I. Gram Panchayat		
1.	Number of Panchayats	225000
2.	Number of total members of Panchayats	2250000
3.	Number of women members (1/3 of the total)	750000
4.	Number of SC/ST members	150000
5.	Number of 1/3 of SC/ST members	50000
6.	Number of chairpersons	225000
7.	Number of women chairpersons (1/3 of the total chairpersons)	75000
II. Intermediary Level		
1.	Number of block Samitis	5100
2.	Number of total members of Block Samitis	51000
3.	Number of women members of Samitis (1/3 of the total members)	17000
4.	Number of chairpersons of Samitis	5100
5.	Number of chairpersons of Samitis	1700
III. District Level		
1.	Number of Zilla Panchayats	475
2.	Number of total members of Zilla Panchayats	4750
3.	Number of women members of Zilla Panchayats (1/3 of the total members)	1583
4.	Number of Zilla Panchayats chairpersons	475
5.	Number of women Zilla Panchayats chairpersons (1/3 of the total chairpersons)	158

Source: Fourth World Conference on Women, Beijing, 1995, Country Report, Government of India, Department of Women and Child Development, New Delhi.

Profile of Panchayat Membership in Karnataka

Unified Karnataka, which is endowed with a rich cultural heritage, was formed on 1st November, 1956. The total population of Karnataka according to 2001 census is 5,27,33,958, out of which, 2,68,56,343 are males and 2,58,77,615 are females. The total literacy rate of Karnataka is 67.04 per cent (3,07,74,988), out of which 76.29 per cent (1,78,17,682) are males and 57.45 per cent (1,29,57,206) are females. In Karnataka there are 27 districts, of which area-wise Gulbarga is the largest and Bangalore is the smallest. On the demographic basis, Bangalore has 6.5 million population, whereas Kodagu has 0.5 million. In literacy, Bangalore is the highest literate district, 83.91 per cent, and Raichur is the lowest, 49.54 per cent. In case of male literacy, Dakshina Kannada stands highest with 89.74 per cent, whereas in respect of female literacy Bangalore stands highest with 54.45 per cent.[7] Administratively, the state is divided into 27 districts and 175 talukas. The Gram Sabha is the basic unit of village administration.

Table 13.2 shows district-wise abstract of Gram Panchayat Elections, Table 13.3 indicates abstract of reservation of seats for women in Taluka Panchayat Constituencies and Table 13.4 shows the abstract of reservation of seats for women in Zilla Panchayat Constituencies in Karnataka as per the records of 2000.

Table 13.5 shows the number of women representatives in Gram Panchayats, Panchayats (Block Samitis) and Zilla Panchayats in Karnataka as per the records of 2000.

Women in Urban Local Bodies

As far as the representation of women in urban local bodies is concerned, one-third seats are reserved for women members in City Municipal Councils (CMCs), Town Municipal Councils (TMCs) and Town Panchayats (TPs).

Table 13.6 indicates district-wise abstract of Urban Local Bodies in Karnataka.

In Karnataka, there are 216 local bodies, among them six are Corporations, forty City Municipal Councils (CMCs), 94 Town Municipal Councils (TMCs) and eighty-six Town Panchayats (TPs). Along with the one-third reservation of seats in total membership for women being granted, the Government of Karnataka, as per

Table 13.2: District-wise Abstract of Gram Panchayat Elections

S. No.	District name	No. of Gr. Pan.	Total No. of Members			SC			ST		
			Gen.	Female	Total	Gen.	Female	Total	Gen.	Fe male	Total
1	2	3	4	5	6	7	8	9	10	11	12
1.	Bangalore (U)	112	958	749	1707	263	181	444	04	112	116
2.	Bangalore (R)	228	1963	1516	3479	4129	315	734	21	230	251
3.	Chitradurga	185	1636	1195	2831	376	255	661	274	258	532
4.	Davangere	230	1603	1308	2911	364	300	664	147	251	398
5.	Kolar	307	2430	1942	4378	680	487	1167	136	294	430
6.	Shimoga	260	1282	1213	2495	206	301	507	09	255	264
7.	Tumkur	321	2824	2108	4932	517	421	938	158	325	483
8.	Chikmagalur	226	1084	1097	2181	219	248	467	09	226	235
9.	Dakshina Kannada	206	1568	1359	2927	64	209	273	39	209	248
10.	Udupi	146	1213	1025	2238	22	147	169	28	148	176
11.	Hassan	258	1853	1598	3451	338	314	652	04	258	262
12.	Kodagu	99	593	550	1143	51	103	154	38	104	142
13.	Mandya	230	2428	1252	3680	249	253	502	–	230	230
14.	Mysore	236	2184	1628	3812	439	343	782	53	245	298
15.	Chamarajanagar	121	1028	834	1922	272	196	468	29	128	157
16.	Belgaum	485	3974	3279	7253	365	547	912	64	498	562
17.	Bijapur	199	1778	1387	3165	366	275	641	08	201	209
18.	Bagalkot	163	1393	1112	2505	230	139	423	06	164	170
19.	Dharwad	127	854	792	1646	28	128	156	02	127	129
20.	Gadag	106	794	662	1456	112	125	237	03	106	109
21.	Haveri	206	1413	1254	2667	153	225	378	39	206	245
22.	Uttara Kannada	204	1170	1162	2332	46	211	257	08	205	213
23.	Bellary	186	1562	1201	2763	234	249	573	152	229	381
24.	Bidar	175	1430	1121	2551	336	244	580	101	185	286
25.	Gulbarga	337	2797	2224	5021	743	536	1279	88	350	438
26.	Raichur	164	1545	1128	2673	297	224	521	153	194	347
27.	Koppal	134	1187	914	2101	178	162	340	53	138	191
	Total	**5651**	**44174**	**35940**	**80114**	**7657**	**7222**	**14879**	**1626**	**5876**	**7502**

Table 13.2: (*Contd.*)

S. No.	District Name	Caste-wise Details						General		
		Gen.	Female	Total	Gen.	Female	Total	Gen.	Female	Total
1	2	13	14	15	16	17	18	19	20	21
1.	Bangalore (U)	244	213	457	104	10	114	343	233	576
2.	Bangalore (R)	493	440	933	218	12	230	812	519	1331
3.	Chitradurga	382	352	734	174	08	182	430	292	722
4.	Davangere	369	382	751	205	08	213	518	367	885
5.	Kolar	536	608	1144	301	05	306	777	548	1325
6.	Shimoga	290	340	630	204	01	205	573	316	889
7.	Tumkur	686	633	1319	311	14	325	1152	517	1867
8.	Chikmagalur	258	295	553	164	05	169	434	323	757
9.	Dakshina Kannada	402	364	766	176	26	202	887	551	1438
10.	Udupi	314	274	588	132	23	155	717	433	1150
11.	Hassan	440	463	903	242	07	249	829	556	1385
12.	Kodagu	135	154	289	94	02	96	275	187	462
13.	Mandya	514	449	963	208	22	230	1027	628	1655
14.	Mysore	569	464	1033	221	18	239	902	558	1460
15.	Chamarajanagar	248	237	521	104	18	122	399	255	654
16.	Belgaum	1032	875	1907	421	94	515	2092	1265	3357
17.	Bijapur	444	396	840	199	22	213	769	493	1262
18.	Bagalkot	343	326	669	154	17	171	660	412	1072
19.	Dharwad	211	215	426	114	12	126	499	310	809
20.	Gadag	195	184	379	98	07	105	386	240	626
21.	Haveri	324	357	681	195	12	207	702	454	1156
22.	Uttara Kannada	290	311	601	168	11	179	658	424	1082
23.	Bellary	366	350	716	174	15	189	5046	385	904
24.	Bidar	331	343	676	174	14	178	498	335	833
25.	Gulbarga	677	660	1337	324	16	340	965	662	1627
26.	Raichur	380	331	711	153	24	177	562	355	917
27.	Koppal	295	269	564	127	13	140	534	332	866
	Total	**10804**	**10285**	**21089**	**5141**	**436**	**5577**	**18946**	**12121**	**31067**

Source: State Election Commission Office, Bangalore.

Table 13.3: Abstract of Reservation of Seats for Women in Taluka Panchayat Constituencies

Sl. No.	District Name	No. of Seats	SC	ST	A	B	Gen.
1.	Bangalore (U)	68 (28)	18 (7)	3 (3)	19 (6)	4 (3)	24 (9)
2.	Bangalore (R)	139 (57)	28 (11)	8 (8)	37 (16)	9 (1)	57 (21)
3.	Chitradurga	115 (48)	27 (11)	22 (10)	31 (12)	8 (3)	27 (12)
4.	Davangere	115 (46)	25 (10)	14 (6)	30 (12)	7 (3)	39 (15)
5.	Kolar	181 (78)	48 (19)	16 (11)	50 (22)	11 (3)	56 (23)
6.	Shimoga	99 (47)	18 (10)	7 (7)	26 (14)	7	41 (16)
7.	Tumkur	195 (80)	36 (14)	18 (10)	53 (20)	13 (6)	75 (30)
8.	Chikmagalur	103 (50)	20 (10)	7 (7)	28 (14)	7 (1)	41 (18)
9.	Dakshina Kannada	115 (48)	9 (5)	6 (5)	31 (12)	7 (3)	62 (23)
10.	Udupi	88 (34)	5 (3)	4 (3)	24 (9)	6 (2)	49 (17)
11.	Hassan	139 (58)	25 (10)	8 (8)	37 (16)	10 (3)	59 (21)
12.	Kodagu	46 (19)	5 (3)	5 (3)	13 (6)	3	20 (7)
13.	Mandya	144 (60)	20 (9)	7 (7)	39 (14)	10 (4)	68 (26)
14.	Mysore	152 (62)	31 (12)	8 (7)	42 (15)	10 (5)	61 (23)
15.	Chamarajanagar	81 (33)	20 (8)	4 (4)	22 (8)	6 (2)	29 (11)
16.	Belgaum	287 (110)	33 (14)	12 (10)	75 (25)	19 (9)	148 (52)
17.	Bijapur	124 (49)	25 (10)	5 (5)	32 (10)	9 (4)	53 (20)
18.	Bagalkot	99 (41)	17 (6)	6 (6)	27 (12)	6 (1)	43 (16)
19.	Dharwad	66 (33)	5 (5)	5 (5)	17 (10)	5	34 (13)
20.	Gadag	66 (32)	9 (5)	5 (5)	18 (10)	5	29 (12)
21.	Haveri	109 (47)	16 (7)	8 (7)	30 (14)	7 (1)	48 (18)
22.	Uttara Kannada	123 (67)	12 (11)	11 (11)	33 (22)	11	56 (23)
23.	Bellary	112 (47)	24 (9)	14 (8)	29 (14)	8 (1)	37 (15)
24.	Bidar	101 (43)	23 (10)	10 (5)	30 (10)	5 (5)	33 (13)
25.	Gulbarga	198 (82)	51 (19)	13 (10)	54 (20)	12 (6)	68 (27)
26.	Raichur	107 (43)	20 (8)	12 (7)	27 (10)	7 (3)	41 (15)
27.	Koppal	83 (33)	13 (6)	6 (4)	22 (8)	5 (2)	37 (13)
	Total	**3255 (1375)**	**583 (252)**	**244 (182)**	**876 (361)**	**217 (71)**	**1335 (509)**

Note: Figures in brackets indicate seats reserved in favour of women.

Source: State Election Commission Office, Bangalore.

Table 13.4: Abstract of Reservation of Seats for Women in Zilla Panchayat Constituencies

Sl. No.	District Name	No. of Seats	SC	ST	A	B	Gen.
1.	Bangalore (U)	17 (7)	4 (2)	1 (1)	5 (2)	1 (1)	6 (2)
2.	Bangalore (R)	38 (15)	8 (3)	1 (1)	10 (4)	3 (1)	16 (6)
3.	Chitradurga	31 (12)	7 (3)	6 (2)	8 (3)	2 (1)	8 (3)
4.	Davangere	31 (13)	7 (3)	4 (2)	8 (3)	2 (1)	10 (4)
5.	Kolar	47 (16)	13 (5)	4 (2)	13 (5)	3 (1)	14 (5)
6.	Shimoga	27 (10)	5 (2)	1 (1)	7 (2)	2 (1)	12 (4)
7.	Tumkur	52 (19)	10 (4)	4 (2)	14 (5)	3 (1)	21 (7)
8.	Chikmagalur	30 (12)	6 (2)	1 (1)	8 (3)	2 (1)	13 (5)
9.	Dakshina Kannada	31 (12)	2 (1)	2 (1)	8 (3)	2 (1)	17 (6)
10.	Udupi	24 (10)	1 (1)	1 (1)	6 (2)	2 (1)	14 (5)
11.	Hassan	37 (14)	7 (3)	1 (1)	10 (3)	2 (1)	17 (6)
12.	Kodagu	26 (9)	3 (1)	2 (1)	7 (2)	2 (1)	12 (4)
13.	Mandya	39 (15)	5 (2)	1 (1)	10 (4)	3 (1)	20 (7)
14.	Mysore	41 (15)	8 (3)	1 (1)	11 (4)	3 (1)	18 (6)
15.	Chamarajanagar	21 (9)	5 (2)	1 (1)	6 (2)	1 (1)	8 (3)
16.	Belgaum	76 (27)	9 (3)	2 (1)	20 (7)	5 (2)	40 (14)
17.	Bijapur	32 (12)	6 (2)	1 (1)	9 (3)	2 (1)	14 (5)
18.	Bagalkot	26 (10)	4 (2)	1 (1)	8 (2)	2 (1)	12 (4)
19.	Dharwad	18 (8)	1 (1)	1 (1)	5 (2)	1	10 (4)
20.	Gadag	17 (7)	3 (1)	1 (1)	5 (2)	1	7 (3)
21.	Haveri	29 (12)	4 (2)	2 (1)	8 (3)	2 (1)	13 (5)
22.	Uttara Kannada	35 (13)	3 (1)	1 (1)	10 (3)	2 (1)	19 (7)
23.	Bellary	32 (12)	7 (3)	3 (1)	9 (3)	2 (1)	11 (4)
24.	Bidar	26 (9)	6 (2)	3 (1)	7 (2)	2 (1)	8 (3)
25.	Gulbarga	55 (19)	14 (5)	3 (1)	14 (5)	4 (1)	20 (7)
26.	Raichur	29 (11)	6 (2)	3 (1)	8 (3)	2 (1)	10 (4)
27.	Koppal	23 (9)	4 (2)	2 (1)	6 (2)	2 (1)	9 (3)
	Total	**890 (339)**	**158 (63)**	**54 (31)**	**239 (84)**	**60 (25)**	**379 (136)**

Note: Figures in brackets indicate seats reserved in favour of women.

Source: State Election Commission Office, Bangalore.

Table 13.5: Number of Women Representatives in Gram Panchayats, Taluka Panchayats (Block Samitis) and Zilla Panchayats in Karnataka

Particulars	*Numbers*
I. Gram Panchayats	
1. Number of Gram Panchayats	5659
2. Total number of members	80627
3. Total number of women members	38305
4. Percentage of women members	43.80
II. Taluka Panchayats (Block Samitis)	
1. Number of Taluka Panchayat	75
2. Number of members	3340
3. Number of women members	1343
4. Percentage of women members	40.20
III. Zilla Panchayats	
1. Number of Zilla Panchayats	27
2. Total number of members	919
3. Number of women members	335
4. Percentage of women members	36.50

Source: 'Karnataka Vikas', Rajyotsava Sanchike, Special Issue, State Rural Development and Panchayati Raj Ministry, Bangalore, November 2000, p. 24.

the directions of Karnataka High Court, announced the list of reservation of posts of Presidents and Vice-presidents to urban local bodies on 6th June, 2001.

Table 13.7 shows reservation of seats for the posts of Presidents in Urban Local Bodies.

Conclusion

Though there are a number of obstacles like family status, caste, class, finance, education, etc., for the participation of women in politics, still they hold important positions in corporations like Mayor, Deputy Mayor, Chairpersons and members of different committees. This is the result of the implementation of 33 per cent of reservation for women at the grassroots level politics. The increased political participation of women is due to urbanisation, democratic education and modernisation. This has substantially contributed in developing political orientation among women. The implementation of reservation policy has increased the number

Table 13.6: District-wise Abstract of Local Bodies

Sl. No.	Name of the District	No. of ULBs					No. of Wards	Female	No. of PS	Total Population	No. of Voters		
		Corpn.	CMC	TMC	TP	Total					Men	Women	Total
1.	Bangalore (U)	01	07	02	–	10	305	114	3741	4099447	1724265	1519013	3243278
2.	Bangalore (R)	–	03	05	01	08	230	85	349	328741	151437	141286	292723
3.	Chitradurga	–	01	02	03	03	124	48	245	223919	95811	91847	187658
4.	Davangere	–	02	–	04	02	127	51	415	439474	178484	166068	344552
5.	Kolar	–	04	05	03	09	284	112	519	522674	205468	198157	403625
6.	Shimoga	–	02	02	04	04	169	67	422	419638	194759	184097	378856
7.	Tumkur	–	01	05	04	06	212	84	419	401699	167675	156110	323785
8.	Mysore	01	–	03	04	04	193	77	762	781494	357148	335059	692207
9.	Chamarajanagar	–	01	02	01	03	92	35	120	135220	52075	50522	102597
10.	Chikmagalur	–	01	02	05	03	141	58	219	181098	80764	73509	154273
11.	Hassan	–	01	04	03	05	169	64	250	255503	110522	105521	216043
12.	Mandya	–	01	03	03	04	154	57	230	245821	102030	94956	196986
13.	Kodagu	–	–	03	–	03	48	20	50	50786	19945	17739	37684
14.	Belgaum	01	02	07	06	10	378	146	618	738299	303003	287437	590440
15.	Bijapur	–	01	04	01	05	147	55	329	307804	123370	113043	236413
16.	Bagalkot	–	02	05	05	07	270	103	378	415292	142527	139885	282412
17.	Dharwad	01	–	01	04	02	153	59	707	735954	285208	261466	546674
18.	Gadag	–	01	03	05	04	187	73	251	297957	109458	107556	217014
19.	Haveri	–	01	04	03	05	179	67	220	256742	86329	79777	166106
20.	Uttara Kannada	–	03	02	06	05	231	89	277	307359	104760	97585	202345
21.	Gulbarga	01	–	07	04	08	279	105	581	599227	252143	235489	487632
22.	Bellary	–	02	01	07	03	228	91	544	558540	225488	213210	438698
23.	Bidar	–	01	05	–	06	145	55	234	271357	112652	95932	208584
24.	Raichur	–	01	02	03	03	138	52	294	300358	131354	125901	257255
25.	Koppal	–	01	01	02	02	84	34	146	143348	56250	51701	107951
26.	Udipi	–	–	02	–	02	81	31	146	157208	58020	59142	117162
27.	D. Kannada	01	–	02	05	03	116	46	144	165099	57762	58369	116131
	Total	**06**	**40**	**84**	**86**	**216**	**4864**	**1878**	**12610**	**13412652**	**5554959**	**5053379**	**10608338**

Table 13.6: *(Contd.)*

Sl. No.	*Local Bodies*	*Nos.*	*No. of Wards*		*No. of Polling Stations*
1.	Corporations	06	Gen.	4864	12610
2.	CMCs	40	Female	1878	
3.	TMCs	84			
4.	TPs	86			
	Total	**216**			

Source : State Election Commission Office, Bangalore.

Table 13.7: Reservation of Seats for the Post of Presidents in Urban Local Bodies

Categories	*General*	*Women*	*Total*
I. City Municipal Councils (CMCs)[1]			
Scheduled Castes	04	02	06
Scheduled Tribes	--	01	01
Other Backward Classes (A)	07	03	10
Other Backward Classes (B)	02	01	03
General	13	07	20
Total	**26**	**14**	**40**
II. Town Municipal Councils (TMCs)[2]			
Scheduled Castes	09	04	13
Scheduled Tribes	01	01	02
Other Backward Classes (A)	14	07	21
Other Backward Classes (B)	04	02	06
General	24	13	37
Total	**52**	**26**	**79**
III. Taluka Panchayats (TPs)[3]			
Scheduled Castes	10	05	15
Scheduled Tribes	02	01	03
Other Backward Classes (A)	15	08	23
Other Backward Classes (B)	04	02	06
General	28	14	42
Total	**59**	**30**	**89**

Sources: 1. *Samykta Karnataka (Kannada) Daily*, dated 4.12.2001.
2. *Deccan Herald Daily*, dated 4.12.2001.
3. *Deccan Herald Daily*, dated 4.12.2001.

of women in local politics but not the quality. Hence to make the participation of women more effective in the grassroots politics as decision-makers the following measures may be taken into consideration:

1. Educated, elected women representatives can better represent the aspirations of women and such representatives can monitor the functioning of local government.
2. The proceedings should be simple and transparent to enable the women representatives to understand their implications for local administration.
3. Only elected women members should be allowed to attend the meetings and proceedings but not by their husbands, sons, brothers and son-in-laws, etc.

4. Some training programme for elected women representatives is necessary to ensure awareness about their duties and responsibilities.
5. In the beginning, the performance of the women members as decision-makers may not be satisfactory; but in the long run it will serve the purpose. In spite of this, it is the responsibility of the governmental and non-governmental organisations to make efforts to organise creative activities to promote political awareness among women.

This study is not conclusive; but it points to the need for extensive and intensive study of the functioning of the elected women representatives in local governing institutions.

NOTES AND REFERENCES

1. R.P. Joshi and G.S. Narwani, *Panchayat Raj in India: Emerging Trends Across the States,* New Delhi, Rawat Publications, 2002, pp. 35-40.
2. Joshi and Narwani, op. cit., p. 34.
3. *Deccan Herald* daily dated 19th January, 2003.
4. Joshi and Narwani, op. cit., pp. 55-56.
5. *Deccan Herald,* 16th September, 2002.
6. *Women's Link,* Vol. 2, April-June 1958, New Delhi.
7. *Provisional Population totals of Census 2001,* Directorate of Census Operations, Karnataka, Bangalore.

14

District Administration in Karnataka

Prospect and Retrospect

S.M. JAAMDAR

Origin of District Administration

For a large territory comprised under a single political unit, some territorial divisions seem inevitable for the convenience of routine administration. The imperial Mouryas, Guptas and Moghuls had within their empires several provinces, and regions within provinces headed by feudal lords or army generals. The Kannada empires—the Kadamba, Chalukya, Rashtrakuta and Vijayanagar—had also provincial and regional units in their territories. The early Chalukyas named them as Desha and Mandala. Rashtrakutas called them Mandal, Vishaya or Nadu. Bahamanis who ruled over a large part of Karnataka organised their kingdom into Sarcars (districts) and Paraganas (taluks). As "administration" in these divisions primarily meant collection of land revenue, maintaining subservience to the king or emperor and occasionally, contributing to the war fund or sending local soldiers to war, the feudal nature of the organisation served well. Such historically "desi" units bear no more resemblance to the modern day concept of district. With distinctly demarcated boundaries, clearly delegated formal authority and systematically organized substate administrative units called "districts" are a creation of the British Rule in India. Such districts were created for the first time in Bengal by a Regulation of the British East India Company dated 14.5.1772 for collection of land revenue in the districts assigned to the Company. As collection of land revenue was the only important duty the head of the district was called "Collector". Over a period of time, the collector and their mentors began to take over one by one more administrative responsibilities in the assigned territories. From "diwani" to "fauzdari", from "administrative" to "political" the sphere of their influence and control spread to the effect of assuming full responsibility and establishing British Rule in a situation that has been described as chaotic. The British district administration brought order amidst chaos and laid foundation for the British Raj in India.

During the expansion and consolidation of the British Rule in India the district emerged as the main unit of administration. The British territories in the United Provinces (the present Uttar Pradesh), the Central Provinces (presently Madhya Pradesh), the Punjab, the Bombay Presidency, the Madras Presidency, etc., were all organized on the district pattern. It proved very successful.

The more and more princely states were annexed and as the British territory expanded, the colonial rulers established their control over vast areas from regionally convenient central locations. Such regions became districts and their central locations were made district headquarters. Districts were generally named after town where the main offices were situated and where a handful British officers wielded power and controlled administration. Reserve police units and often colonial army units were stationed in the district headquarters. Revenue collection was planned, co-ordinated and controlled from the district headquarters. Judicial Courts were also located at the district level. The three basic functions of the state—maintenance of law and order, administration of justice and collection of revenue—were effectively organized at the district level. The District Collector was collector of revenue; as District Magistrate he controlled police; and initially as District Judge he administered justice. Thus a strict, authoritarian and single man controlled district units and provided necessary strength and basis for effective collection and maintenance of highly centralized British Administration in India. Encouraged by this experiment, the district pattern was also introduced in other British colonies such as Burma, Ceylon, and some African countries. District administration is thus a structure from the colonial era.

As exigencies of the situation demanded, the British made convenient adjustments in their policy of annexing native states.

Indirect rule through native kings and chiefs became their policy after 1857. Within the British Provinces, areas comprised in the princely states governed by the local chiefs were left out of district jurisdiction. Such princely states were however controlled indirectly under the so-called Paramountcy doctrine, which in effect meant that the local princes should be subservient to the British Crown whose Viceroy in India would control the princes. A British Agent often designated as Regent or Resident or Commissioner was invariably posted to oversee the governance in the native princely states. Whenever princely administration went haywire or threatened British presence the commissioner took over the administration of the princely state (as in Mysore or later in Coorg). Often the enlightened and progressive princes voluntarily adopted British administrative patterns and legislation. The princely state of Mysore and the Nizam had adopted more or less the British style district administration in their territories although the rigour, manner and content varied widely. The district administration in Karnataka should therefore be examined within this historical context.

Districts in Karnataka

The reorganisation of states in India on a linguistic basis led to the establishment of Karnataka (New Mysore state) as a separate state in 1956. Kannada-speaking people were united into a single state of their own. Contiguous areas populated by Kannadigas, otherwise comprised into diverse and multiple political formations were merged together to form a new state: four districts of Bombay Presidency, two and a quarter districts of Madras Presidency, three districts of the Nizam state and Coorg—a tiny state under the direct control of the President—were merged with nine districts of the erstwhile princely state of Mysore. Thus at the time of its creation on 1st November, 1956, Karnataka then called Mysore state had nineteen districts as its administrative units within a total area of 1,91,791 square kilometers comprising 2,14,20,000 citizens.

Period of Consolidation

Political unification was easier and faster. But effecting consequent administrative uniformity in all the unified regions was more difficult and time consuming. Hurried enforcement of uniformity in laws, rules, administrative organization, designations of hierarchical positions, changing delegation of powers and the like would have disrupted the existing arrangements causing confusion among the people long accustomed to an old systems. It took nearly ten years to enact uniform revenue laws, police laws, jail manual, commercial tax laws, co-operation law, municipal laws, etc. In respect of religious and charitable institutions there are still five different laws applicable to the old regions. Old survey and settlement systems are regionally still different. Existence of uniform central laws relating to criminal and civil justice, police, prisons, probation, juvenile justice, forests, personal laws in respect of marriage, divorce, succession and partnership, trusts, transfer of property, sale of goods, contract law, company law, industrial disputes, registration, stamps, etc., helped in establishing uniformity in the British districts and the districts of former princely states. Similarly, the newly started community development pattern of development administration throughout the country was handy in the creation of uniform institutions for development in the nascent state. From 1956 to about 1966 was thus a period of consolidation of district administration in Karnataka. Consolidation, however, did not alter the area, size, name, or the number of districts. It gradually introduced uniform state laws and rules, designations, pay scales and service conditions.

Reorganization of Districts

Most districts inherited at the time of the formation of Karnataka were too big in area and population and more complex in geographical features. Supervisory tasks and control over administration was more difficult in large districts, which adversely affected administrative efficiency. Moreover, people's participation in administration was limited since a large number of people have had to compete for few elected posts. Often devolution of central funds on the basis of number of districts and Community Development Blocks in the state would be reduced if the districts and Community Development Blocks are fewer because of larger size. Attempts were made to reorganise the districts in Karnataka in the 1970s and 1980s. Gaddigouda Committee and later Hundekar Committee recommended formation of new districts by dividing bigger districts, particularly Dharwad, Belgaum, Bijapur, Gulbarga, Raichur, Mysore, Tumkur and Chitradurg.

In 1986 Bangalore district was divided into Bangalore Rural and Bangalore Urban districts. Bangalore Urban district does not have Zilla Panchayat. Instead, District Rural Development Society looks after the development programmes in three rural taluks—namely, Anekal, Bangalore South and Bangalore North. The Bangalore City Corporation and Bangalore Development Authority manage urban areas.

In 1997 the State Government effected major reorganisation of districts in the state. Seven new districts were created. Bagalkot, Chamarajnagar, Devangere, Gadag, Haveri, Koppal and Udupi became new and compact districts, reducing the size of their previous districts, namely, Bijapur, Chitradurga, Dharwad, Bellary, Raichur, Shimoga, Mysore and Mangalore. The proposed division of Gulbarga and Belgaum districts and the creation of Yadgir and Chikkodi districts was deferred due to dissention and political protests as these two are sensitive border districts. At the present there are twenty seven districts in Karnataka.

The recent reorganisation of districts has made most districts moderate in size: nineteen of the twenty seven districts have seven or fewer taluks. Only five districts have ten or eleven taluks which will be targets for the next division of districts: these are Gulbarga, Belgaum, Tumkur, Kolar and Uttar Kannada districts. (The last one is smaller in population and bigger in area most of which is covered by Wetern Ghats on the one side and the west coast on the other.) The latest picture of districts in Karnataka is shown in the map.

Administrative Culture in Different Districts

The district administration in the newly amalgamated Karnataka presented three distinct politico-administrative cultures. Bombay and Madras Karnataka and, to some extent, Coorg had the British style administration—a strict rule-based rational bureaucracy of Weberian Ideal type. It was a more rigorous administration; civil servants were more punctual, efficient and disciplined; corruption was not so ubiquitous or visible; punishment for defaults was swift,

KARNATAKA
ADMINISTRATIVE DIVISIONS, 2001

Source: Census of Karnataka, 2001.

Table 14.1: The Range of Diversity in 1955-56 in Different Regions of Karnataka

	Bombay Karnataka	*Hyderabad Karnataka*	*Madras Karnataka*	*Kodagu Karnataka*	*Mysore Karnataka*
Area (sq. kms.)	52526	35647	11173	4118	85158
Population (lakhs)	56.70	30.01	16.23	2.53	108.73
Literacy Enrollment	22.3	08.5	23.3	27.2	20.6
- 6 - 11 years	79.2	27.2	74.8	83.8	48.9
- 11 - 14 years	27.8	13.0	30.8	43.2	27.0
Area per primary school (sq. kms.)	8.80	17.09	8.55	18.65	6.73
Population per primary school	931	1434	1250	1146	865
Population per secondary school	44290	166629	25123	23026	40.876
Area per college sq. kms	5793	11882	2794	4118	3276
Population (lakhs) per college	7.1	10.0	4.1	2.5	4.2
Road length per sq. kms. of area	55.9	22.3	67.3	68.1	95.0

Source: Gazetteer of Karnataka 1983.

certain and severe. The civil servants' loyalty was relatively unsuspect. People feared the government and almost every government servant. Since government was largely limited to collection of revenue and maintenance of law and order, it was a smooth administration except for sporadic acts of violence or deliberate refusal to pay taxes during the struggle for independence. The second pattern may be seen in the princely state of Mysore where administration was orderly but not as rigorous as in British districts. Administration was reorganised several times at district and sub-district and taluka levels. People's involvement was considerable. Rich and powerful people were recognized for their contribution to social service and philanthropy. There were also representatives of the people in the Mysore Representative Assembly and later in the Council as well. As the Maharaja was a Hindu and native, people showed more respect to the government than fear. More prosperity and development contributed to the pride of the people and stability of administration. A clear third pattern was in Hyderabad area where administration was lax-it lacked discipline and rigour. Later the parochialism and attempts to muslimize ruined it further. Being the neglected districts in the periphery of Nizam state, people neither respected the government nor feared it. Critical poverty, famines and epidemics made it a minimally governed area.

Table 14.2: Varying Features of Old District Administration

Area	*Designation of district head*	*Language of administration/ education*	*Degree of effectiveness*	*Economic condition*
Mysore	Deputy Commissioner	Kannada	Orderly	Prosperous
Bombay Karnataka	Collector	Marathi	Rigorous	Less developed
Madras Karnataka	Collector	Tamil	Rigorous	Less developed
Coorg	Commissioner	English/Kannada/ Coorgi	Rigorous	Prosperous
Hyderabad Karnataka	Talukdar	Urdu	Lax	Poor

Even after half a century of unified administration, the pre-unification politico-administrative cultures have not vanished. The impact of administration varies in these regions. More politicisation of administration is seen in Mysore area. Laxity still reigns high in Hyderabad Karnataka. There is still more discipline in administration in Madras and Bombay Karnataka districts. Influence of Urdu, Marathi, Telugu and Tamil has dwindled except in revenue records and nomenclature. Kannada as spoken in these regions is marked by regionally specific accent, intonation and mixture of Marathi, Urdu and Telugu words. People of one district or region would not like to work in other regions of Karnataka. One can discern the dislike of government staff for postings in other regions. Not only category 'C' and 'D' employees but also senior officers in A and B categories, Karnataka Administrative Service and the Indian Administrative Service also do not prefer working in Hyderabad Karnataka. Consequently at the district level in most departments, notably health, public works department, irrigation, sericulture, industries and agriculture a large number of posts are vacant which adversely affects implementation of government programmes. Conversely, in South Karnataka districts, particularly, Bangalore, Mysore and Mangalore, government offices are overstaffed with deputationists who do not move out of these districts. This relative lack of mixing among regionally specific "sub-cultures" of administration has resulted in the continuance of old patterns even to this day. Differential development of the regions may be attributed, to an extent, to the varying degrees of administrative efficiency.

Backward and Forward Districts

Compared to the Mysore area, economic backwardness of north Karnataka is more glaring. The four districts of Bombay Karnataka and the three districts of Hyderabad Karnataka are on the border of the former states they belonged to. They were most neglected and under-developed. This sense of deprivation has made those people fight for their unification with Mysore state. When their fight ended in victory they obviously felt exuberant. Contrary to this, the people of the princely Mysore state were highly apprehensive of the formation of wider Karnataka fearing that such unification with poorer but larger areas from "outside" would reduce their own prosperity and progress. Notwithstanding the heated debates against unification in the Mysore Representative Assembly, the greater Karnataka with nineteen districts came into existence on 1st November, 1956 as a fait accompli of the national and natural policy of linguistic states. The new state was baptized as "Mysore State" and the Maharaja of Mysore was made its governor or Raj Pramukh. This was as much to appease the Mysore people as to acknowledge their biggest size, their better off position and influence apart from recognising Mysore as the bastion of Kannada and its culture. Nobody imagined then that this sense of "superiority" and "inferiority", "progressive" and "backward" would one day threaten the unity of Karnataka (as it seems now !).

After nearly four decades of unification the people of north Karnataka districts have sensed that the pace of their development is much slower and lower than that in the southern districts. By the mid-1980s the regional imbalance in development had become a major issue. Discontent in northern districts began to be expressed openly. This led to the creation in the 1990s of the regional development authorities like the Hyderabad Karnataka Development Board followed by the Malnad Area Development Board and the Bayaluseema Development Board virtually covering all districts. That the creation of these bodies was a farce became clear as they could not change the situation much. To arrest the growing discontent, a high power committee has been appointed by the government to check the regional imbalances. In its interim report (February 2001) the committee has recommended sectoral approach at taluka level instead of district level to set right the imbalanced development process. It has suggested that in each sector-education, health, welfare, etc., special allocation of funds and enhanced targets should be made to backward taluks until they reach the infrastructure on part with the developed taluks. If infrastructure is the only factor for their backwardness, certainly they would develop faster. However, the issue is more complex and begs more indepth analysis. The Human Development Index among the districts shows the wide range of variation in northern and southern districts (Please see the map which contains Human Development Index and Gender Development Index).

MAP OF KARNATAKA STATE

Parentheses show ranks of districts

Source: Human Development Index in Karnataka, 1999

Kannada Medium in District Administration

In the newly formed linguistic state, Kannada, the foundation language and its attendant culture, varied widely. Kannadigas had enjoyed longer periods of political unity in Indian history under the Kannada empires of Kadambas (345 A.D. to 540 A.D.), Chalukya (500 A.D. to 757 A.D.), Rashtrakuta (753 A.D. to 937 A.D.), and Vijayanagar (1336 A.D. to 1572 A.D.) empires. Later the fragmentation of the area and their accession to the areas adjoining resulted in being dominated by other languages and in distortion of their language, and has induced wide regional variations in the culture. Marathi, for instance, was the medium of education and administration in Bombay Karnataka. Similarly, Urdu was the official language of Hyderabad Karnataka. In Madras Karnataka, Tamil dominated in Bellary, Mangalore districts and Kollegal taluka. The cultures of these dominant linguistic groups had also influenced the otherwise Kannada "original". Having escaped from such domination, Mysore Kannada remains chaste and superior. The dominance of Marathi, Urdu and Tamil was clearly visible since they were the media in schools and offices of the respective areas. Old records were in those languages. Subsequently, English virtually replaced these languages. Kannada as such remained at the conversation level. In the initial years after unification of the state linguistic chauvinism and sons of the soil notions were not noticeable. Instead, old Mysoreans ostentatiously claimed their sense of cultural superiority over the newly merged areas. It was thus merely a collage of divergent cultures brought together by a common language-though not so common then.

From 1956 to 1985, for nearly three decades, it is an irony to observe that in a linguistic Kannada state, Kannada was not the medium of administration. English was the lingua franca. This led to the appointment of Kannada Watchdog Committee to enforce complete use of Kannada at all levels of administration in the 1980s which revolutionised the scene. Old Mysore districts were quick to adopt Kannada whereas northern districts lagged behind for nearly a decade. In the 1990s Kannada replaced English as the medium of administration except in the Courts. This had a salutary effect in bringing district administration closer to the people and reducing official secrecy. Invention of Kannada typewriters and Kannada computer software has helped faster Kannadization.

Varying Patterns of District Administration

In the years following independence, the first generation of Indian leaders did not see the necessity for tinkering with the style of district administration. The institution of the District Collector was well respected and accepted. There was no easy and viable alternative. Although Gandhiji spoke of Gram Raj and Panchayati Raj there were hardly any democratically constituted Panchayats or experience of running them on democratic lines. Moreover, the need for political cohesion, unity and centralization was more paramount than localization and decentralization. More than five hundred sixty princely states and British territories were reorganised into just fourteen states and nine Union Territories— an act of a highly centralised system. Districts based on centralised control and single line of command were also felt to be far more effective. Thus after independence District Administration Pattern not only continued unaffected but it was further expanded and strengthened. More and more departments were created and their pattern followed the familiar revenue department system. Agriculture department was divided to form separate departments for Sericulture, Horticulture and Fisheries. Newly created Welfare Department spawned several separate departments: Labour Welfare, Social Welfare, Tribal Welfare, Women and Child Welfare, Backward Classes and Minorities Welfare. Education Department was further reorganised into Primary and Secondary Education Department, Department of Collegiate Education, and Directorate of Technical Education. All these departments have their control and coordination functions located at the district level and invariably linked laterally to the coordinative control of the Deputy Commissioner.

While almost all departmental officers are under the control of their respective department or directorate they are subject to the lateral control of the Deputy Commissioner of the District who is also designated as a Major Head of the Department with disciplinary powers over almost every department of the government. Such general powers enable the Deputy Commissioner to exercise general supervision of the entire administration of the district. He can inspect any district or sub-district level office except courts. He can suspend any class-III official. He writes remarks in the annual confidential reports of

Typical Departmental Organisation Chart: Vertical and Lateral Controls

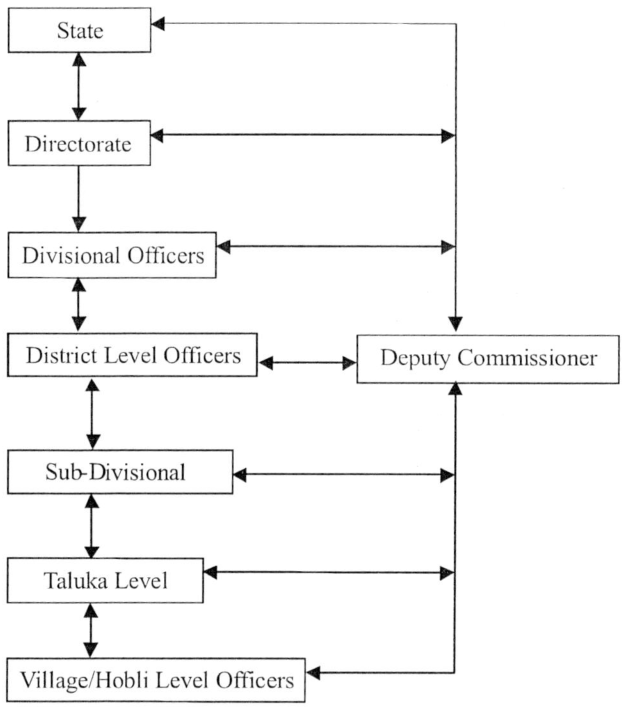

the district level officers of almost all departments. He presides over the meetings of nearly thirty different committees. He coordinates several developmental programmes. Conducting all kinds of elections, maintenance of peace, collection of any governmental dues, management of crises like epidemics, floods, famines, earthquakes and other natural and man-made disasters are basically the functions of the Deputy Commissioner. In such multifarious tasks he galvanises all concerned departments as a leader of complete administration. He represents the government at the district level.

In the 1950s Community Development Programmes and the Panchayat Raj system were introduced in Karnataka like elsewhere in the country. While at the village and taluka levels Panchayats were created and developmental roles and programmes were transferred to these bodies, at the district level the Deputy Commissioner was the Chairman of the District Development Council. All presidents of Taluka Development Boards, MLAs and MPs of the district were its members. Planning, coordination, supervision of all development programmes continued to be done by the Deputy Commissioner assisted by the District Development Assistant. This pattern continued until the early 1980s.

By the 1980s the Panchayats were found ineffective, Community Development movement had almost died down. Poverty was not reduced. More poverty alleviation programmes such as Integrated Rural Development Programme, Small Farmer Development Agency, Marginal Farmer and Agricultural Labourer Development Programme, Rural Landless Labourer Employment Guarantee Programme, and Nehru Rozgar Yojana were introduced. Area development programmes like Desert Development Programme, Drought Prone Area Development Programme, National Rural Employment Programme, etc., were also reorganised. The lapsing of funds at the end of the year if unspent was a routine phenomenon. To overcome this problem District Rural Development Societies were created at the district level. The Deputy Commissioner was made its chairman. Another senior officer from the Indian Administrative Service was posted to implement these programmes through DRDS. Most of the functions of the DDC were performed by the DRDS. All these were within the framework of the Deputy Commissioner as the head of the entire district administration. Indeed, there was loud thinking on the desirability of creating separate cadre or organisation for development administration. But the emphasis in such thinking was still on the administrative machinery with specialized skills and knowledge.

After 1985

In the mid-1980s the change of guard took place in Karnataka. For the first time a non-Congress government came into power. The Janata Party government was more pro-people oriented and emphasised less bureaucracy. A paradigmatic shift took place at the district level administration. A two-tier Panchayat Raj System was created by law. Mandal Panchayats at below-taluka level and

Zilla Parishads at the district level were established through popular but partisan elections. Zilla Parishads were made responsible for all development administration. Government departments were grouped into "Development Departments" and "Regulatory Departments". Indeed nearly two-thirds of the government departments were brought within the ambit of "development" and placed under the control of the Zilla Panchayat. Thus, Education, Health, Social Welfare, Backward Classes and Minorities, Women and Child Welfare, Social Forestry, Rural Engineering and PHE Department, Co-operation, Sericulture, Horticulture, Agriculture, Fisheries, Animal Husbandry, Rural Electrification, Housing, Employment and Training, Dry Land Development, Minor Irrigation, Rural Industries and DIC, Youth Services and Sports, were placed under the control of the ZP. A senior IAS officer equal or often senior to DC headed the ZP administration within the over all control of the elected President and Council of the ZP. Only the Revenue Department, Food and Civil Supplies, Regional Transport Authority, Muzrai, Excise, Police, Jails, Registration, Survey and Settlement and Municipalities have remained with the Deputy Commissioner. There are certain departments like Commercial Taxes, Forest, Labour and PWD whose control at the district level has been left to their own departments and the control of the DC is at best negligible if not altogether absent. The powers of excise, registration, labour and police departments earlier delegated to the DC are now largely withdrawn leaving just a nominal role—more ceremonial than real. Only revenue, food and civil supplies, and municipalities are still considerably controlled by the DC although separate directorates are created for municipal administration as well for food and civil supplies.

Thus, Karnataka district administration today consists of two vertical systems: Development Administration controlled by the ZP independently and the Regulatory administration supervised by the DC as before though diluted. The powers of planning coordination, supervision and control over development departments at the district level delegated earlier to the DC are now transferred to the Chief Executive Officer of the ZP who also writes the confidential reports of those officers. These formal powers of the Chief Executive Officer are weakened by the "informal" manoeuvres of the elected members and Presidents

Current Organisation Chart of District Administration in Karnataka

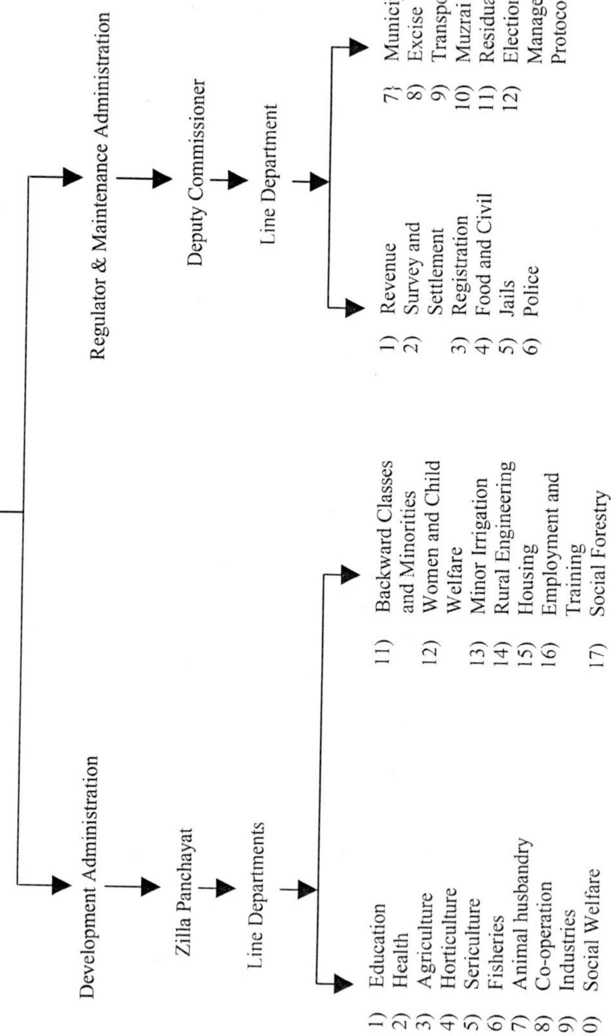

and Committees which often shield the erring officers for extraneous and parochial and often political reasons.

This reorganisation of administration at the district level in Karnataka has rendered the role, power and status of the yet most important Deputy Commissioner diminished considerably. Among the regulatory departments there is a growing tendency to make each department as independent and autonomous as possible. Deputy Commissioner's powers over Excise, Registration, Transport, and Police are largely taken away. Each department acts like a more watertight compartment.

At the same time developmental powers are squarely placed in the hands of elected representatives. The higher echelons of bureaucracy which had experienced "omnipotent" position and "*maibap*" image had to eat an humble pie. Further, they are to work under taluka and district level political leadership which makes the functioning more difficult. Initially there were apprehensions and misgivings. Senior and more experienced leaders who became presidents of Zilla Panchayat in the early years smoothened the ruffled feathers. But now the situation has been reversed. The recent change in the system of reserving positions of Presidents and Vice-presidents to different categories of members for a fixed term has introduced strange features. Most of the women members who become Presidents by virtue of reservation lack experience, courage and most often education and stature. Their position is misused by their husbands, fathers or brothers and not infrequently by other male officers. The situation is similar in case of illiterate, meek and inexperienced members belonging to SC, ST and Backward categories who become presidents by reservation rule. Administrative balance in the Zilla Panchayat is very precarious.

Crisis in District Administration

1. The immediate consequence of the dichotomous system of district administration in Karnataka is the lack of coordination and control of administration at the district level. The division of administration into "Departmental" and "Regulatory" is often illusory and artificial. Without normal conditions, peaceful existence and proper maintenance, implementation of development

programmes is rendered difficult if not impossible. Conversely, lack of infrastructure, imbalanced development or absence of development activities themselves create conditions which breed violence, riots, organised movements which cannot be easily resolved by simple police methods. People picketing for drinking water cannot be arrested like thieves. Students indulging in road blocking demanding better transport facilities cannot be treated like criminals. Hunger strikes organised for obtaining better schooling facilities or irrigation schemes or railways cannot be suppressed as anti-social. It requires balancing development with regulation. Proper and timely coordination between the Deputy Commissioner and Zilla Panchayat is essential.

2. Power to the people is one thing and power in the improper and inexperienced hands is quite another. Election law does not lay down minimum level of education or experience to contest elections. Anybody may get elected. By compulsory reservation, an illiterate, ignorant and incapable person may become the President. Such cases are increasing. The noble objective of "equal" treatment and upliftment of backward sections itself gets defeated. Programmes suffer. People do not get the benefits as intended. Unqualified reservation of the posts of Presidents is carrying equality argument to its illogical extreme.
3. Corruption in the pre-Zilla Panchayat was blamed entirely on the bureaucracy. In the last sixteen years of Zilla Panchayat existence, corruption has become all pervasive and rampant. Bureaucratic disease has infected a majority of elected members and office-bearers. Both are today partners in the nefarious and corrupt practices. Whether it is sanctioning of Janata Houses or house sites, Integrated Rural Development Programme loans or subsidy, special component scheme benefit or selection for training schemes, each beneficiary is to pay the rates fixed by the elected members. Indeed the targets fixed for the Zilla Panhayat/ Taluka Panchayat/Village Panchayat are divided among the members and it is the members who select eventually the "beneficiaries" and in the process many of

them derive the "benefit". Where sectarian interests are uppermost, "equality" before law has become a farce. Most of the civil works like formation or repair of roads, construction of buildings, bunds, bandharas and farm ponds provide abundant opportunities for self-enrichment. In the initial years contractors were fleeced by many members and officers. In recent years most of the members themselves act as contractors in the names of others. Consequently, both quality and quantity of work suffer apart from delay and cost escalation. Transparency in the Zilla Panchayat transactions and adoption of Information Technology have been recommended by the Administrative Reforms Commission (2000) to improve this situation.

4. People's expectations are rising to be juxtaposed by their non-fulfilment. Gram Sabhas in every village provide ample proof of people's frustration which find expression in the virulent verbal and occasionally physical attacks on the elected members of Zilla Panchayats, Taluka Panchayats and Village Panchayats. Zilla Panchayats have become a law unto themselves—neither do they care for the controls of the State Government nor for the criticism of the people. "Power to the people" has meant "power to the elected members". Lack of accountability and commensurate legal sanctions have made mockery of the democratic process.
5. The diminished role and status of the Deputy Commissioner has weakened regulatory administration. Each regulatory department has virtually become a watertight compartment. Lack of coordination, non-cohesive functioning and absence of accountability have rendered district administration in Karnataka very close to the ranks of so-called "BIMARU" states in India. The Karnataka Administrative Reforms Commission has therefore recommended that the position of the Deputy Commissioner should be strengthened and he be given more coordinative role and powers.
6. Failure of the administration to deliver basic services, rampant corruption, lack of transparency and accountability have led to the rise of Non-Governmental

Organisations and Civil Society groups the world over. The demand for reducing the bureaucracy and rolling back the frontiers of the state witnessed in developed countries is widely being imitated in many Third World Countries. Liberalization of trade and industry, privatization of services, outsourcing governmental services, reduction of bureaucracy, etc., are already visible in today's administration in Karnataka. At any case, the day when entire government itself is rendered unwanted and unnecessary will never come except in utopias. It is therefore necessary that early remedies are found for the ills of both the democratic set up and the bureaucratic apparatus at district level.

Conclusion

District administration, as invented by the British, was a contrivance more suited to the demands of colonial objectives. It was adopted by the native rulers since it was more efficient and effective in maintaining minimum administration—limited to maintenance of law and order, collection of revenue and administration of justice. In the initial period after independence, the need for consolidation and centralization were met adequately by the continuance of the old style district administration. Hence, no major changes were introduced in district administration in the first three decades.

District administration in Karnataka more or less followed similar trends in other states of India. First of all, at the time of creation of the new state, British districts were merged with districts of two princely states—Mysore, Hyderabad and Coorg. Such merger created a mixed culture of administration in different regions varying from extreme laxity to high order of rigidity in day to day administration. Effecting uniformity in rules, laws, procedures, designations, pay scales and orderly administration and consolidation was a long drawn and complicated process which took more than a decade in Karnataka to take shape. The legacy of backwardness of the newly merged districts compared to the old Mysore and Madras districts still continues to dog the administration. Several efforts at balanced development of all districts have not yet yielded sufficient results. However,

Kannadization of grass-roots administration has taken deeper roots in almost all districts.

The old style district administration—with heavy emphasis on the deputy commissioner—is altered significantly since mid-1980s. All development departments—nearly two-thirds of the—bureaucracy are brought under the control of the democratically elected Zilla Panchayats. The nine regulatory departments are continued under the supervisory control of the Deputy Commissioner. Thus a nearly unitary system of controlling all administrative departments at the district level is now rendered dichotomous—by separating development administration from regulatory administration. The former is largely participatory and controlled democratically while the latter is more bureaucratic and authoritarian.

15

Socio-Economic Bases of Karnataka Politics

A Historical Survey

S.H. PATIL

Social composition and the nature of economic system affect politics of a nation or a state. The politics of Karnataka state is no exception to this generalization and is determined by social composition and the nature of the economic system in addition to geography, infrastructure, historical legacy, elite structure, institutional set up, etc. Among other determinants of state politics, this article has concentrated on two determinants—social composition and the nature of economic system—which form important bases of state politics. Socio-economic determinants of state politics include caste composition, caste associations, linguistic and socio-cultural groups, ownership of economic means like land, industry and trade, economic pressure groups, etc. These constitute input of the state politics in Karnataka. They affect state politics in terms of socio-economic composition of state legislature, state ministry, zilla parishads, mandal panchayats, municipalities and corporations, choice of the Chief Minister, recruitment and composition of bureaucracy, policy of reservation, land reforms, language policy, party programme, etc. These structural and policy changes constitute output of the politics of Karnataka state.

Physical and Socio-economic Setting

Karnataka is an ancient part of Indian society and its areas were inhabited by people of the stone age, the instruments of which are found in some parts of the state. Karnataka had formed a part of

Ashokan empire and Ashokan inscriptions are found in some parts like Koppal. Its main language, Kannada, belongs to the Dravidian group of languages and its first inscription is found in the fifth century. Reference to the word, Karnataka, is found in Varaha Mihir's Brahatsanhita in the sixth century. Territorial boundaries of the Kannada-speaking people are described in the Kaviraj Marga of Nrupatunga of the tenth century. From the ancient to the medieval period areas of Karnataka were ruled by Satavahan, Kadamba, Chalukya, Rashtrakuta, Hoysal, Gang and Vijayanagar emperors for different periods. Among these some of the rulers of Chalukya, Rashtrakuta and Vijayanagar extended their rule well beyond the present boundaries of the state. After the medieval period, Muslim rulers of Bijapur, Bidar, and Hyderabad, the Wodeyars of Mysore, Hyder Ali and Tipu Sultan, small Maratha, Brahmin, Lingayat and Jain princes ruled. In the eighteenth and nineteenth centuries the British eliminated some rulers and established their direct rule in seven districts (Belgaum, Dharwad Karwar, Mangalore, Bellary and Coorg) but retained the Mysore Wodeyar dynasty in Mysore state and the small princes in Ramdurg, Jamkhandi, Mudhol, Sondur and Savanur, etc., with their suzerainty over those princely states. Three districts of Karnataka—Bidar, Gulbarga and Raichur—were under the Nizam's rule. Thus Kannada people were under nineteen administrative units.

As per the State Reorganisation Act, all these scattered areas (four districts from Bombay province, two districts from Madras province, one Chief Commissioner's province (called part 'C' state) and three districts from Hyderabad state and 9 districts from Mysore state (called part 'B' state) were brought under one administrative unit in 1956. With subsequent creation of one more district, strength of districts in Karnataka has gone up to twenty.

According to physical geography Karnataka state is divided into two parts—the Deccan plateau and the coastal plains and islands—and only two districts (Uttar Kannada and Dakshina Kannada) form coastal regions. The state receives its rainfall from the south-west monsoon and the retreating monsoon. The highest rainfall is received in Karwar (3,129 mm) and the lowest rainfall is received in Bellary (518 mm). The state economy is predominantly agricultural. The state is endowed with suitable climate, soil and rainfall. All kinds of crops are grown here. It has several major and minor irrigation projects like Tungabhadra, Ghataprapha, Malaprabha, Krishnaraj Sagar, Krishna, etc. In addition to these, farmers irrigate their lands from tanks, open wells and borewells. Area of irrigated land has increased. It was 8.4 per cent in 1960-61 but now it has gone up to 17 per cent in 1990-91.[1]

Karnataka state consists of 28 districts and covers an area of 1,91,791 sq. kms. According to the 1991 provisional census report, it has a population of 4,48,17,398. It is more rural than urban: is 3,09,55,766 (69.9%) *Versus* 1,38,50,702 (30.91%).[2] There are 29,400 villages and 306 towns according to the 1991 provisional census.

According to the 1991 provisional census report, 1,72,43,883 constitute the total working force (men and women) in Karnataka state; 59,24,533 are cultivators; 49,57,496 are agricultural labourers; 4,84,323 constitute household industry; and 58,77,531 are other workers.[3] Thus the cultivators constitute 34.36 per cent; agricultural labourers comprise 28.75 per cent; people in household industry form 2.81 per cent; and other workers account for 34.08 per cent. People engaged in industry constitute a small number compared to the number of people engaged in agriculture. Their number was 77,79,000 in 1989-90 and number of factories were 4,441 in 1989-90. According to the provisional census of 1991, workers constitute 41.83 per cent and non-working constitute 58.17 per cent. Per capita income of Karnataka state is Rs.3,602-00 at current prices and is below the national per capita income (Rs. 3,835.00).

Languages spoken in Karnataka are Kannada (65.97%), Urdu (9.00%), Telegu (8.18%), Marathi (4.05%), Tamil (3.38%), Malayalam (1.45%) and Tulu, Konkani and others (7.97%) according to the 1971 census report.[4] According to the census report of 1971, Kannada-speaking people in Bangalore city and Trust Board Area constitute 50.37 per cent with those in Belgaum city form 56.76 per cent. Both are seats of linguistic politics.

Total number of male literates is 1,28,799 (67.25%) and female literates are 81,94,121 (44.24%). The effective literacy is 55.98 per cent according to the provisional census of 1991.

Karnataka racial composition is a mixture of Dravidian, Aryan and aboriginal groups. The Hindus constitute more than 80 per cent while Muslims, Christians, Jains, Buddhists, etc., account for the rest. The following is the table showing caste/region-wise based on Nagangowada Committee Report of 1976.[5]

Table 15.1

Sl. No.	*Caste/Religion*	*Percentage*
1.	Lingayats*	16.57
2.	Scheduled Castes	13.31
3.	Vokkaligas	12.91
4.	Muslims	10.02
5.	Kurubas	06.08
6.	Bedas	04.74
7.	Brahmins	04.28
8.	Remaining religions and castes' population ranges between 0.21% and 2.40%	32.30

* The Lingayats maintain that their percentage is more 15.57%. As the Census enumerators have taken some sub-castes of Lingayats into general Hindu category, the total percentage of Lingayats has gone down, opine Lingayat leaders. There is controversy whether the Lingayats constitute a separate religious group or form a part of Hindu religion.

Political Mobilization

Before 1920 political mobilization for independence was mainly confined to the Brahmins in Bombay Karnataka and Madras Karnataka and the Congress Party was considered as a party of Brahmins. The non-Brahmin movement organised by the Lingayats, Voklaligas and other middle castes and influenced by Justice Party and Dravid Kazagam in Madras province and non-Brahmin movement in southern part of Bombay province was active in Bombay Karnataka, Madras Karnataka and Mysore state. It aimed at the spread of education, entry into civil service and general upliftment of the middle castes. Some of the middle castes did establish educational institutions. Among these, the Lingayats took a leading role and established a number of educational institutions and free boarding and lodging (prasad nilayas) for students. Hyderabad Karnataka and Coorg were politically dormant. To press the claims of the non-Brahmins in civil service and political institutions, Praja Mitra Mandali was established in 1917 in Mysore state.[6]

After 1920 and with entry of Gandhiji in the national movement, the middle castes like Lingayats and Vokkaligas and some upper strata of backward castes joined the national movement in Bombay Karnataka, Hyderabad Karnataka, Madras

Karnataka and Coorg. The Mysore State Congress, a local organisation, was established to secure a responsible government. It worked under the guidance of the Indian National Congress and had also identified itself with the freedom struggle in the rest of India.[7] In small princely states like Ramdurg, Jamkhandi, Mudhol, Savanur and Sondur, Praja Mandals/Praja Sanghas were formally or informally established under the guidance and control of the Congress. Agitation in a small princely state like Ramdurg drew the attention of Gandhiji who wrote an article on it in 1939.[8] The Hyderabad Karnataka people worked for responsible government in Hyderabad state under the leadership of its Congress party (established in 1938) and Swami Ramanand Tirtha who in turn worked under the guidance of the Indian National Congress. They also fought against the atrocities of Razakars. The people of Bellary and Mangalore (South Canara) in Madras province and of Coorg participated in the freedom movement under the banner of the Indian National Congress.

Though the Kannada people were divided into five administrative units, they were united in the freedom movement and the struggle for responsible government. Before 1920, the Congress was dominated by the Brahmins and was confined to the towns and cities. With the entry of the middle castes like Lingayats and Vokkaligas and upper strata of backward castes, the Congress movement reached the villages. The leaders from these middle castes who had come from the villages and had roots in them were successful in mobilizing the rural people in the national movement through folk songs, kirtanas and other popular media. A constructive leader like Hardekar Manjappa, known as Karnataka Gandhi, immensely contributed in awakening the middle castes in general and the Lingayats of Bombay Karnataka in particular for participation in constructive work and freedom struggle.[9] The political mobilization in Karnataka was a part of national mobilization on secular lines. Thus the Congress became a vehicle of political mobilization in Karnataka and has continued to do so even today. With the emergence of Indira Gandhi's leadership in Indian politics, the social base of the Congress was further widened by 1971 and it was demonstrated in the 1971 parliamentary elections. Thus the social base of the Congress Party has been widening from the early 1920s to the present day. The process of politicisation started with the Brahmins in the early

1920s and has taken in its fold the people belonging to the scheduled castes and the scheduled tribes. Now the cycle of politicisation by the Congress has been completed.

Along with the national mobilization for freedom, there was a sectarian but secular mobilization for the unification of Karnataka. It was Kannada literary men who took initiative in starting a movement for the unification of fragmented Kannada-speaking areas. Unification movement got institutional support with the establishment of Kannada Sahitya Parishad in 1915. In terms of caste support for the movement of unification, early initiation came from the Brahmins and later on literary men from Lingayat, Vokkaliga and others took up the cause. Subsequently political leaders and political activists joined the movement for unification. Thus the Kannada people from the various regions had been demanding for a separate Karnataka province since 1916 under the auspices of various organisations like Karnataka Vidyavardhak Sangh, Dharwad, Karnataka Ekikaran Samiti, etc.[10] The movement for unification served as a vehicle for political education. It also gave rise to the emergence of vibrant Kannada literature and linguistic politics.

The movement for unification continued even after independence. Among the various sections and castes, the Lingayats took a leading role in the unification movement in the post-independent period. The Lingayat community which is socially, economically and numerically dominant observed mechanism of parliamentary institutions in the fragmented parts of Karnataka. Some of its leaders became aware of their marginal position in the politics of Bombay and Madras provinces and Hyderabad and Mysore states. They felt that their community could play a dominant role with its numerical strength and dominant position in unified Karnataka. Hence they actively supported unified Karnataka. The Vokkaliga caste which was socially, economically, numerically and politically dominant in the old Mysore state was to become a second force in the politics of united Karnataka. Hence some of the leaders of this caste who were ardent supporters of the movement before independence became inactive in the post-independent period. They feared that the Lingayat community would dominate. What the Vokkaliga leaders feared came true. Before unification three Vokkaligas leaders—K.C. Reddy (1947-1952), K. Hanumantaiah (1952-1956) and Kadidal Manjappa (1956) were Chief Ministers of the old Mysore state. The Vokkalinga leadership had to give way for Lingayat leadership. S. Nijalingappa (Lingayat) became a Chief Minister. Thus unification of Karnataka brought about change in the social composition of the ruling Congress party, state politics and administration.

Domination of Dominant Community (1956-1971)

The Lingayat community which is socially, economically and numerically strong dominated the politics of unified Karnataka state from 1956 to 1971. During this period four Chief Ministers (S. Nijalingappa, S.R. Kanthi, B.D. Jatti and Veerendra Patil) were Lingayats. Nijalingappa became the President of the Indian National Congress during 1967-69. Old Lingayat educational institutions like the KLE Society, the BLD Society, etc., undertook expansion and diversification of educational institutions and a number of local Lingayat educational institutions came up during this period. There was no doubt that other communities/castes were also encouraged to establish educational institutions but the Lingayat educational institutions took a leading role in this sector. A large number of Lingayat youths joined the state services. The Lingayats took a leading role in establishing/managing co-operative institutions, urban banks and local institutions like panchayats and municipalities. They surpassed the Brahmins in administration and the Vokkaligas in the politics. Their domination in education, business, politics, co-operative and local self-governing institutions and the Congress party was very much visible in the districts of old Bombay Karnataka, old Hyderabad Karnataka, Bellary, northern part of old Mysore state like Harihar, Davangere, Chitradurga, part of Shimoga and Mysore districts. In these districts they were managers of the Congress vote banks. The backward castes, the scheduled castes and the scheduled tribes were not politically awakened and were dormant. Lingayat leadership in the north and the Vokkaliga leadership in the south were tacitly accepted by the backward castes, the scheduled castes and the scheduled tribes because of the dominant position of the former castes in socio-economic and political fields. Though the Lingayats had a dominant position in politics, they had not antagonised the Vokkaligas. But, on the other hand, they had constantly sought the support of the latter in maintaining their hold in state politics. The state administration was favourable to the Vokkaligas in establishing educational institutions and in providing important portfolios to the Vokkalaiga leaders in the state ministry.

Politics of Federation of Backward Castes (1972-1978)

The Indian National Congress was split into two parts in 1969. One was known as Congress (R) and was headed by Indira Gandhi and the other was known as Congress (O) and was headed by Nijalingappa. The split affected the Karnataka Congress and politics. Veerendra Patil, the Chief Minister of Karnataka and a close disciple of Nijalingappa, remained with the Congress (O). The Congress (R) carried on its activities in Karnataka under the leadership of Devaraj Urs belonging to small Kashtriya community.

The upper strata of the Lingayat community and Vokkaliga caste remained with the Congress (O) while the lower strata of both communities and other weaker castes were attracted by radical slogans and programmes of Indira Gandhi, the leader of the Congress (R) and Prime Minister of the country. Devaraj Urs who was a second line and dependent leader in state politics started mobilizing the backward castes and minorities in favour of the Congress (R). With the support of these weaker sections and minorities, he wanted to break the political domination of the Lingayats in particular and of Vokkaligas in general. The charismatic personality of Indira Gandhi and her popular programmes, political mobilization of backward castes, scheduled castes, scheduled tribes and minorities by Urs and suppressed desire for political domination by these weaker sections paid rich dividends for the Congress (R) in the parliamentary elections (1991) and the assembly elections (1972). In the parliamentary elections the Congress (R) secured all the twenty-seven seats. Many unknown Congress (R) candidates defeated dominant Lingayat and Vokkaliga candidates of the Congress (O) and were elected with the thumping majority. The hold of the higher castes as the managers of vote banks was loosened by the direct appeal of Indira Gandhi.[11]

Urs became the Chief Minister in 1972 and gave a bigger representation to weaker sections in the positions of power including state ministry and brought them into the network of patronage. He gave representation in the state ministry to politically light weight candidates form the Lingayat and Vokkaliga communities. Thus he established the domination of backward castes for the first time but alienated powerful castes like Lingayat and Vokkaliga which remained with the Congress (O). Though the policy of reservation in old Mysore state was introduced in 1895 for backward castes, the backward castes could dominate the politics of unified Karnataka state only in 1972.

In order to maintain the domination of backward castes and to relegate the dominant castes to the background in state politics, Urs introduced several legislative and administrative measures: (i) a Radical Land Reforms Act was passed in 1973. It provided for establishing of Taluka Land Tribunals which were quasi-administrative and quasi-popular in their composition and functioning. It provided representation to the backward castes in the tribunals. It intended speedy implementation of land reforms and decisions in favour of weaker sections. It took away excess lands of the big landlords and lands of absentee landholders who were mostly Lingayats and Vokkaligas. The Brahmin landlords had already lost their lands under earlier reforms and beneficiary of these reforms were Lingayats and Vokkaligas. Under Urs's land reforms the weaker sections were the main beneficiaries. Thus the land reforms achieved two objectives: (a) It deprived excess lands of these two powerful communities (Lingayat and Vokkaliga) and tried to reduce their political importance in rural areas by levelling them down. (b) It wanted to enhance the socio-economic position of the weaker sections and enable them to participate effectively in politics. (ii) The Urs government appointed the Karnataka Backward Classes Commission in August 1972 under the Chairmanship of L.G. Havanur, a leader from a backward caste. The commission submitted its report in 1975. The report recommended proportionate representation of reservation for backward castes in educational institutions, administration, etc.[12] Some sub-castes of Lingayats were excluded from the reservation while the Vokkaligas were included in the reservation. The Lingayat leaders severely condemned the report. It was alleged that Urs wanted to divide the Lingayat community. The report intended to bring about qualitative change in economic, social, political, administrative and educational lives of weaker sections in the years to come. The expectations of the report have come true to a great extent. The recommendations and implementation of the report constitute a watershed in the history of the backward class movement and in the recent political developments of Karnataka.[13] (iii) The Urs government introduced several welfare measures for the benefit of weaker sections. The 20-point programme of the Indira Gandhi government was also faithfully implemented for the upliftment of weaker sections. (iv) Urs encouraged formation of caste associations of weaker sections. A large number of caste associations belonging to weaker sections came into existence and they politically mobilized their men and women for socio-economic and political benefits. Thus the weaker sections were politicised and became aware of their numerical strength in the politics of Karnataka state. They also formed an informal federation of weaker sections and minorities and the leaders of different weaker sections shared the common platform for political mobilization. (v) In order to preserve the domination of weaker sections in the state politics, the Urs government did not establish Zilla Parishads and Mandal Panchayats. It believed that as the powerful castes like Lingayats and Vokkaligas were numerically dominant in many districts, they might try to dominate district politics through these institutions. (vi) The Urs government put the backward caste civil servants in key positions and placed the dominant caste civil servants in unimportant positions.

Resurrection of Powerful Communities (1983-1989)

The Lingayat and Vokkaliga communities which were relegated to the background in state politics during the regime of Urs (1972-78) started reemerging in state politics by strengthening the Janata Party which had absorbed the Congress (O) during the Chief Ministership of R. Gundu Rao who was a favourite of Indira Gandhi and Sanjay Gandhi. Urs, a champion of the weaker sections, came out from the Indira Congress and formed his own regional party but he soon died. After his death the weaker sections lost ground. R. Gundu Rao, a Brahmin, whose community constitutes 4.28 per cent of the total population of the state, tried to please all sections of the society. During this period of reconcilement, the Lingayats and Vokkaligas started consolidation of their political position under the banner of the Janata Party which had the blessings of Jayaprakash Narayana.

In 1983 assembly elections, the Janata Party and the Kranti Ranga combine secured 98 seats and formed a government with the help of independents. In March 1985 mid-term elections to the assembly, the Janata Party consolidated its position by securing 139 seats while the Congress secured 66 seats. The Lingayats and the Vokkaligas consolidated their position under the Chief Ministership of Ramkrishna Hegde (Brahmin) who was a compromise and acceptable leader to both communities. After his exit from state politics in 1988 (as a consequence of the telephone scandal), S.R. Bommai (Lingayat) became the Chief Minister. Soon there was a struggle for power between Bommai and Devegowda, a cabinet minister in Bommai ministry and powerful leader of Vokkaliga community. It is alleged that Hegde did not play fair in maintaining the harmony of the Janata Dal legislative party. Due to defections from it (Janata Party was renamed Janata Dal in 1988) the ministry headed by Bommai was reduced to a minority and was dismissed by the centre. It was the second downfall of the political hold of these two powerful communities (Lingayat and Vokkalinga) due to intra- and inter-caste feuds. Social cleavage was reflected in the struggle for power.

Between 1983-89 there were no substantial reforms for the weaker sections under the leadership of resurrected powerful communities. However some populist measures for weaker sections and students were introduced and age of retirement for government servants and persons working in aided institutions was raised from 55 to 58. The report of the Third Backward Classes Commission (Venkat Swmay Commission) had excluded the Lingayat and Vokkalinga communities from the list of reservations. The leaders of these communities had carried on an agitation against such exclusion. The Lingayat and Vokkaligan legislators and ministers who constituted an important and vital pillar of Janata/Janata Dal government were able to secure reservations for their communities. Zilla Parishads and Mandal Panchayats were introduced by the Janata government.

Re-emergence of Mellowed Weaker Sections and Subdued Powerful Communities in 1989

After the dismissal of the Janata Dal government, the upper strata of Lingayat and Vokkaliga communities rejoined the Congress

Party and supported the leadership of Veerendra Patil (Lingayat), an able politician and administrator and known for his political maturity. Both the weaker sections and the powerful communities supported the Congress party and the leadership of Patil in the 1989 assembly elections. The Congress secured 178 seats out of total 228 seats in the assembly and came back to power after six years. This was the biggest majority the Congress had ever secured and this indicates coalition of higher and lower castes. By 1989 the weaker sections had mellowed and there was no fire in them as it was during the Urs's regime (1972-78). Similarly, the Lingayats an the Vokkaligas had become subdued and had no dominant outlook as they had during 1956-71. However, the more matured and seasoned leaders of backward castes were waiting in the wings to seize power. When there was difference of opinion between Rajiv Gnadhi (Prime Minister), and Patil, the former asked the latter to step down on the ground of ill health (paralytic attack) and the latter reluctantly stepped down. S. Bangarappa, a leader from a backward caste, was chosen as a Chief Minister. It was expected that he would render a great service to the backward castes by his caste and socialist background. He soon belied the hopes of the weaker sections and antagonised higher castes and various charges were levelled against him. He was asked to resign by the Congress High Command in November 1992 and he did it defiantly. Veerappa Moily, a leader from a backward caste, was chosen as a Chief Minister. The leadership of this backward caste Chief Minister was supported by the ladership of two dominant castes (M. Rajasekhar Murthy, Revenue Minister and a close associate of Veerendra Patil, from Lingayat community, and S.M. Krishna, deputy Chief Minister, from Vokkaliga community) and of the scheduled castes (K.H. Ranganath, PWD minister). The last three were serious contenders to the office of the Chief Minister. There is criticism against the Chief Minister, Moily, that his expanded ministry does not properly represent caste composition and districts. Such social and regional imbalance is a constant irritant to the Chief Minister.

The socio-economic base of the present ruling Congress party is broader than that of the Congress party under the dominant castes (1952-1971 and 1983-89) and under the federation of weaker sections and minorities (1972-83). now the dominant castes are subdued and the weaker sections are mellowed and both the sections are working together under the banner of the Congress Party. Athul Kohli of Princeton University has come to the same conclusion on the changing socio-economic bases of Karnataka politics: "What is significant for our purpose is that Karnataka's dominant groups, the Vokkaligas and the Lingayats, regained some of their lost political prominence during the Janata phase, especially under Hegde. The political situation in the second half of the 1980's was, of course, not identical with that of the 1950s and 1960s when the power of dominant castes went unchallenged. The backward castes and other groups cannot be totally ignored any more. Thus, the ruling group is broader now than it was in the 1950s and 1960s".[14]

Weak Opposition Parties

The Congress had been a dominant party before independence and after independence in fragmented and unified Karnataka except during the Janata/Janata Dal Rule (1983-89). As it is generally supported by the dominant castes and weaker sections, it is strong and formidable. However, it suffered a setback only during 1983-89 when the dominant Lingayats and Vokkalingas joined and nourished the Janata/Janata Dal.

Though the Karnataka state had Lok Sevak Sangh, Janata Paksha, Praja Socialist Party, etc., in the early days of independence, they did not succeed. The Communist Party has been in existence for a long period, but its hold is confined to industrial areas, corporations and municipalities. It plays only a marginal role in state politics. The Congress (O) which was in existence from 1969 to 1977 merged into the Janata Party 1977. The Janata Party/Janata Dal has been in existence in state politics since 1977. Now it is spent up force with about twenty five MLAs in the legislative assembly. However, it is the main opposition party. Jana Sangh was a marginal force in state politics. Bharatiya Janata Party (new form of old Jana Sangh) has done better than the Janata Dal in the last parliamentary elections held in 1991 and had four candidates elected to the Lok Sabha. One of the four elected candidates is S. Mallikarjunaiah and is the deputy speaker of Lok Sabha. The success of the BJP in the recent parliamentary elections is not due to the Hindutva card but as an alternative party to the Congress in view of downfall of Janata Dal at the national and state levels.

Earlier the support base of the BJP was mainly continued to the Brahmins but in the recent parliamentary elections the base was extended to the Lingayats and the Vokkaligas to some extent. The success of BJP in Karnataka politics will depend not on Hindutva but on weak position of other political parties. Samajavadi Janata Party is marginal party in state political. Influence of Muslim League is mainly confined to the Gulbarga city corporation and it has one MLA in the legislative assembly. Influence of Tamil parties like AIADMK is confined to a few pockets in Bangalore city.

Politics of Pressure Groups

The socio-economic bases of the various pressure groups affect state politics to smaller or greater extent depending upon the extent of their support base and the issues involved.

The linguistic pressure groups affect language policy of the state. Though there is a Kannada Sahitya Parishad to promote Kannada literature and language, there have been occasional movements to take up the cause of Kannada language. There were movements like Gokak Chaluvali (agitation), Kannada Chaluvali, etc., which fought for primacy of the Kannada language in state administration and education. There are institutions/associations like the Karnatak Vidyavardhak Sangh, Dharwad (established in 1890), Kannada Shakti Kendra, etc., which have influenced language policy in the state. The Maharashtra Ekikaran Samiti (MES), a Marathi linguistic pressure group in bordered districts like Belgaum, has been very vocal in local politics and is marginally active in state politics. It gets four to five candidates elected to the Karnataka state legislative assembly from 1957 till today.[15] Its main aim is to get the Marathi speaking areas in the border districts merged with the Maharashtra state. Further it intends to protest the interests of Marathi-speaking people in Karnataka. In view of the agitations of MES and counter agitations of Kannada people, Belgaum city draws the attention of the whole nation. Earlier leadership of the MES was dominated by Brahmins and now it is dominated by Marathas who are ruling and are dominant group in the politics of neighbouring Maharashtra. There are literary associations for Urdu, Konkani, Tulu, etc., which marginally affect the language policy of the state. Among fan associations of film stars, the Raj Kumar Fans Association is vocal on Kannada language, culture and films.

There are various professional associations like Raith Sanghas, Chambers of Commerce and Industry, Government Employees Associations, Teachers Associations, etc. These represent economic interests of their members affect state politics. Among these associations, the Karnataka Rajya Raith Sangh is very powerful and its roots are wide spread. It has been vocal and has influenced the policies of government relating to agriculture. It has two representatives in the Karnataka state legislative assembly. Farmers of the Kaveri belt, the economic and political heart-land of Vokkaliga community, are well organised and have influenced the government's attitude and policy towards Kaveri water dispute with Tamil Nadu.

In recent years the educated youths belonging to the scheduled castes, the scheduled tribes and other backward castes have formed an organisation called Dalit Sangharsh Samiti (in 1978) whose ideology is that of Ambedkar and of socialism. It had wide base and is vocal on many issues affecting the Dalits. It is essentially a social movement to fight against socio-religious discrimination and atrocities against the socially suppressed sections.

Various caste groups have orgnaised themselves into caste associations. After independence a large number of caste associations have come up. Probably there is no community with a sizable number of people without an association. These have been fighting for various benefits for their members. Their demands relate to reservation in administration and educational institutions, ruling party tickets, ministerships, etc., for their men and women.

Conclusions

These facts and analysis prove that the changing socio-economic determinants have been responsible for changes in Karnataka state politics in terms of leadership, mobilization of castemen, the place of official language, land reforms, the awakening of farming class, socio-economic composition of bureaucracy and political parties, etc. (i) State leadership in terms of Chief Ministership has shifted from dominant castes to backward castes. New leaders and new elites have emerged from weaker sections. However, the leadership of dominant castes is not replaced at various political levels and in institutions. It has accepted and welcomed leadership from the weaker sections and both of them co-exist and work jointly in certain fields like political parties, bureaucracy, etc. (ii) In the last five decades a large number of caste associations have come up and have been becoming active and mobilizing on behalf of their men and women for political, administrative and educational benefits. They have continued to influence state politics in terms of the composition of council of ministers, distribution of party tickets in the elections, policy of reservation, etc. (iii) With influx of weaker sections into politics and education, emphasis has shifted from English and Sanskrit to Kannada, the language of common people. (iv) Landlordship of the dominant castes has been abolished and land owners from these castes are now only middle and marginal farmers. With benefits of irrigation, some of them continue to dominate rural politics. (v) The farmers who form the backbone of the state economy have been politically mobilized and are a force to reckon with. (vi) Bureaucracy which was once mainly dominated by the higher castes has accommodated the weaker sections. (vii) The weaker sections which were politically dominant, economically exploited and easily suppressed have made some progress in socio-economic and political fields.

Thus the changing socio-economic bases of Karnataka society are reflected in the politics of the state.

NOTES AND REFERENCES

1. *Karnataka at Glance 1990-91,* Bangalore, Director of Economics and Statistics, 1991, p. 26.
2. *Census of India 1991, Series 11, Karnataka,* Provisional Census, Bangalore, Director of Census Operations, Karnataka, 1991, p. 19.
3. *Ibid.*, p. 134.
4. *Census of India 1991, Series 14, Mysore,* Bangalore, Director of Census Operations, 1977, p. 121.
5. *Report of Mysore Backward Classes Committee,* (Popularly known as Nagangowda Committee)), quoted by Patil Oklay, B.B., "Karnataka: Politics of One Party Dominance", in Iqbal Narain (Ed.), *State Politics in India,* New Delhi, Meenakshi Prakashan, 1976, p. 130.
6. Manor James, *Political Change in an Indian State Mysore 1917-1955,* New Delhi, Manohar Books Service, 1977, p. 59.
7. Patil, S. H., *The Congress Party and Princely States,* Bombay, Himalaya Publishing House, 1981, p. 58.

8. Gandhi, M.K., *To the Princes and their People,* (Ed.), Anand T. Hingorani, 1942, p. 405.
9. Patil, S.H., *Swatantra Chalavi: Vidhayak Karya*, in Kalburgi, M. M. {Ed.), *Karnataka Gandhi: Hardekar Manjappa*, Bangalore, Kannada and Sanskrati Nirdeshanalaya, Government of Karnataka, 1989, pp. 267-69.
10. Diwakar, R.R., *et al., Linguistic Provinces and the Karnataka Problem,* Hubli, Karnataka Ekikaran Mahasamati, 1948, p. 12.
11. Patil Okaly, B.B., *Karnataka Politics of One Party Cominance,* in Iqbal Narain's (Ed.), *State Politics in India,* New Delhi, Meenakshi Prakashan, 1976, p. 145.
12. Report, *Karnataka Backward Classes Commission,* in four volumes, Popularly known as Havanur Commission, Bangalore, Government of Karnataka, 1975.
13. Hebsur, R.K., *The Havanur Commission on Backward Classes: An Analysis,* The Indian Journal of Political Science, Vol. XLII, No. 4, October-December 1981, Hyderabad, The Indian Political Science Association, 1981, p. 28.
14. Kohli Atul, *Democracy and Discontent India's Growing Crisis of Governability,* Cambridge: Cambridge University Press, 1991, p. 97.
15. S.H., Patil, *Maharashtra Ekikaran Samiti: A Case Study of a Linguistic Pressure Group in the politics of Karnataka 1946-1980,* Journal of Karnatak University Social Sciences, Vol. XXIII, 1987, Dharwad, Director, Prasaranga, Karnatak University, 1987, p. 35.

16

Party System in Karnataka

S.S. PATAGUNDI

After independence India adopted the federal system of government. The powers of both the centre and the state are clearly enumerated in the Constitution. Each state has its own internal administrative structure with the Governor as the nominal head, the Chief Minister as its executive head. However, as the territory, population, literacy level, caste, class composition, etc., differ from one state to another, they have an impact on the working of the political system of that state. Therefore, it is pertinent to understand the politics of each state. Karnataka is an important state well-known with the advancement it has made in the field of Information Technology.

Since politics is a major constituent of the federal system, it reflects the national as well as the grassroots level politics. Political scientists and anthropologists have increasingly come to recognize that the modern and modernizing societies belong to many levels in a political system and the states in a federal system are important links connecting village, town and city politics to the national political system.[1] Politics of each state is distinct from the politics of other states. In southern states like Tamil Nadu and Andhra Pradesh regional political parties like DMK, AIADMK, TDP, etc., play an important role. In Kerala also the regional political parties aligning with national parties play their significant role in determining state politics.

However, the states share a common legal system, a common Constitutional framework, a common administrative structure and common international environment; but their internal political patterns vary considerably.[2] Efforts were made to form regional political parties, such as, Janata Paksha, Karnataka Kranti Ranga, Karnataka Congress Party, Kannada Nadu; but no party was successful in Karnataka. The Kannada Nadu has been formed by Vijay Sankeshwar, a former BJP Member of Parliament from Dharwad, North Karnataka, in the year 2003. It failed miserably in the 2004 Assembly and Lok Sabha elections.

The party system plays an important role in state politics since it involves interaction among political leaders in affairs of public importance. The effectiveness of this interaction is primarily influenced by the nature and character of the party system. In this paper an attempt has been made to examine such nature and character of the party system in Karnataka state. For this purpose we have to understand the number of parties, their strength in the state legislature and the competitiveness among themselves. All these significantly determine the nature of interaction which is crucial to the party system. According to the *International Encyclopaedia of Social Sciences,* the study of a party system involves the understanding of the competitive interaction among the parties.[3]

The working of the party system can be understood based on their number and strength. In this context, the political process plays an influential role. For this purpose, we have considered the number of parties which participated in the Lok Sabha and the Assembly elections in Karnataka. Besides, we have considered the impact of the personality of the leaders on the factional politics in Karnataka which within the Congress party was reflected the internal working of the Congress party.

Post-Independence Karnataka

After independence, efforts were made for the unification of Karnataka. Dharwad was the centre of this movement and Allur Venkatrao was the brain behind it. Finally, the Fazal Ali Commission was appointed, and, according to its recommendations, united Karnataka came into existence on 1st November, 1956, and was named Karnataka in 1973, a long cherished aspiration of Kannadigas.[4]

A large number of people in Karnataka are dependent on agriculture. Lingayats constitute the largest caste group.

"According to the 1991 census there were 73,69,279 Scheduled Caste members in the state (54,45,186 Rural and 17,24,093 Urban) which is about 16.48 per cent of the total population of the state. There were 19,15,691 Scheduled Tribes (16,29,496 Rural and 2,86,195 Urban) which is about 4.26 per cent. The literacy percentage in the state according to the 1991 census is 47.05 per cent as against 38.41 per cent in 1981, 31.52 per cent in 1971 and 25.40 per cent in 1961. These figures indicate that there is a steady increase in the proportion of literates to the total population."[5] Kannada is the official language. Hinduism is the major religion along with it Jainism, Buddhism, Christianity, Islam and Sikhism also flourish.

One Party Dominant System from 1952-1983

In the first general elections the opposition parties did not prove to be a significant force in any of the regions except, to some extent, in old Mysore area where all the opposition parties and the independents together were able to win about 25 per cent of the assembly seats.[6] The Table 16.1 given below summarizes the comparative data in this regard.

The Table 16.1 shows that the Congress party was able to muster the largest number of seats in all the four assembly elections and three Lok Sabha elections indicating the necessary characteristics of One-Party-dominant system. Functionally there were five parties in 1957 and 1962 Legislative Assembly. There were seven parties in 1967 Legislative Assembly. The opposition was fragmented and weak. The Congress party was dominant during this period. After the 1952 assembly elections in the Mysore state, the Congress formed the government under the leadership of K. Hanumanthaiah. He had to face problems from within and outside the Congress party. "K. Hanumanathaiah kept on counter-acting the moves of his opponents by establishing contacts with the leaders in the other regions which were going to be incorporated into the Karnataka state. But he did not prove himself to be equal to the task and was thus forced to tender his resignation on 19th August, 1956, just a few months before the integrated state of Mysore was to come into existence."[7] Kadidal Manjappa succeeded him as Chief Minister. But he had to resign soon after the emergence of the integrated state. S. Nijalingappa who had played

Table 16.1: Party Position in the State Assembly Since 1952

Party	*1952 (old Mysore State Only) Total Seats 99*	*1957 Total Seats 206*	*1962 Total Seats 206*	*1967 Total Seats 216*
Congress	74	145	136	126
SOC	03	--	01	06
KMP	08	--	--	--
CPI	01	01	03	02
SCF	02	02	--	--
Swatantra	--	--	09	16
PSP	--	17	20	19
Jana Sangha	--	--	--	04
Republic	--	--	--	01
LSS	--	--	04	02
MES	--	--	06	--
DMK	--	--	--	--
Janata Paksha	--	--	--	04
Independents	11	38	27	34
PWP	--	02	--	--
United Front	--	--	--	02

Source: Iqbal Narain (ed.), *State Politics in India*, Meenakshi Prakashan, Meerut, 1976, p. 131.

an important role in the unification of Karnataka and also had the sizeable support in all the regions assumed Chief Ministership of the new state.

In the 1957 general elections he played a significant role in selecting candidates for elections and was also able to secure party tickets to his supporters. As a result, he enjoyed the majority in the Congress Legislative Party and became the Chief Minister for the second time. Soon he had to resign in 1958 because of the discontent among the legislators, which helped B.J. Jatti to become next Chief Minister.

Nijalingappa was able to establish his control over the party organization. This made the group led by Jatti to turn its attention towards capturing party organization. However, the party High Command intervened and brought about a compromise between these two sections before the 1962 general elections. But the bitterness between these two groups did not disappear and every group was competing to secure party tickets to ensure its majority. Because of its control over the organizational wing the faction led by Nijalingappa, it succeeded in allotting party tickets to his supporters. Though a majority of the party legislators were elected, he was himself defeated in his home constituency in the assembly elections which were held after the 1962 general elections. As a result, S.R. Kanti was temporarily made the Chief Minister till the results of the bye-elections were declared. In 1962, for the third time, Nijalingappa became the Chief Minister. Now he was able to complete his tenure.

"On the eve of the fourth general elections, the rival groups again became active. Realising that they would be able to regain control over the organization many members of the Jatti faction thought of forming a separate state level political party."[8] This resulted in the emergence of the Janata Paksha. In spite of the efforts of opposition parties to defeat the Congress, it emerged as the majority party. Nijalingappa became the Chief Minister. But, soon he vacated his office and made Veerendra Patil—a young Congressman and a loyal follower—his successor. During this period it was found that intra-competition or factions within the Congress was more influential than inter-party competition.

The split in the national Congress as Congress (O) and Congress (R) considerably affected state politics in Karnataka. The entire organization pledged its loyalty to Congress (O) and the dissident Congressmen joined Congress (R). As a result, the control of the state went to Congress (O). The situation tended to expect a basic change in the One-Party-Dominant system hoping that a two or multi-party system may emerge. Numerically there was no change in the party system in Karnataka and there were only five parties. In the elections of March 1972, the Congress (O) was defeated and the Congress (R) won majority. The performance of the opposition parties was as in previous elections. As a result of this the One-Party-Dominant system continued. Devaraj Urs became the Chief Minister. The results of 1972 Assembly elections are given in Table 16.2.

From Table 16.2 it becomes clear that though Congress (R) got majority, other parties' performance was not satisfactory. In the first three assembly elections the competition was among the Congress leaders for power. But with the split in the state level and

Table 16.2: Party Position After 1972 Legislative Assembly Elections

Year	Party	No. of seats contested	No. of seats won	Percentage of votes polled
1972	Indian National Congress (R)	212	165	52.17
	Indian National Congress (O)	176	24	26.22
	Bharatiya Jana Sangh	102	--	04.30
	Socialist Party	29	03	01.69
	Swatantra Party	28	--	00.57
	Communist Party of India (CPM)	17	--	01.03
	Communist Party of India (CPI)	04	03	00.99
	Janata Paaksya (JP) (A local party)	02	01	00.16
	Independents	250	20	12.87
	Total	**820**	**216**	**100.00**

Source: S.R. Honnalingaiah, *A Handbook of Karnataka*, Karnataka Gazetteer Department, Bangalore, 2001, p. 59.

national level Congress the situation became tough for the Congress party to continue its domination.

After a short period of emergency rule from 1975 to 1977, in February 28, 1978 assembly elections were declared after the general elections in 1977. Party position as on 1.12.1977 is shown Table 16.3. "Of the three parties which made an attempt for power, the Janata Party had its candidates in 222 constituencies, the Congress (I) in 214 and Congress (O) in 208 constituencies. CPI and the Republic Party (Gavi Group) fielded 6 candidates and one candidate respectively."[9]

Table 16.3: Party Position as on 1.12.1977

Total seats	*216*
Vacant	11
Congress	161
Janata	35
CPI	03
Indepenents	06

Source: Shiv Lal, *Elections Under the Janata Rule*, The Election Archives, New Delhi, 1978, p. 12.

In spite of the claims made by the Janata party leaders, the Congress won majority in the state assembly. The Congress declined in terms of the percentage of votes in the Lok Sabha elections in 1977 and the Assembly elections in 1978 in Karnataka from 56.80 to 44.25. Although the Congress (I) had been swept back to power with a two-thirds majority in the new 224-member assembly, a steep fall in the popular votes is in the March 1978 elections was enough to shake its leaders and the euphoria of their success.[10] Table 16.4 shows the party position after 1978 elections.

Table 16.4: Party Position after 1978 Elections

Total Seats	*224*
Congress (I)	149
Janata Party	59
Congress (O)	02
CPI	03
Maharashtra Ekikaran Samiti	05
CPI (Gavi)	01
Muslim League	01
Independents	04

Source: Shiv Lal, *Elections under the Janata Rule,* The Election Archives, New Delhi, 1978, p.12.

For a brief period from 1972 to 1977 the state was ruled by the Congress party under the leadership of Devaraj Urs. From December 31, 1977, to February 28, 1978, the state was under President's rule for the second time. From 1978 to 1980 Devaraj Urs again became the Chief Minister. The Urs Congress was defeated in the 1980 Lok Sabha elections and the Congress (I) came to power under the leadership of Gundu Rao. Therefore, it is not quite accurate to say that the 1983 elections brought an end of Congress rule for the simple and obvious reason that the Congress before the split cannot be identified with the different Congress factions. In this sense the replacement of Congress (I) by the Janata Ranga or Janata Party in 1983 belongs to the One-Party-Dominant period began in 1969.[11] Table 16.5 shows the party position in Legislative Assembly after 1983 elections.

Table 16.5: Party Position in the Legislative Assembly after 1983

Party	*No. of seats contested*	*No. of seats won*	*Percentage of votes polled*
Janata Party (JNP)	194	95	33.08
Indian National Congress (INC)	221	82	40.42
Bharatiya Janata Party	110	18	07.93
Communist Party of India (CPI)	07	03	01.25
CPI (CPM or Marxist)	05	03	00.90
AIADMK	01	01	00.13
Independents and others	747	22	16.28
Total	**1,365**	**224**	**100.00**

Source: S.R. Honnalingaiah, *A Handbook of Karnataka*, Karnataka Gazetteer Department, Bangalore, 2001, p. 60.

During this period, 1978 to 1983, the number of parties in the Legislative assembly was the same, i.e., five. But there was a basic change in the Congress party under the leadership of Indira Gandhi which significantly influenced its working in Karnataka. The Janata party was a strong opposition in terms of electoral strength as well as the strength in the Legislative Assembly as compared to the position of the opposition in the Legislative Assembly in the past.

It was first a non-Congress government in Karnataka. However, it did not survive for long. Mid-term elections were held to the Legislative Assembly in 1985. Based on the electoral strength as well as strength in the Legislative Assembly it was predicted that this may tend to the emergence of two party system in Karnataka. The Congress became a strong opposition during this period.

Though in 1984 the Lok Sabha election the Congress won more seats, in the Assembly elections of 1985 the Janata party with 139 seats became the largest party in the state. Again Ramkrishna Hegde became the Chief Minister. As Chief Minister between 1983 and 1985 and again 1985 and 1988, he became an active votary of state rights within a federal set up, but one who made no concession to regional or linguistic chauvinism.[12] Table 16.6 shows the party position in Legislative Assembly after 1985 elections.

"In February, 1986, Mr. Hegde had resigned as Chief Minister following the adverse verdict of the Karnataka High Court in the Liquor Bottling case. He withdrew the resignation following pressure from his party legislators. Mr. Hegde's resignation as Chief Minister came again on August 10, 1988, when he accepted moral responsibility for the tapping of telephone of prominent politicians of the state by the state intelligence."[13] After his resignation, S.R. Bommai became the Chief Minister from 1988 to 1989. But his duration was very short. On 21st April, 1989, for the third time President's rule was imposed. In 1989, general elections were declared for both the Lok Sabha and the State Legislative Assembly. The two party system emerged in Karnataka in 1985 and it was quite satisfactory from 1985-1989. Table 16.7 shows the party position in Legislative Assembly after 1989 elections.

Table 16.6: Party Position in the Legislative Assembly after 1985

Party	*No. of seats contested*	*No. of seats won*	*Percentage of votes polled*
Janata Party	207	139	43.84
Indian National Congress	224	66	41.10
Bharatiya Janata Party	117	02	03.84
Communist Party of India (CPI)	08	04	01.08
Communist Party of India (CPM)	07	02	00.86
Indian Congress (Socialist) (ICS)	05	--	00.08
Lok Dal (LKD)	37	--	00.42
Republican Party of India (RPI)	--	--	--
All India Anna DMK	02	--	00.18
Independents	1188	11	08.57
Total	**1795**	**224**	**100.00**

Source: S.R. Honnalingaiah, *A Handbook of Karnataka*, Karnataka Gazetteer Department, Bangalore, 2001, p.61.

The results of the 1989 elections tended to revive the One-Party-Dominant system in Karnataka. The opposition became weak. From 1989 to 1994 once again the Congress came to power in Karnataka under the leadership of Veerendra Patil. Factional politics within the Congress (I) considerably increased. As a result, from 1989 to 1994 Karnataka had three ministers, namely, Veerendra Patil, S. Bangarappa and Veerappa Moily. Moily assumed office in 1992. Again there was pressure from party members for a change of Chief Ministership. Congress President Narasimha Rao on December 22, ruled out change in leadership.[14]

Table 16.7: Party Position in the Legislative assembly After 1989

Party	*No. of seats contested*	*No. of seats won*	*Percentage of votes polled*
Indian National Congress	219	176	43.77
Janata Dal	208	24	27.30
Janata Party	215	02	11.40
Bharatiya Janata Party (BJP)	119	04	04.13
Karnataka Rajya Raitha Sangha	111	02	03.63
CPI	18	--	00.59
Communist Party of India (CPM)	07	--	00.54
AIADMK	01	01	00.18
Muslim League	13	01	00.43
Republican Party of India (RPI)	10	--	00.10
Bhahujan Samaj Party (BSP)	04	--	00.03
Independents and others	1086	12	07.90
Total	**2011**	**222**	**100.00**

Source: S.R. Honnalingaiah, *A Handbook of Karnataka*, Karnataka Gazetteer Department, Bangalore, 2001, p. 62.

"The dissident members of Moily government including the Deputy Chief Minister S.K. Krishna tendered their resignations to the Governor on January 3. On the day that is January 3 dissident legislators' meeting was held in the residence of S.M. Krishna where they chalked out a strategy to bring pressure on the high command to effect a change of leadership in the state."[15] The central leadership decided to retain Moily as Chief Minister, but curtailed his power.[16]

Meanwhile dissident leader S. Bangarappa was expelled from the Congress party membership for six years. On December 22, 1994, he formally announced the formation of Karnataka Congress Party (KCP).

The factional politics in the Congress was a major factor which made the people of Karnataka switch over to the Janata Dal. The Janata Dal came to power in the 1994 elections. H.D. Deve Gowda became the Chief Minister from 1994 to 1996. When the United Front elected Deve Gowda as its leader, be became the Prime Minister. He tendered his resignation as Chief Minister and J.H. Patel succeed him. In the 1994 Legislative Assembly elections, the BJP emerged as an important opposition party which contributed to change the nature of the party system in Karnataka. The position of the parties in the Legislative Assembly made the people hope for the emergence of a multi-party system. Table 16.8 shows the party position in the Legislative Assembly after 1994.

Table 16.8: Party Position in the Legislative Assembly after 1994

Party	*No. of seats contested*	*No. of seats won*	*Percentage of votes polled*
Janata Dal	221	115	33.56
Bharatiya Janata Party	223	40	17.00
Indian National Congress	223	36	27.40
CPI (M)	13	01	00.49
CPI	08	--	00.23
Janata Party	36	--	00.16
AIADMK	04	01	00.24
Bharatiya Republican Party	03	01	00.13
Bahujan Samajwadi Party	78	01	00.76
Karnataka Congress Party	218	10	07.28
Karnataka Rajya Raith Sangh (KRRS)	112	01	02.73
Independents and others	1358	18	10.04
Total	**2497**	**224**	**100.00**

Source: S.R. Honnalingaiah, *A Handbook of Karnataka*, Karnataka Gazetteer Department, Bangalore, 2001, p.63.

After the 1999 elections S.M. Krishna, leader of the Congress party, formed his ministry, "His E-governance measures have been extremely successful and have brought in transparency. The state of governance has improved remarkably under his leadership and the satisfaction with his mode of functioning is visible".[17] Krishna inaugurated the first ever Krisi Marata Vahini website of the Agricultural Marketing Department and the State Agricultural Marketing Board, (maratavahini.kar.nic.in). The state is said to be the first in the country to launch a website to implement e-governance to provide reliable data on daily arrivals of agricultural commodities with minimum and maximum prices in all 142 APMCs in the state of which 70 are to be computerized.[18] In spite of this the Congress party was not able to get majority in the Legislative Assembly in the 2004 elections. Table 16.9 and 16.10 show party position in the Legislative Assembly after 1999 and Karnataka Assembly Elections 2004 results.

The party system in Karnataka in terms of the number of parties in the Legislative Assembly continued almost the same from 1952 to 2004 and the number of parties increased from five to seven. No party was in a position to form support each other. Both parties agreed on seat sharing. The Congress leader Dharam Singh became the Chief Minister and Janata Dal (Secular) leader, Sidharamaiah became Deputy Chief Minister and the BJP is the opposition. "The

Table 16.9: Party Position in the Legislative assembly After 1999

Party	No. of seats contested			No. of seats Won			Percentage of votes polled
	Men	Women	Total	Men	Women	Total	
Indian National Congress	210	13	223	126	06	132	41.06
BJP	144	05	149	44	--	44	20.69
JD(U)	108	04	112	19	--	19	13.52
JD(S)	193	10	203	09	--	09	10.42
CPI (M)	08	--	08	--	--	--	00.39
CPI	11	--	11	--	--	--	--
BSP	84	01	85	--	--	--	--
KCVP	07	02	09	--	--	--	--
AIDMK	11	02	13	01	--	01	--
KRRS	09	--	09	--	--	--	00.04
Independents	450	25	475	19	--	19	11.78
Other Parties (13)	43	--	43	--	--	--	--
Total	**1278**	**62**	**1340**	**218**	**--**	**224**	**100.00**

Source: S.R. Honnalingaiah, *A Handbook of Karnataka*, Karnataka Gazetteer Department, Bangalore, 2001, p.64.

Bharatiya Janata Party (BJP), the single largest party in 224-member House with 79 members together with its ally, the Janata Dal (United) with five members, will have 84 members on its side. This is the first time in the history of the State Assembly that the single largest party will be sitting in the opposition."[19]

In politics participation constitutes a major issue. Here participation refers to that of the people as well as of the elected representatives. There cannot be meaningful participation of the people in the political process unless they develop some critical thinking about the public policy issues. It calls for a serious attention to the implication of the public policy decisions. An elected representative cannot make a meaningful contribution to the public policy making unless he pays serious attention to the issues on which he wants to express his views on the floor of the house. Several elected representatives seem to be reluctant to get in touch with the people in a meaningful way. Their fear seems to be that of an intimacy with the people may lead to the reduction of their authority. Hence, they seem to maintain distance. Consequently, our representatives do not satisfactorily understand

Table 16.10: Karnataka Assembly Elections 2004 Results

Party	*Constituency*	
	Contesting	*Won*
BJP	198	79
BSP	102	00
CPI	05	00
CPM	05	01
INC	224	65
JD (S)	220	58
JD (U)	26	05
ADMK	02	00
AIFB	01	00
AITC	01	00
CPI (ML) (L)	02	00
MUL	06	00
SHS	11	00
SP	15	00
AIFB (S)	01	00
ANC	02	00
BPJP	01	00
BPNSNP	01	00
ICSP	01	00
JP	155	00
KCVP	05	01
KNDP	188	01
KRRS	10	00
LJNSP	04	00
MP	01	00
PPI	01	00
PPOI	03	00
RPI	03	01
RPI (A)	09	00
SPSP	03	00
USP	02	00
USYP	65	00
IND	442	13
Total	**1715**	**224**

Source: http://www.indian-elections.com/assembly-elections/result-karnata...

or represent the aspirations of the people and this is a weakness in the public policy-making process. All these get reflected in the working of the party system.

NOTES AND REFERENCES

1. Myron Weiner, *Political Development in Indian States, in Myron Weiner (ed.), State Politics in India,* Princeton University Press, New Jersey, 1968, p. 5.
2. *Ibid.*, pp. 4-5.
3. David L. Sills, *International Encyclopaedia of Social Sciences,* The Macmillan Company and The Free Press, New York, 1968, p. 436.
4. S.R.Honnalingaiah, *A Handbook of Karnatak,* Karnataka Gazetteer Department, Bangalore, 2001, pp. 57-58.
5. *Ibid.*, pp. 70-71.
6. Iqbal Narain (ed.), *State Politics in India,* Meenakshi Prakashan, Meerut, 1996, p. 131.
7. *Ibid.*, p. 132.
8. *Ibid.*, p. 134.
9. Shiv Lal, *Elections under the Janata Rule,* The Election Archives, New Delhi, 1978, pp. 8-9.
10. *Ibid.*, p.12.
11. K. Raghvendhra Rao, *Social Structure and Political System in Karnataka,* in George Mathew (ed.), *Shift in Indian Politics,* Concept Publishing Company, New Delhi, 1984, p. 15.
12. *The Hindu*, January 14, 2004.
13. *Ibid.*, January 13, 2004.
14. *Indian Recorder*, 1(2), January 8-14, 1994, p. 27.
15. *Ibid.*, 1994, p. 44.
16 *Indian Recorder*, 1(5), January 29—February 4, 1994, p. 77.
17. *The Hindu*, February 12, 2004.
18. *Ibid.*, June 16, 2002.
19. *Ibid.*, June 9, 2004.

17

Tenth Assembly Elections in Karnataka
An Analysis

H.M. RAJASHEKARA

Democracy and Elections

Elections are the alchemy of democratic political process. They play a meaningful role for an orderly succession of rulers and for securing legitimacy to governance. Michael Brecher has rightly observed: "elections provide the means for the peaceful and orderly transfer of power, for dealing with the vexing problem of succession, for the routinization of political change".[1] According to another scholar, "the question of elections is at the centre of politics everywhere".[2] Norman D. Palmer has observed:

> Elections are particularly conspicuous and revealing aspects of most contemporary political systems. They highlight and dramatize a political system, bringing its nature into sharp relief, and providing insights into other aspects of the system and the basic nature and actual functioning of the same as a whole.[3]

"The stability of any given democracy" writes Lipset, "depends not only on economic development but also upon the effectiveness and the legitimacy of its political system".[4] Therefore, elections may be described as the foundation of democracy. Myopic view of elections as marginal and peripheral political events undermines the doctrine of popular sovereignty and the theory of "mandate".

Elections in India

Under the Indian democratic system the Lok Sabha elections and several state assembly elections have been conducted. The electoral behaviour and the experience reveal that the elections in India have contributed tremendously for the satisfactory working of democracy. After the second general election to the Lok Sabha (1957) the Election Commission of India noted "the degree of political maturity displayed by the electorate even in many backward areas of the country". Despite several loopholes in the existing electoral system, India seems to be developing what V.D. Key, Jr., calls, "responsible electorate". Rajni Korhari's observation is worth recalling:

> India's experience with elections has produced "a mature and demanding electorate" and that there has taken place a growing awareness of issues among the people, an inclination to punish parties and leaders that are unable to deliver the goods, a break down of community based loyalties and voting patterns, the growth of secular identities and allegiances and accelerating process of political interest, information, evaluation and hard bargaining on the basis of party commitments and their ability to translate them into reality.[5]

Assembly Elections in Karnataka

From 1952 to 1994 Karnataka has witnessed 10 elections to the assembly. In these the electorate has done reasonably well to strengthen the foundation of democracy.

To the 224 member House, the 10th election was conducted in two phases on November 26th and December 1st, 1994. The estimated total electorate was 3.07 crore.[6] The Congress (I) had fielded 224 candidates, the BJP 223, the Janata Dal 222, and the Bahujan Samaj Party 78. The regional parties—Karnataka Congress Party (KCP), Karnataka Rajya Raitha Sangha (KRRS) and Kannada Chaluvali Vathal Paksha (KCVP) had fielded 218, 111, and 46 candidates respectively. There were 58 candidates from other parties and 1,317 independents.

This article analyses the electoral victory of the Janata Dal on the basis of the following hypotheses:

Table 17.1

Sl. No.	*Election year*	*Number of contestants*	*Percentage of votes polled*
1.	1952	394	50.08
2.	1957	560	52.44
3.	1962	675	59.46
4.	1967	727	62.89
5.	1972	820	61.64
6.	1978	1165	71.96
7.	1983	1356	66.69
8.	1985	1795	67.21
9.	1989	2043	67.93
10.	1994	2497	68.49

Source: Sandeep Shastri: An Analysis of the Karnataka Assembly Elections, 1994, pp. 33, 45.

(a) Anti-ruling party syndrome.
(b) Rejection of the one-party rule theory.
(c) Electorate's preference for the Janata Dal as an alternative to the Congress (I).
(d) Rejection of regional parties.

II

The Indian electorate has shown its maturity and capability in judging the performance and political prudence of the ruling party at the time of elections. The ballot revolution against the ruling party for its ineffective governance or dismal performance is also called as the "iron law of the Indian democracy" (Ashis Nandy), and the "incumbency syndrome" (Prannoy Roy). In 1957, it was palpable for the first time in Kerala. In the post-Nehru period it has become a common phenomenon in the Indian electoral politics. In the parliamentary elections of 1977, 1980, 1989 and 1991 the electorate had voted against the ruling party. At the state level, people voted for change in Tamil Nadu in 1967, 1977, 1989, and 1991. Since the 1960s in Kerala, Andhra Pradesh, Karnataka and in many other states this has been the common trend. In most of the assembly elections held during the past five years people have dethroned the ruling parties from power.

The Indian National Congress has enjoyed almost unparalleled political dominance in Karnataka for more than three decades. Its historic role in the freedom struggle, its fight for the establishment of popular rule in the princely state of Mysore, its composite and secular image, its widely accepted socio-economic philosophy and the charismatic and dynamic leadership of Jawaharlal Nehru and Indira Gandhi at the national level largely contributed to the uninterrupted Congress rule in the state until 1982. Moreover, the state Congress leaders such as K. Hanumanthaiah, and S. Nijalingappa did give better governance and competent leadership during their tenure as Chief Ministers. James Manor has rightly observed: "Hanumanthaiah's style of leadership during his tenure of office greatly accelerated the transformation of politics in Mysore".[7] Under the stewardship of Nijalingappa Karnataka had made big strides in the field of irrigation and agriculture.

Table 17.2: Congress Party's Position after Assembly Elections

Sl. No.	*Year*	*Total seats of the house*	*Seats won*	*Percentage of votes*
1.	1952	208	164	49.45
2.	1957	208	150	52.08
3.	1962	208	138	49.83
4.	1967	216	126	48.14
5.	1972	216	165	53.56
6.	1978	224	149	44.25
7.	1983	224	82	40.42
8.	1985	224	66	41.10
9.	1989	224	178	44.00
10.	1994	224	35	27.34

Source: Shiv Lal: Elections to India's State Legislature since 1952, Election Archives and Institute, New Delhi, 1978, and "The Hindu".

It was under the able and affable leadership of Veerendra Patil the Congress (I) came back to power in 1989 with a massive mandate after a gap of 6 years. After he assumed office as Chief Minister for the second time on November 30, 1989, Patil proved himself a first-class administrator and within a short span of time he restored credibility to the regime and improved the financial position of the state. He was widely respected for his efficient administration, secular outlook and etiquette. His sudden illness and difference, with Rajiva Gandhi damaged the political prospects of the Congress in Karnataka. He was dethroned by the party High Command on October 19, 1990.

Many reasons could be attributed for the defeat of Congress (I) in the 1994 assembly election. The first reason for the anti-Congress (I) wave was the frequent change of Chief Ministers and the uncontrollable politics of dissidence within the Congress (I). S. Bangarappa who became the Chief Minister after the removal of Patil was Rajiv Gandhi's choce. As he had no majority support in the party he could not curb the dissident activities of his party men. In fact, he became a victim of factional politics and he was replaced by Veerappa Moily in November, 1992. He also did not have majority support in the Congress Legislature Party. If there had been an election for leadership S.M. Krishna would have got 138 votes and Moily had 40.[8] Secondly, the postponement of Panchayat Raj elections created dissatisfaction among the people. Fourthly, the projection of the "pro-poor image" by the Bangarappa government received little attention in the state. Fifthly, the Ayodhya incident of 1992, the Idgah Maiden controversy in the state and the Urdu news telecast episode on the eve of the assembly election created the "insecurity syndrome" among the Muslims in the state. From the Congress only one Muslim candidate was elected out of 14 Muslim candidates. Thus, the majority of Lingayats, Vokkaligas and Muslims who had extended their support to the Congress (I) in 1989 assembly election revolted against it in the 10th assembly election. S.M. Krishna observed: "The Vokkaligas left us, the Lingayats wreaked revenge on us and finlly even the Muslims deserted us over the Urdu news bulletin issue".[9] Finally, the people of Karnataka wanted a changed and they had visualised that the Janata Dal could provide an alternative stable government.

The Congress (I) bastion was rudely shaken and it was badly mauled by the electorate in 1994. It was routed in the districts of Mandya, Mysore, Coorg and Uttara Kannada. It could win one seat each in Bidar, Kolar, Bangalore, Chikmagalur, and Shimoga districts. Even in north Karnataka it experienced unexpected disaster. It was reduced to the third position with 35 seats in the new house. The voting swing against it was about 14.8 per cent, whereas the swing in favour of Janata Dal was only 2.7 per cent.[10]

III

"The one-party rule theory" put forward by the Congress (I) president was not received favourably by the Karnataka electorate.

In the election campaign at Mandya on November 13, 1994, P.V. Narasimha Rao said:

> The party needs 5 to 10 years of peace and harmony in the country to take it to its full potential. .... The people could ill afford to change the ruling party when the process of development is going on in full swing.[11]

At Hiriyur in Chitradurga district he observed:

> The Congress (I) alone can maintain the integrity and sovereignty of the country, ... it is the only party that can ensure a stable government. The progress of the states and the country as a whole could only be possible if there is the same party government at the centre and in the state.[12]

In its election manifesto, the Congress (I) had focused its attention on political stability, economic development, the benefits of the liberalisation policy, and social peace. But this manifesto did not influence the voters decisively in favour of the Congress (I). Ramakrishna Hegde had ridiculed the Prime Minister's statement that the same party government at the centre and in the state would be helpful for all and dubbed it as "disastrous" for the federal country.

IV

People's preference for the Janata Dal in 1994 was based on several factors: Firstly, Janata Dal's unity and solidarity since mid-1992 and collective leadership did project its image as a viable and capable alternative to the Congress (I). Unity became paramount to contain the growing influence of BJP which polled 28 per cent of the votes and bagged 4 seats in 1991 Lok Sabha elections, and also to capitalise the anti-Congress (I) mood of the electorate. Moreover, the Janata Dal leaders knew that the politics of groupism within the party was one of the main reasons for its debacle in 1989 assembly election. The top leaders had toured the state unitedly covering all districts for more than a year and promised the people, "if the Janata Dal is voted to power, it will set an example to the administration down the line with its leadership conducting itself in an exemplary manner". Ramakrishna Hegde, a stalwart with all-India stature and image said: "We have demonstrated our solidarity in our conduct to enable the voters to repose confidence in us once again".[13] S.R. Bommai, a leader from north Karnataka, had toured this region extensively and intensively along with Hegde and others. In this Lingayat-dominated part of the state, the Janata Dal leaders received overwhelming response. The party wrested 50 out of 96 seats allotted to this area. Moreover, 33 Lingayat candidates were elected from its tickets.

Secondly, elevation of H.D. Deve Gowda, as the president of the state unit of the Janata Dal on August 9, 1993, was an act of prudent political strategy to get massive support from Vokkaligas. Janata Dal's electoral performance in the southern part of the state was very impressive and spectacular. It secured a stunning majority in the Vokkaliga-dominated districts of Bangalore (it captured 15 out of 25 seats), Mandya (7 out of 9), Mysore (11 out of 16), Hassan (5 out of 8), and Chikmaglaur (4 out of 6 seats). 31 Vokkaliga candidates belonging to this party were elected. Altogether, the Janata Dal obtained 66 out of 128 seats allocated to old Mysore.[14] It polled about 57 per cent votes in this part of the state.

Thirdly, the election manifesto of the Janata Dal made a considerable impact on the rural masses. Like many other parties it also indulged in the politics of "competitive populism" to woo the voters. Its manifesto promised to:

1. launch "Nirmal Karnataka" project under which community latrines would be opened in every village;
2. provide potable drinking water to every village through taps and the installation of an underground drainage system in phases;
3. provide "Yellow" cards to the rural and urban poor who are below the poverty line, free medical check-up twice a year, and the group medical insurance;
4. establish an "employment fund" for the rural craftsman and artisans;
5. provide 25 per cent of the working capital for setting up of cottage and tiny industries in rural areas;
6. reserve 70 per cent of jobs to the rural, educated unemployed youths;

7. give working capital, Rs.50,000, for self-employment to eligible unemployed youths;
8. provide low interest loans to the deserving farmers with an ultimate aim to render them debt-free;
9. fix fair and reasonable power tariff for the electricity supply to irrigation pump sets and to ensure supply of uninterrupted power for a minimum of 10 hours a day;
10. evolve a scientifically viable reservation policy to usher in social justice;
11. enact legislation to reserve 25 per cent of seats for women in the assembly and 30 per cent of jobs in the government;
12. supply rice at the subsidised rate of Rs. 3.20 a kg. to all green card-holders; and
13. introduce measures to curb migration of people from other states and to give preference to the Kannadigas in government jobs and in other sectors.

Lastly, there was wide support to the Janata Dal in 1994 from SCs, STs other Backward Communities and Muslims who constituted about 16 per cent, 3 per cent, 27 per cent and 11 per cent of the state population respectively. Out of 35 SC successful candidates 26 were from Janata Dal. Of the 6 ST elected candidates 3 belonged to it. Out of 24 elected legislators from OBCs 7 were elected from the Janata Dal tickets. 3 Muslim Janata Dal candidates also won the election.

Table 17.3: The Position of Janata Party/Dal as a Ruling Party in Karnataka

Sl. No.	*Year*	*Seat won*	*Percentage of votes secured*
1.	1983	95	33.00
2.	1985	139	44.00
3.	1994	116	33.00

V

Karnataka's post-independence history has demonstrated that regional parties do not take root and flourish in its soil. Some reasons can be attributed to this state of affairs. Any kind of regional movement that has taken place in Karnataka has been assimilated into the national movement. Secondly, many regional parties in the state have been formed by the leaders who severed their connection from the national parties due to various reasons. Surajya party founded by K. Hanumanthaiah during the last phase of his political career did not receive the attention of the people and went into oblivion within a short time. Karnataka Kranti Ranga, formed by D. Devaraj Urs and his close associates during early 1980s disappeared from the political scene after the 1983 assembly election. Removal of S. Bangarappa from Chief Minister's post in 1992 made him to form his own party, Karnataka Congress party. It wrested only 10 seats[15] from the districts of Gulbarga (3), Shimoga (2), Chitradurga (1), Uttara Kannada (1), Dakshina Kannada (1), Tumkur (1), and Dharwad (1). It secured about 7.1 per cent of votes polled. The Karnataka Rajya Raitha Sangha, which emerged as a pressure group in the earlier decades, is now struggling hard to become a potential rival to national parties. But its influence is confined to few districts. It was able to get only one seat in 1994 election as against 2 in 1989. Its subsequent poor performance in the Panchayat elections dealt a severe blow to its claim as a rural-based party. Kannada Chaluvali Vathal Paksha is only one man's party without mass support. It may be considered as a pressure group rather than a regional political party.

Conclusion

The 10th Assembly election in Karnataka was a watershed in its political history. It was a democratic revolution to unseat the erring ruling party from power. The Congress High Command's high-handedness in the imposition and removal of Chief Ministers, unhappy performance of the government in the post-Patil period, negligence of grass-root level democracy, indulgence in wrangle and absence of competent leadership at that time chiefly contributed for the sagging image of the Congress (I) and its defeat in the election.

The Janata Dal's emergence as a cohesive and revitalised party with a collective leadership became a turning point in its chequered political history. It received wide support from all sections of the state for its declared faith in democratic values, social justice, secularism, decentralisaion of power and ethics of governance. It became obvious that the secular spirit had influenced the voting pattern in its favour. It wrested 90 seats from 190 general constituencies. It was given only a working majority of 116 instead of a stunning majority to judge its capability of governance and fulfilment of electoral promises.

NOTES AND REFERENCES

1. Michael Brecher, *Succession in India: The Routinization of Political Change*, Asian Survey, July 1967, p. 147.
2. Machenzie, W. J. W., *Free Elections: An Elementary Text Book*, 1958, cited in Norman D. Palmer: Elections and Political Development, New Delhi, Vikas, 1976, p. 4.
3. *Ibid.*, p. 1.
4. Lipset, *Political Man*, New York, Doubleday & Co., 1960, p. 77.
5. V. D. Key, Jr., *Democracy in Perspective: Significance of Recent Elections in India*, India and Foreign Review, 1972, cited in Norman D. Palmer: *Ibid.*, p. 46.
6. The Hindu, 01.11.1994.
7. James Manor, *Democracy in Perspective: Significance of Recent Elections in India*, India and Foreign Review, 1972, cited in Norman D. Palmer: *Ibid.*, p. 46.
8. Sunday, 18-24 December, 1994, p. 31.
9. *Ibid.*, pp. 31-32.
10. India Today, December 31, 1994, p. 81.
11. The Hindu, 14.11.1994.
12. *Ibid.*, 22.11.1994.
13. *Ibid.*, 10.11.1994.
14. India Today, December 31, 1994, p. 81.
15. Five KCP MLAs later defected to Janata Dal.

18

Citizens' Awareness of their Elected Representatives

SANDEEP SHASTRI and HARISH RAMASWAMY

The process of democratic engineering in India and the efforts to expand the democratic space have occupied the spotlight of attention in any analysis of Indian democracy in general and the dynamics of electoral politics in particular. In recent years, survey research has provided a window of opportunity to assess the multi-track factors that have contributed to the ushering in of a new phase of competitive democratic politics across the country. One important trend in this new phase of competitive politics in the citizen's attitude towards the 'dividends' of democracy and more particularly their response to the role and performance of their elected representatives.

In this paper the findings of the State and Society Project Survey on the public awareness of and confidence in elected representatives in Karnataka is analysed. One of the questions in this study sought to measure the level of awareness among the respondents about the representative elected to the local body, the state legislature and the Lok Sabha. They were further asked whether the elected representative took care of the interests of all, some or none at all. Finally, if they mentioned that the elected representative looked after the interests of a few, their response was sought on who those few were. While the study was conducted in 20 states of India, the finds in Karnataka with regard to the above-mentioned issues are reported in this paper.

It is important to record the fact that when the respondents in Karnataka were asked the name of their elected representative in the Lok Sabha, the Legislative Assembly and the local body, the response varied significantly. While sixty per cent of the respondents were able to identify the name of their elected representative in the state legislature correctly, less than half of them knew the name of the Lok Sabha members from their constituency. More than eighty per cent of the respondents knew the name of their elected representative in the local body. There appears to be a direct correlation between the respondents' capacity to identify correctly their elected representative and the level at which these representatives were working. The closer the level they were operating at, the name likely that the respondents identified them correctly.

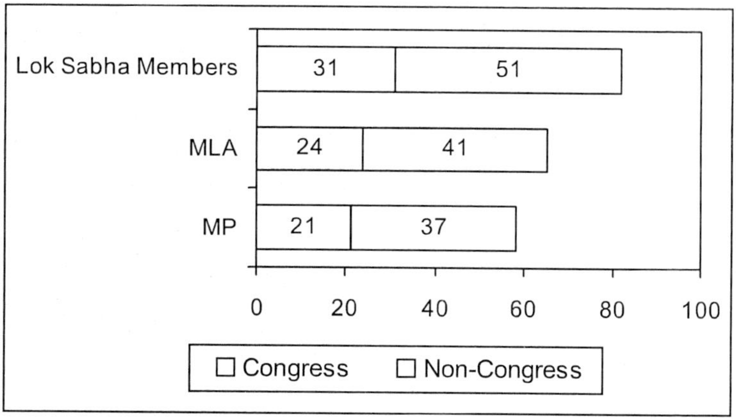

Fig. 18.1: Who is your Lok Sabha MP, MLA and Representative in the Local Body

When asked whether the elected representative took care of the interests of all, or some or none, the percentage of respondents who were unsure of the answer increased as they commented on an elected member who represented them at a more distant level. Nearly two-thirds of the respondents were unsure of the nature of interest that their Lok Sabha member served. While more than half the respondents were similarly ambiguous about the role of their MLA, there was much greater clarity when it came to their representative in the local body, with only one-third being unsure of what stand to take.

A majority of the respondents believed that the local representative served the interests of all. One of every three respondents believed that the MLA served the interests of all and there was a seven percentage point decline when it came to the evaluation of their MP. A little over 10 per cent of the respondents categorically stated that their local body representative served the interests of a few or none. This percentage remains more or less the same in the case of the MLA and the MP.

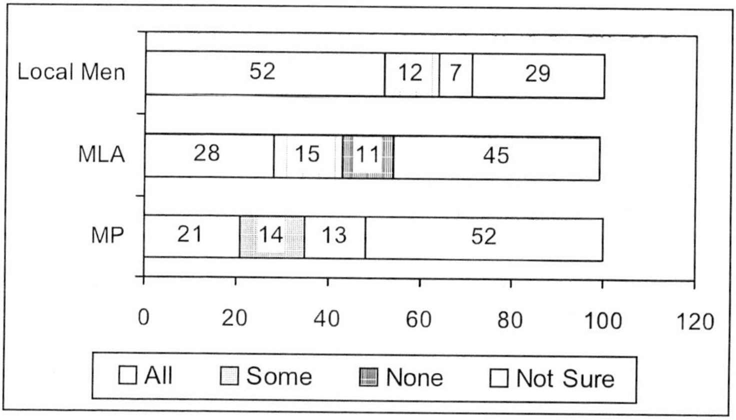

Fig. 18.2: Whose interests does your Lok Sabha MP, MLA and Representative in the Local Body Serve?

Among those who felt that the elected representative served the interests of only a few, the trend did not vary significantly in the case of all the three elected representatives. A majority of those who felt that the elected representatives served the interests of a few, pointed out to the special treatment meted out to those belonging to the party of the representative. The second group rated as being the most favoured by the elected representatives were those who were affluent. Those belonging to the caste of the elected representative were the third most privileged group.

Do all segments of people in the state have a similar degree of information about their elected representatives and there are variations in their assessment of their role ? To account for the variance in the distribution of sentiment on the above factors, the role of education, gender, age, caste and place of residence were analysed. Critical differences emerged with regard to the above demographic variables.

Who is your MP, MLA and Representative in the Local Body: Correct Response Across Gender.

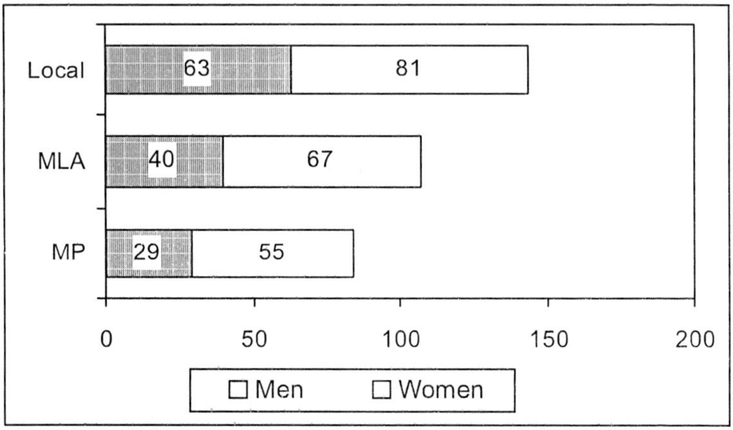

Fig. 18.3: Who is your Lok Sabha MP, MLA and Representative in the Local Body: Correct Response Across Gender

The level of difference between men and women in their awareness about the elected representative was striking. While less than 30 per cent of the women respondents were able to mention correctly the name of the Lok Sabha member from their constituency, the percentage rose—though marginally (to a little over 40 per cent) in the case of the member of the legislative assembly. More than three-fourths of the women respondents were able to correctly recall the name of elected member of the local body.

The difference between men and women in their level of awareness about their elected representative is more than double in the case of the MP. The difference reduces marginally in the case of the member of the legislative assembly and reduces significantly in the case of the local body representative (12% percentage points).

There appears to be a clear link between the social background of the respondents an their level of awareness about their elected representative. Awareness about the elected representative to the Lok Sabha was significantly higher among the Forward Class,

Dominant Castes as compared to the Other Backward Castes and the Dalits. On the other hand, the level of awareness about the representative at the local body was the highest among the Dalits as compared to the Other Backward Castes, Dominant Castes and Forward Castes.

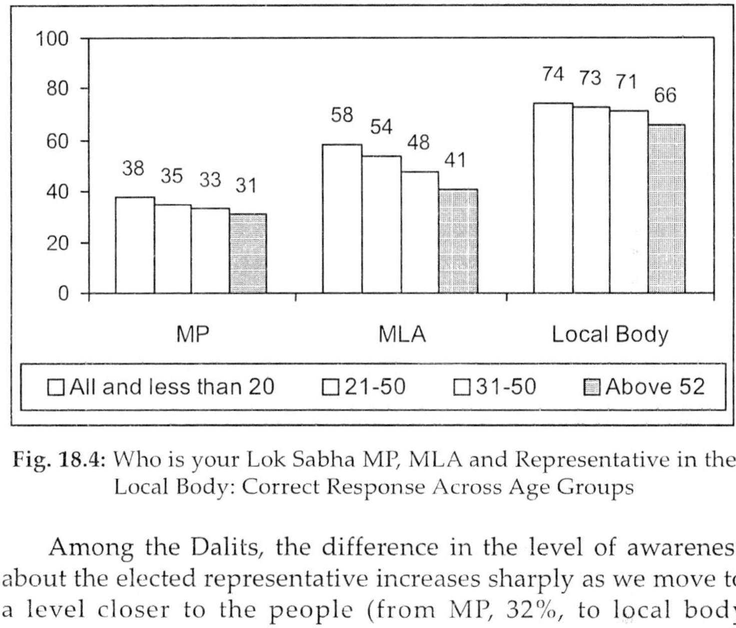

Fig. 18.4: Who is your Lok Sabha MP, MLA and Representative in the Local Body: Correct Response Across Age Groups

Among the Dalits, the difference in the level of awareness about the elected representative increases sharply as we move to a level closer to the people (from MP, 32%, to local body representative, 86%). Similarly, in the case of the Other Backward Communities the level of awareness about the elected representative doubles when one moves from the MP to the local body representative (42% to 84%). This difference is not as skewed in the case of the Dominant Castes and Forward Castes (60% in case of MP and 80% in case of local body representative).

There is a clear link between the level of education and the awareness about the elected representatives. The higher the level of education the greater is the change of the respondent being able to name the elected representative. The only exceptions seems to be in the case of the local body representative. The difference between the level of awareness about elected representatives among the illiterates and the degree holders is pronounced in the case of Lok Sabha members (67 percentage points) and legislators

(40 percentage points). When it comes to the awareness about the local body representative the level of awareness is marginally lower among those who have had the benefit of college education. Among the illiterates there is a much greater likelihood that they are able to name their local representative rather than their state legislator or Member of Parliament. On the other hand in the case of those who have acquired a college degree, the likelihood of their being able to recall rightly the name of their elected representative to the Parliament and the Assembly is much higher as compared to the name of their representative in the local body. This factor is possibly linked to the place of residence (those with the benefit of college education are more likely to be found in urban areas), which is discussed in the next session.

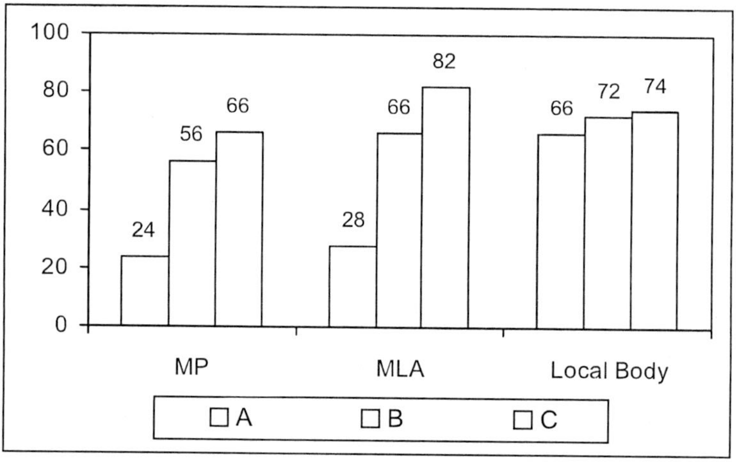

Fig. 18.5: Who is your Lok Sabha MP, MLA and Representative in the Local Body: Correct Response Across Education Groups

When the place of residence of the respondents is taken into account, a unique pattern is noticed. With regard to the elected representative to the Lok Sabha and the Legislative Assembly, there appears to be greater awareness in the towns and cities as compared to the villages. The trend gets reversed in the case of the elected representative in the local body. Here, the level of awareness is higher by 6 percentage points in rural areas as compared to the cities and towns.

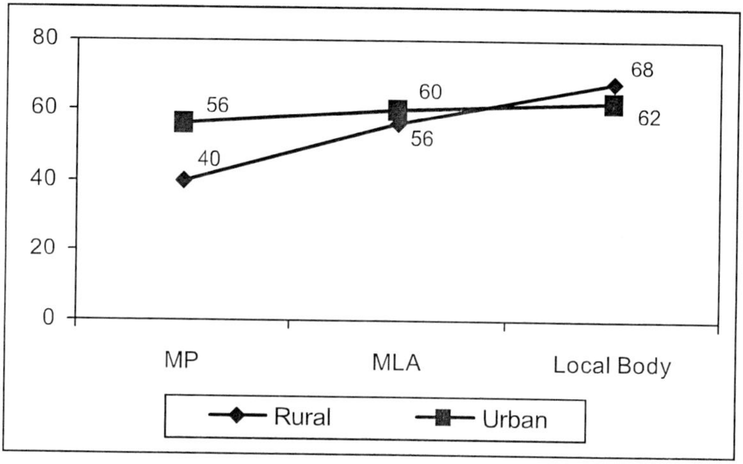

Fig. 18.6: Who is your Lok Sabha MP, MLA and Representative in the Local Body: Correct Response and Place of Residence

Significant difference in perception among the respondents was noticed when the issue, whose interests did the elected representative take care of, was measured. The variation was clearly evident in the case of three important variables—level of education, caste and place of residence. The unhappiness with the performance of the elected representative was the highest among the more educated and gave room for greater optimism as the level of education of the respondent reduced. Among those who had the benefit of college education, more than 20 per cent felt that their elected representative took care of the interests of a few people or none at all. In the case of the illiterates, similar sentiments were expressed by less than 10 per cent of the respondents. The ambiguity with regard to the role played by elected representatives declines among the illiterates as one moves to levels of representation closer to the people.

A similar trend is noticed when the response of those belonging to different social groups is measured. More than 20 per cent of the respondents from among the Forward Castes and Dominant Castes felt that their elected representatives served the interests of a few or none. The degree of pessimism among the Dalits is significantly lower. Further, among the Dalits, the ambiguity in response declines significantly as the respondents are asked to evaluate a representative who works at a level closer to them. It is also noticed that among the Dalits the unhappiness with the functioning of the elected representative is the highest at the level of the local representative—more than 10 per cent felt that the local representative served the interests of some or none.

The survey results also provided proof of the fact that the degree of frustration with the elected representative was significantly higher in urban areas as compared to the villages. There was a fifteen percentage point difference in the response in urban and rural areas on whether the elected representative served the interests of a few or none, with respondents is urban areas being more critical. This pattern holds good for elected representatives at all the degree of ambiguity on the role in representing the interests of society was more pronounced in the urban areas.

A few tentative conclusions could be arrived at from the above findings. These conclusions have important implications for the quality of representation in the state and the perception of the common citizens in this regard.

There is a direct co-relation between the respondents to identify correctly the elected representative and the level at which the elected member represents the people. Respondents were more likely to be aware of who their representative in the local body and less likely to recall correctly their representative in the state legislature and parliament.

Men were more likely to know the name of the elected representative as compared to women. The difference between the level of awareness between men and women is more pronounced when representative at the state and national level are taken into account.

The social background of the respondent is linked in significant ways to the level of awareness about the elected representative. Awareness about the elected representative to the Lok Sabha was significantly higher among the Forward Castes, Dominant Castes as compared to the Other Backward Castes and the Dalits. On the other hand, the level of awareness about the representative at the local body was the highest among the Dalits and marginally lower among the Other Backward Castes, Dominant Castes and Forward Castes.

There appears to be a direct relationship between the level of education of the respondent and their awareness of their elected representatives in the Parliament and the state legislature. The lower the level of education, the lesser the likelihood of their being aware of who their elected representative was. The position gets reversed when it comes to the local government representative.

Urban voters were more likely to be aware of their Lok Sabha and Assembly representative than their rural counterparts. The converse is true in the case of awareness about selected representatives in the local bodies.

The respondents were more likely to be ambiguous when commenting on the performance of their elected representative in the Lok Sabha and State Legislature as compared to the one in the local body.

The unhappiness with the performance of the elected representative was the highest among the more educated and those belonging to the forward and dominant castes.

The lack of faith in the capacity of the elected representatives was much higher in urban areas as compared to the villages.

Among those who felt that the elected representatives served the interests of a few, the "few" essentially included party workers, the rich, those belonging to the caste of the elected representatives and their relatives.

1. The survey was conducted as part of the "State and Society Project", coordinated by the Bangalore University. Dr. Sandeep Shastri was one of the Principal Coordinators of the Project and Dr. Harish Ramaswamy was the Karnataka Coordinator. A rigorous scientific methodology was employed to generate the sample for the survey. A target sample of 8,388 citizens was identified and detailed face-to-face interviews were conducted. The survey was conducted in 18 states of India, which covered nearly 97 per cent of the nation's population. 73 districts were identified for the purpose of the survey. The 73 districts were spread across the 18 states in which survey was conducted keeping in mind the population of the states, even while ensuring that a minimum of two districts were survey in each of the 18 states. In Karnataka, the survey was conducted in 4 districts chosen by random sampling (PPS: probability proportion to size). A target sample of 480 was generated for the state.

2. Respondents are divided into three categories on the basis of their education level: (a) illiterate; (b) Some School (primary pass, matriculate, intermediate); (c) some college (diploma holder, graduate, post-graduate degree). On the basis of place of residence, respondents are divided into (a) Rural and (b) Urban with a further sub-classification of urban into those living in towns and cities.

19

Change of Priorities in Planning

Karnataka

D.M. NANJUNDAPPA

Is there need for Planning?

The rationale of the New Economic Policy is that the government makes a departure from the involvement of the state extensively in economic development keeping the private sector at bay. Yet, under the various Five Year Plans including the VIII, the private sector was presumed to be investing the same proportion as that of the public sector which had extended its arm to a large segment where the private sector could have easily been made to play a bigger role. Planning and markets are complementary both in the national economy and Karnataka's economy, the concept of the mixed economy has produced a framework which would weather the effects of the macro policy adjustments and the much projected restructuring in the national and the regional economies. The fact that the public sector in Karnataka, as in the case of India, has continued to function in several cases with administered prices and central planning of investment thereby distorting to some extent the market mechanism has culminated in various imbalances that are also to be attributed to the imperfections of the market. With such disenchantment, the questions that arise are: *Do we need an approach to the IX Plan?*

What for do we plan it?

The changing perception reflected by the economic liberalisation since 1991 calls for a reorientation of the approach to development. There could be no reversal of the direction which has already been taken and should be sustained during the IX Plan in spite of what the pleaders of a reduction in income inequalities and more employment wish for. At the national level, more of centralised planning, which permeate Indian economy so far will yield place to more of indicative planning, focussing on the future perspectives and allowing the states to have a greater say in the development process. The areas where direct state involvement is required still continue to be same in which a great deal remains to be done. They are, broadly, poverty alleviation, reduction of unemployment, ensuring year-round drinking water facility, expansion of public health services, primary education aimed at a resolute elimination of literacy, construction of badly needed access roads to rural areas, providing housing for the poor and a massive employment generation for the creation of purchasing power among the people. These sectors crying out for attention are very much linked to one another. The farming out of the tasks in the other equally viable areas of industry to the private sector, both Indian and foreign, road transport and communication, infrastructure, power generation and distribution, oil exploration and refining, etc., to mention a few, will ensure that the planning process takes much better care of the vulnerable sections. Further, it is observed that even when investment is thrown open to the private sector, there is hardly any indication of the flow of capital to key infrastructures like irrigation for a strong agricultural foundation, roads and a marketing network where returns at the moment appear not very much attractive for private initiative, domestic or foreign.

Karnataka, therefore, should develop an approach that can take care of the failure of the markets to provide the guidance for investment flow and at the same time propose massive investment in agriculture, rural development and social infrastructure where it is the government intervention that can achieve the desired results. Thus, planning becomes necessary both for accepting direct responsibility for investment in areas appropriate to government through proper resource planning and also for taking care of the depressed areas and the poor for whom the market is not friendly.

Lessons of the Past

The major thrusts in the IX Plan are dictated by the lessons which Karnataka has to learn from its previous plans.

1. Net domestic product at constant prices has been increasing at 5.4 per cent per annum during 1980-94 with instability in the yearly growth rate. The per capita net domestic product at constant prices has been growing at about 3.5 per cent per annum. Here also one notices instability in the yearly growth rate. The growth rate of primary sector, especially of agriculture, is 3.2 per cent. The growth rates of forestry and mining are negative at 1.12 per cent and 2.9 per cent respectively. These are also punctuated by instability in yearly growth rates. The secondary sector has been growing at 7.11 per cent with manufacturing growing at 8.57 per cent. The tertiary sector consisting of transport, trade, banking, insurance, public administration, etc., has been growing at 7.24 per cent. Karnataka has shown the highest growth rate at 11.59 per cent in the financial sector like banking and insurance. It is to be noted that agriculture and public utilities are growing at rates lower than the growth rate of the net state domestic product. Such a record of growth in Karnataka is observed although the broad priorities for allocation of plan outlay both among different sectors and intra-sectors has more or less remained roughly the same.
2. With increasing population and inflation, the higher outlays provided in the plans, especially VIII Plan in comparison with the VII Plan, *reveal* that the infrastructure facilities have, *by and large, deteriorated* during the VIII Plan. In the social infrastructure there is a decline in the facilities per lakh population between 1989-90 and 1995-96 in respect of primary schools, medical sub-centres, hospital beds, borewells with hand pumps, piped water supply scheme, mini water supply scheme and even in financial infrastructure like the bank branches. Irrigation and power have improved marginally while continuing to be very inadequate compared to the need. This is so notwithstanding the rhetoric of the need to develop their

full potential, if Karnataka is to progress *speedily* both on the agricultural and industrial fronts.

3. There is high unemployment which is of great concern. Employment generated is far from adequate when compared to the demand for the work force which is around 1.7-1.9 crore. According the Employment Exchange data and after allowing for the adjustments, more than 8-10 lakh persons are in the category of educated unemployed.
4. In the matter of irrigation, large investments have been made in the public sector but have unfortunately been spread too thinly over a large number of on-going projects and new projects for which token provisions are made. This created a situation of more expenditure but less of commensurate benefits and no resource mobilisation due to removal of all levies on the use of water and the capital gains accruing to land under irrigation. Large leakages are also reported. As for power, the state is reeling under severe shortage. For over two years, there is more of talk about foreign investment in power projects of one type or the other. They are still unborn apart from opposition from environmentalists. There is greater uncertainty surrounding the probable increase in the generation of power in both the private and public sectors. The problem is further compounded by the huge loss incurred by the Karnataka Electricity Board and non-payment to the Karnataka Power Corporation for power supply. There is a dead-lock, as it were, in the matter of resources and firm decisions in solving them.
5. Massive investment in irrigation, power and transport are not taking place contrary to expectations of liberalisation. No doubt, announcements made about investment have put Karnataka at the top place (Rs. 1,11,464 crore). But, investment under implementation in the states is only 6.5 per cent (Rs. 26,063 crore) compared to 15.4 per cent in Gujarat, 7.7 per cent in Madhya Pradesh, 12.4 per cent in Maharashtra, 9.7 per cent in Uttar Pradesh, and 7.2 per cent in Andhra Pradesh out of the total investment made under implementation of Rs. 4,00,692 crore in the country. The direct foreign investment in the state, as per available

data, is only around Rs. 10,000 crore (from August 1991 to June 1999) in comparison with more than Rs.57,000 crore in Maharashtra, Rs. 4,200 crore in West Bengal, Rs. 3,700 crore in Tamil Nadu. Obviously, this suggests the need for better and greater resource planning within the state in so far as the foreign capital flows have been limited.

6. Industrial policy heavily relies on foreign investment and the various incentives offered by the state for the prospective investors. Anxiety coupled with enthusiasm to attract as much foreign investment as possible should not blind us to the adverse repercussions that are likely to follow after some time. The tendency to provide vast lands by way of incentive needs some restraint. Similarly, the Korean case, which has demonstrated that foreign capital would flow once they are convinced about the profitability of the projects even when the state determines the areas in which foreign capital is welcome, should hold out a lesson both for the country and for Karnataka. Investment in service sector like Insurance or Hotels of one type or the other is not helpful to growth and employment generation. While encouraging foreign investment in the state, in the ultimate analysis, domestic resources are to be mobilised for achieving a sustained level of investment. A well thought out policy in regard to foreign investment suited to Karnataka is necessary.
7. Rural development is considered yet a non-starter in so far as the multi-sectoral development in rural areas has not taken place to throw up a scenario of total development of villages thereby contributing to the quality of life of the people inhabiting them. Poverty alleviation measures including IRDP and employment scheme are reported to have reached only 15-20 per cent of the target group. Implementation has come under severe criticism. Rural roads and other infrastructure present a frustrating picture. The rate of urbanisation in Karnataka is increasing and it is likely to touch about 40 per cent in the next five years from the present level of about 26 per cent. Consequently, urban infrastructure is under great strain. Apart from this, sustainable development without harming the environment is somewhat elusive. Pollution

in a city like Bangalore has almost reached the maximum permissible limit fixed by WHO, viz., 200 micro gram/M^3. If left uncontrolled, it can very soon double to reach the intolerable situation prevailing in Calcutta and Delhi where the WHO limit has been already crossed to reach levels like 460 micro/M^3. The lesson is that not only infrastructure in rural and urban areas has to improve, but the environment has to improve or be protected in order to prevent its deterioration to unmanageable and intolerable limits that can soon hit the state and the capital city.

8. The level of poverty is still around 33 per cent and the poor have not enough income to meet their needs. Social infrastructure like health, services, literacy, primary and secondary education, housing and the like is falling short of the estimated requirement both in magnitude and in quality.
9. Panchayat Raj system has been introduced and along with it decentralised planning. But District Plans and Block Plans are not so prepared as to ensure integration of the sectoral and spatial components and realisation of effective implementation. In fact, the focus now should be more on decentralised and micro planning. Serious concern is voiced at all levels about poor implementation and leakages. Proper planning of implementation is more important now than ever before.
10. Even where priorities have been right like irrigation and power, the butter has been spread thinly over a large number of projects, especially river projects. This has contributed to a double crisis. One is that even when a larger allocation of available funds is made to irrigation, the projects are not completed so that benefits can be reaped. The cost overruns and the time overruns have played havoc in irrigation investment. Even with 25 per cent allocation in most of the plans including the VIII Plan outlay for irrigation, the net area irrigated is still around 25 lakh hectares as against an ultimate potential of about 50 lakh hectares. This coupled with unsatisfactory results in the power sector have pushed the resource position of the state to a very precarious situation. This emphaises

the importance of resource planning.

11. In the context of liberalisation and proper management of the Balance of Payments at the macro level, states have to plan for a bigger contribution in the export sector. With Karnataka having an export potential of about Rs. 8,000 crore in agriculture, an *Export Policy* is also to be evolved to get dovetailed with the national policy.

Planning a Policy Regime

The above illustrates that planning now will have to be more *in terms of designing proper policies* and generating more savings within the economy, while external financing will still be inevitable, but in the process, investment pattern between the public and the private sectors in Karnataka will have to be somewhat different from what has been indicated at the national level. The Planning Commission has proposed that the public and the private investments are to be in the ratio of 36 : 64, which in itself is a great deviation from pre-1996 situation of something like 48 : 52 obtaining in the Indian economy so far. A reduction in the public investment of the order of 14 per cent to 34 per cent from a level of 48 : 50 per cent in the VIII Plan creates its own problems both in resource generation and for establishing of an equilibrium.

The major reason for such a design is that private capital, domestic and foreign, is not flowing to irrigation as well as to agriculture. There is evidence of the flow of capital from the external sector to the power projects. Even after admitting the enormous delays in the crystallisation of such project investments, there are the power projects, which are half-through in the public sector, and they are to be completed quickly in the interest of Karnataka's economy. Efforts to have joint ventures are desirable provided the legal bottleneck is removed quickly, and this can to some extent relieve the pressure on public investment. Even then, the IX Plan outlay has to provide not less than 16-18 per cent for generation of power. This is on the heroic assumption that foreign investment and domestic private investment is readily forthcoming of the order visualised. Public investment in agriculture and allied activities, transport, especially, state highways and rural roads, the marketing network and social infrastructure covering health, education, housing, nutrition, rural electrification and sanitation is inevitable and this demands a bigger outlay in the public sector. Therefore, the public and private sector investment ratios will radically differ in Karnataka compared to the National Plan as well as some of the other states. A careful consideration of the relevant segments and their priorities seems to suggest that public sector investment in Karnataka cannot be less than 45-46 per cent.

Given the imperative of obtaining optimal results from the free market forces, even with considerable resources that are to go into public investment, the focus of planning should be of designing a *Policy Regime* rather than indulge in determining the size of the plan, and the growth rate. The two follow without much labour if available recourses are known and we adopt an ICOR. Moreover, the Planning Commission has already indicated that for the IX Plan, it is not going to determine the total size of the State Plans. It will tell the states about how much of central assistance for the plan is likely to become available and ask the states to finalise the outlays by themselves. Given the other component of funds flowing to the states by way of devolution on the basis of the recommendations of the Tenth Finance Commission, it will be entirely the responsibility of the state to determine the outlay for its plan depending upon its own revenue surplus and additional resource mobilisation that can be attempted by it.

Recent estimates of savings are not available for Karnataka. Adopting the national average, even a 24 per cent or 25 per cent savings may turn out to be difficult to achieve in so far as surpluses from the government sector are becoming negative. Anticipated contributions from some of the public sector undertakings have also been negative and they themselves are in need of budgetary support. While it is true that investment expenditures have an impact on the total development, both the state's economy and its people, higher outlays alone do not guarantee commensurate output. The targeting approach, even after the eighth Five Year Plan has landed the state in severe shortfalls, and exaggerated achievement with lesser impact on the quality of life. It is true that quality of life does not depend upon income only. It is the total environment that registers an improvement, including changes in values and attitudes. If we are to adopt the Human Development Index based on life expectancy, educational status and per capita income, Karnataka's welfare stands at a lower pedestal compared to some of the other progressive states. The Physical Quality of

Life Index based on life expectancy at age one, infant mortality rate, illiteracy rate and per capita income for Karnataka is a little above the all-state average (32.8 to 48.9) but below that of states like Kerala, Punjab and Maharashtra. This should be one of the primary concerns of the state for policy formulation.

It is well-known that we have to use our rights in the *Krishna Basin before 2000 AD*. All on-going projects for their completion may require about Rs.10,000 crore. It should be made clear that unless a very strict prioritisation is made, leakages are stopped and resources mobilised for recycling the funds, Karnataka might face a serious destabilisation in this sector which affects the total economy also. The focus shall not confine only to methods of raising resources from the capital market, greater attention should be given to proper utilisation and for getting benefits as early as possible. Although irrigation helps in the development of agriculture and the rural areas, better management or irrigation investment should not be lost sight of. Not recognising the importance of timely completion of projects and deriving benefits therefrom both by way of additional agricultural output and revenues from appropriate user charges, massive investment getting earmarked for irrigation, as a high priority, appears to have contributed, *inter-alia*, to the financial difficulties of the state. The total cost of the projects which are on-going, including new projects incurred so far and the balance needed to complete them at the *present prices* are given below:

Sl. No.	*Name of the Basin*	*Present estimated cost* *Rs. crore*	*Expenditure up to Mar. 96* *Rs. crore*	*Balance needed* *Rs. crore*
1.	Krishna Basin on-going projects and new projects	9,602	2,957	6,749
2.	Cauvery Basin on-going projects and new projects	3,811	1,853	1,957
3.	Godavari Basin on-going projects and new projects	323	168	156
4.	Other Basins on-going new projects	530	18	512
	Total	**14,266**	**4,996**	**9,374**

Source: Adapted from a note sent by the Irrigation Department to the State Planning Board.

It will be seen that as against the total cost of Rs.14,266 crore, only Rs.4,996 crore has been invested so far on the on-going and new projects. The balance of works at the present cost require yet another Rs.9,374 crore including all new projects. Even when on-going projects themselves are not getting enough funds for completion, the investment pattern has led to high investment without yielding commensurate returns. It is quite certain that by the time these projects are completed the cost would almost double and the expectation of deriving full benefits from irrigation investment would get postponed to a very long time in future.

At present the revenue receipts from irrigation do not exceed Rs. 20 crore. When related a total investment of about Rs. 10,000 crore, these receipts do not even cover the maintenance cost. The net consequence has been a deterioration in the maintenance of the irrigation system and at the same time enhancement of the expenditure on irrigation spread over a large number of projects which are not getting fructified within a reasonable period. Hence, there is need for a thorough review of the irrigation investment, priorities and charging for the water supplied as well as for value added to the land resulting from the irrigation facility. In this direction, resources available for irrigation should be allocated to all those projects which can be completed in all respects within the next three years. Then, the other projects, which can be completed in five years, will get the required funding. Under no circumstance, new irrigation project should be taken up nor should tokenism continue in the matter of approvals of new irrigation projects. It is absolutely necessary for optimising the results in irrigation from the scarce resources, one-fourth of which are getting earmarked for irrigation.

Resource Planning

Karnataka's resources have been highly strained. The major reason is that the state has to find nearly 80 per cent of the plan funds from its own tax and non-tax revenues while central assistance is getting stagnant around 20 per cent. Market borrowings are yet to become a balancing factor in plan finance. Assuming some flexibility in borrowings, it is time that a *Note of Caution* is struck about the increasing financial instability that have been funded by debt has to be assessed with real urgency. The policy of the state should be to avoid a high *Debt Service* eating into the resources otherwise available for plan schemes.

It is distressing that year after year Karnataka's original plan outlays approved have been revised by reducing the plan size by nearly Rs. 400-Rs. 500 crore in order to escape the clutches of a possible proportionate reduction in central assistance. VIII Plan approved outlay was reduced by nearly Rs. 1,800 crore and obviously this has severely affected both development and employment generation. It will be startling to know while Karnataka has been reducing its development plan by as much as Rs. 400-500 crore per annum, progressive states like Maharashtra, Tamil Nadu, Gujarat, West Bengal, Kerala, Punjab and Haryana have managed their development plans more efficiently and with no cuts in their plan outlay. Even a state like Rajasthan has maintained its original plan outlays without resorting to any cuts.

From the viewpoint of development, larger plan outlays are required. But the financial management has gone astray in different spheres. The non-plan expenditures are rising with the increase in the share of salaries and wages, interest on loans and repayment needs. The worst is that Karnataka's finances are causing great concern notwithstanding the fact that the per capita tax revenue as per cent of per capita income (Tax effort) is at 17.6 per cent, the highest in the whole country. We have reached the dead-end as it were in the matter of raising more resources from taxation.

The resource crunch is further compounded by the state policy of not applying the benefit cost principle in the matter of user charges for supplying even economic inputs like water for irrigation, power for the IP sets, and transport for commuters. In irrigation investment there is a highly skewed scenario and has enhanced social injustice over the years since the abolition of water rate and betterment levy. This has not only caused disrepairs to the water distributories as well as the dam structures, but has also led to deterioration in the maintenance of these assets. No serious attention has been given to even safe policy recommendations from the State Planning Board to the evolving of a system of user charges for supply of economic inputs. Leakages in power earnings through power theft and high T&D losses of KEB have further added to the agony. Finally, the State Public Undertakings in which there is an investment of about Rs. 13,500 crore are not contributing to the surpluses for re-investment. On the contrary, these incur a loss of nearly Rs.1,600 crore.

The state is following schemes of subsidisation without even a single evaluation of these subsidies ever since they were instituted. On the plan side, the subsidy is more than Rs. 600 core and on the non-plan side, it is around Rs.110 crore leaving our hidden subsides, which exceed about Rs.1,200 crore. Together, nearly Rs.2,000 crore are spent without any attempt being made to assess its impact on output and objective and to determine whether they are to be continued in the coming years. An immediate evaluation of all the subsidy schemes (overt to covert) should be an important policy decision. One of the key elements of resource planning should be to stop budgetary support for all public sector undertakings and adopt a general policy-making most of them to function like commercial enterprises.

Prudence in irrigation investment management demands that there should be a return of at least 6 per cent on the capital invested, if not 12-15 per cent. Even at 6 per cent, about Rs. 800 crore can be raised from the irrigated lands. In so far as the value of the irrigated land has increased enormously over these years, in equity, there is justification for a betterment levy, which once was prevalent in Karnataka, but was abolished. Its re-introduction even at a low rate of Rs. 5,000 per hectare to be paid once in five years. This can bring Rs. 1,250 crore in a five year period or Rs. 250 crore annually. Again power supply to IP sets should be charged reasonably. Even at a rate of no loss no profit for the power supply to IP sets more than Rs.1,000 crore can be raised. Levy of a water rate at Rs.1,000 per hectare can yield Rs. 500 crore per annum altogether for irrigation and power investment. The state should make efforts to mobilise at least Rs. 2,000 crore without imposing much of a burden on the beneficiaries of irrigation investment. For ensuring social justice as between beneficiaries of irrigation and dry land farmers, the proposed returns from irrigation investment are imperative. Otherwise, the state would be subjected to unpardonable neglect and irreparable damage to its growth.

In short, non-tax revenues have to be relied up to a larger extent in the next five or more years. For "Resource Planning" the following approach will be necessary:

(a) Implementing proper user charges for supply of water for irrigation,

(b) Levy of proper user charges for supply of power for IP sets,
(c) Reduction in subsidies after a thorough evaluation of the effects of the subsidies which have been there continuously over decades,
(d) Stricter prioritisation of investment, in particular irrigation investment. No new project shall be taken up unless the on-going projects are completed. Even among the on-going projects, priority should be given to those which can be completed in the following two or three years. This implies diversion of resources out of the outlay to such projects. Balance outlay, if any, must be allocated to projects that can be completed within two years thereafter,
(e) Order energy audit in all KEB circles,
(f) Reduce T&D losses of KEB by at least 2 per cent,
(g) Stop budgetary support for all State Public Sector Undertakings and adopt a general policy by which a package of measures including autonomy, proper pricing, professional management, fixing responsibility for showing a 16 per cent return on the investment and the like. This can include Disinvestment up to 49 per cent in those undertakings where public interest is involved. In all other cases, disinvestment can be done up to 100 per cent. Where service corporations are necessary, they should function on a *no loss no profit basis.*

The state cannot afford to be complacent about its resource position. Introduction of even partial prohibition may lead to a revenue loss of about Rs. 500-600 crore. Continuing to meet the losses of public sector undertakings including irrigation takes away another Rs. 200 crore or so. This apart, project implementation has resulted in both cost over-run and time over-run and leakages. The resource position is very disturbing and cannot be allowed to continue as it is without serious adverse repercussions on the future development of the state and the welfare of its people.

Regional Development Policy

Karnataka has followed in some form or the other regional planning with the adoption of District Planning Approach since the middle of the 1970s. However, it cannot be said to be perfect due to the non-availability of appropriate instruments and precise data for "Decentralised Planning". With the introduction of the Panchayat Raj system in 1986, an institutional framework has been provided for decentralised planning, with the District as the third-tier, the fourth and the fifth coming at the block/taluk level and the Panchayat/Village level respectively. Massive investment has also been made in irrigation projects in the backward districts of Karnataka. Separate boards like Hyderabad-Karnataka Development Board, Malnad Development Board, Maidan Development Board, and the like have been set up with separate budgetary allocations to give an additional thrust for *speedier* development of the backward areas and thus reduce regional imbalances in the state.

Taking Karnataka as a whole, a recent study published in "Productivity" journal puts Karnataka at the fifth place with the state's competitiveness index at 56.19 as against 82.80 for Punjab, 60.63 for Gujarat, 67.71 for Kerala, 39.80 for Rajasthan, 48.77 for Maharashtra, 25.27 for Uttar Pradesh and 22.36 for Bihar. The progress achieved in terms of income generated in the different regions and districts and the distance covered in reaching the highest per capita income among different districts is given in the following table:

District Per Capita Income in Karnataka at Current Prices

Sl. No.	*District*	*1970-71*	*1980-81*	*1990-91*	*1996-97*
1.	Bangalore	699	2114	7164	17915
2.	Bangalore Rural	--	--	--	9040
3.	Belgaum	559	1407	4575	10235
4.	Bellary	797	1586	4478	9971
5.	Bidar	503	1335	3197	6770
6.	Bijapur	479	977	3765	8351
7.	Chikmagalur	1176	1865	6655	15732
8.	Chitradurga	674	1628	4088	9087
9.	Dakshina Kannada	786	1704	5682	11381
10.	Dharwad	586	1289	3705	9333
11.	Gulbarga	622	1386	4098	9568
12.	Hassan	674	1385	3884	8967
13.	Kodagu	1851	3079	10447	19437

(*Contd.*)

(*Contd.*)

Sl. No.	*District*	*1970-71*	*1980-81*	*1990-91*	*1996-97*
14.	Kolar	481	862	3387	7071
15.	Mandya	607	1599	3924	7402
16.	Mysore	742	1466	4305	10615
17.	Raichur	751	1452	4538	7874
18.	Shimoga	968	1810	4531	12097
19.	Tumkur	514	1179	3681	8349
20.	Uttar Kannada	869	1673	4941	10465
	Karnataka State	**685**	**1528**	**4696**	**10504**

Source: Economic Survey, Planning Department for concerned years.

It will be seen that barring Kodagu and Bangalore which have to be considered in the context of other features like coffee plantations in Kodagu and Urban agglomeration in Bangalore, all other districts have been substantial improvement in per capita income between 1970-71 and 1996-97. What is significant is the growth of per capita income is not the same for all the districts between one decade and the other. Although the per capita incomes have risen in all the districts substantially, still several districts (Tumkur, Mandya, Bellary, Kolar, Hassan, Gulbarga, Uttar Kannada, Dharwad, Chitradurga, Raichur, Bijapur, Bidar, Belgaum) continued to have per capita income below the state average even after more than two decades of development. Such districts should receive higher priority in the allocation of plan resources and planning of projects. The extant criteria for distribution of plan funds should be revised with a view to facilitating further weightage being given for the relatively backward districts, measured in terms of per capita income and supplemented by a comprehensive Development Index built on indicators of backwardness.

In formulating the IX Plan the routine approach of the District Allocation on the basis of an objective criteria now followed may have to be supplemented by equalisation grants. In other words, instead of relying only on the finances provided, efforts should be made to equalise the level of services obtaining in the backward districts in comparison with the state average and also reduce intra-disparities. This is to be achieved by looking into the actual physical level of various services including, social and infrastructural, to make a more effective dent into regional disparities. The Panchayat Raj institutions are to be fully involved in the formulation and implementation of schemes of all sectors within the district and also the utilisation of equalisation of grants for achieving better intra-district balance in the matter of development.

Employment Policy

Unemployment, the other side of the poverty coin, is yet another matter of serious concern. The spectre of increasing unemployment in the state is baffling to policy-makers. Creating employment opportunities at the right place, at the right time and at the right number for the target groups should permeate the new thrusts for employment planning. The NSS data indicate that Karnataka has registered an overall growth rate of employment of 2 per cent per annum while the labour force has grown at the rate of 2.8 per cent per annum. The gap between the two gives an overall measure of the demand for working in relation to the supply of work opportunities. Paucity of data and lack of precise estimates of unemployment confront the planning process with too many constraints. Estimates of labour force, employment and unemployed in 1993-94 are given in Table 3 and 4, referred to earlier.

According to the Live Registers of employment Exchanges' Data, adjusted for deficiencies, would still give a figure of around 17 lakh as unemployed. Of these, the educated unemployed is as high as about 10 lakh. Unemployed Diploma Holders and ITI Certificate holders have increased *six times* between 1980-1997. During this period, post-graduates, who are unemployed, have increased almost *three times*. Even unemployed graduates have increased more than *two times*. The least increase is among below matriculates, implying a lesser growth of unemployed among the less skilled categories. Approach to employment policy should fully reflect the severe poverty conditions and without getting bogged down by the lack of precise estimates of unemployed and employment generated under different schemes, the IX Plan should aim at offering "*An Employment Guarantee Scheme*" thereby claiming the right work as a constitutional obligation. This alone can be a reliable antidote to poverty besides the developing the rural infrastructure by utilising all employment schemes and other development projects in an integrated manner under an area approach. Karnataka should make a determined bid to achieve full employment by the end of the IX Five Year Plan.

A Happy Society: Social Services

It is not just the growth rate which matters if a good society is to be established in the state. The social services covering general education, technical education, medical and public health, family welfare, water supply and sanitation, housing, nutrition, labour and employment, ought to get higher priority so that human resources development takes place at the required pace to achieve a higher growth in the NDP of Karnataka. In the planning process, notwithstanding the restrictions imposed by the Planning Commission on allocation for the social services, the state showed greater understanding by allocating a higher proportion than what was approved for the social services. Consequently, there is an appreciable growth in the social services. It goes to the credit of Karnataka for having introduced "Rural Housing Scheme" and "employment Assurance Scheme" for the poor in the early 1970s.

With liberalisation, more public investment should go to social services. This depends upon the development outlay under the Five Year Plans. The total plan outlay has increased from Rs. 145 crore in the Second Plan to about Rs. 11,000 crore in the Eighth Plan. For a recent period like 1989-94 when there is considerable exhortation about the need to improve social services, the total expenditure rose from Rs.1,286 crore in 1989 to Rs.2,677 crore in 1993-94. As a proportion of the total budgeted expenditure, it showed an improvement from 48.3 per cent to 53 per cent; but these are lower than the All States' average ratio of expenditure on social services to total budgeted expenditure. If one were to go deeper, especially comparing the needs of the state, the sectoral expenditure on education increased hardly by 5 per cent to 6 per cent. Expenditure on secondary education is more than double. But even this is inadequate compared to the needs of the state. Expenditure in technical education has drastically declined and this is a highly disturbing feature. Expenditure on universities and higher education went up from 3.1 per cent to more than 17.6 per cent. There is, however, a reduction in recent years. This has not been reconciled to by the advocates of larger allocation for higher education, keeping in view, international scenario and also the lower proportion of the population getting into higher education in Karnataka or in India. Expert opinion differs on the issue of relative priority for higher education. State resources need not go to subsidise higher education in so far as the monetary benefits get localised in the individual although there is diffusion of social benefits. Funds for higher education should come from fees linked to costs with enough scholarships and freeships for the poor and merited. More serious attention should be given to the evolving of a "Self-financing System" of higher education in the state with proper regulation and safeguards to prevent quality deterioration.

Even within education, removal of illiteracy, especially among women should receive the highest priority. As part of the educational reform, determined action should be taken for teaching through nature, geography, history, birds and forests, the contents of elementary and primary education. Karnataka should achieve 100 per cent literacy and compulsory primary and secondary education by the end of IX Five Year Plan. This must be attempted even if necessary by reducing outlays on irrigation by a couple of crores to provide Rs. 500 crore more for primary education. As for vocational courses, government should privatise the ITIs and involve the Chamber of Commerce and Industry in giving training in the various vocations needed on the lines presently followed with great success in Germany.

Karnataka's Health Service has come under great criticism. The hospitals and medical institutions maintained by the government have deteriorated considerably in terms of the facilities and the quality of service. It is astonishing to note that the number of beds per lakh population has declined from 106 in 1987 to 77 in 1997. Similarly, sub-centres per lakh population have also declined from 18 to 16. The per capita outlay on health is Rs. 104 in comparison with a state like Punjab where it is around Rs. 120. Karnataka once occupied the pride of place in health services. Unfortunately, over the years, while the total physical facilities have increased in respect of number of doctors and PHCs, the status of buildings of PHCs and sub-centres, resources for drugs and health workers, the position in Karnataka is unsatisfactory compared even to some of the neighbouring states like Andhra Pradesh, Kerala and Tamil Nadu. Compared to the national average per capita expenditure on health including water supply and family welfare, that of Karnataka was lower in 1985-86 and continues to be so even now. It goes without saying that larger resources are needed for the health sector too.

Among the various schemes of social service, housing has been given a big push in the state in the VIII Five Year Plan. Larger allocations have, no doubt, been made for drinking water supply. The policy-makers have failed to note that the villages are also gradually growing with the state's Housing Policy for the poor and this coupled with an increase in population would demand further new outlets for potable drinking water.

It is encouraging that nutrition has maintained a higher share and by the beginning of 1990s its share touched about 5 per cent with tendencies to grow higher. This should be made an adjunct to population control measures.

Notwithstanding the shortfall in the social service sector in a state like Karnataka which had ascended to a higher level in the national scenario earlier but had declined in later years, concerted efforts are being made in the areas of Human Resources Development like education, health, housing, rural electrification, rural roads, rural water supply, nutrition, removal of illiteracy, village sanitation, etc. Development should be around the people and not the other way. Focussing improvement of the quality of life for the people should be a strong feature of Karnataka's policy formulation. The state should make social services one of the crucial sectors for developing its future growth strategy.

Urban Development Policy

The most pressing problem of the state, apart from power, irrigation and agriculture, seem to be those of urban transportation and rural housing. There is haphazard growth of traffic while the road infrastructure is totally insufficient. Problems of pollution are increasing; they are yet to be tackled. Mega projects have been drawn up for Urban Mass Rapid Transit System; but they are unlikely to fructify even in a medium term like 5-10 years mostly due to severe resource constraints. The immediate requirements have to be met. In this context, one suggestion could be that a Radial Railway system should be provided for Bangalore *immediately* utilising the present railway network. The needs and their estimation should be based on the anticipated growth in rural housing and the increase in the population of villages. Neglect of these factors has led to a situation where Karnataka, which was the first state at one stage in the whole country to provide adequate drinking water supply to all the villages in the state, has been confronting now an unenviable reputation. The latest available data show, that there are still about 6,000 villages which have no drinking water facilities. All such villages should be covered fully in the first two years of the IX Plan. Also a major dent should be made in planning for protected piped water supply to at least 30 per cent of the villages by the end of the IX Five Year Plan.

Rural Development Cries for a New Vision

Notwithstanding very large outlays on rural development under different schemes, there are grave deficiencies in Karnataka. In particular, sanitation has not made any dent in rural areas and some kind of a crash programme is required on the lines recently adopted in China. In the IX Plan, 50 per cent of villages should get sanitary facilities and all villages should be covered within 10 years from now. Rural development being a multi-sectoral activity, the approach should be one of integrated development bringing the various components of rural uplift under a well-knit scheme to be implemented by the Panchayat Raj institutions. In particular, rural roads, cultural centres and youth clubs have to get special attention.

Mass Rapid Transit system which involves astronomical investment is to be accepted with a pinch of salt. While any long-term solution of this type should form a part of the strategy, what could be done immediately with or without any marginal investment should be given the highest priority. The railway network should be able to provide radial services in three directions like Bangalore-Kengeri, Bangalore-Yeshwantpur and Bangalore-Krishnarajapuram. Electric Multiple Units should be deployed on these radials. This would handle substantial commuter traffic. The road transport services handled by KSRTC should be rearranged making the start off from the centres served by the radial railway station. Simultaneously, railways must start work on establishing a fourth corridor from Jayanagar to Rajajinagar. During the IX Plan at least 10 or 12 growing towns and cities should be developed with the required infrastructure to function as counter magnets to metropolitan cities in the state.

Restraint on Non-Plan Expenditures

It is often mentioned that that the non-plan expenditure is on the rise and if this is not reduced, there is little hope of finding more resources for development. Even as late as 1996-97 in Karnataka, development expenditure as per cent of total expenditure is 70.5 per cent. This implies that non-development expenditure forms nearly 30 per cent or roughly one-third of the total expenditure. It is not that all non-development expenditure can be controlled. They relate either to the use of funds on the non-plan side for capital works (like Cauvery basin river projects) or for providing interest and repayment of loans and meeting revised emoluments of bureaucracy. The whole gamut of expenditures should be reviewed to develop norms for efficiency and save every rupee of non-productive expenditure. Probably, this demands an "Expenditure Commission" which can go into the growth of expenditure over these years, examining the manner in which loans have been utilised, what returns to capital expenditures are obtained, what is the level of user charges for economic services and to what extent subsidies that distort production and distribution can be either eliminated or rationalised. In fact, government should turn its attention *to doing more with less* instead of only preaching it to others. The state will do well if it appoints an "Expenditure Commission" immediately to report within one year, a time-bound affair.

Political Will

The development of Karnataka is not purely a matter of economic and social policies. It is equally connected with the political aspects. For a successful functioning of a democracy and with it the development process, political decision-makers and the bureaucrats should function in a detached manner free from any selfishness. Unfortunately, developments in Karnataka are somewhat disheartening. Dr. Ambedkar, the architect of our constitution, while listing out conditions for a successful functioning of democracy in India, included the following two along with others. (1) A Statutory Moral Order and (2) The functioning of a Social Moral System in Society. It is high time that the politicians and the bureaucrats take note of them for a stricter observance in their conduct and behaviour.

There is an obligation on the part of elected representatives and appointed bureaucracy to explain to the people the development of the state, the policy measures needed to achieve the objectives set up in the development plans and assist in the generation of a willingness on the part of the people to accept measures of resource mobilisation either by way of an additional levy or a charge for inputs provided like water or electricity by the Department/Undertakings of the State Government that are to function on a commercial basis for their self-sustenance. On the contrary, if an environment of reticent response is directly or indirectly created, it will run counter to the developmental objectives and to the very welfare of the people in the long run. Unless credit supply, payment of user charges, repayment of loans and the like are made to move smoothly with understanding and appreciation from the people as a whole, the wheels of development are bound to get clogged. It is unfortunate that Karnataka is going through such a procrustean process due to political developments. The bureaucracy is also demoralised. Corruption and political turncoatism have played havoc striking at the very vitals of democracy and this should be stopped. Dissent can and should be in respect of policy aims and objectives; but should never be on personal considerations and survival exigencies. Motherland is more exalted than heaven, an observation of Sri Bankim Chandra Chatterji, the father of nationalism, should ever be reverberating in the minds of both the elected representatives and the appointed bureaucrats to prevent any deviations from the path of dedication, equity, service and sacrifice.

Conclusion

The IX Five Year Plan of Karnataka has been prepared at a time when its resources are very much strained, implementation being very poor, decision-making getting procrastinated and a general sense of demoralisation in the socio-economic scenario affecting the democratic system as well as the bureaucratic dedication. The approach suggested in this paper replies heavily on policy-making and its contents than on indicating what the total outlay or the growth rate for the IX Plan should be. Given these policies and the resources in sight for the next five years, one can expect a reasonable improvement in the growth of Karnataka's economy. Whether the growth rate should be 6.0 per cent or 7.0 per cent or more need not be a redherring in developing our approach to the planning within the broad framework of indications of the future shape of things and detailed micro planning under the Panchayat Raj system. The policy regime discussed in this paper would call for large public investment in agriculture, irrigation, rural transport and basic minimum needs including housing and a special priority for 100 per cent literacy and compulsory primary and secondary education to be achieved by the end of the IX Five Year Plan. The needs are that agriculture should grow at 5 per cent, industrial growth at 16 or 18 per cent, reducing urban-rural disparities to the barest minimum with an approach of equalisation of the level of services in the matter of grants to different regions. There should be massive free flow of private (domestic and foreign) capital to power, urban transport, roads, ports, irrigation, agricultural marketing network with some social obligations as found in the South Korean Policy frame. Power generation should reach 7,500 MW by 2000 AD and this will be a necessary condition for fulfilling the broad directions reflected in the change of priorities. *Inter-alia*, utilising science and technology to reduce poverty and unemployment, providing full employment by making employment a *fundamental right* along with rural development, giving an Education Guarantee Scheme (up to PUC), informing all authorities and respondents about people friendly management culture, developing a vision of the state's trade both with other states in India and abroad, aiming at a higher export target, focussing on better infrastructure, credit, and technology for agricultural and industrial production emphasising cost-efficiency and time-efficiency, offering requisite facilities for sports and cultural programmes specially in rural areas, giving an exposure for specialised skills from both within the country and from outside and crowning it all with education-employment focus in social and economic development policies, primary and secondary education getting a larger share of public funds, improving the quality of life particularly in rural areas and of weaker sections of society and restoring moral values in public policy flashing the richness of the societal outcome are to be the major components of the perspective of the New Plan. They expect a strong and effective Monitoring and Evaluation Mechanism, supported by involvement of voluntary organisations, generating a sensitive public response and a commitment to people's welfare on the part of the bureaucracy and the elected representatives at all levels.

20

The Karnataka Right to Information Act, 2000

B.K. CHANDRASHEKAR

An Act to provide for the right of access to information to the citizens of the state and in relation to the matters connected therewith or incidental thereto. Whereas as right to government held information is accepted by the Supreme Court as a part of the right to speech and expression guaranteed to the citizens in the Constitution. And whereas providing the right of access to information to the citizens of the state promotes openness, transparency and accountability in administration and ensures effective participation of the people in the administration and also makes democracy meaningful. And whereas it is expedient to provide for the right of access of information to the citizens of the state and in relation to the matters connected therewith or incidental thereto and for the purposes hereinafter appearing: Be it enacted by the Karnataka State Legislature in the fifty first year of the Republic of India as follows:

1. Short Title and Commencement—(1) The Act may be called the Karnataka Right of Information Act, 2000.

(2) It shall come into force from such date, as the State Government may, by notification, appoint, and different dates may be appointed for different provisions of this Act.

2. Definitions—In this Act, the context otherwise requires:

(a) "Competent authority" means the head of the office or any officer or person as may be notified by the State Government for the purpose of this Act:

Provided that where the Competent Authority transfers applications to any officer or person under the proviso to sub-section (2) of Section 5, such officer or person shall be deemed to be the "Competent Authority".

(b) "Information" means information relating to any matter in respect of the affairs of the administration or decisions of a public authority;

(c) "Public authority" means:

   (i) all offices of the State Government including the Karnataka Public Service Commission;

   (ii) all local authorities, all authorities constituted by or under any Act of the State Legislature for the time being in force, a company, Corporation, trust, society, any statutory or other authority, Co-operative society or any organisation or body funded, owned or controlled by the State Government, but does not include:

      (i) offices of the Central Government;

      (ii) any establishment of the armed forces or Central Para-military forces;

      (iii) any body or corporation owned or controlled by the Central Government;

(d) "Right to Information" means right of access to information from any public authority:

   (i) by obtaining certified copies of any records;

   (ii) by obtaining diskettes, floppies or any other electronic mode or through print-outs where such information is stored in a computer or any other device;

   (iii) in such other manner as may be prescribed.

(e) "record" includes:

   (i) any document, manuscript or file;

   (ii) any microfilm, microfiche and facsimile copy of a document;

   (iii) any reproduction of image or images embodied in such microfile (whether enlarged or not); and

   (iv) any other material produced by a computer or by other device.

(f) "Trade secret" means information contained in a formula, pattern, compilation, programme, device, product, method, technique or process which is not generally known and which may have economic value.

3. **Obligation of Public authorities**—Every public authority shall:

(a) maintain all records in such manner and form as is consistent with its operational requirements duly catalogued and indexed;
(b) publish at such intervals as may be prescribed:
  (i) the particulars of its organisation, functions and duties;
  (ii) the power and duties of officers and employees and the procedure followed by them in the decision-making process;
  (iii) the norms set up by the public authority for the discharge of its functions;
  (iv) the details of facilities available to citizens for obtaining information;
(c) publish all relevant facts concerning such of the important decisions and policies that affect the public as may be prescribed while announcing such decisions and policies;
(d) before sanctioning or initiating or causing to sanction or intimate any project scheme or activity as may be specified by the State Government, publish or communicate to the public generally or to the persons affected or likely to be affected by the project, scheme or activity in particular in such manner as may be prescribed, the facts available to it or to which it has reasonable access which in its opinion should be known to them in the best interests of maintenance of democratic principles;
(e) publish such other information as may be prescribed.

4. **Right to Information**—(1) Subject to the provisions of the Act every citizen shall have the right to information.

(2) Notwithstanding anything contained in sub-section (1), no person shall be given:

(a) information, the disclosure of which would prejudicially affect the sovereignty and integrity of India, security of the State, strategic scientific or economic interest of India or conduct of international relations;
(b) information, the disclosure of which would prejudicially affect public safety and order or which may lead to an

incitement to commit an offence or prejudicially affect fair trail or adjudication of a pending case;

(c) information relating to Cabinet papers including records of the deliberations of the Council of ministers, Secretaries and other officers:

Provided that information regarding the decisions of the Cabinet along with the reasons leading to the decision shall be made available and every Government Order issue on the basis of the cabinet decision shall be accompanied by a statement explaining the reasons for and circumstances under the decision is taken;

(d) information the disclosure of which would harm, frankness and candour of internal discussions including inter-department or intra departmental-notes, correspondence and a paper containing advice or opinion as also of projections and assumptions relating to internal policy analysis:

Provided that information regarding minutes or records, advice including legal advice, opinion or recommendation made or given in respect of the executive decisions or policy formulations shall be made available after an executive decision is taken or policy formulation is done.

(e) information the disclosure of which would prejudice the assessment or collection of any tax, cess, duty or fee or assist in avoidance or evasion of the tax, cess, duty or fee;

(f) information the disclosure of which would constitute a breach of privilege of the Parliament or the State Legislature:

Provided that the Competent Authority shall before withholding information under this clause refer the matter to the Karnataka Legislature Assembly Secretariat or the Karnataka Legislative Council Secretariat, as the case may be, for determination of the issues and act according to the advice tendered by the Secretariat:

Provided further that in computing the period of thirty working days under sub-section (2) of Section 5 for the purpose of this clause, the time required for determination of issues under the first proviso shall be excluded;

(g) information regarding trade or commercial secrets protected by law or information, the disclosure of which would prejudicially affect the legitimate economic and commercial interests or the competitive position of a public authority; or would cause unfair gain or loss to any person;

(h) information regarding any matter which is likely to;

(i) help or facilitate escape from legal custody or affect prison security; or

(j) impede the process of investigation or apprehension or prosecution of offenders.

5. Procedure for Supply of Information—(1) A person desirous of obtaining information shall make an application to the competent authority in the prescribed manner, along with such fee, in such form and with such particulars, as may be prescribed:

Provided that the fee payable shall not exceed the actual cost of supplying information.

(2) On the receipt of an application requesting for information, the competent authority shall consider it and except for justifiable reasons, pass order thereon either granting or refusing it, as soon as practicable and in any case within fifteen working days from the date of receipt of the application:

Provided that where the competent authority does not have the information, he shall within fifteen days from the date of receipt of application transfer the application to the office or person with whom such information is available and inform the applicant accordingly and thereafter such officer or person to whom such application is transferred shall furnish information within fifteen working days from the date of receipt of the application from the competent authority.

(3) Where a request is rejected under sub-section (2), the competent authority shall communicate in writing to the person making the request:

(i) the reasons for such rejection;

(ii) the period within the appeal against such rejection may be preferred;

(iii) the particulars of the appellate authority.

6. Grounds for Refusal to Supply Information in Certain Cases—Without prejudice to the provisions of Section 4, the competent authority may also reject a request for supply of information where such request:

(a) is too general in nature and the information sought is of such nature that it is not required to be ordinarily collected by the public authority:

Provided that where such request is rejected on the aforesaid ground, it shall be the duty of the Competent Authority to render help as far as possible to the person seeking information to reframe the request in such a manner as may facilitate the supply of information;

(b) related to information that is required by law, rules regulations or orders to be published at a particular time; or

(c) relates to information that is contained in published material available to public;

(d) relates to personal information the disclosure of which has no relationship to any public activity or which would cause unwarranted invasion of the privacy of an individual except where larger public interest is served by disclosure:

Provided that the information relating to returns of assets and liabilities filed by the Government servant shall be made available to the public.

7. Appeals—(1) Subject to such rules, as may be prescribed, any person:

(i) aggrieved by an order of the competent authority may, within thirty days from the date or receipt of such order; or

(ii) who has not received any communication within a period of fifteen working days from the date of making application under Section 5, may within thirty days next after such period;

appeal to such authority as may be prescribed:

Provided that no appeal shall lie against an order of withholding of information under clause (f) of sub-section (2) of Section 4.

(2) The appellate authority may, after giving the person affected a reasonable opportunity of being heard, pass such order as it deems fit.

(3) Any person aggrieved by the order of the appellate authority under sub-section (2) may prefer an appeal to the Karnataka Appellate Tribunal.

(4) Appeals referred to in sub-sections (1) and (3) shall be disposed of within thirty days from the date of receipt of such appeals.

8. Power to Remove Difficulties—If any difficulty arises in giving effect to the provision of this Act, the State Government may by an order make such provisions not inconsistent with the provisions of this Act and appear to them to be necessary or expedient for removing the difficulty:

Provided that no such order shall be made after the expiry of two years from the date of commencement of this Act.

9. Penalties—Where any competent authority without any reasonable cause fails to supply information sought for within the period specified under Section 5 or furnishes information which is false with regard to any material particulars and which it knows or has reasonable cause to believe it to be false:

(i) the authority immediate superior to the competent authority may impose a penalty not exceeding two thousand rupees on such competent authority as it thinks appropriate after giving him a reasonable opportunity of being heard and such a penalty shall be recoverable from his salary or if no salary is drawn as arrears of land revenue; and

(ii) he shall also be liable to disciplinary action under the service rules applicable to him.

10. Bar of Jurisdiction of Courts—No Court shall entertain any suit, application or other proceeding in respect of any order made under this Act and no such order shall be called in question otherwise than by way of an appeal under this Act.

11. Act to have Overriding Effect—The provisions of this Act shall have notwithstanding anything inconsistent therewith contained in any other law made by the State Legislature in respect of any matter falling under State list or concurrent list except the provisions of any existing law or a law made by Parliament in respect of any matter falling under concurrent list.

12. Power to Make Rules—(1) The State Government may, after previous publication by notification, make rules to carry out the provisions of this Act.

(2) In particular, and without prejudice to the generality of

the foregoing power, such rules may provide for all or any of the following matters, namely:

(a) the fee payable under Section 5;
(b) any other matter which is required to be, or may be prescribed.

(3) Every rule made under this Act shall be laid as soon as it is made, before each House of the State Legislature while it is in Session for a total period of thirty days which may be comprised in one session or in two or more successive sessions and if before the expiry the session in which it is so laid of the session immediately following, both the Houses agree in making modification in the rule or both Houses agree that rule should not be made thereafter, shall have effect only in such modified form or be no effect, as the case may be, so however, that any such modification or annulment shall be without prejudice to the validity of anything previously done under that rule.

13. Repeal and Savings—(1) The Karnataka Right to Information Ordinance, 2000 (Karnataka Ordinance No. 9 of 2000) is hereby repealed.

(2) Notwithstanding such repeal anything done or any action taken under the said Ordinance shall be deemed to have done or taken under this Act.

STATEMENT OF OBJECTS AND REASONS

(As appended to at the time of introduction)

The Karnataka Right to Information Bill, 2000, among other things provides for the following:

(i) Requiring public authorities to make voluntary disclosure of certain information referred to in clause 3.
(ii) Listing exemption from giving information under certain circumstance as mentioned in clause 4.
(iii) Specifying the procedure for supply of information;
(iv) Specifying the grounds for refusal to supply information in certain cases.
(v) Imposing a penalty on the competent authority up to two thousand rupees for failure to give information without any reasonable cause.

(vi) An appeal is provided against the order of the competent authority and a second appeal lies to the Karnataka Appellate Tribunal.

Certain incidental provisions are also made.

Since the matter was urgent and the Karnataka Legislature Council was not in session, Karnataka Right to Information Ordinance, 2000 (Karnataka Ordinance No. 9 of 2000) was promulgated to achieve the object.

Hence the Bill.

FINANCIAL MEMORANDUM

There is no extra expenditure involved in the proposed measure.

EXPLANATORY STATEMENT AS REQUIRED BY SUB-RULE (1) OF RULE 77 OF PROCEDURE AND CONDUCT OF BUSINESS IN THE KARNATAKA LEGISLATURE COUNCIL

It is considered necessary to have a legislation to provide the right to access to information to the citizens of the State which would promote openness, transparency and accountability in administration and ensure effective participation of people in the administration.

MEMORANDUM REGARDING DELEGATED LEGISLATION

Clause 3: In Clause 3 —

(i) sub-clause (b) empowers the State Government to make rules regarding the intervals at which the particulars organisation functions, powers and duties of its officers and employees and details of facilities available to citizens, etc., are to be published.

(ii) sub-clause (c) empowers the State Government to make rules regarding the important decisions and policies which are to be published.

(iii) sub-clause (d) empowers the State Government to make rules regarding the manner in which the projects, scheme or activity, which affects the public, in general have to be published.

(iv) sub-clause (e) empowers the State Government to make rules regarding such other information to be published.

Clause 4: In sub-clause (2)—

(i) the proviso to item (c) empowers the State Government to make rules regarding cabinet decisions along with reasons to such decision which will be made available to the public.

(ii) the proviso to item (d) empowers the State Government to make rules regarding the minutes, or records, advice including legal advice, opinion or recommendation.

Clause 5: Sub-clause (1) empowers the State Government to make rules regarding the manner, in which an application may be made by any person to obtain any information.

Clause 6: The proviso to sub-clause (d) empowers the State Government to make rules regarding the circumstances at which the assets and liabilities filed by any government servants shall be made available to public.

Clause 7: Sub-clause (1) empowers the State Government to make rules regarding the circumstances under which and the authority to whom an appeal may be preferred by the person aggrieved by an order of the competent authority or a person who has not received any communication within a period of thirty days from the date of his application for information.

Clause 13: Clause 13 empowers the State Government to make rules after previous publication in general and in particular regarding fee payable under Section 5 or any other matter which is required to be or may be made.

The proposed delegation of legislative power is normal in character.

21

New Social Movements in Karnataka

History, Strategies and Discourses

MUZAFFAR ASSADI

Unlike the other parts of India, Karnataka witnessed very few social movements, the post-colonial period. One such preceding the colonial period was the Lingayat movement led by Basavanna (Ishwaran: 1983). His protest was against caste discrimination and it was for social equality. It was popularly called Bhakti movement. It was one movement that brought a paradigm shift in the socio-cultural practices of Karnataka.

However, until the end of the British rule, there were sporadic peasant or farmers' revolt. The first came to surface during 1800 when the British introduced a new tax system in the coastal belt (Assadi: 1997: 25). Peasants adopted a novel method of immigrating to other areas. Nonetheless the massive peasant movement arose in the 1830s in the Old Mysore province called Nagar Division in the present Shimoga district. It all began when the princely state introduced "Sharath System" of selling the land to the highest bidder. Interestingly, this struggle also combined such other issues as nepotism, anti-upper caste hold over the state, etc. It was the one that had tremendous effect on the princely state. In fact, the British used the pretext of peasant discontent to their advantage, and took over the state. For the next thirty years the Mysore princely state was under the British rule. However, until the end of 1920, there wasn't any peasant struggle. During 1920 the peasants of Mandya district took out a long march to Bangalore to redress their grievance. During the nationalist movement peasants did participate in Forest Satyagraha, civil disobedience, non-co-operation. etc.

Nonetheless, other social movements such as the one by tribals was embedded with the sepoy mutiny of 1855. On the contrary, ecological issues mediated through the nationalist movement. Since they were a part of a larger struggle, they had no separate identity.

This calls for an explanation as to why very few movements came to surface in Karnataka until the end of the British rule. First, there was uneven development between and across the regions. This made the task of uniting different social categories difficult. Secondly, the experience of exploitation also varied due to the presence of various rural/agrarian structures and social set up. Most important was the fact that the state, princely state, was a liberal state, which would accommodate different social categories into its fold by providing spaces in the state administration. This largely contained the discontent simmering from below. This is the reason why Gandhi called Mysore state as "Ram Rajya". Finally, during this decade the state did not witness different forms of crises such as the ecological/ environmental of urban space, of working class, including the fact that the state did not witness massive growth of industries. This is the reason why majority of the social movements occurred came to surface during the post-independence period.

Nonetheless, post-independence movements are popularly called "New Social Movements" (Brass: 1995). This conceptualization is done on the basis of the following:

- Unlike the earlier movements the "New" social movements are concerned with the larger issues afflicting social categories.
- These movements believe in undivided social categories and thereby advocate class harmony and unity among the categories.
- New Social Movements are no more confined to the rural areas rather their operational areas have expanded to reach global level.
- They believe in forming larger collectives both at the national and international level.
- They have distinct notions about history and the future.

- New Social Movements basically believe in retrieving an autonomous space for different social categories from within the civil society.
- Although New Movements throw up large number of ideologies, they all vouch for Gandhism or its variants.
- The strategies that they employ are also new—Gav Bhandi to Jal Samadhi or ransacking the multinationals and their properties.
- They believe in analyzing issues both from within and the larger perspectives, such as from globalization, etc.

These movements need to be located in a particular context and period. In fact some of the social movements came to surface during 1970s (Dalit Movement). However, other social movements surfaced during 1980s/1990s. There are many issues that made the possibilities of social movements emerging: terms of trade going against agriculture, growing depletion of the environment, globalization, growth of militant social categories and finally, growing fear of loss of identity, loss of culture, loss of social space, loss of social life and loss of nature. Nonetheless, post-1970s saw many new social movements: ecology, farmers, dalits, tribals, etc. This is a common phenomenon throughout the country including Karnataka.

Environment or Ecology Movement

The concern for environmental issues emerged during the early 1980s, although its symptoms were present much earlier. The depleting green cover, water levels and forest lands, massive industrialization and the attendant pollution and other issues created conditions of environmental movement. However, there are multiple groups that took up the cause of environment. This shows that Karnataka unlike north India was not able to throw up a comprehensive environmental movement. Most of the time issues raised were specific to areas or to local culture.

Movement for Social Forestry

One important issue that received much attention in the environmental movement during 1980s was of social forestry. It all began when the Karnataka government under the massive aid from the World Bank introduced social forestry, which later on was converted into the monoculture of eucalyptus plantation to serve the interests of rayon and paper industries. The latter was supposed to provide fuel, fodder, timber, manure, fruits, oil, fibers and raw materials for the rural people. But the transformation of social forestry into a monoculture had multiple effects on the ecology: it tended to dry up the water and the fertility of the soil in and around the planted area. it acts as an ecological destabilizer, it excludes the growth of vegetation under it, it creates deficit in food crops and invites draught. The toxic element adversely affects ecology. More than that, eucalyptus plantation transforms a self-sufficient economy into a market oriented deficit economy, including the fact that it increase rural unemployment and poverty. One important movement which opposed eucalyptus plantation was "Kittiko Hattiko Chalavali" or popularly called "Kasunur Horata" in Dharwad district during the 1980s. This struggle began when the Karnataka government leased out 30,000 hectares of land to the Harihar Polyfibre Company to plant eucalyptus saplings. Samaja Parivarthana Samudaya took up the cause of the peasants who were displaced and rendered unemployed. On November 4, 1987, peasants destroyed thousands of saplings in Kasanur village. As a result of the struggle the government ordered closing down the company. Nonetheless, other social movements also took up the issues of social forestry. One such movement was the farmers' movement led by the Karnataka Rajya Raitha Sangha. Even Dalit Movement joined the agitation as the plantation economy had evicted large number of Dalits from the lands on which they had no legal title. For other such as Mannu Rakshanan Koota, Karnataka Sarvodaya Mandal, Guddagadu Abhivraddi Samiti, etc., it was purely an ecology issue such as retaining the fertility of land. The struggle against Eucalyptus plantation was at its peak during the early 1980s. It took the form of destroying samplings, cutting down trees and courting arrest. The agitation centered on certain districts such as Chickmagalur, Hassan and Shimoga. Interestingly women and children participated in large numbers, as they would become the first victims of ecological disaster in the countryside.

There were other environmental issues that the KRRS and other social movements picked up: mining, dumping, urban space, air pollution, etc. Nonetheless, in recent years, the environmental issues are mediating through resisting the Bt. Cotton and patenting of bio-diversity by the multinationals. In the former case arguments centre on the toxicity of the cotton plants, changing pattern of the culture of production and the ecological imbalance that the Bt. Cotton would create. In the case of patenting bio-diversity, the issues are conversion of bio-diversity into a private property of western capital, growing monopoly over bio-diversity, loss of culture, loss of identity, loss of rights over production, distribution, etc. The resistance took the form of attacking the multinationals or destroying the properties of multinationals including the Bt. Cotton crop in different parts of Karnataka.

Save the Western Ghat and agitation Against Mega Industries

One of the earliest environmental struggles was Save the Western Ghat March in 1989. This march was necessitated as the Western Ghat was coming under severe pressure due to rampant urbanization, industrialization, deforestation, inappropriate utilization of natural resources and mining. Subsequent to the march a spate of new movements began to grow in the erstwhile Dakshina Kannada district in the coastal areas. Mega industries such as Cogentrix (Assadi: 1996: 2129), MRPL, Nagarjuna, Ispat, Indo-Gulf Fertiliszer Ltd., and others came under severe contestation. In all these cases pollution, increasing stress on the eco-sensitive district, loss of fauna and flora, acid rain, etc., became major issues. In Dakshina Kannada the struggle against the mega industries was led by Nagarika Seva Samti, Dakshina Kannada Jilla Parisaraskti Okkuta, (Dakshina Kannada District Environmental Federation), Dakshina Kannada Meenugarara Parisara Samiti. As a result of a series of agitations such as protests, street plays, pamphleteering, jathas, lobbying, cycle jatra, and bandhs, some of the companies were made to withdraw from Dakshina Kannada and the coastal areas.

Similarly, Uttara Kannada saw a series of agitations during 1980s. An important one was the "Appiko Chalavali" (Hug the trees) against deforestation. This campaign received its inspiration from Chipko Movement of North India. The campaign began from Balegadde Village in Uttar Kannada and continued for 38 days. The second important struggle was "Against Bedthi" Project as it would have destroyed much forest land and displaced much population. However, during 1990s "Uttara Kannada Ulisi

Andolana" (UKUA), opposed Kaiga Power Plant, Karwar Port, and the Eco Tourism of the Taj Group that would have taken away lands from peasants and fishermen. It is in this context that the UKUA came out with twenty demands: declaring Uttara Kannada as forest agriculture-fisheries district, declaring the district as non-alcoholic district, giving up the tourism plan, including the construction of five star hotel in and around Gokarna, giving up privatization of Karwar and Ankola ports, rejecting thermal power project, rejecting Bedthi Gangavali power plant and also the Sharavathi Tail Range power plan, reconstruction of forestry, rejecting mining, declaring Tadhadi, Ankola Belikeri, Honnavar Bhatkal as Fisheries Port, giving the right to collect shells to fishermen than to the capitalist, stopping Kaiga nuclear plant, proper rehabilitation to those who were displaced from the Konkan Railways, Supa, Sea Bird, Kaiga, etc., stopping mining in Kesar Rock by Chaugule Company, rejecting plan to allow chemical industries, stopping aqua culture, stopping illegal felling of trees in the name of progress and development, cleaning the urban centres affected by the pollution, supporting traditional cottage industries, supporting Joint Forest System, establishing schools, colleges which support traditional crafts, declaring Uttar Kannada free from alcohol, supporting solar power, etc.

Even North Karnataka witnessed movements against mega industries and industrial pollution. One such agitation was the Kolar industrial area struggle in Bidar district against air and water pollution caused by the discharge of chemical industries. The warehouse of one of the chemical companies was attacked as protest. Nonetheless, similar agitations are discernible in Raichur in north Karnataka, Bangalore and Mysore in southern Karnataka. Interestingly in Mysore district the environmental movement also opposed Bangalore-Mysore Infrastructure Corridor Project on the ground of displacement and ecological imbalance. Even issues like depleting water levels, diversion of water to the industries are picked up by the environmental movement (e.g., movement against Bannary Amman Factory in Nanjangud taluk in Mysore).

Agitation against Mining in Kudremukh

One of the important struggles in recent years where large number of environmental groups entered Kudremukh. This was centred on opposing further extension of leasing to the Kudremukh Iron Ore Company in the Kudremukh region of Chickmagalur district. Their opposition also combined other multiple issues: the Kudremukh Iron Ore Company, a profit making public sector, is involved in ecocide from time to time. Further, environmentalists also argue that this company was said to be causing serious damage to the irrigation potential of the Bhadra River, an important lifeline of Karnataka. Finally, their argument centred around the fact that, "mining over the past twenty five years has depleted the Shola forest and replaced them with heaps of mined waste, several naturalists accounted for the disappearance of many varieties of fish, decline in the agricultural productivity, due to deposition of mine tailings. Communities complain of sickness and disease due to pollution of a river, a major source of potable water".

Nonetheless, there are other important issues involved: (a) converting Kudremukh region as a National Park and (b) Tribals living in the vicinity of Kudremukh region. There are two streams in the environmental movement, other than the intellectuals who had sympathized with the larger issues of Kudremukh region: Dakshina Kannada Parisarasktara Okkuta—Organization of Environment Interested of Dakshina Kannada, Environment Support group, Kalpavriksha, Environment Action group represents one stream. It is a conglomeration of modernist, liberals and Gandhains, Civil Society groups. However, radical discourse/ group come from Kudremukh Rashtriya Udayana Virodhi Okkuta. (Organisation against Kudremukh National Park) and Thunga Vulist. The movement resorted to different strategies such as long march, cycle jatha, Bandhs, Neerigagi Jatha, etc. However, the Kudremukh issue has come to a stand still with the order of the Supreme Court, the latter declined to give extension.

Dalit Movement

Unlike other social movements, the history of dalit movement can be traced to the early 1970s. Initially it took the form of literary protest, which was popularly called "Dalita Bandaya". The Dalit movement, which later on translated into Dalit Sangharsha Samiti, was the product of four important factors. one, the radial land reforms measures. This brought into focus the intense conflicts between the landed gentry and dalits on the issue of owning land.

These conflicts manifested in different forms —land grab struggles or rape, killings, destruction of properties, etc. In fact, land became one of the issues of identity-formation of dalits *vis-a-vis* the dominant caste. Secondly, during this decade the effect of emergency was also felt in Karnataka. It was during the emergency that the Dalit movement spread far and wide. More than that it was during this period that a new generation of cultural constructionist among dalits began to identify with Lohia, through JP's total revolution, Marx and Ambedkar. Even the Dali Panthars of Maharashtra influenced the Dalit intellectuals. Fourthly, episode of "Boosa" where Kannada literature was equated with cattle fodder. This incident triggered off a major controversy and ended up in the resignation of a state minister.

Nonetheless, during the 1970s and 1980s the regional specificities of culture and social relations also contributed towards the growth of a militant Dalit movement or the politics. In Raichur district, for example, the Dalit movement emerged against the cultural practices of nude worship, domination and confiscation of land. In Chickmagalur the issues of "Bagar Hukum" land, destruction of property by the dominant castes controlling common grazing of "gomal" lands created conditions for the Dalit movement to grow. In Gulbarga the dalit movement developed against the practice of bonded labour, special boycott, practice of untouchability in hotels and nude worship. In Bangalore it started as a protest against increasing discrimination in the workplace, atrocities, prohibition to enter into temples, prevailing bonded labour, land alienation and confiscation of common grazing land.

Nonetheless, the Dalit movement did not revolve around one particular issue while resorting to agitational politics. It led five types of agitations over the years (Krishnappa: 2002, Chandala: 2002, Munivenkatappa: 1998, Mogalli Ganesh: 1999).

Land struggles

Until the end of the 1980s the Dalit movement resorted to many land struggles. One is known as Sidlipur Land Struggle of 1977. This compelled the government to introduce the Prevention of Land Alienation Act. The second important struggle was Honnali Land struggle in Shimoga district, which ended up in issuing tenancy letter to the landless peasants; Bidari Kavli land struggle of the 1980s in Hassan district was largely a "land grab struggle"; similar was the Chandgod and Kooduvalli struggle in Chickmagalur in 1979, Medikanala struggle centred on confiscating tank land in 1984, Mohammad Nagar struggle of 1987 in Bellary district was against encroachment by the sugar baron. The most important struggle was Nagasandra struggle in Kola in 1985. Its success lies in the fact that the government ultimately agreed to distribute six hundred acres of land to the Dalits. These struggles, however, also combined the issues of distribution of sites to dalits.

Struggle for Student Hostels

This was the result of discrimination and unfavourable treatment meted to the Dalit students in different hostels. These struggles also combined the issues of scholarship or freeship to Dalit students. Some of the famous struggles were Dharwad Vyasrajpura struggle, Kolar-Hunsur, Mysore struggle.

Struggle against Untouchability

This was mainly to oppose untouchability practised at different levels—hostels, social interaction, public places, etc. Struggles in Kundur, Alaud, Kada Kothnahalli and Hirenaganur were important.

Struggle against Rape

Some of the important rape cases that the movement took up were the cases of Ansuyamma, Nagamma Chintamani, Kakkeli Tayamma.

Agitation against Globalization

For the last couple of years, the Dalit movement is concerned with the effects of globalization. Its undertakings include a critical analysis of globalization. There are three inbuilt arguments *vis-a-vis* the globalization: loss of identity, loss of culture and loss of their economy and/or employment.

Nonetheless, like the farmer's movement, the militancy of the Dalit movement has been muted over the years. One of the reasons is the growing sharp differences from within the movement leading to the split. One of the issues is the politics—supporting or opposing a particular political party. These differences can be seen even on the issue of international reservation or what is called "reservation within reservation" for "Holeyas" and "Madigas". For the last couple of years each group is demanding reservation in proportion to its numbers. All these have made the Dalit movement lose its identity as a powerful social movement.

Farmer's Movement

One of the most important movements which went beyond the national boundaries to join international collectives is the farmers movement of the 1980s under the Karnataka Rajya Raitha Sangha (KRRS) which began as a protest against the terms of trade going against agriculture, the declining purchasing power, increasing cost of input prices, declining per capita income, increasing indebtedness, unremunerative prices for the agricultural crops, uneconomical holdings, losing proportion of agriculture, the increasing poverty level and finally the urban bias of the state. Till the end of the 1980s the KRRS resorted to many agitations: Non-Tax agitation (1980-85), Road Block agitation (1981), Road and Jail Bharo agitation (1982), Long March (1982), Dharna in Vidhana Soudha (1983), Rail and Rasta Roko (1984), Long March (1984, 1985), Jail Bharo agitation (1987), Rail and Rasta Roko agitation (1989). All these agitations revolved around certain major issues: remunerative prices, writing off loans, attachment of the property of the defaulters, removing the restriction placed on the movement of grains, urban bias in policies, alienation of land, imposition of agricultural tax and higher wages to agricultural labourers. At the same time the farmer's movement was much concerned about the externally linked issues such as industrial capital. Nonetheless, until the end of the 1980s the issues of globalization never became major. In fact a complete break came during the 1990s when the Indian government became a party to globalization.

Globalization and the Farmer's Movement

Farmer's movement under KRRS resorted to different strategies, beginning with organizing seminars to adopting resolutions to direct attack and forming international collectives at the global level. All these strategies had one larger meaning other than contesting globalization: to claim the authenticity of representing the natives/locality/nation and nationality. In other words, farmers = natives = locality =nation =nationality became an inseparable entity in the discourse. This representation, nativity/ocality/nation/ nationality, is discernible in such popular slogans as "Farmer means India: India means Farmer", "Farmers are the owners of the country and the bureaucrats are the workers of the farmers".

Sometime these claims went beyond the boundaries of a nation to the international level.

In the first, organizing seminars and conferences, the movement demonstrated its clear-cut anti-globalization position by pinpointing the larger consequences and the larger agendas behind globalization. This is apparent in the following statement: "Major decisions that affect our farmers are no longer being made by farmers and their organizations or by state legislatures or even by Parliament. Decisions are being taken in Washington and Geneva at IMF and World Bank headquarters and at the GATT Secretariat with no popular participation. We seem to be entering a new era of colonization with our production and consumption and our natural resources being increasingly controlled by multinational corporations for producing luxury good." Further, it argued that from being autonomous producers with control over resources like land and seeds farmers are being transformed into low wage labourers for agri-business. We see the threat to the small farmer's independence as a threat to the freedom of our country. It is our rural society which gives rise to the diverse cultures which make India a distinctive civilization. The displacement of the small farmers is destruction of our culture, our sociology, and our economy.

In the second, adopting resolutions, the matter of opposing globalization, mediating through the Dunkel Draft and multinationals was clear-cut. In one of its resolution submitted to the Prime Minister of India in 1992 the KRRS demanded the following:

1. No decision should be taken on any aspects of the Dunkel Draft relating to agriculture without consultation with representatives of all the farmer's organizations in the country.

2. No decision should be taken on any aspects of the Dunkel draft relating to agriculture without consultation with all state legislatures, since agriculture is a state subject.
3. No patents or similar forms of Intellectual Property Protection should be accepted on living organisms. There should be no interference of any kind in the rights of farmers to produce, modify and sell seed.
4. A ban must be imposed on the entry of multinational companies in the seed sector.

Other than the above, the movement came out with six important issues to confront the Dunkel draft: violation of Human Rights of Farmers, Imperialist jurisprudence, reversal of burden of proof, constitutional misconduct and constitutional anomaly. In the case of Violation of Human Rights of the Farmer's the argument centres around the following: "... that patenting of genes and plants, as envisaged by the Dunkel Draft rests in the creation of monopolies over seed production and bio-technology in general and in the field of bio-fertilizers and bio-pesticides in particular, to the total exclusion of the individual farmer's right to produce his own seeds and fertilizers. It would also lead to privatization and commercialization of research and as a consequence capitalist censorship of knowledge for profit. Knowledge being the product of societal activity, patenting is clearly an act against human right. Right to information being an integral part of the right to freedom of thought and expression, patenting which has the same effect as censorship would be a clear violation of a valuable and indispensable human right. Right of the individual citizen to live with dignity and liberty as contemplated in a democracy imposes on the state the corresponding duty to provide the necessary means of production to the individual. The Dunkel draft on the contrary, deprives the individual farmer his right to produce his own means of production, namely, seeds and fertilizers by allowing monopolies, thus violating the basic human right of the individual to practise any trade, profession or occupation of the choice to live with dignity."

One more important form was resorting to "Seed or Beeja Satyagraha". This was resorted to in 1992 and it was equated to "Second stage of Salt Satyagraha of yesteryears". "If Charka was the symbol of the Indian independence, the seed is the symbol of protection of this Independence and also the protection of farmer's culture" declares the KRRS. Asserting Collective Intellectual Property Rights or Sanad by beating traditional drums and trumpet precipitated the agitation. In addition, the "Seed or Bija Satyagraha" culminated in what is called "Dehali Muttige" (Seizing Delhi) or Satyagraha at Delhi. This is a part of nation wide "Seed Satyagraha" agitation. At this moment six important issues came under sever contestations of the KRRS: one, issues of transforming the categories into bonded labour "category". two, withdrawal of subsidy and the pressure of the western hemisphere to import the goods. Three, patenting on the bio-diversity. four, continuing the urban and industrial biased policy and finally, issues of loss of peasant or farmer's culture in the midst of the loss of autonomy to produce, sell and hold the seeds. The "Dehli Muttige" (Seizing Delhi) agitation was joined by the different farmers movements at the all India level such as BKU of UP, Rajasthan Kisan Sangathana of Rajasthan, Kisan Mazdoor Sangathana of West Bengal, Samata Sangathana of Orissa, etc. This rally came out with a Charter of Demands which stressed (1) Total rejection of Dunkel Draft Treaty; (2) Amendment of the Constitution of India to make it mandatory for international treaties to be ratified by the Indian Parliament and the State Legislatures; (3) Scientifically calculated parity prices for agricultural produce; (4) Liquidation of the so-called "debts" of farmers; (5) Restriction on import of agricultural and dairy products; (6) Restriction on diversion of prime lands for non-agricultural purposes; (7) No agricultural lands should be given to multinational corporations. Some of the issues that the farmers movement raised were stereotyped in nature, some of them belong to the early decade of its inception such as scientific price policy and writing off of loans. Interestingly, the farmers' movement was concerned about two important issues for the first time—which in fact were the principal arguments of the new Agricultural Policy of Karnataka. These issues were restriction on diversion of prime lands for non-agricultural purposes and the handing over the agricultural lands to the multinational corporations.

The "Seed Satyagraha" was followed by a world conference of farmers in 1993 at Bangalore. A strategy for preserving the traditional seeds, bio-diversity, rights of individual farmers, alternative and sustainable agriculture was mooted with the symbolic exchange of money, water and traditional seeds among farmers representing third world. This conference was attended by large number of farmers from different parts of the country, including international scientists and representatives of farmers from Indonesia, Thailand, Malaysia, Sri Lanka, Zimbabwe and Nicaragua. The following resolutions were adopted:

1. Initiate a third World Farmers Campaign to fight against TNCs Monopoly as promoted by the Uraguay Round of GATT negotiations, and to promote farmer's community Intellectual Property rights.
2. Launch an international Neem Campaign as the beginning of a people's movement against the patenting of the Third World's plants, seeds, genetic and biological resources.
3. Reject the concept of patenting of all forms of life, including plants, animals, micro organisms, human beings or their parts whether occurring naturally or in a modified form.
4. Declare that the seeds, plants, and biological material and biological wealth are part of the Common Intellectual Property of the people of the third world and of the world, and protect developing and advancing these Common Intellectual Property Rights.
5. Collect and share information on ecologically sound and traditional agricultural practices as an alternative to the Green Revolution and the new agricultural bio-technologies.
6. Programme of research and training and spreading of experiences to build sustainable agriculture that is environmentally sound and socially just and equitable.
7. Support initiative to promote the exchange of seeds among farmers with and across countries.
8. Set up community Seed Banks and restore bio-diversity in agriculture in the third world.

Nonetheless, the most important strategy to confront globalization came in the form of resorting to direct attack and destroying the properties of multinational companies operating in Karnataka (Assadi: 1999). Monsanto and Cargil twice came under attack. Kentucky Fried Chickens was attacked once—as these companies represent the larger agenda of globalization. In the first case, the company's warehouse was destroyed in Bellary as well as in Bangalore. In the case of KFC property, located in Bangalore, was targeted. Finally in the case of Monsanto, attack was centred on destroying Bollgard cotton crop in Maledagudda village in Raichur. The latter was chosen as one of the 40 locations in India for the Bt. Cotton trial. Bt. Cotton seeds were burnt in Davangere too.

Finally, strategy came in the form of taking out "Caravan" of farmers to Europe, and also joining international collectives including opposing globalization in the centres of global capital such as Washington D.C., Geneva, New York, etc. In the former case KRRS along with other organizations took out a Caravan in 1996 to Europe: Germany, Belgium, France, Italy, Spain, Czech, Poland, Switzerland, Netherlands by buses and by walk. This was basically meant to protest together, "with local people against the world economic system, against gene technology, against war, against the nuclear threat", and, in the process "regain control over countries, over communities, and the future to be colonized by the transnationals." This Caravan consists of landless movement of Bangladesh, human rights and environmental group of Nepal, Mexican Zapatista support group, Black community movement of Columbia, Rainbow keepers of Ukraine and activists from Brazil and Chile. The action, strategies, and tactics the Caravan adopted varied: they participated at the demonstration of the Euro March, a big alliance of unemployed people; participated in the counter summit against the EU summit; participated in the resistance camp, etc. The action taken by the caravan interestingly included "demonstration in front of the headquarters of multinational corporations such as Novartis, Monsanto, Cargil, Nestle and others, at institutions such as WTO, the FAO and the European Central bank. Some direct action such as the destruction of two fields of genetically modified crop and one bio-technology laboratory in collaboration with the Fresh peasants confederation of the painting Novartis Building in Barcelona. Further, the strategy included visits to test fields, meeting and exchanging views with women, students, refugees, migrants and biological farmers. Nonetheless, two organizations at the global level made the Karnataka movement transform into a global movement: via Campensia and People's Global Action. The former is an international movement of farmers, small and medium peasants and agricultural labourers, rural women and indigenous community from Asia, Africa, America, and Europe. Unlike Via Campensia, PGA is an evolving collective of social movements. All these made the movement to go beyond the national boundaries, to join the international collectives and thereby social movement has ultimately become global in character.

Nonetheless, issues of globalization has had one deep impact on the movement: it vertically divided the movement with one section stressing more on the local problems and the other one on globalization. This division has diluted the militant farmers movement in Karnataka.

Tribal Struggles or the Movement

For the past few years the tribal struggles have become sharp with the globalization entering into the domain of culture, nature and environment. This is because tribals have been confronted with new forms of contradictions. Historically their immediate contradiction has been the state—earlier it was the colonial state and after the independence it has been the Indian state (through the means of forest officials) (Assadi: 1998: 2210). In recent days the entry of World Bank and global capital under the garb of eco-development project has added one more dimension to the contradiction. This has come out at a time when the Indian state was giving up the model of "command economy", succumbing to the pressure of globalization and western capitalism. In addition, the recent Supreme Court verdict to vacate the lands occupied by the tribals in the forest region has further sharpened the contradiction between the Indian state and the global capital and the tribals.

Unlike the colonial period, the tribals in recent years have formed many organizations to resist and to advance their claims: Rajya Moolanivasigala Budakattu Janara Vedike, Girijanara Jilla Samiti, Nagarhole Budakattu Janara Hakku Sthapana Samiti, Budakattu Krishiakara Sangha and Karnataka Rajya Moolanivasigala Budakattu Janara Vedike. However, their struggle all these years have taken different forms—dharnas, protest marches, defying the law and submitting memoranda. Some of the most important struggles that the tribals waged in recent years are as follows:

Movement against Eco-Development Programme

This is a World Bank project aiming at converting the Nagarhole areas into a National Park or Protected Area (PA). The project has five important objectives (Assadi: 1996b: 2722): to improve the capacity of PA management to conserve bio-diversity and to increase opportunities for local participation in PA management activities and decisions; reduce negative impact of PAs on local people and increase collaboration of the local people in conservation efforts; more effective and extensive support for PA eco-development to ensure effective management, prepare bio-diversity to ensure effective management and finally prepare bio-diversity project. However, the larger implication of Eco-Development projects are different one, it makes the tribals living on the core areas to vacate the forest areas; it will increase cultural alienation and the alienation between the tribals and the nature, loss of the self. Nonetheless, tribal struggle against Eco-Development Project was sharp during later years of 1990s. Tribals resorted to series of demonstrations, strikes, long marches to cities to enlighten the urbanites. This struggle also brought other demands such as uniform law for the protection of forest areas, declaring natural resources the common property of tribals, providing facilities like telephone and transport to the Haadis, bringing to a halt the construction of dams and roads inside the forest areas, total rights over forest produce, providing basic facilities like hospitals, dispensary, water and schools. Interestingly, it was during this time that the tribals also opposed the construction of Taj Resort in the middle of a thick forest.

* *"Enter the Forest" Movement:* This is a part of asserting the "self rule" in 1995 in the vicinity of Nagarhole National Park in south Karnataka. The major claim was that the tribals were denied the traditional right to collect fuel, fodder and also to worship nature. The most important argument was that, "The forest which was our home in the past has become the property of forest department, it is high time we re-established our self rule in the forest". In fact, tribals symbolically asserted their claim over the forest areas by declaring self rule inside the forest region.

* ***Struggle against Eviction:*** The Supreme Court in its recent judgment has made it mandatory to vacate the forest lands occupied by tribals and peasants. This case was strengthened with the declaration of Kudremukh region as national park (Assadi: 2002: 1956). The tribals in National Park areas of Kudremukh region as well as the tribals of North Kanara have resented the eviction notices. This has taken an organized form of associations such as Male Kudiyas Sangha, Kudremukh Udyanavasi, Male Kudiyara Horata Samiti, and Zilla Adivasi Hithrakshana Samiti. In the Kudremukh region the tribals have come out with six important demands including the demand to involving the tribals in Joint Forest Programme, sup-porting the tribals for collecting forest produce, non-obstructing the tribals from doing agricultural works, reserving seats in the assembly, Zilla Panchayats and local bodies, and finally, awarding the ownership of lands to those who have been cultivating forest lands for the previous ten years. They also demanded the scrapping of the Kudremukh National Park programme, protecting the fundamental rights of the tribals, and declaring Karnataka as Scheduled Areas.

Land Struggles

Land has been the major concern for majority of categories in Karnataka. Despite the introduction of Land Reforms Act in the 1970s by the late Devaraj Urs, the land question has remained unresolved for varieties of people. This is because of the fact that the Land Reforms Act itself was defeated by the landlord categories by using the loopholes inherent in the Act. This is one of the reasons why Land Reforms Act never destroyed feudalism in Karnataka. The presence of feudalism can be seen in the way caste atrocities have been perpetrated by the dominant and upper castes over the Dalits, the presence of bonded labour and the caste struggles. It can be seen in even the forced labour and presence of different land structures or relations. It is in this context Karnataka saw the simultaneous presence of two social formations: feudalism on the one hand and capitalism on the other.

Nonetheless, land issues have become important for varieties of social categories for three important reasons. One, it provides the required ground for identity formation in the countryside; two, it helps in the transformation of rural economy and three, it creates spaces for the growth of autonomous individuals in the countryside. This is the reason why different social groups including the left parties took up the cause of land.

In fact left parties during the 1970s took up the land question through the mediation of "Land Gram Movement". (Assadi: 2002b: 56). This was a part of an all India struggle waged by the Communist Party of India. This land occupation struggle includes constructing houses for homeless agricultural labourers and Dalits in the vacant land. In some districts (South Kanara) the struggle was waged jointly by the Kisan Sabhas, Trade Union Council and the Communist Party. "In Bidar the activists occupied the land called Akkapetti, Nimbi, Mala and Nagar beed". It was during this struggle that the party demanded the fixing of ceiling and abolition of land revenue on all uneconomic holdings and lands below 100 acres.

The Dalit movement took up the land question from the very inception. For the DSS land issue was part of the anti-feudal struggle and also a part of creating spaces for the identity of the Dalits. Some of the important struggles that the Dalit movement waged were Chendugodu struggle of 1978 in Chickmagalur, Siddlipur Land Struggle of 1975-78, Bidarkaval Struggle in Hassan District, Devalpura Struggle of H.D. Kote, and Nagasandra Struggle of Kolar district.

The other tribals addressed the issues in a different way. For them more than feudalism, identity becomes important. Therefore their struggle against land mediated through opposing the state policy of eviction and rehabilitation and conversion of forest lands into reserved lands. Their struggle is as old as the 1960s, when they demanded proper rehabilitation due to construction of dams across the rivers such as Kabini, etc. However, a new twist came in recent years with the state notifying the eviction from the lands occupied by the tribals in the forest region. The struggle is now centred around Kudremukh and Nagarhole in Uttar Kannada, Dakshina Kannada, Udupi and Chickmagalur districts. The small and marginal farmers in Dakshina Kannada, Uttara Kannada, Udupi, Chickmagalur and Shimoga districts are facing similar situation. In these districts the farmers who have been tilling the lands for years together are struggling to retain hold over land. It is in this context that land becomes the symbol of identity, existence and social life.

Conclusion

The preceding shows the increasing growth of social movements in recent years. Nonetheless, these social movements are not without weaknesses which are:

- These social movements failed to bring about radical transformation both at the grass root levels and at other structural levels. Whatever the changes they have brought about are half-hearted and are not effective to bring about over all changes.
- These social movements have not been able to overcome the sectarian interests and thereby they have not been able to form a strong, larger collective at an all Karnataka level.
- Most of the struggles have remained localized, class, caste and area specific.
- They have not spread evenly between different regions. This is because their effects are different. If environmental movement is powerful in the coastal belt, the same is not true in the north-western region.
- They have not been able to address the issues within a clear-cut framework both theoretically and ideologically.
- Most important is the lack of unity within the social movements. This has led to the split and dilution of militancy.
- Finally, limited agenda of the movements has also prevented them from becoming effective.

NOTES AND REFERENCES

Assadi, Muzaffar, (1996), *Politics of Cogentrix,* Economic and Political Weekly, Vol. 32, No. 32, August 10, pp. 2129-31.

____ (1996b), *Tribals on War Path: Confronting Eco-Terrorism,* Economic and Political Weekly, Vol. 31, No. 40.

____ (1997), *Peasant Movement in Karnataka,* Shipra, New Delhi.

____ (1998), *The State and Tribal Rights: Confrontation Over Land Question,* Economic and Political Weekly, Vol. 33, No. 33-34.

____ (1999), *Third Attack on Multinationals: Badkaku Bandavala's Re-enactment of Gandhian Violence,* in Ashish Gosh, ed., Dalits and Peasants: The Emerging Caste-Class Dynamics, Gyan Sagar, Delhi.

____ (2002), *"Kudremukh: of Environment and Mining"*, Economic and Political Weekly, Vol. 32, No. 18, pp. 4988-91.

22

Impact of Language on Karnataka Politics

MIDATALA RANI

Introduction

State politics in Indian polity has been taking shape in clear-cut way after the reorganisation of the states in 1956 on linguistic basis. As part of the Indian federation, Karnataka has also been experiencing various changes since its inception. State politics is affected by constitutional requirements, national leadership, national party politics and by national events. Apart from these factors, local factors like caste, religion and language also shape the state politics. Particularly the language factor has come to the fore after the reorganisation of the states.

Karnataka is Indian miniature. Historically the Kannada-speaking people were scattered in a number of other language speaking territories. They were brought together and re-grouped as one entity in 1956.

Up to 1856, the language factor had been a substratum. The politics of old Mysore was determined more by the caste factor. The language issue has not ended with reorganisation. It has rather made a beginning. Also since then the politics in Karnataka, there has been an upsurge in language politics in terms of various demands and pressures both organised and unorganised on the successive governments. The pro- and anti-Kannada pressure groups have influenced the language policy discussions and decisions since 1956. In post-1970s and -80s language has emerged as a potent force to influence the electoral fortunes and bring about a change of government. So it is today.

Karnataka has a rich historical background. Many rulers like the Kadambas, Gangas, Chalukyas, Rashtrakuta, Hoysalas, Rulers of Vijayanagar, the Wodeyars of Mysore fostered the Kannada language and have significantly contributed to Kannada language, art, architecture, literature and culture.[1] Even during the rule of Mohammadans and Bahamani Sultans, Kannada was well in usage in the various fields. Later during the British rule Kannada was widely used for administrative.

The influence of English was first felt during the Commissioner's Rule (1831-1880) in Mysore. This was followed by Rendition of the State to Wodeyar's family. Then subsequently modernization of the state under the far-sighted rulers led to the growth of English as an official language. Yet the use of Kannada was encouraged in administration at the lower level even by some British Officers.[2] Wodeyars were patronisers of Kannada and its culture. Until 1956, Mysore had a majority of Kannada speakers. It was the citadel of Kannada culture and also a rallying point for the growth of Kannada consciousness which in turn led to the Ekikarana (Unification) movement.[3]

Role of Kannada in the Unification

Most of the supporters of the Karnataka unification movement were nationalists. This provided a link between the struggle for national freedom and the Karnataka unification movement. As early as 1920, the Indian National Congress (INC) organised itself on linguistic basis at the provincial level. The Gandhian movement relied on regional languages which encouraged the Kannada linguistic movement. Consequently, the Karnataka Provincial Congress Committee (KPCC) was established on linguistic basis. The INC session held in 1924 clearly indicated two ideas. First, Kannadigas irrespective of their division into various administrative units stood behind Mahatma Gandhi in the freedom struggle. Secondly, there was firm determination to secure a separate united province for Kannadigas.

The first in a series of agitations and mass movements in this region was the strong demand for a responsible government in Mysore. The demand was first put forth in a newspaper *Satyavadi* in 1918.[4] Subsequently it was reiterated on a number of occasions. However, this movement did not receive ample support from all quarters. The Praja Samyukta Paksha (1934) kept away from the Congress by calling the "National Congress Organisation" as a party of Brahmins.[5] Also the relations between the Congressmen of Mysore and Bombay Karnataka were not cordial. The Mysoreans felt that Mysore was a model Kannada speaking area compared to the backward Bombay presidency. Secondly, the former believed that the scope for cultural development of Kannada language lay in Mysore.[6]

This situation continued up to 1937. In that year, the Congress party formed popular ministries in the Madras and Bombay presidencies. This development brought a change in the attitude of Praja Samyukta Paksha. It joined the local Congress party, and the Mysore State Congress party was formed. The policies of the INC were accepted.[7] The Mysore State Congress organized its sessions in 1938 (Shivpur) and in 1939 (Vidhuraswath) demanding a responsible government. Later the Congress intensified its agitation by organizing "Flag Satyagraha" and "Mysore Chalo" to force the Maharaja of Mysore to agree for Mysore's accession to the Indian Union. Violence increased and many Congressmen were arrested. It was only after the country attained independence in 1947 that a responsible government in Mysore came into existence. Its emergence increased the role of the people's voice in the government. This laid the foundation for the majority Kannada-speaking people of Karnataka to demand an expanded role for Kannada in Karnataka.

Historically in determining the language demand and policy, the role of Kannada renaissance and the Kannada Ekikarana movement has to be taken into consideration. The Karnataka renaissance took place in the nineteenth and twentieth centuries. It was part of the Indian renaissance. The introduction of the printing press, railways and the modern education system contributed to it. The rise of the national awakening and the recalling of the past historical and cultural glory of Karnataka in particular and India in general also contributed to it. The role of the model Mysore state under the enlightened Wodeyars and Dewans of Mysore as the hub of Kannada language and culture was also important. The Kannada renaissance expressed itself in the coming of a "new Kannada" language, "new Kannada" literature, new books on Karnataka history and culture and newspapers in Kannada. These threw light on the past glory and the present divided and backward plight of Kannadigas. The Ekikarana movement flowed from this.

The Karnataka Ekikarana movement was the first and a long drawn language-based movement. The Ekikarana movement which began in the first decade of the twentieth century culminated in the state's reorganisation and the creation of the unified state of new Mysore on 1st November, 1956. In this long struggle a vast reservoir of Kannada consciousness and pride was built. Various organisations political and non-political, the Kannada press, personalities—political and literary—and miscellaneous influences played a role in shaping Kannada consciousness which later became foundations for new demands and policies.

Dominant Castes and State Politics

In the formation of the present unified Karnataka, Kannada language played an important role. But in running the unified state, conduct of elections, party politics, language is playing a secondary role. Caste plays a more predominant role.

In a state like Kerala or West Bengal class is more important. But not so much in Karnataka. This issue has been well-covered by James Manor.[8] Pointing out that class has no role to play in Karnataka, M.N. Srinivas and M.N. Panini[9] go to the extreme extent of saying that Karnataka has proved to be a barren field for leftist social movements. On the other hand the theoretical approach provided by K. Raghavendra Rao[10] view the 1983 assembly elections in Karnataka as an increase of "Materialization" of the people's culture and the growing shift from caste to class as the focus of identity. However, a detailed analysis of Karnataka politics clearly shows that caste is a more important factor. Studies supporting this view are many.[11]

In the pre-reorganised Mysore, Vokkaligas were the largest single caste and until then all the successive three Chief Ministers were Vakkaligas. The enlargement of the state in 1956 to include the heavily Lingayat dominated districts of Bombay, Karnataka and Hyderabad Karnataka allowed the Lingayats to achieve dominance in politics. The Vokkaliga Chief Ministers were followed by five Lingayat Chief Ministers. The Congress party dominated by these caste groups relied upon the leverage which the Vokkaligas and the Lingayats derived from land control and key positions in villages. On the other hand, the party forged ties with selected leaders of the other social groups to reduce the grievances of those excluded sections of the society. This arrangement worked well. So the period between 1956 to early the 1970s can be called as a period of Lingayat dominance (with Vokkaliga support) in which the two dominant groups had smooth going based on politics of "consensus".

In 1969 there was a split in the Congress party at the national level, resulting in the formation of the Congress (O) headed by S. Nijalingappa and the Congress (R)[12] headed by Indira Gandhi. At the state level Devaraj Urs Indira Gandhi's Congress (R). At that time Indira Gandhi wanted new leaders who did not belong to the numerically large castes.[13] Urs who belonged to the backward community soon revealed his capacity for leadership. After Indira Gandhi's success in 1971 mid-term elections, Urs engineered defections from the ruling Congress (O) party in the state. He also nominated many individuals from small and backward castes and schedule castes and tribes and minorities to contest the Karnataka Assembly elections in 1972. His strategy worked well and his party swept the polls and Urs became the first Chief Minister from a non-dominant caste.

While forming his ministry Urs carefully chose many from the non-dominant castes. Thus the socio-political power structure in Karnataka underwent a dramatic change after the 1972 elections.[14] Much has been written about Urs's caste equations, the pragmatic, progressive policies pursued by him and how he tried to break the strangle hold of the dominant castes in state politics.[15]

Socio-economic policies adopted by the Urs regime instilled a new consciousness among the non-dominant castes of the backward classes and the minorities. Thus Urs sowed the seeds of radial change in Karnataka. As James Manor rightly put it, "politics can enjoy a certain autonomy and occasional primacy as an agent for change".[16] Thus the success of Urs proved it and his period was categorized by the dominance of backward class-caste politics in the state. This view has been shared by Manor in his article too.[17]

The alliance between Urs and Indira Gandhi broke in 1979 owing to political developments within the Congress party and differences between the two on national issues. Urs started his own party called Congress (U). But most of his supporters went back to Congress (I) fold led by Mrs. Indira Gandhi. As a result in 1980 Lok Sabha elections most of the Congress (I) candidates won, but none of Urs's nominees were returned.

Gundu Rao, then the transport minister in the Urs cabinet, set up a rival Congress party in the assembly which was loyal to Indira Gandhi and started to win legislators to his side. Urs realized that the victory of Indira Gandhi in the elections would lead to a new wave of defections to Rao which would give the latter a majority. So Urs resigned as Chief Minister. Consequently, the Congress (I) won the 1980 assembly elections and Rao belonging to the Brahmin community became the Chief Minister of the state with the active support of Indira Gandhi and her son Sanjay Gandhi.

With the coming to power of Rao, the struggle for power and influence between Vakkaligas and the Lingayats surfaced once again. Initially the Lingayat leaders tried to establish close links with Rao. But the farmers' agitation in the Ghataprabha and Malaprabha areas in which most of the Lingayat farmers were involved and the manner in which Rao's government tackled the situation caused a set back to the relations between Rao and the Lingayats. Taking advantage of the situation, the Vakkaligas tried to move closer to Rao. But realizing that Rao belonged to the Brahmin community, the Lingayats and the Vakkalingas joined together in a common cause to prevent the Brahmins from dominating state politics.

Manor has well traced the functioning of Rao's government and the political developments in the state during 1980-84 in one of his articles.[18] His government was forced to tackle major movements. In dealing with these movements his government exhibited lack of determination. As a result, he and most of his cabinet colleagues lost in the 1983 elections.

Meanwhile Urs wanted to capitalize on a combined platform of Kannada language and backward castes by forming the "Kannada Kranti Ranga". But his death in the early 80's weakened it. Yet his successors like S. Bangappa in his party pressed on and won some seats in the 1983 elections and even joined the government in alliance with the Janata party. The Janata Kranti-Ranga combine was a shrewd alliance of Vakkaliga-Lingayat-backward caste groups. After the electoral success the conflict among these groups was resolved by electing Mr. Ramakrishna

Hegde a Brahmin as the leader of the legislature and the Chief Minister. A shrewd balancer Hegde consolidated this alliance and his power base by seeking and securing tactfully a clear mandate in 1985. In spite of many achievements he could not complete his term. He had to face continuously attempts by the dominant castes to regain power. When he resigned S.R. Bommai, a Lingayat, succeeded him. But within a few months the Vokkaliga intransigence undid his government and the Janata party. The President's rule was imposed on the state. This lasted for a few months. In the ensuing elections the Janata party lost power to the Congress. Thus, the caste dynamics continued to affect Karnataka politics even during the Janata period.[19]

The success of the Congress (I) was itself the result of a shift in Lingayat votes in favour of the Congress which campaigned under the leadership of Veerendra Patil, an ex-Chief Minister and a Lingayat. Even though the state again came under the Lingayat domination, it did not last long. In October 1990, Bangarappa who belonged to backward caste became the Chief Minister. He lost power in 1992 owing to dissidence in his party. He was succeeded by Veerappa Moily who also faced continuous pressure from the dominant groups. The Congress (I) lost the 1994 assembly elections. The Janata Dal voted to power. However, in the 1999 assembly elections, the Congress (I) regained power and formed the government under the leadership of S.M. Krishna. While this proved to be an advantage to the Vokkaligas, the other dominant community in the state, the Lingayats, have been demanding their share of power. In recent times, the government is forced to tackle the issue of neglect and deprivation of the north Karnataka region which is heavily dominated by the Lingayats. The issue started with the demand for the establishment of a permanent Bench of the High Court at Hubli-Dharwad to meet the needs of litigants of north Karnataka. Thus the caste factor plays a more predominant role in Karnataka politics than any other factor.

Language Based Parties and Party Politics

The influence of language on party politics in Karnataka is low, because the language-based parties in Karnataka have been few and ineffective in the politics. In Karnataka the major political parties including the Congress and the Janata party have stolen the language thunder. However, the language-based political parties have been very few, weak and ineffective in electoral politics except the MES (Maharashtra Ekikarana Samiti) in Belguam, the AIADMK (All India Anna Dravida Munnetra Kazhagam) in Bangalore and Kolar districts and the Kannada Chaluvali Paksha in Bangalore.

Kannada Chaluvali Paksha

The Kannada Chaluvali Paksha came into being in early 1960s. From 1967 onwards it picked up momentum. But the Chaluvali Paksha has not put up more candidates in different elections in the state. Only its own leaders and strongmen of the Chaluvali movement, Vatal Nagaraj and G. Narayan Kumar have been contesting the elections in the state since 1972. Also the Chaluvali Paksha is an unregistered and unrecognized party. As such its leaders have been contesting the elections as independent candidates. It is only from 1994, Nagaraj has contested as KCVP (Kannada Chaluvali Vatal Paksha) candidate. Even through the Kannada Chaluvali movement is an old force in the state, its electoral fortunes have not been bright.

Kannada Desha of A.K. Subbaiah

The language issue was the corner stone of the Gokak agitation. Taking advantage of it and the situation that existed then, A.K. Subbaiah (a person with pro-Kannada attitude) roped in the Kannada matinee idol Rajkumar and gave a new dimension to the Gokak agitation. Subsequently, he even planned to start his "Kannada Desha"—a language-based political party in the state by roping in the Kannada film stars and other pro-Kannada personalities. However, his efforts did not succeed. However, with his powerful speeches, he influenced the minds of Kannadigas about their language and the safeguards it needed.

Kannada Paksha of Nanjunda Swamy

The Karnataka Rajya Raitha Sangha came into existence in the 1980s to protect the interests of the farmers in the state. Being a rural farmers' association, the Raitha Sangha exhibited not only a pro-

Kannada approach but also staunchly supported the Gokak movement. The leader of the Raitha Sangha, Professor N. Nanjunda Swamy planned to link the peasant movement and the pro-Kannada wave into a new regional party. It led to the formation of the "Kannada Paksha". But it did not have impact on state politics.

Kannada Kranti Ranga of Devaraj Urs

The Kannada Kranti Ranga, a regional political party founded by in 1979 became a symbol of the aspirations of the Kannadigas. Urs founded it after he parted company with the Congress and Indira Gandhi in 1979. This was an attempt to establish a strong regional party. But the death of Urs was a great blow to it. Bangarappa who succeeded him could not help. The Kranti Ranga contested the 1983 elections in the state in alliance with the Janata party.

The Janata Kranti Ranga combine won ninety-four seats out of one hundred ninety-three seats that it contested. Supported by the Bharatiya Janata Party and the Communists, the Janata Kranti Ranga formed the government in the state. The electoral victory of the combine was due to several reasons.[20] They were:

(a) The pro-Kannada policies pursued by the Urs government.
(b) The mishandling of the Kannada agitation by the Congress(I) government which alienated not only the minorities but also Kannadigas.[21]
(c) The pro-Kannada thrust provided by the Janata party in its election manifesto.

Despite this positive trend, the government faced constant threat of withdrawal of support by the Bharatiya Janata Party and the Communists. Added to this in the 1984 Lok Sabha elections in the state, most of the Janata party candidates were rejected by the voters. Consequently, Ramakrishna Hegde who was heading the government then resigned and sought a fresh mandate from the people. Judging the performance of the Janata Party government, the voters returned it to power in 1985 elections with a comfortable majority. Apart from this development, the passing away of Urs in 1982 and the Kranti Ranga supporters led by Bangarappa rejoining the Congress (I) sealed the political fortunes of the Kranti Ranga in state politics. The Kannada Kranti Ranga was thus short-lived.

Insignificance of Kannada Parties

In Karnataka most of the Kannada parties emerged only when the interests of the Kannadigas were threatened. In fact the Kannada Desha, Kannada Paksha, Kranti Ranga came into being at the height of the Kannada language movement. While the first two never took a concrete shape or form, the Kranti Ranga became a recognized regional political party, won the 1983 elections along with the Janata Party and formed the coalition government. But the fortunes of the Kranti Ranga were also short-lived. It is only the Kannada Chaluvali Vatal Paksha which is still paying a limited role in state politics. Thus the Kannada parties in the state have been few, weak, *ad hoc*, insignificant and ineffective.

In the post-1956 Karnataka politics, while the role of language factor has been marginal, caste has played a more important role. In the context of the deep rooted caste divisions, regional differences and modern national political parties and developmental situation, language may never become a primary factor in Karnataka politics.

Impact of Language on Electoral Politics

The language issue is also linked with electoral politics. In Karnataka, the Congress party used the language issue in getting the state reorganised and Karnataka unified, renaming the state as Karnataka, giving primacy to Kannada language (by the Devaraj Urs government). The language issue had the potential to be a major political factor in the elections. But its influence is confined to (a) rattlings in election manifestoes, (b)certain pockets either in border areas or in a minority dominated urban areas like Bangalore or Kolar Gold Fields where linguistic minorities are in big numbers. It is in these pockets that the language issue and pressure groups are active, (c) specific elections such as the one in 1983 coming after the Gokak agitation, made the language issue one of the focal issues.

Elections form an integral part of a democratic political system. As part of Indian democracy, Karnataka has experienced the electoral process. The election manifestoes brought out by the political parties reflect their stands on the various socio-economic and political issues.

It was in the year 1952 that the first general elections to the Mysore Legislative Assembly were held. Most of the political parties including Indian National Congress, Communist Party of India, Kisan Mazdoor Praja Party as well as the independents gave prominence to the demand for formation of linguistic states in their election manifestoes.[22]

During the 1957 elections, the twin issues of stability and development of the state were given prominence. This was because the new state of Mysore had just come into formation fulfilling a long cherished dream.[23] A big issue before the electors in 1962 elections was the geographic integration of the Kannada-speaking people brought about in 1956. This issue was given importance for occasional remarks that were expressed both in public and private that integration of Kannadigas had not been a total success, regional imbalances persisted, the principle of linguistic states did not hold good forever, etc.[24] Such views were expressed because of non-inclusion of the outlying Kannada areas in Mysore.

Mysore border dispute was an important issue during 1967 elections. In its manifesto, the Congress (I) said that it would resolve the border issue if it was voted to power. The opposition parties including the Swatantra Party, Jana Sangh, Praja Socialist Party, Samyukta Socialist Party described the Congress (I) assurance a gimmick.[25] However, the Congress (I) emerged victorious.

During the 1972 assembly elections, the opposition parties laid stress on issues like greater autonomy for the state, anti-centre posture, step motherly treatment meted out to Myosre by the centre on the Maharashtra-Mysore border problem, distribution of Cauvery water and other questions.[26]

The 1978 elections basically centered on the series of reforms introduced by Devraj Urs. Due to the populist policies he introduced, including renaming the state as Karnataka, his party was voted back to power in the 1978 elections in the state.

The 1983 elections were held in the backdrop of the Gokak movement. As such the language issue became a focal point. The Janata Party stated in its election manifesto that if it was voted to power, it would give primacy to Kannada at all levels. It also promised that it would protect in spirit and substance all the rights given by the constitution to linguistic and other minorities.[27] The Janata Party won substantially and in alliance with others formed the government.

However, in December 1984 Lok Sabha elections in the state, most of the Janata Party candidates were rejected by the electorate.[28] Keeping his commitment to value-based politics, Ramakrishna Hegde sought a fresh mandate from the people. This paved the way for the holding of the 1985 assembly elections in the state. Sympathy for Hegde was very alive. Hegde's popular slogan of "giving power back to the people" fetched him lot of public sympathy.[29]

The electorate of Karnataka cleverly returned the Janata party to power at the state level, even though they had voted for Congress (I) in the 1984 Lok Sabha elections. Having won the elections with a comfortable majority, the Hegde government took a series of policy decisions to improve the position of Kannada in the state.

In 1988, there was dissidence in the Janata Dal.[30] It resulted in political instability and imposition of the President's rule in April 1989. The Congress party lost power in 1983 mainly due to the Gokak movement and how it handled it. On the use of Kannada language the party promised (a) to set up a full-fledged Doordarshan Centre for the state, (b) to use Kannada at all levels of administration, (c) to vest ownership of fertile land with the people from the state, (d) to increase employment opportunities to Kannadigas.[31]

The Congress (I) got elected and the government was formed under the leadership of Veerendra Patil. Of course, language issue was not the sole factor for the result. Significantly the election manifestoes of the Janata Dal, the Janata Party, the Bharatiya Janata Party and others did not mention anything about language.

During 1994 assembly elections, the Janata Dal in its election manifesto gave more importance to economic issues. Significantly the Bharatiya Janata party tried to capitalize on the two pre-election developments.[32] The Congress (I) lost its power in December 1994 assembly elections in the state. The Janata Dal was voted to power. However, in the October 1999 elections the Congress (I) was returned to power in the state.

Language and Electoral Behaviour

Language as an emotional issue is a potential determinant of voting behaviour. However, the link between the two comes into sharp focus only in some elections. For instance, in Karnataka language was one of the important issues in 1983 elections because of the aftermath of the Gokak agitation. The mishandling of it was one of the factors for the fall of the Congress (I) government. Apart from the 1983 elections, the impact of language on voting behaviour during other elections in the state was very low. But in the state legislative elections particularly in the linguistic minority dominated constituencies in Bangalore, Kolar Gold Fields and in border areas language seems to have played a determining role continuously.

Electoral Fortunes of Kannada Chaluvali Candidates

The Kannada Chaluvali movement gave fillip to the pro-Kannada organisations to put up their own candidates in the successive elections to the state legislative assembly. As a result, Chaluvali candidates started contesting elections to the state. This was done with the idea that, if the Chaluvaligars got elected they could influence the government more effectively. With such intentions the two strongmen of the Chaluvali movement, Vatal Nagaraj and G. Narayan Kumar have been contesting the general elections in the state since 1972 mainly in Bangalore city constituencies. Nagaraj contesting and winning from the Chamarajanagar constituency in 1994 is an exception. Out of seven elections in which he has contested, he has won only once from Bangalore, i.e., in 1972 and twice in 1989 and 1994 from Chamarajanagar. Narayan Kumar has also won twice—once in 1983 and again in 1985 from the Binnypet constituency in Bangalore. This indicates that the Kannada Chaluvali leaders have some influence mainly in Bangalore city where a big number of non-Kannadigas reside and the language issue is a burning one. Anyway the Kannada Chaluvali is not an important force in Karnataka electoral politics.

Impact of Language on Karnataka Politics

In Karnataka, the language factor has influenced regional politics. Particularly after 1956 the place of language as a factor is enhanced. The pro-Kannada policies pursued by successive governments in the state is responsible for this trend. However, the influence of language is secondary to caste politics. The language factor is prominent only in certain pockets.

Further, language as a factor: politics has been prominent only in certain periods in the state. For instance, the Kannada Chaluvali movements in 1960s, the Gokak agitation in 1982 and the Cauvery agitation in 1991-92. That is why Kannada language as a political factor is only at the pressure group level and has not emerged into a statewide political party. Moreover, a consensus is often expressed by political parties in the state that Kannada language must be given importance increasingly with due consideration for minority linguistic interests in the state. The interests of linguistic minorities are also protected by constitutional provisions, courts and their own active pressure groups. So, language in Karnataka politics is not an issue of much conflict and division.

Caste can play a factional role within national parties. Language is too amorphous, wide spread and structureless base when compared to caste and religion. Its thunder can be stolen by any party or group. The role of language as a base of politics is stable and strong only in regional pockets. Therefore, there is no effective separate regional language based party in Karnataka. The caste factor is too old, an anachronistic and divisive to form the base openly and exclusively of an effective regional party.

NOTES AND REFERENCES

1. For a detailed study, read, Karnataka State Gazetteer, Part II, Bangalore, Government of Karnataka, 1983, pp. 868-908, 1029-1097.
2. Mahadev Banakar, *Anglara Adithadalli Kannada,* (Kannada), Directorate of Kannada and Culture, Bangalore, 1986.
3. R.R. Diwakar, *Karnataka Ekikaranada Kathe,* (Kannada), Hubli, Lok Shikshana Trust, 1956.
4. Cied in Suryanath U. Kamat, A Concise History of Kannada, Bangalore, Archana Prakashana, 1980, p. 266.
5. S. Chandrashekar, *Old Mysore in Karnataka—The Reluctant Unification,* Deccan Herald, 30 October, 1983.
6. Loc. cit.
7. For a detailed role of the Congress Party in the unification movement, read K. Rahavendra Rao, *Linguistic Politics and the Congress Party in Mysore State: 1947-1956,* unpublished Ph. D. Dissertation, Toronto, 1969.
8. James, Manor, *Karnataka, Caste, Class Dominance and Politics in a Cohesive Society,* in Francine R. Frankel and M.S.A. Rao (Ed.)

Dominance and State Power in Modern India—Decline of a Social Order, Vol. I, Oxford University Press, Delhi, 1989, pp. 322-361.

9. M. N. Srinivas and M.N.Panini, *Politics and Society in Karnataka,* Economics and Political Weekly, Vol. XX, No. 44, November 1985, pp. 69-75.
10. K. Raghavendra Rao, *Social Structure and the Political System in Karnataka—A Sociological Perspective on the Elections to the Seventh Vidhana Sabha in Karnataka,* in George Mathes, (Ed.), Shift in Indian Politics 1983 Elections in Andhra Pradesh and Karnataka, New Delhi, Concept Publishing Co., 1984, pp. 13-33.
11. Mention may be made of Lalitha Nataraj, V.M. Nataraj, James Manor, M.N.Srinivas and others who have recognised the importance of caste factor in Karnataka politics in most of their works.
12. The symbol of the Congress (R) was used initially to distinguish Indira Gandhi's break away the Congress from the present Congress (O), short for Organisation Congress. Later Indira Gandhi's Congress came to be referred as Congress (I), "I" for Indira. Subsequently, when Devaraj Urs broke away from Mrs. Indira Gandhi and formed his own group it came to be known as Congress (U), 'U" for Urs.
13. This was because Indira Gandhi wanted her influence to penetrate more effectively to regional and sub-regional levels and to build a phalanx of backward castes against dominant upper castes.
14. M.N. Srinivas and M.N. Panini, *Politics and Society in Karnataka,* op. cit.
15. Lalitha Nataraj and V. K. Nataraj, *Limits of Populism—Devaraj Urs and Karnataka Politics,* Economic and Political Weekly, Vol. XVII, No. 37, 11th September, 1982, pp. 1503-1506.
16. James Manor, *Karnataka, Caste, Class, Dominance and Politics in a Cohesive Society,* in Francine R. Frankel and M.S.A. Rao (Ed.), Dominance and State Power in Modern India — Decline of a Social Order, op. cit., p. 348.
17. James Manor, *Structural Changes in Karnataka Politics,* Economic and Political Weekly, Vol. XII, No. 44, 29th October, 1977, pp. 1865-1869.
18. James Manor, *Blurring the Lines between Parties and Social Bases—Gundu Rao and Emergence of a Janata Government in Karnataka,* Economic and Political Weekly, Vol. IX, No. 37, 15th September, 1984, pp. 1623-1632.
19. This view has been shared by Lalitha Nataraj and V. K. Nataraj, *Backward Classes, Minorities and the Karnataka Elections,* in George Mathew, (Ed.), Shift in Indian Politics—1983 Elections in Andhra Pradesh and Karnataka, op. cit., pp. 35-60.
20. Narendra Pani, *A Review of State Elections—Negative Vote Against Congress (I),* Deccan Herald, 8th February, 1983.

21. The Kannada Chaluvali Paksha candidate Mr. G. Narayan Kumar who contested on Janata party ticket won the Binnypet seat by defeating the siting Congress (I) MLA is a pointer to this.
22. Cited in D. Balagopalan, *25 Years of Elections in Karnataka 1952-1977,* Department of Cabinet Affairs, Bangalore, pp. 4-5.
23. Loc. cit.
24. Shivlal, *Encyclopaedia of Elections,* Elections Archives, New Delhi, 1975, p. 119.
25. Loc. cit.
26. Loc. cit.
27. Deccan Herald, 24th December, 1983.
28. Most scholars attribute this to the sympathy wave generated after the tragic assassination of Mrs. Indira Gandhi on 31st October, 1984.
29. A. M. Rajashekaraiah, P.S. Jayaramu and Hemalatha Jayaraj, *Ideology and Politics in Karnataka,* Indian Journal of Political Science, Vol. XLVIII, No. 4, October-December, 1987, p. 591.
30. The polarisation of political forces paved way for merger of a few major opposition parties at the national level and the formation of the Janata Dal. Sri Devegowda and his supporters declined to join the Janata Dal, thus leading to a split in the Janata Party in Karnataka.
31. Deccan Herald, 20th November, 1989.
32. One of them was the Hubli incident on the independence day where the police fired on a mob during hoisting of the National Flag at the controversial Idigah Maidan in which six people were killed. The other issue was the telecast of ten minutes Urdu news bulletin by the Bangalore Doordarshan Kendra from 2nd October, 1994 which led to large scale violence in Bangalore and the subsequent withdrawal of the telecast of Urdu news bulletin.

23

Communal Issues and Minorities

MUMTAZ ALI KHAN

India is a multi-structured society where religious pluralism and cultural dualism prevail. While 80 per cent of the population consists of Hindus, Muslims account for 12 per cent and the rest belong to other religious groups. Thus, Muslims constitute the major group among the minorities. While, in general a majority of both are reasonably sensible and responsible, a small group among both pollute the entire social and cultural atmosphere. This leads to the often-repeated tensions and conflicts. Thus, apparently there seem to be Hindu and Muslim communal conflicts. But in reality it would be wrong if a general conclusion is drawn that Hindus or Muslims of India are at loggerheads and indulge in clashes. The ground realities need to be objectively examined, analysed and understood.

Generally, there is a feeling that the partition of India the genesis and spread of communalism in India. But, the available historical records point out that communal considerations were witnessed during the pre-partition days as well. The growth of fundamentalism became inevitable with the emergence of fanatic groups among the Muslims as well as Hindus. In a sense, both these fanatic groups bring disgrace to their religions. Muslims, by and large, are very sensitive to religious issues. Any slight attempt to say something against Islam will not be tolerated by the very groups of Muslims who do not practise what Islam stands for. Let us take the case of an article that appeared in Deccan Herald, a leading newspaper in Karnataka. The title of the article was "Mohmmed, the idiot". Within a couple of hours this led to a vitiated atmosphere and a large number of Muslim youths appeared on the scene to attack the office of Deccan Herald and cause heavy damage. The police were forced to fire and seventeen youths were shot dead in a couple of minutes. The situation became uncontrollable. The episode deserves explanation.

The appearance of the article in Deccan Herald was totally misconstrued by Muslims and communal leadership spread the news fast and this corrupted news message was sent to many mosques where it was broadcast. Frenzied Muslims lost their balance and gave a call for attack. Thousands of Muslims gathered in front of Deccan Herald office. They wanted to lay seize to it and destroy the whole building. They did not have patience to read the article objectively. The story written in the article had been published about a decade ago in a newsmagazine in Malayalam language in Kerala. Nothing untoward had happened. But strangely, it took a different shape when the article appeared in English. The author of the article used the name of Mohammed while describing the role of some person. There could be any number of Mohammeds who are idiots. The name Mohammed is not copyrighted and as such any body irrespective of his behaviour and background could have this name. To this extent, there was nothing wrong. But unfortunately, the author used some names while describing the members of the family and this had reference to the family to the Holy Prophet Mohammed. It is this reference that made all the difference.

Religious Procession

Taking out a religious procession is an integral part of a religion as it is practised in India. It is a part of cultural behaviour. A large number of people have sentimental attachment and therefore participate in it. Why should then this religious procession cause disturbance? It is again the handiwork of the polluted or corrupted people. One specific incident is narrated here.

About 25 years ago one of the worst communal disturbances took place in an urban area, Munireddy Palya, in Bangalore city. This area is inhabited by both Hindus and Muslims whose population is more or less equal. There are both educated and uneducated people. For a long time both the groups had lived in peace and harmony. But, suddenly there was a total transformation in the behaviour of some people in both the groups. It was an occasion of Dasara festival. As usual, elaborate arrangements had been made to observe the festival where a procession of the deity is a very important part of the celebration. The procession was taken out in the evening in the main street of the locality. There are two Hindu temples and one mosque in this street. The procession was started with music. As the procession passed the mosque, prayer was going on in the mosque. The processionists starting beating the drum made loud nose. This caused annoyance to the Muslims. Call for stopping the music fell on the deaf ears of the processionists. Very soon the Muslims attacked them. It became a free-for-all. There was a rain of stones. There was a loud cry in the name of God. The anti-social elements took advantage of this and started looting the shops. Then, they entered the houses, pulled out men and women and battered them. Women including young girls were molested, irrespective of other considerations. Hindu women became the targets of Muslim men and *vice versa*. There was no end to this fanatism.

The government made an appeal to all the religious leaders to bring the situation under control. Police used its brutal force to harass the people. It was said that the police failed in their duty. It was alleged that police sided with the Hindus. Muslim leaders demanded withdrawal of the police officers and the force working in this area. They wanted a police force from outside the state. The situation became normal in course of time. Today, both the Hindus and the Muslims are living peacefully.

The communal riot of Munireddy Palya raised a few fundamental issues. These are: (1) should religious processions be banned? (2) should the peace committees be formed after riots or before the riots? (3) other religious groups also have a symbolic participation in the process.

As said earlier, religious processions cannot be banned. If there are alternative routes, a safer route convenient to both Hindus and Muslims should be used. Music is a part of the procession. But, when the procession with music comes in front of the religious institution, it is desirable that music is stopped for a couple of minutes until the procession crosses the area of the religious institution. This change of mind is not to be based on legal issues. This should be more on human consideration and the need for respect and tolerance for all religions. Mala fide intentions will cause havoc. The religious leaders of the Hindus and Muslims should play a vital role. They have to explain to members of their religious communities about the need for harmony and co-existence. Political leaders should take the lead to unite people, not to divide them for political gains. A government should take all possible measures for maintaining religious understanding and harmony. Peace committees should be established on a permanent basis. Such committees should include the leading lights among the Hindus and Muslims.

Cow Slaughter

Cow slaughter is one of the major causes for concern and conflict. For the Hindus in general the cow is a sacred animal and is worshipped. They have a sentimental in this regard. Muslims do not have any such sentimental values. It is true that cow slaughter is practised by Muslims, but not by all. Islam permits cow slaughter, but no mandate is given. While the Constitution of India discourages cow slaughter under the Directive Principles of State Policy, the fact that cow slaughter is not brought under Fundamental Rights does give room for slaughtering cows. In some states laws have been enacted to prevent slaughter of cows. Despite these prohibitions and restrictions, cow slaughter is still seen not only among Muslims but also among some Hindus.

Killing of cows leads to tensions and conflicts. More than this, the relationship between Hindus and Muslims is strained. Whether the Muslims are right in asserting the legitimate and religious claims over cows or whether the Hindus are right in prevention of cow slaughter is a knotty problem. Though the meat of the cow is halal, Muslims need to practise some self-control. They have to respect the sentimental feelings of their Hindu cousins. They have other animals whose meat is available in plenty and where there are no objections. Islamic mandate is that law of the land should be respected. Similarly, the sentiments of the non-Muslims should not be hurt. This is not a difficult exercise. Even if it amounts to some sacrifice, it is worth for preserving unity and understanding.

Consider two extreme cases. The first relates to the attitude of some Muslims of Alipur in Karnataka. This is a small place where 90 per cent are Muslims. The remaining 10 per cent are Hindus. The Muslims eat beef. They slaughter animals other than sheep and goats also. But they slaughter animals far-away from the place of residence and bring the meat in bags and vessels, not exposed to the Hindus. This is only to prevent any hurt to the sentiments of the Hindus.

On the other hand, there is a different case. Years ago, a Muslim and a Brahmin families lived together as neighbours with a common courtyard. Holy festival was celebrated by the Brahmin family. Wood was burnt throughout the night, besides there were songs and dances by the members of the family. The Muslim neighbour appealed to his Brahmin neighbour to stop this, as his children had to prepare for the examination. But the Brahmin gentleman did not yield saying that the holy festival comes once in a year. This disturbed the Muslim gentleman who became desperate. After some time, Bakrid festival appeared. He brought a cow and started slaughtering it. The Brahmin gentleman told him that cow was sacred and therefore this should not be slaughtered. But the Muslim did not yield saying that his religion permits him. There was a quarrel between the two, which acquired greater proportion and ultimately it became a well-spread communal riot.

Thus, a communal riot took place over religious rights. But this is not the spirit of Islam. Cow slaughter could be avoided, not because of force but because of a need. In a country with a Hindu majority and Muslim minority, there is a need for living together with dignity, self-respect and mutual understanding. Islam will not be offended if cow slaughter is voluntarily given up, as an act of tolerance, respect to other religion and magnanimity.

There are certain segments of the population who believe in destruction and disturbance. These mischievous segments have satanic power and the good people is not important to them. Some people kill a pig and throw it into the premises of a mosque. Muslims dislike pig as a condemned animal. Its very presence irritates them. Muslims become furious at such an incidence indulge in arson and looting. In a short time the peaceful social environment gets transformed into a dreaded one. Many innocent and economically poor people become the victims of attack and counter attack. Madness supersedes sanity.

Similarly, some mischievous Muslims prove that they are not far behind their mischievous Hindu cousins. They kill a cow near the temple or throw parts of the dead animal into the temple. This vitiates or pollutes the sanctity of the temple. This is intolerable. Hindu reaction is swift. Innocent men and women as well as children become target of their attack. Hatred replaces love, anger substitutes peace and humanism gets converted into barbarism.

Urdu Language

Urdu language is associated with the Muslims of India. But, when its origin and growth is examined, it becomes very clear that it has nothing to do with Islam. It was born in India for a different purpose and it was patronized by both the Hindus and Muslims. However, Muslims claim it to be their language and it has become an emotional issue. If this language is not encouraged by the government and if it creates any hurdles for its development, Muslims in general take this amiss. It is also true that they make allegation against the government in this regard.

One significant incident is narrated here. A couple of years ago the Bangalore Doordarshan relayed Urdu news from Delhi at a particular time meant for programmes in Kannada language. This conveyed wrong signals to the Kannada propagandists. There was a hue and cry. Protest was organised. Finally, it resulted in violence. A dispute between the Kannada propagandists and the Doordarshan authorities was converted into a clash between Hindus and Muslims. In a short spell several Hindus and Muslims were involved in mutual attack. Many transport vehicles were set on fire. Shops were looted. There is no end to such mischievous designs.

Doordarshan authorities decided to stop relaying all India Urdu news. After a few days, peace was restored. In this incident Muslims were not at fault. They did not ask the Government of India to cut short the time meant for Kannada programmes to be relayed by Bangalore Doordarshan. The Government could have relayed Urdu news by utilising the time meant for Government of India's news in Urdu. But, this lack of social vision led to communal clashes. Even to this day those who suffered remember those black days.

It is also true that Muslims claim for a separate department for Urdu language. The government accepts the demand. But, Kannada propoganists oppose this. There is also a demand for Urdu as the second language of the state administration. The Governments of Uttar Pradesh and Andhra Pradesh have already implemented this. In Karnataka also such a demand is made from time to time. This creates irritants in the minds of the opponents of Urdu. Recently, the Government of India took a decision to start a Urdu University just as there are a Kannada University and a Tamil University.

But the question is whether there is need for a Urdu university when millions of Muslims are illiterate. Who will be the beneficiaries of these Urdu universities? These issues should not be blown out of proportion. If universities are started in many Indian languages, there should not be any opposition for Urdu universities. Logic should prevail. Emotions do not help. Urdu is one of the languages of India. Every language deserves attention.

Prayer Call

Prayer call in the early hours of the day, that is by 5.00 a.m., has become an issue of controversy. When the prayer call is given from a mosque by using a loud speaker, people who are sleeping get disturbed and feel annoyed. In the earlier days there was no need for using loud speakers because people used to stay in a small area and very close to the mosque. But now, particularly in the urban areas, people are scattered and without mike they cannot hear the prayer call. Therefore, loud speakers have become inevitable. But some Hindus have raised objections and challenged this system. It is true that under the Police Act, there is a provision to regulate use of loud speakers. Normally, this is not allowed between 10.00 p.m. and 5.00 a.m. But, this restriction is not generally followed.

Recently, this issue went even to the Supreme Court where the priests of the mosques of Calcutta had challenged the order of the government. But, finally Supreme Court upheld the order of the government. Some Muslims point out that the Hindus also use loud speakers during the day time when they observe major Hindu festivals. The argument is that why the government does not control the Hindus ? This argument seems logical. But, controversy has the effect of dividing the Hindus and Muslims.

Eve Teasing

Eve teasing is a well known phenomenon. When young girls are walking on the road, young boys happen to tease them. If a Muslim boy teases a Hindu girl or *vice versa*, the concerned community youths make it a major issue and create problems. The incident assumes the form of communal riots.

This is a very unfortunate sociological phenomenon. There are quite a number of Muslim boys teasing Muslim girls. Is their action justified? Why then Muslim youth become so emotional if Hindu boys tease Muslim girls? Recently, I noticed some Muslim girls out of school. I asked them for a reason. They narrated horrible stories. Their parents are also very unhappy. Then, where is the justification? This behaviour of the Muslim boys is something that needs to condemned.

Indo-Pakistan Matches

The results of the Indo-Pakistan hockey or cricket matches have devastating effects on the behaviour of Muslims; and Hindu reactions follow. For some time it was observed that some of the uneducated Muslims with poor knowledge of Islam were siding with a Pakistani team. They would even rejoice its victory. This gave wrong signals to some of the Hindu groups who would generalise this behaviour and dub them pro-Pakistanis. Though it was not the intention of the Muslim youths to enjoy the defeat of Indian team, their behaviour indicates this. Therefore, this made some of the Hindu groups feel and openly say that Muslims are not loyal to the country. They are pro-Pakistanis. However, in course of time efforts were put in to educate the Muslim youths that their behaviour was against Islam. The spirit of "Watan" is emphasised in Islam.

Conflict Over Religious Places

With the emergence of the BJP led government at the centre, Hindu-Muslim relationships are strained. Though the Prime Minister Atal Bihari Vajpayee had adopted a liberal attitude pinning his faith in the secular fabric of Indian society, some groups were bent upon destablising the Indian society. Among such groups are the Vishwa Hindu Parishad (VHP), the Bajranga Dal and the Hindu Jagruti Manch. They raise fundamental issues which cause worry the Muslims. They are not prepared to accept the secular characteristics or the Indian Constitution. They have a built-in grouse against the

Muslims. They are against conversions. They argue that Indian Muslims are also Hindus. They oppose special rights conferred on the Muslims in the Indian Constitution. They do not accept Indian Muslims as honourable and equal citizens of the country. The Ram temple in Ayodhya at the disputed site where the Babri mosque had stood has created tension. They are preparing for a Ram temple even without obeying the government or the Supreme Court.

Recently, serious problems were faced at Baba Buden Giri Hills in Karnataka. Baba Hayat Khalander was a Sufi saint who stayed there nearly a few centuries ago. After his death the cave in which he used to stay became a sacred place. Both Hindus and Muslims visit this place to offer their respects. The Hindus say that this was a place that belonged to Dattatreya who was worshipped by them. Every year the Muslim priest would hand over the custody of this sacred place to the Hindu priest for 3 days to perform annual Pooja. Till last year there was absolutely no controversy about the sacred place. Both the Hindus and Muslims were reconciled to the situation. But this year the Bajarang Dal activists created problems. They wanted the sacred place to be handed over to the Hindus as it originally belonged to them. But the Muslims were not prepared for this. Tension prevailed to such an extent that the whole nation expressed its concern. It should not become another Babri mosque episode. The area was fully protected and finally no untoward incident happened. The Bhajarang Dal withdrew its agitation at least for this year. It is unfortunate that what has been going on for a long period without any problem is now facing a crisis.

Idgah Ground Conflict

Chamarajpet is a very prominent part of the city of Bangalore. It has a mixed population of Hindus and Muslims, the former having a higher percentage. In this area there is a big ground which was under dispute for sometime and finally the Supreme Court gave its judgement in favour of the Muslims. But, in spite of this judgement, some Hindu groups wanted this vast piece of land out of the control of Muslims. This ground is primarily used by Muslims for offering prayers twice a year, Ramzan and Bakrid festival prayers. In between there is no activity excepting children playing. The ground remains virtually unused, though it is a valuable piece of land in the heart of the city. Some politicians instigated the Hindus which led to a communal clash. The police had to resort to lathi charge and firing too. Though the situation was brought under control, bitterness prevailed between the two groups for a long time.

Inter-religious Marriage

Inter-religious marriage is not still openly encouraged. It is not even tolerated by some. Marriage between a Muslim boy and a Hindu girl is a not a pleasant one for both Hindus and Muslims. In spite of it all, sometimes inter-religious marriages do take place. It is possible that this could lead to communal tension and conflict. One such very important incident is presented here.

Chintamani is a town in Kolar district of Karnataka. A Muslim youth fell in love with a Hindu girl. Both of them were not much educated. This Hindu girl by name Mahalakshmi married this boy out of her free will. There was no coercion or fraud. But, some of the Hindus picked it up seriously. Her parents lodged a complaint with the local police. The girl told them that she had married on her own. The parents went to the court. The court allowed her to stay with her parents till the case was taken up. When the case came up for hearing, Mahalakshmi told the judge that she was forcibly married. She said so, reversing her earlier stand, because her parents had finally made her say so. The case was decided. The judgement went against the Muslim youth who was given a sentence of imprisonment. Then it led to communal tension and conflict. A large number of Muslims and their property suffered. This incident became well known and was a big lesson for youngsters who liked to have inter-religious marriages.

Conversion

Conversion from one faith to another is on the increase and often it results in tensions and conflicts. Conversion at the individual level does not generally create problems. But, group conversion generally results in communal problems. The trend of the conversion movement is that the Hindus get converted to Islam or Christianity and the *vice versa* is almost absent.

A couple of years ago there were massive conversions in south India. A large number of scheduled castes people gave up Hinduism and embraced Islam. Was it because of petr-dollar? My book *Mass conversions of Meenakshipuram: A Sociological Enquiry*; deals with the subject at length. Conversions are only because of self-respect. But still some Hindu organisations like Hindu-Munnani were very unhappy and tried to prevent conversion. They created a poisoned atmosphere so much so that hatred between some Hindus and Muslims was inevitable. It should be said that Islam does not permit forced conversions. It is these two factors that motivate the educated think of giving up Hinduism where the practices of untouchability, social stigma and social distance prevail.

Common Civil Code (CCC)

One of the serious concerns faced by the Muslims is the constant demand by some Hindu groups for enacting a common civil law governing the Hindus and Muslims. Article 44 of the Constitution lays down that the state shall endeavour to implement common civil code. It is this constitutional provision that enables some to force the government to implement it. Their argument is that there cannot be two different sets of laws for the Hindus and Muslims governing marriages and divorces. Muslims are equally opposed to it. Their main contention is that they are governed by the Shariat Laws. The Muslim Personal Law now enforced in India is based on the Shariat. The Holy Quran is a revealed book. What is made by God cannot be undone by man. Muslims do entertain the fear that slowly they will be forced to accept many changes suggested by the Hindus. The tussle has also assumed political colour. The BJP and its Sangh Parivar were insisting on this till recently. But of late this issue seems to have lost force, ever since the BJP came to power. It could also be said that here a vast majority of the Hindus do not support the demand of the BJP. Muslims as a whole are totally opposed to CCC.

But, something has to be done to control the ground realities. Muslim society is currently a deviant society. Muslims do not follow the true spirit and letter of Islam in matters relating to marriage, divorce, inheritance of property, etc. Whimsical plural marriages and divorces are on the increase. There is no one to counter this movement, advise the Muslims and guide them properly. Leadership whether political, religious or intellectual has miserably failed to rise to the occasion and do something to avoid conflict. One important suggestion that generally emerges is that there is an imperative need for reforms within Muslim society. These reforms should be undertaken by Muslims themselves. Confidence-building exercise among the Muslims is needed now. Common Civil Code may not see the light of the day, but reforms are inevitable. If reforms are implemented, this would remove the tension between Hindus and Muslims.

In this article some major issues which have relevance to Hindu-Muslim conflicts are presented in brief. What is needed is preservation of a stable Indian society. The relationship between the majority and minority people should not be allowed to be strained. Efforts should be put in to remove misgivings, misconceptions, and ultimately harmony and understanding should prevail. The minority cannot be appeased and the majority need not be made to feel so. Both these groups should understand the need for unity, tolerance, respect for different religions, etc. Inter-faith organisations should be roped in to propagate respect for humanism as well as all religious groups.

24

Demand for Separate State—Issues and Problems

A Study of Hyderabad Karnataka

CHANDRAKANT YATANOOR

Demand for the creation of a separate state in Hyderabad Karnataka comprising the districts of Bidar, Gulbarga, Raichur and Bellary has evoked mixed response from the people living both inside and outside the region. While some have held it as a right step taken after considerable time, others have expressed some doubts that if the demand is considered and a state is created more and more separate and smaller states will soon emerge. India would be once again divided into several hundred states reminiscent of the pre-independence 562 princely states. The idea of separate state may encourage more people to demand separate states. This may lead to weaken the polity and the nation. The separate state may not always be economically viable in view of its small size and lack of enough resources.

No doubt, there is an acute sense of relative deprivation in the underdeveloped regions of many states. This perception of lack of development has transcended the linguistic cohesion which was a strong cementing force in the initial years of the post-colonial era of political development. There is a growing dissatisfaction among the people of the Hyderabad. Karnataka region in recent years due to the fact that they have been feeling the pinch of underdevelopment. The region still has its identity as "Hyderabad-Karnataka", which means that it is yet to come up to the standards of Karnataka state.[1]

Historical Background of Hyderabad Karnataka

If we look at the history through the ages, different rulers have neglected the region during pre-independent and post-independent periods. As we know the whole nation celebrates the Independence Day on 15th August every year since 1947, but the people of Hyderabad Karnataka celebrate Independence Day on not only 15th August, but also on 17th September since 1948. Even after India's independence Hyderabad, Karnataka was under Nizam's rule. The people of Hyderabad, Karnataka have had to fight for their independence not only against the British but also Hyderabad Nizam who supported the Razakars. The freedom movement in the region was in no way at low profile, it was as serious as in other parts of the country. But unfortunate nobody highlighted this aspect in the history of the freedom movement.

Hyderabad, Karnataka region originally consisted of three districts—Bidar, Gulbarga and Raichur (and recently Koppal district) which belonged to the Hyderabad state and later merged in Karnataka state. These districts along with Bellary form the Gulbarga division in the state (though culturally Bellary is different from the other). These districts on the border areas of the Nizam state did not receive proper attention of the rulers and hence remained backward and neglected.

The Hyderabad state, the largest and the richest of the Indian princely states was a relic of medieval autocracies. The form of administration was absolute monarchy. But the state was governed by an irresponsible bureaucrat, with an executive council at the top. During the rule of the last Nizam, viz., Usman Ali Khan Bahadur, the Hyderabad state was a reflection of social schisms, political upheavals, economic exploitation and religious atrocities. There was neither freedom of speech nor that of an association. People were deprived and denied of their fundamental rights. They did not enjoy the economic liberty owing to the deep-rooted feudal system and its henchmen. The minority enslaved the majority. The Nizam and Ittehad formulated such of the policies which aimed at establishing an Islamic state in a Hindu majority state. He did not grant the religious freedom to Hindus.

Social life was tinctured with communal feelings, which reached its climax, before the accession of the Hyderabad state to the Indian union, in the form of the "Razakar movement".[2] It was privilege to be a Muslim. He was considered superior in the socio-political status to his Hindu counterpart who lived as a second grade citizen in the state. Swamy Ramananda Tirtha, in his memoirs of Hyderabad Freedom Struggle, states that the Muslim fanatics treated the Hindus as slaves. The life of the people was controlled by the Muslim oligarchy. Muslims were allowed to use weapons. Much discrimination was shown in the application of law against the Hindus, whereas, Muslims enjoyed special treatment in the administration of justice. Private enterprise in education was almost forbidden and it was looked upon with disfavour. Kannada language and culture were reeling under the influence of Urdu, the official language of the state. The press, which is the mirror of public opinion, did not enjoy the freedom to publish articles on nationalism and liberty.

The struggle for independence and integration was more or less a struggle against the communalism of the Nizam government. The spirit of nationalism in the minds of the people emerged out of their instinct to protect their religion. In Hyderabad Karnataka the Swadeshi movement found its expression in the establishment of national schools. The leaders clearly perceived the permanent necessity of an ideological basis for the freedom movement. Against the political odds created by the Nizam government the nationalists of this region struggled successfully to establish five national schools.

In the history of the Hyderabad struggle, the founding of Hyderabad State Congress and the entry of the Swamy Ramananda Tirtha coincided not by an accident, but as a result of a series of seemingly non-political movements meant for the political preparedness of the people of Hyderabad Karnataka to launch direct action against the autocratic rule of the Nizam. This helped to develop political consciousness and national spirit among the Kannadigas of Bidar, Gulbarga and Raichur districts.

The Police Action was a historic event in the history of independence movement in Hyderabad state. To restore law and order and to grant the responsible government and to integrate the state with the union of India, a Police action become imperative. At this juncture, Sardar Vallabhbhai Patel ordered this step under the Command of Maj. Gen. J.N. Choudhari on the early morning of Monday, 13th September, 1948. The Hyderabad army surrendered to the Indian forces on same day and on the next, the

Nizam Usman Ali Khan Bahadur signed the instrument of accession, the incorporation of the Hyderabad state into the Union of India. Thus, with the Police action, an era of tyranny, communalism, political chaos and confusion in the state came to an end.

The problems of the people of the Hyderabad Karnataka did not find any solution with the merger of Hyderabad in the Indian Union. The question of freedom from Muslim autocracy was a minor question in comparison with the question of these Kannadigas finding their rightful place in the new Karnataka state. There could be no place for them until they were allowed to merge with their linguistic kinsmen. Thus, efforts were made by the Nizam's, Karnataka Parishad to encourage the people of Bidar, Gulbarga and Raichur who were losing their cultural distinctiveness to extend their whole-hearted support for the formation of United Karnataka. The Kannada Sahitya Sammelan held at Gulbarga in March, 1949, passed a resolution for the formation of the united Karnataka by merging in it the area of Hyderabad Karnataka. The people of Hyderabad Karnataka toiled hard to integrate their territory to form "Vishal" Karnataka. They firmly believed that a linguistic province produces what democracy needs, viz., the social homogeneity.

It may be recalled that in the first round of states reorganisation, states had been created largely on the linguistic principle. V.P. Menon, who was a witness to this entire process of reorganisation wrote, "We had demolished the artificial barriers between the states, inter se and the test of India and had indeed laid the foundation for an integrated administrative and financial structure. But the real integration had to take place in the minds of the people. It would take sometime for the people of the erstwhile states to outgrow the regional loyalties and to develop a wider outlook and broader vision. That task requires great vision and patience. The best-governed state is the one that possesses a sound political system and an efficient administrative system. Each of these is indispensable, if the state is not to fall into anarchy".[3]

Since 1956 we have seen that the state reorganisation has failed to resolve problems. Sentiment for language and culture has given way to the urge for speedier economic development. Ironically, most backward regions of some of the states are actually the richest in terms of natural resources. It was the articulation of this strong sentiment which is treated as an "Internal colony". Such articulation has led to the demand for more and more separate states. The much published "Kerala Model" in the south and the "Punjab-Haryana-Himachal Model" in the north gave the necessary impetus to this concept of "Small is Good".[4] It is sometimes believed that the demand for separate and smaller states can bring speedier economic development. It should be noted that even in the much discussed Uttarakhand movement and the long drawn Jharkhand movement the driving force was the strong sentiment against decades of non-development.

After the creation of the three new states of Chattisgarh, Uttaranchal and Jharkhand, the demand for separate states has been intensified. The most powerfully argued cases have been those of Telangana and Vidarbha in Andhra Pradesh and Maharashtra respectively. Any large scale reorganisation is also likely to give impetus to demands from other regions like Konkan and Marathawada in Maharashtra, Sourashtra and Kutch in Gujarat, the tribal dominated backward plateau region of Western Orrisa, besides smaller regions like Gorkhaland and Kamatpur (or Udayanchal) in West Bengal, Bodoland and Karbi Anglong and Cachar in Assam and Ladakh and Jammu in Jammu and Kashmir.[5] In Karnataka alone, there are a number of demands for the creation of separate states, like the old Mysore region, Coorg (or Kodagu), North Karnataka (comprising of the districts of Dharwad, Belgaum, Karwar, Gadag, Haveri, Bijapur and Bagalkot) and Hyderabad Karnataka (comprising the districts of Bidar, Raichur, Gulbarga, Koppal and Bellary).

Now, let us examine the possibilities of the various demands being made. Paul R. Brass, an American political scientist, has observed in his study of Indian politics, that the Central Government has followed some four unwritten rules while conceding the demand for separate statehood. These are the following: the demand should not be based on the communal principle, should have no secessionistic tinge, should not have been opposed by any major population group in the region, and, finally, should have a popular mass support in the very area.[6] While the first two conditions have become somewhat redundant in view of secession and communalism no longer being the basis of such demands in the current political scenario, the last two points still remain relevant, and in fact two more points may be added to these, namely, the size of the proposed state and the non-problematic criterion of separation.

The demand for a separate state and construction of regional identities in Indian politics were on the basis of demands put forth by the regional linguistic elites. The unilingual distribution of resources and neglect of economic development were always highlighted as reasons enough to carve out separate states. In some of the linguistic non-Hindi states, the movements for separate statehood have ironically been anti-language as the demand for creation of separate states of Vidarbha, Marathawada and Telangana are more economic than socio-cultural. The economic factor may constitute a necessary condition for the creation of new state. This may be true in the case of Telengana and Vidarbha. But the situation in the Hyderabad Karnataka is slightly different. In addition to the economic backwardness, this region lags behind in the socio-political and cultural fields.

Though, in fact, the area (Hyderabad Karnataka) produced the first Kannada book called Kavirajamarga written by Sri Vijaya, who lived under the rule of Rashtrakoot king, Sri Amoghavarsha Nrupatunga of Manyakheta (the present Malkhed in Gulbarga district). During this time, the Manyakheta was a famous cultural centre. Throughout history, the "Hyderabad Karnataka" area has been very famous for its socio-cultural and religious activities. The area was also known as the place of "Sharanas" of the twelfth century under Kalyana dynasty. Bijjala was a famous king and his prime minister, Basavanna, has done a great service to mankind in the removal of inequalities and establishing a casteless society. Basavakalyana (which is part of Hyderabad Karnataka region), was the cultural centre of Sharana movement. It is under the Nizam rule that this region was totally neglected; and after independence of the country nothing changed.

The history of this region is a saga of sufferings and backwardness and a long spell of stagnation both in economic and social sectors. However, the region was expected to have a bright future. Because large scale and rapid development was expected to take place when the Tungabhadra and Upper Krishna Projects were completed. But, unfortunately, the projects were not completed even after the completion of the period.

This region has remained neglected even in the new set up as it was woefully neglected in the erstwhile Nizam's Hyderabad state. The area is full of potential, talent and material resources. After its integration with the state, considerable effort has been made to promote development in this region by State Governments through the five-year plans. Even so, till 1980, all the three districts occupied the bottom position except Bellary (placed 10th place in per capita income). The continuous backward position of this region consequently led the authorities to undertake some specific efforts for development. These include the preparation of development plan by the Hyderabad Karnataka Development Board (HKABD) in 1992, for implementation of schemes in this region.

Demand for Separate State: Issue and Problems

It is a matter of justice that the region should get a fair share in the total resources according to population. But the Gulbarga division in Hyderabad Karnataka does not get its due share in respect of many facilities. For example, its share in the population in the state is 18 per cent, whereas, its share in banks in the state is only 13 per cent, in credit it is 7 per cent, in primary schools 15 per cent, and so on. Only for some indicators such as irrigated area, health centres, the region has its due share. Further, in respect of many indicators such as literacy, percentage area under irrigation, availability of communication facilities, educational facilities, etc., the region is well bellow the state average (see Table 1).

As far as Human Development Index (HDI) and Per Capita Income (PCI) are concerned, the districts of Hyderabad Karnataka are lagging behind as compared to other districts of the state and the state as a whole. The people of Bangalore have the highest per capita income followed by Kodagu, Dakshina Kannada, Chikkamagalore and Mysore, whereas the districts of Hyderabad Karnataka region 17th, 19th and 20th place. Bellary is slightly better (at 10th place) and the state per capita income is much above the per capita income of these districts (see Table 2).

Table 24.1: Divisional-wise Availability of Social Infrastructure (1997-98)

Name of the division	*% share in area*	*% share in population*	*% share in primary schools*	*% share in high schools*	*% share in PHC*	*% share in hospital beds*	*% share in post office*	*% share in telephone*	*% share in road \length*	*% share in banks*
Bangalore	25.18	33.63	38.08	39.29	27.60	30.62	26.65	51.09	28.48	35.32
Belgaum	28.41	24.98	22.21	24.43	24.75	21.16	26.48	16.84	24.44	23.26
Gulbarga	23.73	17.87	14.84	12.39	17.27	15.62	19.20	07.90	15.94	13.14
Mysore	22.68	23.52	24.77	23.89	30.38	32.60	27.67	24.17	31.16	28.28
State	100.00	100.00	100.00	100.00	100.00	100.00	100.00	100.00	100.00	100.00

Table 24.2: Per Capita Income

Sl. No.	*Name of the district*	*PCI*	*Rank*	*Remarks*
1.	Bangalore	25,740	01	
2.	Kodagu	24,623	02	
3.	Dakshina Kannada	20,167	03	
4.	Mysore	14,576	04	
5.	Shimoga	13,970	05	
6.	Bellary	12,200	10	
7.	Gulbarga	9,516	17	
8.	Raichur	8,688	19	
9.	Bidar	7,861	20	
10.	Whole state	13,621		

Source: DES, Karnataka at a Glance, Bangalore, 1999-2000.

With reference to the HDI, once again the districts of Hyderabad Karnataka are last in the list. Though life expectancy is more, the HDI value is less when compared to the state's average and of the other districts. Here, the important aspect is, how do we live rather than how long we live. The district of Kodagu has higher HDI value followed by Bangalore, Dakshina Kannada, Uttara Kannada and Chikamagalore (they are in 2, 3, 4 and 5 places), whereas Bellary, Bidar, Gulbarga and Raichur occupy 17th, 18th, 19th and 20th places (see Table 3).

Table 24.3: Human Development Index

Sl. No.	*Name of the district*	*HDI*	*Rank*	*Remarks*
1.	Kodagu	0.630	01	** Four districts of the HK region are below the state HDI value.
2.	Bangalore	0.601	02	
3.	Dakshina Kannada	0.592	03	
4.	Uttara Kannada	0.533	04	
5.	Chikamagalore	0.524	05	
6.	Bellary	0.429	17	
7.	Bidar	0.419	18	
8.	Gulbarga	0.412	19	
9.	Raichur	0.399	20	
10.	Whole state	0.470	**	

Source: Government of Karnataka, HDI report, 1999.

Disparity in the Field of Education

According to HDI Karnataka 1999, a book published by the Planning Department, Government of Karnataka, Mysore, was a more progressive region even before India's independence. Modern educational system was introduced in 1833. Thereafter English medium schools were started in Bangalore, Tumkur, Hassan and Shimoga. When women's literacy was a dream, the London Mission opened the first school in Bangalore in 1840. A Government Girls' school was a milestone in Karnataka's education. The Mysore University was opened in1916. As a result, when India's literacy rate was 16.6, old Mysore's literacy rate was 20.3 before independence. A single district in Hyderabad Karnataka had a degree college when this region was assimilating with old Mysore. The literary rate of Hyderabad Karnataka was 8.5 compared to Kodagu Karnataka 27.2, Madras Karnataka 23.3, Mumbai Karnataka 22.3 and Mysore Karnataka 20.6 during 1955-56 and women literacy rate was 7 when in other districts it was between 18 and 19. Mysore region's first Government High School was opened in 1858 in Bangalore. By 1871 their number rose to 11 and by 1911 there were 16 government high schools.

In Gulbarga, the first high school was opened in 1885-86 and in Bidar in 1891. By 1956, in the whole region of Hyderabad Karnataka only 19 high schools existed. In this way, this region began to remain backward. This disparity was found in the appointment of high school teachers also. In a recently concluded recruitment of high school teachers, very few candidates were appointed from Hyderabad Karnataka. In a total allotted 636 seats in Gulbarga division only 137 candidates are selected from this region. This is most regrettable. The statistics of temporarily recruited teachers' list shows this disparity (see Table 24.4).

Pre-University Education

Pre-university education is an entry to higher education. In many places there is a death of basic facilities like laboratories and libraries. In pre-university colleges there is acute shortage of lecturers. The reason is that while recruiting lecturers for pre-university colleges and high schools not many candidates of this area are selected. The selected candidates of other regions get transferred within a year or two and the posts remain vacant. Hence, the standard of education suffers hindering the academic career of students for competing for the professional courses. The solution to these problems lies in declaring the PUC result at divisional level with recruitment and admission at divisional level. In this regard, there is a demand for a separate SSLC and PUC Boards in Gulbarga for many years.

Table 24.4: Tentative Selection List of High School Teachers of Gulbarga Division for the Year 2001-2002

Subject	*Gulbarga district*	*Bellar district*	*Raichur district*	*Koppal district*	*Bidar district*	*Total*
Kannada Art	07	04	02	03	03	19
Kannada Pandit	07	03	02	--	02	14
English Pandit	06	01	02	02	02	13
Hindi Pundit	15	03	03	01	17	39
Urdu Pandit	01	--	01	--	--	02
Urdu C.P.Ed.	--	01	--	--	01	02
Marathi C.P.Ed.	--	--	--	--	01	01
Kannada CBZ	04	03	08	07	01	23
Physical Ed.	01	02	--	--	--	03
Grade I	10	05	03	01	01	20
Grand Total	52	28	15	13	20	137

Source: Government of Karnataka, Primary and Secondary Education Department, 2001-2002.

Higher Education

There was lot of disparity in higher education even before the state's reorganisation. Mumbai and Madras universities were far-away for the students of Gulbarga and the students seeking higher education were to depend on Osmania university, Hyderabad. The State's First College, Saint Aloitious College, opened in 1879 in Mangalore. In 1875 the Bangalore High School was upgraded to degree college called Central College. Maharaja College was opened in Mysore in 1864. Christian institutions entered the education field during the 1880s. The Catholic Church opened Saint Joseph College. But in Belgaum and Gulbarga not a single college was opened even at the end of 19th century.

When higher education was spreading in other parts of Karnataka, Gulbarga region had only intermediate classes during the 1930s. At the time of the states reorganisation in 1956, 70 colleges existed in the entire state, whereas only 5 colleges existed in the Gulbarga region. Due to such reasons the candidates of this area were not able to compete with the candidates of other universities. This injustice prevailed in the recruitment of lecturers also. When the recruitments are held at the state level, the medals and ranks are given at the universities' level. While the KPSC see the aggregate marks in recruitment, Gulbarga university was awarding ranks based on final year's marks until 2-3 years ago. Because of this reason, the students of this area did not get even a call letter from the KPSC. As at the university level Bangalore, Mysore and Mangalore give the marks liberally. Due to all these reasons only one or two candidates from Gulbarga get selected by the KPSC.

In the index of education, we see many disparities. The 1991 education index predicts the state's index as 596, whereas Bangalore alone has 773 and is ahead of all districts. The indices of Hyderabad Karnataka districts are Bellary 516, Bidar 489, Gulbarga 421, Raichur 383. These districts have figured at the end of the list and have remained backward for at least two decades compared to other districts of south Karnataka.

Women Education

A formal school for girls was opened in Bangalore by London Mission in 1840; a Kannada medium school was also opened in Bangalore thereafter. In 1918 the percentage of school-going girls was only 4.8. The same Mission opened many schools in Belgaum and Madras areas. The South Canara popularised primary education rapidly and by the end of 1931-32, 134 primary and 7 high schools were opened in that district. In the Gulbarga region Christian missionaries' activities were limited and they opened a school for girls in Raichur only in 1957. School College Statistics, p. 22.

TCH/B.Ed. Education

The injustice done in the recruitment of high school teachers is already stated. Likewise in the recruitment of TCH teachers of this area also has remained in the last place. There are 131 TCH colleges in the state, while Hyderabad Karnataka has only 13. Region-wise there should be at least 20 colleges. The total number of TCH entrants is 7,006 in the state. On an average at least one thousand students from this area should get through the TCH course. But only 626 students have been admitted. The free seats in the state are 3,700. At least 925 seats should go to this area. But only 500 seats are allotted. In this way right from the admission to the TCH injustice is being done to students. The solution to such problems lies in direct recruitment of teachers at district and taluka levels.

At B.Ed. level also injustice has been done. Among the 67 B.Ed. colleges existing in the state, this region has only 9 colleges. In these 9 colleges the number of students from this region is very less. For example, out of 6,700 seats at least 1,600 to 1,700 seats on an average should be allotted to this area. But only 900 students get admission. Among 3,700 free seats in the state, this region should get at least 925 seats, but only 500 seats have been allotted. In this way, in admission to the TCH and B. Ed. colleges, and in the teachers' recruitment, injustice prevails.

The government expenditure on education also shows disparity compared to south Karnataka. The government spends Rs. 2,700 per year per student in south Karnataka, whereas it spends only Rs. 900 per student per year in north Karnataka. Former primary and higher education Minister, H. Vishwanatha, agreed with this fact. At many places in this area, many schools have no building, no playground, no library and no laboratory facilities in the schools and colleges. Often schools exist on only papers. Schools are added by the government but it has no control over them. When such disparity was brought to the notice of the government (including Bijapur and Bagalkot), a Directorate was opened in Gulbarga. The purpose of this Directorate is to spend at least 50 per cent of the educational fund on educational development of 7 districts of North-Eastern Karnataka, viz., Bidar, Gulbarga, Raichur, Koppal, Bellary, Bijapur and Bagalkot. But, so far nothing has been done concretely except opening an office with a few chairs and tables.

Health

As it is stated earlier, discrepancy is seen in health also. The total number of in the government hospital is 43,868 and in the private hospitals beds 40,900. Among these in Gulbarga there are 2,020 and

1,492 respectively, in Raichur government beds are 1,180, private beds are 567, in Bidar government beds are 800, private beds are 734, whereas the government and private beds in the district of the South Karnataka are much higher by any comparison. The basic facilities in health services show low health index. The government intention to minimise these disparities through planning and non-planning media has not made any headway. In the recruitment of medicos representation has not been given to the candidates of this area. The doctors and the dentists' recruitment is being done at state level. Not even 5 per cent doctors of this area were appointed by the government. In the last two recruitments among the 558 and 550 medical officers, only 54 and 40 candidates are from here. Among 180 dentists only 12 are from Hyderabad Karnataka and again during last recruitment, among 80 dentists, only 2 are from here.

Industries

Since the beginning, this region has received a step motherly attitude from the government in the establishment of major industries. Though the region is rich in resources, not a single notable public or private industry is established so far. Raw material for cement is available abundantly, but the government owned cement industries are not working properly. MSK Mill, which served meals for many workers, is closed for many years. The Shahabad ACC cement factory is closed likewise. The government has not made sincere efforts to restart these. Whichever industries are here, a majority of the employees is from outside the state. Locals are not given preference. So, land is ours, but outsiders are exploiting and extracting the available resources by establishing industries with only profit motives.

Transportation facility in Hyderabad Karnataka is the worst. One cannot at all compare it with other areas of the state. The government announces without any result. Even today, many villages in the region do not have proper roads or buses. For example, Bangalore division has 638 kms. of National Highways, Mysore has 416 kms., Belgaum 715 kms., whereas Gulbarga has only 238 kms. This region does not have good bus depots, and many of the depots are without buses. Only few new buses are plying and rest of the buses are not safe for journey. There is no proper maintenance and after purchasing new buses, the government will give only a few buses to these districts.

Due to disparity and negligence on the part of the government and the successive elected representatives, the people of this area, under the leadership of Vaijanath Patil, formed a committee called Hyderabad Karnataka Development Agitation (HKAHS). It started demanding a separate state, consisting of the districts of Bidar, Gulbarga, Raichur, and Koppal. In this regard, the leaders of HKAHS, decided to hoist a separate flag on 1st November, 2001 and released the map of the proposed separate state (please see map). According to Vaijanath Patil, initially their agitation is confined to the five districts of the Gulbarga division. Later on, they want to spread it to Bijapur and Bagalkot. That is, they want to include Bijapur and Bagalkot districts under their umbrella as these districts are socially, culturally and economically similar in character.

After this hue and cry for a separate state, the Home Minister and the Gulbarga district in-charge minister including the Chief Minister called the Kannadigas for the unity of the state and announced various measures to remove the regional imbalances. Accordingly, under the chairmanship of the noted economist, D.M. Nanjundappa, a Commission for the removal for the regional imbalance was constituted few years ago. The commission has done a scientific study of north Karnataka in comparison with south Karnataka (old Mysore). It has made sincere effort to bridge the differences. Nanjundappa says, "if the officers sitting in responsible positions discharge their duties in utmost care and sincerely, the problems in this regard could have been solved".[7] Keeping the state average as an yardstick, the commission in its report, has recommended Rs.1,247 crore additional amount.[8] But the government has not reserved any amount during the last two years budget, though the report was with the government well before the 2001-2002 budget session.

Conclusion

Though the government has suggested a number of ways to remove the regional imbalances, these are only on paper. By only lip service the disparity in development will not disappear. The successive governments in Karnataka have not properly identified the priority areas and the local expertise has not been included while formulating policies and constituting commissions to look at the matter. The allocation of regular budget to these districts from the government has come down drastically. On an average 10 to 15 ministers from this region have been (6 from Gulbarga district) in the council of ministers. Due to lack of commitment and political farsightedness on the part of these leaders, no time-bound development has taken place. The government and the officers should build confidence among the people by showing their real commitment.

For speedy and proper development of the region, the demand for the creation of a separate state will not help. Rather, the people should agitate for the right cause and put pressure on political leaders to do their duties and force them to keep their promises. The youths should come forward to lead the agitation without self-interest. A kind of social movement in spreading awareness and establishing corruption- free society is the need of the hour. Right to information, accountability, transparency and objectivity must be introduced in the administration. Vaijanath Patil, who spearheaded the agitation for the creation of separate state, also argues that the demand for separate state may not materialise immediately; but the ultimate aim is to seek speedy development on par with other parts of the state. He further argues that the government should immediately implement Dr. Nanjunappa Committee's report. Otherwise the agitation for the creation of a separate state will be intensified further.

NOTES AND REFERENCES

1. Chaya, Degaonkar, *A Region in Transition,* Deccan Herald, November 24, 2000.
2. B.C. Mahabaleshwarappa, *Integration of Hyderabad Karnataka (1946-1956),* Ph. D. thesis (1992), p. 269.
3. V. P. Menon, *"Integration of the Indian State",* New Delhi, Oriental Longman, 1985, p. 490.
4. Pradeep Kumar, *Demand for New States,* Economic and Political Weekly, August 26, September 2, 2000, p. 3079.
5. *Ibid.,* p. 3081.
6. Pradeep Kumar, *Do We Need More States in India?,* Mainstream, October 21, 2000, p. 26.
7 Kannada Nudi—By Kannada Sahitya Parishat, Bangalore, January 2002, p. 7.
8 *Ibid.*

25

Movement for Statehood in Kodagu

P.E. SOMAIAH

Agitations or movements for statehood and autonomy are not a new or recent development, they have existed right from the days of independence in different parts of India which number about eighteen.[1] Amongst them, three movements succeeded in getting statehood. The nation witnessed the emergence of Chattisgarh, Uttaranchal and Jharkhand as twenty-sixth, twenty-seventh and twenty-eighth states of the Indian Union respectively in November 2000. With this development, movements for statehood elsewhere in the country are in an upbeat mood.

A section of the warrior community of Kodavas (Coorgs) in Kodagu are preparing to breakaway from Karnataka and a movement for statehood or restoration of statehood to Kodagu is very much alive. Day after day the debate about the movement is becoming bigger and bigger and the media attention to the movement is also on the increase.

All prominent leaders of the district and state and the respective State Government have somehow ignored the movement as an insignificant one. Some are very critical about the developments taking place in the district. Under these circumstances an attempt is made here to present certain basic facts about Kodagu and analyse the statehood movement objectively.

Area and Population

Kodagu district has an area of 4,109 sq. km. and is one of the smallest districts, next only to Bangalore urban district. Out of the total state area of 1,91,791 sq. km., it constitutes only 2.14 per cent. As per 1991 census it had a population of 4,85,229. This constituted only 1.08 per cent of the state's population. The population density per sq. km. was only 118. The district has been divided into three taluks, namely, Madikeri, Virajpet and Somarpet.[2] Madikeri is the district headquarters.

History

According to legendary and puranic sources Kodagu was known as "Matsyadesha", "Brahamadesha" and "Krodhadesha". The early history of Kodagu is not clear and specific; but according to several inscriptions discovered and published in Epigraph a Carnatica (Vol. 1, 3rd edition) Kodagu was ruled by the Gangas, Cholas, Hoysalas, Kongalavas and Changalavas. During the Vijayanagara period, there were a number of petty "palegars" or chieftains in Kodagu. Regarding the early administrative units of Kodagu the traditional belief is, the kingdom was divided into 12 "kombus" (districts) and 35 nadus (sub-divisions) which encompassed an area larger than today.[3]

Kodagu attained a separate identity under the Wodeyars of Kodagu or the Rajas of Kodagu who originally belonged to the Keladi Nayaka Royal family. As they started their rule from a small place called Haleri, they are also proclaimed as Haleri Rajas. Twelve rulers from this dynasty ruled Kodagu from 1600 A.D. to 1834 A.D.[4] The third king of the Haleri dynasty, Mudduraja, got a hillock levelled and constructed a fort and a palace in 1681. The new township was named as Muddurajakeri which became Madikeri in course of time. The capital was thus shifted from Haleri to Madikderi. At that time Periyapatna was a part of Kodagu.[5] In early 1780, Lingaraja died. On this occasion on the pretense of being the guardian of the minor prince, Haidar Ali occupied Kodagu kingdom. With this began a long struggle which lasted 9 years. It was during this period that Tipu Sultan (who had in the meanwhile succeeded Haidar Ali) is said to have taken 70,000 Kodavas as prisoners and shifted them to places outside the district and at the same time tried to populate Kodagu with Muslims brought from outside. During this period, the rightful king Vera Rajdendra was imprisoned and kept in confinement in Piriyapatna. In 1788, Vira Rajendra escaped from the prison and established friendship with the British. Subsequently, at the conclusion of the III Mysore War between the British and Tipu Sultan of Mysore, the latter was forced to hand over the possession of Kodagu to the British, who, in turn, restored the kingdom to Vira Rajendra. From then on till 1834, Kodagu was ruled by the Haleri Rajas under the suzerainty of the British. Doddaveerappa Raja extended his kingdom's boundary to Amarsullya and Puttur of the present Dakshina Kannada district. After acquiring Panje and Bellare belonging to the same district from Hyder Ali, boundaries between Kodagu and Mysore districts were demarcated. Lingaraja defeated the Mysore army and annexed Yelu Saviraseeme located in the vicinity of Kodlipet to his kingdom.[6]

Table 25.1: Area of Each Taluk During Dodda Veerarajandera's Period (1781-1809 A.D.)

Sl. No.	*Name of the taluk*	*Sq. kms.*
1.	Yelusaviraseeme	238
2.	Kiggatnadu	811
3.	Kodagu proper (Kasba)	3056
4.	Sullya (including Amara)	717
5.	Puttur	785
	Total	**5607**

Source: Kodagu District Gazetteer, 1993, p. 5.

Kodagu under the British

King Chikkaveeraraja was deposed by the British on 13th March, 1834. The Company's government took over the territory of Kodagu along with administrative responsibility. Colonel Fraser was named the Commissioner of Kodagu. It was considered a non-regulated province of the Government of India. The provision was that all the regulations that were passed by the Government of India need not be given effect in this region. But any legislation could be effected by means of special enactment. The Commissioner of Kodagu was designated Chief Commissioner in 1869.

In the wake of national uprising during 1857-58 the natives of Kodagu, as per the directions of Mark Cubbon, the Commissioner of Mysore, stood by the British, in suppressing the revolt in

Srirangapatna and its surroundings. This loyalty of the Kodavas towards the British was appreciated by Mark Cubbon and he permitted them to possess guns without licence, contrary to the Arms Act of India, a privilege which continues even today in the independent India.

During the British administration there was all-round progress in Kodagu. Education, transportation and communication, received tremendous boost from the British administration. They introduced coffee cultivation and its export from Kodagu increased year after year. Education spread very quickly and by 1901 the literacy rate was 14 per cent. The Kodavas as a result of their contact with European coffee planters were inclined to westernization and they came forward in large numbers to serve in the Army. At Virajpet and Madikeri, hospitals were opened by the British in the year 1870 to popularise the western medical system. The District Board was established in 1901. The co-operative movement in Kodagu made a beginning in 1905 and became popular even before Indian independence.[7]

When the British took over Kodagu, on popular demand and for effective administration, Puttur and Amarsullya (having a total area of 1,502 sq. km.) taluks were re-transferred to Dakshina Kannada District in 1834. The rest of the district was divided into six taluks consisting of twenty-four nadus (units similar to hoblis). The nadus were again sub-divided into gramas or villages.

The total area of Kodagu has remained the same since 1834, though there have been several changes from time to time in the internal divisions to suit administrative convenience. In 1894 all the three hoblis of Yelusaviraseeme were merged with Nanjarayapatna. The five taluks were reduced to four in 1921 by combining the two taluks of Padi-Nalknad and Yedenalkand into one, giving the name Padi-Yednalknad to the new taluk. There was yet another change in 1922, when the two taluks of Padi-Yedenalknad and Kiggatnad were combined into one to form the new south Kodagu taluk with effect from 1st September, 1922. In 1926, the two taluks of Madikeri and Nanjarayapatna were also amalgamated into one taluk, under the name of North Kodagu. After this change there were only two taluks.[8]

Freedom Movement and other Developments

Lack of genuine interest in the welfare of the masses, discrimination against Indians in employment, promotions and pay scales shocked the educated Kodavas. They grew suspicious about the sense of justice of the British, which culminated in the development of strong anti-British feelings. To fight the British discriminatory

Table 25.2: Details of Six Taluks of Kodagu as in 1834

Sl. No.	*Taluk/Nadu*	*Area in sq. km*	*No. of villages*	*Seat of Kacheries*
1.	**Madikeri Taluk**	**541**	**57**	**Madikeri**
	a. Mercera-Halerindad	127	15	Madikeri
	b. Kagodlunad	104	06	Thalatmane
	c. Horuru-Nurokkalnad	101	11	Boykeri
	d. Hudikeri, Kanta-Murnad	127	14	Murnad
	e. Uluguli-Mudigeri	83	11	Shuntikoppa
2.	**Padinalknad Taluk**	**1070**	**57**	**Napoklu**
	a. Padinalknad	368	12	Nalkunad Palace
	b. Kadiyat Nad	132	12	Bhavuli
	c. Tavunad	360	09	Bhagamandala
	d. Benganad	109	11	Kolegadala
	e. Kuyin Keri	101	13	Palur
3.	**Ydenalknad Taluk**	**544**	**49**	**Virajpet**
	a. Yedenalknad	238	22	Virajpet
	b. Beppunad	106	08	Arameri
	c. Ammattinad	199	19	Ammatti
4.	**Kiggatnad Taluk**	**1036**	**63**	**Hudikeri**
	a. Anjikernad	231	15	Hudikeri
	b. Thavalkerinad	285	15	Thavalkeri
	c. Hatutgatnad	290	13	Ponnampet
	d. Betietnad	231	20	Kuntagrama
5.	**Najarayapatna Taluk**	**679**	**114**	**Fraserpet (Kushalnagar)**
	a. Surlabbi-Gadinad	293	21	Madapur
	b. Yedavanad	243	37	Somvarpet
	c. Nanjaraya Patna	142	26	Fraserpet
	d. Ramaswami-Kanive	N.A.	30	Kampur
6.	**Yelusaviraseeme Taluk**	**236**	**168**	**Shanivarsante**
	a. Kodali Hobli	70	55	Kodlipet
	b. Bilhada Hobli	47	40	Shanivarsante
	c. Nidhata Hobli	119	73	Gaudhalli
	Grand total	**4105**	**508**	

Source: Richter, G., The Coorg Manual 1870, p. 367.

policies and to draw their attention, the Coorg Agricultural Society was formed in 1909 by Kodanda Madaiah and Biddnada Ganapathi. In the year 1912 it was transformed into Coorg Zamindars' Association. This association became the nucleus for the nationalist movement in Kodagu. In the year 1929, yielding to the pressure of the people, a legislative council was created by the Government of India. It had thirteen members elected by restricted voting and two members were nominated. The establishment of Kodagu District Congress Committee in 1925 gave further fillip to the freedom struggle in Kodagu. C.S. Venkappaiah, Paravanda Kushalappa, Pandyanda Belliappa, Kotera Chinappa, Sripathi Rao, Jammada Madappa, Ajji Kuttira Thammaiah and many others were in the forefront of the freedom struggle in Kodagu. The opposition to the British rule was near total. Kannada Sahitya Sammelana was held at Madikeri under the presidentship of Dr. D.V. Gundappa, after which a Kannada Sangha was established in 1933. This brought Kodagu much closer to the then Mysore princely state.

The Merger Controversy

The Legislative council which existed even before independence had no powers other than giving approval and consent to the local matters brought before it. However, from the early 1930 it witnessed serious difference of opinion amongst its members whether Kodagu should merge with Mysore princely state or Madras province or should it remain an independent state. Interestingly, the council supported the resolution of merging Kodagu with Mysore state, even before independence in spite of stiff opposition from some prominent leaders.

In the year 1946, when the process of forming a constituent assembly to draft a constitution started Kodagu got an opportunity to elect a member to the central constitution-making body. C.M. Poonacha, a Congress candidate was elected. After independence in August, 1947 the Chief Commissioner's rule continued. The Indian Constitution recognised Kodagu as a Group 'C' state and entitled to possess a responsible government with a twenty-four member legislative assembly. Apart from Coorg there were nine other Group 'C' states in the country.[9] This system came into existence in 1952.

The elections for the 24 members' assembly took place in 1952 as it was held in other states. Out of the 24 seats the Congress was able to win 15 seats under the leadership of C.M. Poonacha. The anti-merger group (group which desired to keep the identity of Kodagu as a separate state from the beginning) lead by Pandyanda Belliappa secured nine seats. Nidamane Somanna, a Congress candidate, was elected as member of the Lok Sabha from Kodagu. The council of ministers consisting of C.M. Poonacha as the Chief Minsiter and K. Malappa as minister assumed office the same year.

The Congressmen of Kodagu gave their support for the unification of Karnataka. Kodagu Congress Committee was within the jurisdiction of the Mysore Pradesh Congress for a long time. The Kannada Sanghas and Kannada literary activists were in favour of merger of the Coorg state with the Mysore state. As merger became a reality Pandyanda Belliappa, A.C. Thimmaiah and other leaders, opposed the merger of Kodagu with Mysore state. Even Kodagu Congress Committee passed a resolution against the merger in 1953. But in 1955, when a merger resolution was brought before the legislative assembly, 22 voted for and two against it. The States Reorganisation Commission recommended the merger of Kodagu in the proposed new Mysore state (Karnataka) and suggested that Kodagu should be retained as a separate district. With the formation of Mysore state, as per State Reorganisation Commission's recommendations, Kodagu became one of the districts of new Mysore state on 1st November, 1956.[10] The merger of Kodagu with the Mysore state, thus appears to be very mysterious.

Why Demand for Restoration of Statehood Now?

When Coorg was a part 'C' state for four and half years, from March 1952 to November 1956, it witnessed tremendous progress and development, not evidenced during the time of any earlier princes of Kodagu or the British. Five year plans and community development projects came into force. As Coorg was able to secure enough financial assistance from the centre, bridges, roads, schools and hospital buildings were built; poultry farming, agricultural development, plywood industry, bee-keeping, co-operative movement and many other activities flourished.

Bridges were constructed across the Cauvery at Balamuri, Mottamudi and Kondageri and to the Lakshmana Theerth at Mallur and Kanur. Thousands of acres of government land, at the rate of 300 rupees per acre, were also released. According to I.M. Muthanna, the income of the Kodagu Government was Rs.104 lakh and the expenditure was Rs.140 lakh in the year 1953. This period is very often hailed by many senior citizens of Kodagu as the "Golden Era" in the history of Kodagu.

With effect from 15th December, 1953, the internal divisions of Kodagu state were re-grouped to facilitate effective administration. The third taluk known as Madikeri taluk comprising Madideri Nadu and Bhagamanda Nadu of the north Kodagu taluk (33 villages and one town) and Napoklu Nadu of the south Kodagu taluk (37 villages) came into being. The remaining portions of the north and south taluks were merged to form Somvarpet taluk (135 villages transferred from north Kodagu taluk and four villages from the south Kodagu taluk) and Virajpet taluk (103 villages and one town transferred from the south Kodagu taluk).[11]

Discontentment

Kodagu district after its merger with Mysore state in 1956 has been neglected at every level by all successive State Governments in spite of being rich in resources and having the highest per capita income in the state of Karnataka.[12] The district has 70,000 hectares of coffee plantations and records an annual coffee production of about two lakh tonnes, which constitutes 1/3 of the total coffee production in the country, worth Rs. 600 crore. The total annual turnover of Indian coffee trade is Rs.1,800 crore. Coffee is the second largest traded commodity in the world after oil. There is a general feeling among the people that the district is not being given any importance and no proper developmental work is being undertaken. Apart from this Kodagu has certain unique problems. In this context an analysis of different problems confronting the district causing discontentment will be appropriate here.

1. The overall infrastructure of the district is in a very bad shape. The roads throughout the district are in a pathetic condition full of craters and massive pot holes. Though the number of

vehicles have increased by manifold, the existing roads are neither widened nor tarred. The district has 1,115 km. of road coming under the Public Works Department. Various NABARD schemes have been launched to boost the development of roads in Kodagu during recent times under Rural Information Development Fund (RIDF); but most of the projects have made little progress. This is attributed mainly to the non-receipt of the letter of credit in time, inadequate budgetary support from the State Government (which is required to contribute 10 per cent of the total project cost) and delay in settlement of contractors' bills by the PWD and so on.[13] The terrain of Kodagu is full of rivers and streams, which necessitates the construction of big, medium and small bridges at many places. Unfortunately, the successive governments and the peoples' representatives have done very little in this regard. For instance, the Barapole bridge which is expected to reduce 20 km. of distance from Virajpet to the Badagarakeri Cross, which in turn connects T. Shettageri, Srimangala, Birunani and other areas, benefiting the people living in 20 villages, has remained incomplete and abandoned due to the objection of the forest department. A sum of Rs. 20.21 lakh has been spent so far on the work.[14] Apart from this the district is the only one in the state not provided with a railway line.

2. The hospitals and health centres of the district are in a highly neglected state, lacking equipment and staff. In spite of being the richest district of the state, it lacks a modern hospital with latest equipment and speciality services.

Table 25.3: Growth of Medical Institutions from 1960-61 to 1996-97 in Kodagu

Sl. No.	*Year*	*Number of medical institutions*
1.	1960-61	48
2.	1970-71	44
3.	1980-81	45
4.	1990-91	43
5.	1996-97	47

Source: Human Development in Karnataka Report–1999, p. 239.

If the number of Government Medical Institutions has increased in all other nineteen districts of Karnataka since 1960-

61, it has come down by one in Kodagu district which is a very disturbing fact.

3. The educational needs of the youngsters are another area of total neglect. Although there are a few colleges and ITIs, they continue to offer traditional and outdated courses which are inadequate to the present needs. This has deprived the youngsters of better job opportunities in the job market. Many youngsters are forced to move out of Kodagu in pursuit of their studies. After a long wait the first technical institute for higher education by name Coorg Institute of Technology has come into being from August 2000 at Ponnampet.

Table 25.4: Number of General and Professional Colleges in Kodagu

Sl. No.	*Category*	*1991-92*	*1996-97*
1.	General Degree	05	07
2.	Law	00	00
3.	B.Ed.	01	01
4.	Engineering	00	00
5.	Polytechnics	02	02
6.	IITs	02	02
7.	Medical	00	00
8.	Pharmacy	00	
9.	Dental	00	00
10.	Nursing	00	00
11.	Ayurvedic	00	00
12.	Homeopathy	00	00
13.	B.P.Ed./M.P.Ed.	00	00

Source: Human Development in Karnataka Report—1999, pp. 288-290.

4. The job opportunities for the Kodav youths in the government departments has become very limited due to the different employment policies adopted by the government. They are forced to compete with a larger segment of candidates as they fall under the general category. Several youths after completing their education by spending huge amount of money in cities like Mysore, Mangalore and Bangalore are forced to return to Coorg, as they find it difficult to secure jobs outside the district. Enrolment of Kodava youths to the police and armed forces is also on the decline. Unrest among youths is visible everywhere, as they have lost all hopes.

5. According to KPTCL authorities Kodagu consumes least units of electricity when compared to all other districts at Karnataka. In spite of this the people of Kodagu suffer from inadequate power supply and frequent power shutdowns. Some households which are electrified in remote villages have electricity connection but no power. Kodagu occupies 19th position out of 20 as far as the percentage of households electrified as on 1991. Only 36.28 per cent of households are electrified which is next only to Raichur district which is 32.51 per cent of households electrified, as against the state average o 52.47 per cent.[15]

6. Kodagu district stands fifth in the state in respect of forest area and 20 per cent of the total forest area of the state. Of the total geographical area of 4,102 sq. km. forest constitutes 1,259.52 sq. km. forming 30.43 per cent protected forests 27.14 sq. km. and 95.92 sq. km. of unclassified forests.[16] The forests are disappearing mainly due to extensive exploitation by foreign companies and tycoons in the name of development. Precious trees are smuggled out of Kodagu forest every now and then by the timber mafia with the connivance of the forest department personnel and the police. The forest department has failed miserably in safeguarding the precious forest wealth of Kodagu. The smuggling of 12 pristine teak trees worth Rs.18 lakh from Kolangere section of the Kallala range of the Nagarahole National Park by smugglers during December, 1999 could very well be the tip of an iceberg.[17]

Over 1,200 sacred groves popularity known as "Devarakadu" in the district are facing serious threat to their existence due to large scale encroachments, timber felling, government policies and change in the attitude of the local people. Between 1873 and 1905, the area of the groves increased from 10,865 acres to 15,506 acres, before it was transferred to the revenue department from forest department. In 1985, it was decided that the sacred groves should be handed back to the forest department by the State Government after declaring them reserve forests. However, the land had been reduced to 6,299.61 acres and about 352.38 acres were officially recognised as encroached.[18]

7. Kodagu has a rich heritage of wild life. It has wild life sanctuaries located at Brahmagiri (181.29 sq. km.), Purhspagiri (102 sq. km.) and Tala Kaveri (105 sq. km.) apart from the famous Nagarhole National Park (642 sq. km.). Due to large scale poaching during the last two decades wild life in the sanctuaries has

depleted. Elephant poaching has become an inter-state operation. Separate gangs operating from Kodagu and neighbouring Periyapatna in Mysore district are believed to be involved in poaching. The masterminds located in Kodagu send their henchmen to kill elephants. The tusks are then removed and sold to parties in Mysore who later transport them to Hyderabad and Kerala. The forest and police department personnel have totally failed in checking large scale poaching activities.

8. Kodagu district faces another peculiar problem, Elephant-Human conflict. The district has 1,730 elephants spread over a protected forest area of 1,588 sq. km. Wild elephants raiding paddy fields and farms is a common phenomenon. Apart from the loss of paddy and plantations, human injuries and deaths are on the increase. Between 1992 and 1996, losses because of crop depredation by elephants effected 222 different villages involving 2,146 cases. The average annual number of crop damage cases range between 400 to 500. The most commonly raided crop is paddy (48.2%) followed by coffee (17%), cardamom (10.5%), coconut (8.61%) and banana (6.2%)[19]. The affected people are paid meagre compensation by the forest department after a long wait and several visits to the concerned departments.

9. During every monsoon, floods create havoc in most areas of Kodagu district. The Cauvery river submerges the bridges and roads and the movement of people and vehicles come to a stand still. Human casualties are also reported. The most flood prone areas are Bhagamandala, Balmuri and Karadigod. In other places like Guhya, Nellihudikeri, Kakot-parambu and Kadnur, flood water submerges vast tracks of paddy fields. Most of the time the victims are the migrant labourers. When the river Cauvery is in spate, the affected families are shifted to temporary rehabilitation camp at nearby schools. This has been going on for several years. Revenue officials run from pillar to post to ensure safety of the affected people; mechanised boats are pressed into service all involving huge expenditure. If the bridges were to be well planned and built in time, much of the tragedy could be averted in the district during the rainy season. To cite an example, the Kalur Bridge, where two persons were washed away last year in flash floods, remains as it is till date.[20] There is lack of genuine concern for effecting long-lasting remedial measures on the part of the district administration and the State Government.

10. Kodagu district has a good potential for tourism industry. The natural beauty of its landscape, the variety of wild animals in its sanctuaries, the place of origin of the Cauvery, Tala Cauvery, and places on the banks of the Cauvery like Bhagamandla, Nanjarayapatna, Balamuri and Suntigutti are some of the captivating sites for the tourists. The beauty of the water falls such as Abbi, Abbi Matha Falls, Baraple and Irpu must be enjoyed. The temples at Bagamandla, Padi Igguthappa with rare wood sculptures, the Gaddige Mausoleam's of the former rulers of Kodagu and the Raja set botanical garden at Madikeri are other attractions. Unfortunately the State Government has not exploited this tourist potential. The approach roads to all the above mentioned tourist attractions are in a very bad shape, accompanied by poor or no facilities for tourists. Even the basic safety measures too are not initiated in these places. For instance, till the end of October, 2000, fifty-five tourists have drowned to death in the famous Abbey Falls near Madikeri. Funds allocated for promotion of tourism by State Government are meagre.

11. The Kodavas constitute the most important portion of population in the district. Kodava customs, traditions and practices are unique. Being a warrior race, they possess soldierly inclination by blood. Kodava language comprises a mixture of Kannada, Malayalam, Tamil and Tulu words. The First and Second Karnataka Backward Class Commission in 1972 and 1984 put the Kodava population figures at 86,266 and 70,193 respectively in the district. Apart from the Kodavas there are 18 other groups of people who speak the Kodava language, like Amma Kodava, Airi, Meda, Peggade, Kaniya, Kapala, Kembatti Poleya, etc. Due to hypocratic and vicious policies such as world human good, globalization and secularism postulated as a conspiracy by invisible forces have generated unnatural and unrealistic circumstances, relegating the customs and traditions of the natives to the background. Due to the influence of westernisation and the onslaught from outsiders, the original inhabitants of Kodagu are joining the ranks of an endangered species and the very Kodava identity has been lost. With the influx of outsiders to the district the natives have been relegated to the position of second-class citizens in their own district.

12. The district has been politically neglected during the last four decades. Kodagu district was attached to Mangalore Lok

Sabha Constituency in 1957. Since independence only two people from Kodagu, namely, Nidamane Somanna and C.M. Poonacha have been elected to the Lok Sabha. Poonacha is the only person from the district, since independence, to be appointed, as a minister in the Union council of ministers. Virajpet constituency of the district has been notified as a reserved constituency since last twenty-three years, though it has a significant Kodava population. Since 1956 four people from the Kodava community were able to secure berths in the Karnataka state council of ministers. Due to the common reservation policy of the State Government, Kodava stand a limited chance of getting elected to the Grama Panchayats, Taluk Panchayats and the Zilla Parishads. Most of the representatives in these bodies are rank outsiders.

13. The financial allocations for the developmental work of the district from the Central and State Governments remains inadequate. The district generates Rs. 400 crore of revenue every year and not even 20 per cent of it is earmarked for its development. For instance, the state and central allocations for the Zilla Parishad for the financial year 1999-2000 stood at Rs.27.93 crore, out of which Rs. 14.26 crore and Rs.13.67 crore remained as the Central and State Government allocations respectively.[21]

14. The common people are a harassed lot by the administrative officials at the taluk and district level. This is mainly due to the fact that most of the officials are from other parts of the state and they find it very difficult to understand the problem of the locals and their sentiments. The cultural gap between the officials and the public is another reason for officials being insensitive to the locals.

Movement for Statehood

Disgusted with inaction on the part of the successive governments and utter neglect of the area both administratively and politically over the last 44 years, there is a cry for a separate homeland. The Coorg National Council (CNC) formally called Kodagu Rajya Mukti Morcha (KRMM) and Liberation Warriors of Kodagu (LIWAK) respectively, are spear-heading a struggle for a separate homeland, a Kodagu state, within the Indian Union, under the leadership of N.U. Nachappa, a lawyer by profession. This frontal organisation is in the news since October, 1991, and in the recent years has established itself as the main voice and a forum of the natives of Kodagu.

Nachappa, the General Secretary of CNC argues: Coorg's districts, historical, cultural, racial, ethnic, linguistic and social fabric has been destroyed by successive governments; separate state of Coorg would be economically more viable; political representation alone can bring prosperity to the region which can happen only if Coorg gets statehood. He also says that all they want is a political and not economic package for the development of the district, accompanied by a constitutional guarantee for their land, language and race as they face an identity crisis.

The CNC has held several rallies and hundreds of meetings within Coorg and outside to educate the people about the movement and for mobilisation of popular support. It organised a "Delhi Challo" with 5,000 strong delegates on 16th November, 1998, to submit a memorandum to the then Prime Minister Atal Behari Vajpayee highlighting separate statehood for Kodagu. A "Bangalore Challo" event, with 10,000 strong delegates was organised by CNC on 8th November, 1999, to draw the attention of the Karnataka government. It has also held a public rally in Delhi on November 21, 2000, to make another plea for a separate Kodagu state, after the creation of three new states of Chattisgarh, Uttaranchal and Jharkhand. It has also submitted representation in this regard to the Home Minister L.K. Advani and to the constitution Review Commission Chairman M.N. Venkatachallaiah. The main demands of the CNC are as follows:

(a) Re-establishment of Coorg state with rights as on the day it was amalgamated to the then Mysore state.
(b) Reservation for Kodavas as a non-religious racial minority in order to get them reservation for government jobs and constitutional protection.
(c) Inclusion of Kodava language in the VIII Schedule of the Constitution.
(d) A separate parliamentary constituency for Kodagu.
(e) Guarantee under Article 371 of the Constitution and not a mere statutory guarantee, to protect their homeland which it claims being sold to outsiders.

(f) Establishment of an autonomous university in Coorg on the lines of Aligarh Muslim University or Benaras Hindu University.

(g) The Kodavas must be guaranteed land, language, culture, heritage, economic and political freedom of their own in the purview of the V Schedule of the Constitution.

(h) Union territory status for Coorg as an interim arrangement if the process at establishing a full-fledged Coorg state were to be a time-consuming affair.

Is the Demand for Coorg State Justified ?

Open criticism of all successive governments for the neglect of the district, the mission of preserving the language and cultural identity, appeal for more political representation and the goal for rebuilding Coorg undertaken by CNC are really laudable. The Secretary General of CNC needs to be complimented for sustaining the movement all these years against all odds. However, the demand for a separate state or the restoration of statehood:

1. Apart from the Kodavas there are also other groups of people with substantial population like the Muslims, Christians, Gowdas and Veerashaivas. The population composition of Kodagu is illustrated in Table 25.5.

Table 25.5: Population Composition of Kodagu

Hindus	4,04,785
Muslims	66,573
Christians	16,271
Buddhists	06
Jains	86
Sikhs	11
Others	285
Religion not stated	438
Total	**4,88,455**

Source: 1991 Census Report.

The Kodavas who are considered Hindus number about 90,000 to 1,00,000 in Kodagu according to unofficial estimates. In this context the question is asked by many is whether CNC has taken these groups into confidence and enjoys the majority support of these groups in the statehood movement? The rivalry between CNC and Kodagu Praja Vedike (a group which opposes statehood) comprising non-Kodavas is complicating the whole matter of popular support.

2. The geographical area and population of Coorg is another limitation for statehood. The district which measures 4,102 sq. km. is little larger than Goa state, but has comparatively smaller population than Goa. Table 25.6 gives a clear picture about the area, population, number of districts and number of seats in assembly, Lok Sabha and Rajya Sabha respectively.

Table 25.6: Facts about the Smallest States of the Indian Union

Sl. No.	*State*	*Area in sq. km.*	*Population in lakh*	*No. of districts*	*No. of seats in state assembly*	*No. of seats in LS*	*No. of seats in Rs*
1.	Goa	3,702	11,69,793	02	40	02	01
2.	Sikkim	7,096	4,06,457	04	32	01	01
3.	Tripura	10,486	27,57,205	04	60	02	01
4.	Nagaland	16,579	12,09,546	07	60	01	01
5.	Mizoram	21,081	6,89,756	03	40	01	01
6.	Manipur	22,327	18,37,149	08	60	02	01
7.	Meghalaya	22,429	17,74,778	07	60	02	01
8.	Himachal	55,673	51,70,877	12	68	04	03
9.	Arunachal	83,743	8,64,558	11	60	02	01

Source: Limca Book of Records.

Table 25.7: Factors about Three Newly Created States of Indian Union

Sl. No.	*State*	*Area in sq. km.*	*Population in lakh*	*No. of districts*	*No. of seats in state assembly*	*No. of seats in LS*	*No. of seats in RS*
1.	Chattisgarh	1,25,100	176.15	16	90	11	05
2.	Uttaranchal	55,845	70.45	13	70(31)	05	03
3.	Jharkhand	79,714	218.44	18	81	14	06

Source: The Hindu, 5th November, 2000, p. 14.

Based on the facts, illustrated by tables six and seven, it is contended by many that Coorg is too small in terms of its area and population to be granted statehood. It is also debated that grant of statehood to Coorg will naturally strengthen many other statehood movements in different parts of the country, leading to large scale complications resulting in secessionist tendencies.

3. Any statehood movement to succeed needs support and sympathy of major political parties, prominent political leaders, intellectuals, statesman and literary orgnisations supporting the statehood movement, with a few exception of outside forces, the credibility of the movement is severely questioned.

4. It is also debated that Coorg was not the only Part "C" state prior to 1956. There were nine other Part "C" states with Coorg, out of which Manipur, Tripura and Delhi had according Union Territory status first and later on were elevated as states. If Coorg is restored with statehood now, then all the pre-1956 Part "C" states of Ajmer, Bilaspur, Bhopal, Kutch and Vindya Pradesh, too stand a chance for the same, along with many others. A day may soon come when India would be once again divided into several hundred states.

5. The main source of income to Coorg is from coffee plantations and other agricultural activities. There is no other alternative source of income from the industrial and other allied activities, as there are no big industries in Coorg with the exception of few agro-based industries. Establishment of large scale industries will result in large scale deforestation and environmental degradation which will be strongly opposed by environmental groups from outside leading to litigations, delays and stagnation. Depending only on plantations and agricultural activities for income, without any other alternative source, will be a risky proposition, leading to over-dependence on other states and the centre for the basic needs, causing a lot of hardship to the common man. Thus the argument that Coorg can develop well on its own is also questioned.

6. The idea of smaller states as being economically viable, better administered and panacea for development is also severely questioned. Many argue that had size alone been the major casual explanation, the small states of north-east would not have performed so badly on the administrative and economic fronts. Small states like Punjab, Haryana, Himachal Pradesh and Kerala are progressive states not because of their smallness alone, but due to various other factors like dynamic leadership, the green revolution, land reforms and large scale migration respectively.

In conclusion it can be said that the need of the hour is to channelise the energies and resources for the development of Kodagu. The problem faced by the Government of Karnataka and the centre. It only requires a prompt administrative action, a special package for the development of the district and strong political will on the part of both the governments. All demands put forth by the Coorg National Council, with the exception of the demand for restoration of statehood, are worth considering, by both the State and the Central Governments. The CNC today is not alone in voicing these demands, as the Bangalore Kodava Samaj, on behalf of the members of the Kodava Samaj all over the world and on behalf of the people of Kodagu in its Memorandum to the Prime Minister submitted through the Union Minister Dhanjaya Kumar on 13th November, 1999 has endorsed the CNC demand of separate parliamentary constituency for Coorg and the inclusion of Kodava language in the Eighth Schedule of the Constitution of India. Chief Minister S.M. Krishna who has already responded well to the problems of the people of Coorg by inducting three representatives from the district in his Council of Ministers, will do well again if he invites the CNM activists for talks, which can help assuage the feelings of the activists and the people of Kodagu on the apparent neglect of district over he years.

REFERENCES

1. Memorandum of Kodava Samaj Bangalore dated 13.11.1999, submitted to the P.M. through the Union Minister Dhananjaya Kumar.
2. Palaksh Kumar, *New States*, The Week, Vol. 18, No. 37, August 27, 2000, pp. 12-13.
3. Swaraj Basu, *Is Creation of New States the Answer to People's Aspirations?*, Mainstream, Vol. XXXVIII, No. 9, September 16, 2000, pp. 9-12.
4. Pradeep Kumar, *Do We Need More States in India?*, Mainstream, Vol. XXXVIII, No. 44, October 21, 2000, pp. 21-27.

NOTES

1. Pradeep Kumar, *Demand for New States*, Economic and Political Weekly, August 26–September 2, 8.2000, Vol. XXXV, No. 35-36, pp. 3078-3082.

2. Kodagu District Gazetteer (R.E.) 1993, pp. 2-3.
3. *Ibid.*, pp. 50-51.
4. They were: (1) Veeraraja, (2) Appaji Raja, (3) Mudduraja, (4) Doddaveerappa, (5) Chikka Veerappa, (6) Mudduraja II and Muddai Raja (Joint rule), (7) Devappa Raja, (8) Linga Raja, (9) Dodda Veera Raja, (10) Linga Raja II, (11) Devamaji, (12) Chikkaveera Raja.
5. Presently Periyapatna falls under Hunsur Taluk of Mysore District.
6. Kodagu District Gazetteer (R.E.) 1993, p. 4.
7. *Ibid.*, p. 92.
8. *Ibid.*, pp. 6-7.
9. They were—Ajmer, Bilaspur, Bhopal, Delhi, Himachal Pradesh, Kutch, Manipur, Tripura and Vindya Pradesh.
10. Kodagu District Gazetteer (R.E.) 1993, pp. 103-105.
11. *Ibid.*, p. 8.
12. Kodagu has the higher per capita income of Rs. 20, 120 as against Rs.9,384 of the state. Source—Human Development Report of Karnataka, 1999.
13. NABARD schemes boost development of roads in Kodagu, The Hindu, 15th July, 2000, p. 5.
14. Forest Department object halts work on Baraple Brdige, The Hindu, 8th August, 2000, p. 7.
15. "Human Development in Karnataka Report", 1999, p. 375.
16. Kodagu District Gazetteer (R.E.) 1993, p. 30.
17. *Plunder of precious timber comes as a shock*, The Hindu, 26th February, 2000, p. 5.
18. Is Devarakadu facing Extinction ? Deccan Herald, 19th October, 2000, p. 4.
19. *Hunger forces elephants to raid farms: A Study*, The Hindu, 29th October, 2000, p. 5.
20. *Lack of Concern for Flood in Kodagu*, The Hindu, 12th August, 2000, p. 6.
21. Shakti Kannada Daily of Kodagu, 12th April, 2000, p. 4.

26

Backward Classes and Minorities in Karnataka Politics

V.K. NATRAJ

Karnataka is a relatively new area in the research agenda of social scientists who for long treated it as insufficiently volatile. Hence they sought their material in the more turbulent waters of Kerala, West Bengal and Tamil Nadu. However, there is one feature of Karnataka's socio-political ethos which has attracted the attention of scholars, namely, the backward class movement. This, along with the policy of positive (protective) discrimination, has been the subject of learned treatises.[1] In the last decade and a half there has been considerable research effort expended in analysing the implications of the backward class movement for the state's political structure. Also, the entire issue of who constitute the backward classes and what benefits they should be entitled to under articles 15(4) and 16(4) of the Indian Constitution has assumed very complex dimensions. What is, however, clear is that the issue of reservations is alive, and Karnataka's political configurations are noticeably influenced by the alignments among the state's *backward classes* themselves as well as among forward and backward classes.

The basic purpose of this article is to examine the relative gains and losses, in electoral terms, of different caste groups in Karnataka. The first part sketches a portrait of caste groups in Karnataka and briefly outlines the nature of positive discrimination in the state. The second part analyses the representation of different caste groups in the state assembly from 1952 onwards. The third part discusses these developments in a theoretical perspective. The final part sums up the discussion and hazards some speculations.

Background

Caste in Karnataka is ubiquitous. While the dominance of caste sometimes draws attention to the exclusion of other factors germane to Karnataka's political and social life, there is little doubt about its relevance to any study of the politics of the state. For purposes of this analysis Karnataka's castes can be usefully divided into the following groups: Brahmin, Lingayat, Vokkaliga, other backward classes (OBC), scheduled castes and scheduled tribes and Muslims. In the former princely state of Mysore, which constituted the social and territorial core of Karnataka before independence, the Vokkaligas were the single largest group, followed by the Lingayats. These two groups traded places after the unified state was formed in 1956. They are recognised as being the dominant castes in the state. Despite their numerical weakness, Brahmins have enjoyed a pre-eminent position in education and state services although protective discrimination has resulted in limiting their opportunities to some extent. The scheduled castes and tribes are classified separately because of their special status. The OBC category consists of all other Hindu castes, communities and tribes, in recent years, especially since the early 1970s: this constellation of castes has been attempting to fight the dominance of the upper castes. It is unnecessary to justify grouping the Muslims separately. Table 26.1 shows the percentage of selected castes to the state population and also their distribution through the twenty districts of the state.

The first committee to inquire into the grievances of the non-Brahmins regarding inadequate representation in service under the state was the Miller Committee. In 1918 it initially classified all non-Brahmin cases as backward. The Brahmins were thoroughly dissatisfied with Miller. The non-Brahmins in the 1920s and 1930 felt that the Miller recommendations had not been properly implemented. It is during this latter period that signs appeared of the fragility of the non-Brahmin alliance. However, the basic structure recommended by Miller continued with modifications till after independence. And so did the fragile alliance among the non-Brahmin groups.

Table 26.1: Percentage of State Population and Co-efficient of Variation (CV) of Selected Castes

Castes	*Percentage to state population*	*CV*
Agasa	1.00	62
Adikarnataka	5.37	117
Adidravida	1.59	75
Meda	2.75	99
Banjara	1.18	96
Brahmin	3.81	73
Vodda	1.53	82
Devanga	0.74	70
Besta	2.80	123
Idiga	2.54	201
Kumbara	0.70	96
Ganiga	0.45	103
Uppara	1.31	112
Kuruba	6.92	65
Vaisya	0.77	86
Yadava	1.46	139
Rajput	0.15	172
Marathas	3.20	142
Nayinda	0.60	73
Neygi	0.65	77
Darzi	0.33	81
Vokkaliga	11.68	124
Lingayat	16.92	88

Source: Report of KBCC-1.

The second milestone was the Mysore Backward Classes Committee, popularly known as the Nagan Gowda Committee (after its Chairman, R. Nagan Gowda), which submitted its report in 1961. The radical feature of this report was that it recommended deletion of the Lingayats from the list of backward classes. Predictably, this the Lingayats resisted vehemently. They have always been a political power and, after the enlarged state was created, they became the single largest caste as well. The government finally yielded to the pressure of the Lingayats and, in subsequent orders, included the Lingayats among the backward classes. The Nagan Gowda Committee thus illustrates the problems which arise when a dominant caste long encompassed by protective discrimination is deprived of that benefit.

In the years immediately following the Nagan Gowda report, there were several cases of litigation in the High Court of Mysore as well as in the Supreme Court. It was during this period that there began to merge the semblance of opposition to Lingayat-Vokkaliga dominance from the other non-Brahmin groups. Gradually a clamour arose for a review of the existing reservation policy. Matters reached a climactic level as a result of several synchronous developments. Disaffection with the inequitable sharing of benefits of positive discrimination started to become evident in much clearer perspective than before. At the national level, there was Prime Minister Indira Gandhi's strident insistence, during the 1971 national elections, on *garibi hatao* (abolish poverty) accompanied by an equally emphatic commitment to the welfare of SCs, STs and the minorities. The Congress split of 1969 had also added to this scenario. In Karnataka the Congress stayed with Congress (O) rather than joining the Prime Minister in the Congress (R) which initially commanded little effective support in the state.

Into this vacuum stepped Devaraj Urs who took over the stewardship of the party. An experienced politician who had been a minister for some years between 1962 and 1968, he assumed the mantle of leadership of the Congress (R) in the state. He belonged to a small community, the Arasus, who claim Kshatriya status given that the Mysore royal family belongs to this community. He was thus not seen as a threat by the dominant caste communities. But he had a sufficiently high ritual status to be accepted as an appropriate leader. Urs proved to be a perceptive student of caste in the state's politics and was endowed with enviable patience. With Indira Gandhi's support, he built up the Congress (I) and won the state assembly elections in 1972. He is frequently credited with having altered the structure of politics of Karnataka (Manor, 1980; Natraj and Natraj, 1982; Manor,1984). He commenced a political journey which was to culminate in his recognition as the most articulate and astute statesman of the OBCs (Srinivas and Panini, 1984).

The most important concrete step taken up by Urs was the appointment of the Karnataka Backward Classes Commission in 1972 (hereafter KBCC-I). He was keen on a comprehensive review of reservations but, being the sagacious politician that he was, he waited until there were public demands for such a review. He found an able ally in L.G. Havanur, a lawyer by profession, who over the years had developed an articulate resentment to Vokkaliga-Lingayat dominance. It was Havanur who was largely instrumental in creating a demand for a fresh look at reservations. The Urs-Havanur axis worked in tandem and the two shared, by all accounts, a common philosophic outlook on protective discrimination.

The Havanur Commission came out with its report in 1975 but once again Urs displayed his political acumen in not issuing a government order until 1977, the eve of the fifth general election. The Havanur report excluded the Lingayats from the list of beneficiaries of protective discrimination while it retained benefits for the Vokkaligas and classified the OBCs into three groups—backward community, backward caste and backward tribe. For the latter three, the distribution of reservations was recommended at 16, 10 and 6 per cent respectively. The government order issued in 1977, however, made two significant alterations in the Commission's recommendations. First, Muslims were included among the backward communities although the Commission had expressly argued against it. Second, a new group, termed the backward special group, was added to the three recommended in the Havanur report. Inclusion into this group was based not on caste but on occupation and income. With these two master strokes, Urs won the support of the Muslims and succeeded in placing some sections of the forward castes who could claim benefit under the Backward Special Group. There was, as could be expected, opposition to both the Havanur report and the subsequent government order, but the substance of these two pronouncements and the debates about them resulted in the creation of a broad public consensus on the moral obligation of championing the cause of the OBCs. The opposition to the Urs-Havanur scheme manifested itself in very many ways, but it was unable to disengage this developing consensus.

Urs parted company with Indira Gandhi in 1979 and resigned from the Chief Ministership in 1980 when his party, the Congress (U), failed to secure a single seat in the mid-term elections to the parliament. His successor as Chief Minister, Gundu Rao, neither shared his commitment to the OBC cause nor did he possess his substantial political skills. It was during Rao's stewardship (1980-83) that the signs of dominant caste resurgence began to appear. The Lingayats were constantly complaining about the injustice done by KBCC-I to their caste and took the matters to the Supreme Court in a writ petition (*K.C. Vasantha Kumar* vs. *State of Karnataka*).

During the arguments in this petition, the Rao government committed itself to appointing a commission to examine the question of listing beneficiaries for reservation *de novo*. Soon thereafter, however, the Janata government took office and deferred the undertaking given by its predecessor with consequences which can only be described as cataclysmic.

The Janata government of Ramakrishna Hegde appointed the Karnataka Backward Classes Commission-II (KBCC-II) under the Chairmanship of T. Venkataswami. Three factors distinguish KBCC-II from KBCC-I. First, the public debate which had surrounded the latter and in a sense prepared the ground for acceptance of its report was missing in the case of KBCC-II. Secondly, KBCC-II lacked homogeneity because of the presence of several ministers who expressed their dissent whereas KBCC-I had only one such minister who dissented only on a minor point. Thirdly, the KBCC-I report and the government order following it had the protection of the national emergency while KBCC-II had not.

The Venkataswami Committee presented its report early in 1986 but it was made public only in September of that year. It divided the OBCs into two groups. A and B, comprising fifteen and twenty communities each with reservation benefits of fourteen and thirteen per cent respectively. What is significant is that both the Lingayats and the Vokkaligas were deleted from the list of OBCs. The report was greeted with one of the most effective protests ever seen in the state, the most vocal opposition coming from the Vokkaligas with the Vokkaliga Sangha in the vanguard in mobilising opinion against the report. The highway between Bangalore and Mysore was blocked for nearly two weeks at Mandya, the traditional headquarters of the Vokkaligas. Ultimately the State Government announced, on 8 October that it was withdrawing the report and that an *ad hoc* list of OBCs would be in operation until a new commission examined the question. Under this order, the beneficiary castes are grouped as follows: (a) sixty-two backward tribes as specified in KBCC-I and a few additions, (b) one hundred twenty eight backward tribes included earlier and seven new communities including Idigas, (c) backward communities including Muslims and Vokkaligas, (d) new communities including Lingayats, and (e) backward special group.

Nearly ninety six per cent of the state's population is now brought under the ambit of reservation, though the actual number of beneficiaries is smaller because of the income ceiling from which only group A is exempt. A remarkable feature of the post KBCC-II development is that the Lingayats who were deleted from the OBCs in 1973 by KBCC-I made a re-entry through the new arrangement. This is remarkable given the fact that their contribution to the anti-KBCC-II agitation was muted compared to that of the Vokkaligas.

Representation in the Assembly and Lok Sabha—A Historical Account

Against this background we now turn to an analysis of the representation of different caste groups in the state legislative assembly. The data are presented with respect to the Lingayats, Vokkaligas, Muslims, OBCs, SCs, STs, Brahmins, Christians and the Marathas. The analysis is guided by the following questions:

1. What has been the quantum jump, if any, in the representation of the OBCs in the state legislature in the last three decades, and especially since 1972—the beginning of the Urs era?
2. Among the OBCs which groups have received the most substantial gains?
3. What is the magnitude of political influence of the backward classes in Karnataka, in general, and what is its impact on the state's political behaviour, in particular ?

Tables 26.2 through 26.5 present detailed information about representation of "other backward classes" in the state legislative assembly. For example, in 1972, as Table 26.2 shows, OBC representation was three times what it had been at the time of the first general elections held twenty years before. In subsequent elections further advances were registered by the OBCs, reaching peaks of forty five in 1978 and 1985. It is a clear indication of the working of the Urs effect that has operated in Karnataka to improve political representation of the OBCs. However, it is necessary to point to the virtual constancy of the representation after the big jump between 1967 and 1972. Table 26.6 presents the Lok Sabha picture. No significant jump is seen in this case, but there is a steady increase in OBC, SC and ST representation during the period under review.

Table 26.2: Representation of Selected Castes and Groups of Castes in the Karnataka Legislative Assembly Since 1952

Castes	*1952*	*1957*	*1962*	*1967*	*1972*	*1978*	*1983*	*1985*
Lingayats	18	73	69	70	58	53	65	65
Vokkaligas	42	46	57	47	47	47	54	52
Brahmins	06	18	12	18	14	16	16	11
Marathas	--	09	08	09	09	07	11	05
SCs and STs	19	29	29	29	32	37	35	35
Muslims	--	09	07	08	13	17	02	09
Christians	--	02	01	03	03	03	03	03
OBCs	12	16	17	18	36	45	36	45
Total	**97**	**202**	**200**	**202**	**212**	**225**	**222**	**224**

Source: S. Bhiemappa: 'Analysis of Elections', Times of India, (Bangalore), 23 April, 1987.

Table 26.3: Assembly Elections—1978: Analysis by Caste and Party

Caste	*Janata*			*Congress*		
	Seats allotted	*Seats won*	*Percentage of success*	*Seats allotted*	*Seats won*	*Percent-age of success*
Lingayats	65	18	28	49	31	63
Vokkaligas	53	19	36	43	23	53
Brahmins	11	03	45	16	09	56
Marathas	08	00	00	12	07	58
SCs and STs	35	08	23	37	26	70
Muslims	14	02	14	--	--	--
Christians	02	01	50	03	02	67
OBCs	23	05	22	54	40	74

Source: S. Bhiemappa: 'Analysis of Elections', Times of India, (Bangalore), 25 April, 1987.

There are additional factors to reckon with. The OBC category, it had been noted earlier, is amorphous and consists of several quite desperate groups. In terms of population, the leading castes are Kuruba (6.92 per cent), Bea (5.1 per cent), Maratha (3.2 per cent), and Idiga (2.3 per cent). There are others whose share in the state population is miniscule. In terms of social and economic status, there are also enormous differences. A feature of interest not generally noticed is the geographical distribution of castes and communities (OBC and others) throughout the state. Table 26.1 shows that the service castes are well distributed as are several others such as the Kurubas, Bedas and, of course, the Brahmins. Further, if the data are examined by *taluk*, it will be found that if the Kurubas are well represented, so are minority groups like the Upparas. Detailed information on these relative concentrations is not readily available but it can be forcefully argued that all these factors exert powerful influence in the state's politics.[2]

Table 26.4: Assembly Elections—1983: Analysis by Caste and Party

Caste	*Janata*			*Congress*		
	Seats allotted	*Seats won*	*Percentage of success*	*Seats allotted*	*Seats won*	*Percentage of success*
Lingayats	68	26	38	54	28	52
Vokkaligas	44	27	61	43	15	35
Brahmins	12	06	50	14	03	21
Marathas	07	03	43	11	07	64
SCs and STs	35	19	54	36	12	33
Muslims	06	01	17	18	01	06
OBCs	25	14	56	40	16	40

Source: S. Bhiemappa: 'Analysis of Elections', Times of India, (Bangalore), 25 April, 1987.

Table 26.5: Assembly Elections—1985: Analysis by Caste and Party

Caste	*Janata*			*Congress*		
	Seats allotted	*Seats won*	*Percentage of success*	*Seats allotted*	*Seats won*	*Percentage of success*
Lingayats	64	47	73	48	11	23
Vokkaligas	53	36	68	45	10	22
Brahmins	10	08	80	17	-3	18
Marathas	04	01	25	08	02	23
SCs and STs	35	23	66	35	11	31
Muslims	02	00	00	02	02	100
OBCs	32	22	69	48	20	42

Source: S. Bhiemappa: 'Analysis of Elections', Times of India, (Bangalore), 25 April, 1987.

Table 26.6: Assembly Elections—1952-84: Analysis by Caste

Caste	*1952*	*1957*	*1962*	*1967*	*1971*	*1977*	*1980*	*1984*
Lingayats	08	07	07	06	07	06	04	07
Vokkaligas	03	04	06	08	09	09	06	04
Brahmins	01	09	06	04	03	03	03	03
Marathas	--	01	01	03	02	02	03	02
SCs and STs	02	03	03	04	04	04	04	05
Muslims	--	01	01	--	--	--	01	01
OBCs	--	01	02	01	02	03	05	05

Source: S. Bhiemappa: 'Analysis of Elections', Times of India, (Bangalore), 25 April, 1987.

If we keep these variables before us, the data presented in Tables 26.2 to 26.5 yield more interesting results. The Marathas have enjoyed impressive representation going back to 1957, their representation consistently exceeding their share in the state's population. The Marathas are mostly found in the erstwhile Bombay Karnataka districts (Belgaum, Dharwar and Uttara Kannada). Interestingly, the KBCC-II classified Marathas as a forward group, but they were included in the *ad hoc* OBC list of October 1986. In 1957, 1962 and 1967 the Marathas accounted for nearly one-third of all OBC legislative assembly members. From 1972 to 1985 their share of OBC MLAs has fluctuated between 25 and 11 per cent. These details are presented in Table 26.7.

Table 26.7: Percentage Share of Marathas in OBC Representation in the Assembly

Year	*Percentage*
1952	00
1957	56
1962	49
1967	50
1972	25
1978	17
1983	30
1985	11

Source: Times of India, 25 April 1987.

Another striking feature is the position of the Kurubas. They constitute a major group among the OBCs in terms of population. They are rather evenly distributed throughout the state, are well organised, and have made their presence felt in state politics for a number of years, having had representation in almost every ministry. Yet they have only five members in the legislative assembly at present. In the 1985 elections a total of twenty six seats were allotted to the Kurubas — sixteen from the Congress and ten from the Janata. Four Janata candidates and one Congress candidate won. One would normally have expected the Kurubas to have a much larger slice of the OBC cake. Their representation in 1978 and 1983 was seven and nine respectively (for details see KBCC-II, Report). A very plausible explanation for this is that the Kurubas have tended to alienate other OBC castes, specially the numerically small groups, and since their areas of concentration overlap in several places, the non-Kuruba population has tended to vote against Kuruba candidates. This explanation has also a theoretical plausibility. The OBCs have rarely shown cohesion and it should not be surprising if numerically tiny groups fear the conversion of this numerical strength to political power on the part of the Kurubas. To this may be added the possibility that minorities among the OBCs attempt to use politics as a means to alleviate any dependency relationship they may have *vis-a-vis* the dominant caste. This is certainly a fruitful area for further investigation.

Of the forty seven MLAs from the OBCs elected in 1985, the largest single group is that of the Idigas. Toddy tappers by profession, the more affluent among them take to wholesale liquor trade (excise contractors). At present there are eleven Idiga MLAs, though this caste's share of the state population is but 2.5 per cent. Their representation has registered a steady increase—1978 (6), 1983 (8), and 1985 (11).

Second in size are the Bedas, a tribe agitating for inclusion in the scheduled tribe list. The KBCC-I estimated their population at over six per cent of the state total but the KBCC-II puts it at 2.75 per cent. The difference is caused by the manner in which those using names synonymous with the Beda are classified. If the KBCC-I method is utilised we can count six MLAs in 1985 and ten in 1978 but comparison is rendered difficult for the reason advanced above. Once again the falling numbers among Beda MLAs can be explained with reference to the same factors as have been advanced in the Kuruba case, and the same caveat applies here as well.

There has been a feeling in Karnataka politics that the backward classes phenomenon is essentially a Congress phenomenon and that the Janata has remained an urban and relatively dominant caste-oriented party. Tables 26.3 to 26.5 give the distribution of seats allotted and seats won by the Congress and the Janata in 1978, 1983 and 1985. The data provide some support to this view, but much more important is the fact that while the Congress has not reached the 1978 level in terms of seats allotted, the Janata has shown a steady, if wholly unspectacular, increase in allotting tickets to representatives of backward classes. If the Congress and the Janata are considered together, there is striking evidence of the rise in the number of OBC candidates fielded by both the parties.

If we ignore party affiliation and merely look at aggregate numbers, it is immediately discernible that, while the number of OBC candidates has been rising, their rate of electoral success has declined perceptibly. The explanation for this has to be sought in the decline of the Congress' success rate. The data also yield the conclusion that the success rate of the OBC candidates pivots around their party's general performance. Since the Congress had generally fielded more OBC candidates and has also fared badly from 1983 onwards, the overall success rate of this group has dwindled. A final and obvious point is that as the number of candidates for a relatively stable set of positions increases, the proportion of those successful, by immutable mathematical logic, declines.

What is the picture that emerges when we look at the fortunes of the dominant castes and the Brahmins in assembly elections since 1957, the data of the first election in the state as currently comprised? The most striking features are:

Table 26.8: Caste/Community-wise Break up of OBCs in the Assembly Elections, 1983 (% to state population in brackets)

Caste/Community	*Percentage*
Idiga	11 (2.54)
Kuruba	05(6.92)
Beda	06(2.75)
Besta	03(2.80)
Uppara	03(2.80)
Sadar	02(0.06)
Kamma	04(0.25)
Devadiga	01(0.29)
Baliya	01(1.33)
Golla	03(1.46)

(Contd.)

(*Contd.*)

Halwakki Wakkal	01(0.19)
Kumanapalk	1 M.A.
Gowli	1 M.A.
Kumbara	01(0.70)
Not known	04

Source: Complied from Times of India, op. cit., and Report of KBCC-II.

First, Lingayat representation in the assembly has stayed more or less constant if we ignore 1972 and 1978 when they touched a comparative low. Second, Vokkaliga representation has also remained more or less at the same level, particularly since 1967. Third, the jump in OBC representation between 1967 and 1978 coincides with noticeable fall in Lingayat representation from seventy to fifty eight in the same period. Fourth, the preceding point is supported by qualitative analysis. This was the period when the Congress split with state continuing under Congress (O) governance. Urs, the Congress (R) leader in the state, found it difficult in the beginning to attract the dominant castes, in particular the Lingayat. Fifth, 1983 marks a watershed. Both the dominant castes gained over the Lingayats by twelve seats in 1978 and the Vokkaligas by seven—while the OBCs lost nine seats. Muslim representation dropped precipitously from seventeen to two. Largely these losses became the dominant castes, gain. Sixth, it is significant to note that, between 1978 and 1983, the Congress allotment of seats for the OBCs itself decreased from fifty four to forty. After the 1983 elections several the Congress leaders blamed the party's poor showing on what they termed the neglect of the Devaraj Urs formula.

Towards a Theoretical Construct

The empirical analysis presented above leads to some general theoretical constructs. The evidence available, impressive in itself, demonstrates considerable gains made by the OBCs in the post-1972 period. However, we notice that since then there has been a slackening or at best maintenance of the *status quo*. This evidence is reinforced by the observation of Karnataka's political scene. The earlier parts of this paper have focused on two characteristics of OBCs—their inability to achieve political coherence and the amorphous nature of their group. As a category the OBCs contain several divisions within. These are mutually reinforcing features. Additionally, some of the OBCs are so small in number and so weak economically that over time they have developed dependence on the major castes. This has led to several noticeable emergent trends. They are discussed below and, wherever possible, illustrated with examples.

If Urs forged an alliance among the OBCs, he was in no small measure helped by his circumstances—the Indira wave in 1971-72, the Emergency, and Indira's assiduous championing of the SC-ST cause. While he created an atmosphere in which the OBC casue became a household issue, the structure remained fragile to the end (Natraj and Natraj, 1982). After Urs' political eclipse and his death, the fervour so obvious in his time on behalf of the backward classes suffered a decline, particularly so during the Rao regime (1980-83) when a resurgence of dominant castes took place. It is possible that, commitment apart, Rao could hardly compare with Urs in skill in handling the OBC-dominant caste equation. In other words, even if Gundu Rao shared Urs' zeal for advancing the OBC cause (which is doubtful), he was compelled by political circumstances, and his limited skills as to gravitate towards the dominant castes.

This becomes obvious when we compare the fate of KBCC-II (Venkataswami) with KBCC-I (Havanur). Throughout its functioning, KBCC-I made its presence felt. The Chairman, L.G. Havanur, lost no opportunity to speak of the backward classes, the coincidence of castes and class (often mistakenly), the need for reservation and a host of related issues. No one was left in doubt that he enjoyed the confidence of the Chief Minister (interview with L.G. Havanur, 2 January, 1982). Apart from the important contribution of Urs and Havanur, the political climate was favourable. Urs managed the Emergency so cleverly that it had virtually no adverse consequences for him in the 1978 poll. Until 1979 when Urs broke from Indira Gandhi and resigned in 1980, the state witnessed several rallies, meetings, seminars and demonstrations in favour of the Havanur report.

In contrast, the KBCC-II started with disadvantages. In a sense the Commission was totally unnecessary. KBCC-I had made a fairly elaborate survey and listed thirteen backward communities, one hundred twenty-eight backward castes, and sixty-two backward tribes. For good measure mention was made of three hundred eighty six castes, communities and tribes whose population could not be ascertained. While not perfect, the KBCC-I had given a comprehensive scheme and had muscled the Lingayats out of the OBC list. A successor Commission, it was obvious, would run into problems. The genesis of KBCC-II has been discussed earlier in this paper. The consequences of the appointment of the latter have also been pointed out. And lest the present author be accused of hindsight, he would like to cite from an earlier paper of which he is a co-author. "Also it is in (sic) the cards that the second KBCC, will be forced to make some concessions to Lingayats, currently the most vociferous group demanding the backward tag" (Natraj and Natraj, 1984). This projection came true although some prophetic injustice was done to KBCC-II. What actually happened was that the Commission declassified the Vokkaligas and drastically reduced the quantum and coverage of reservations. However, the forecast proved correct since the government was confronted with a very difficult situation and ultimately had to reject the report.

This rejection was inevitable for several reasons. First, the changed atmosphere which KBCC-I created was absent during the tenure of its successor. Second, the report played into the hands of its critics by adopting a methodology easily open to question. Third, the OBCs did not put up a spirited enough defence in favour of the report. Wholly absent was the crescendo of well-blended OBC voices which had, a decade ago, conferred on the Havanur report the halo of a credo. What little support was expressed was drowned in the babel of voices stridently denouncing it. The Havanur and post-Havanur days had witnessed a remarkable proliferation of backward class (caste) associations. All this became a thing of the past after the early 1980s. KBCC-I enjoyed a perverse piece of luck. Most members of the Commission evinced little interest in its work.

The government order of October 1986 has, as noted above, declared almost all groups backward. Given the present state of development in the state, the major beneficiaries of this new bonanza will be the relatively more advanced among the castes now included among OBCs. One of the tragedies of both KBCC-I and KBCC-II is that neither paid any attention to the imminent need of preparing a base for those OBCs which are still in a nascent state of development. A large percentage of reservations in the A, B, C and D groups will benefit only the relatively developed ones.

The backward classes have not been able to show Hegde that he can rule the state with their support. It would appear that one of the lessons. Hegde has learnt from the experience of Urs is that excessive dependence on the OBCs will create problems of political survival. Nothing else can explain the indifference with which the government watched the road blockade during the anti-KBCC-II agitation. Hegde is generally accused of dependence on three of his dominant caste colleagues—Deve Gowda, Bommai and Patel.

Another dimension of this vexatious problem relates to the general minority caste perception of social reality. They are invariably prone to anti-Brahminism and can be classified to be anti-dominant caste. At the same time they are suspicious of SCs and STs. Finally, even amongst themselves they perceive some as threats. The problem is exacerbated by their poor economic status. To put it briefly, their attitude is one of the sullen resentment. Their suspicious are known but not their preferences.

It would, therefore, be appropriate for activists committed to the case of the backward classes to explore practical and feasible method of putting them in a position where they can reach out for the benefits of reservations. This may help them achieve more cohesiveness. It is here that we see the limited nature of the reforms carried out till now. The economic condition of many of the minority groups has recorded little improvement and this, in many ways, makes them unfit for effective participation. Numerical strength is no panacea but it does appear to be a reasonable placebo.

There is one further point of significance. The minorities including the SCs and STs necessarily depend upon the dominant castes for support. This necessity often compels their traditional leaders to plead the cause of dominant caste candidates for party tickets. In 1983 and 1985 this was quite in evidence. The result once again is that minorities and dominant castes form alliances.

In conclusion, it can be said that Devaraj Urs was the key figure in the rise of the OBCs. He was fortunate in finding an environment favourable to his ideas during his leadership. However, his skills, notwithstanding his stratagem of strengthening the OBCs, were at all times hedged in by limitations. The root of the problem obviously lies in the difficulty which bedevils any attempt to restructure the social base of politics while leaving the economic base more or less untouched. After Urs, a phenomenon of reservations for the dominant castes has developed. The reflection of the report of the KBCC-II is but one pointer in this direction. The fragility of the alliance, when any of the different groups constituting the non-dominant OBCs is visible, has increased more now than was the case during the Urs era. Of crucial importance here is the absence of any meaningful attempt at creating an alliance between the OBCs and the SCs.

The future course of events is likely to be influenced by two developments. The first is the experiment launched by the State Government in developing substantial power to new institutions of local government, namely, the Mandal Panchayats and Zilla Panchayats. The former comprises a group of villages, the latter a district. At both levels there is mandatory quota prescribed for SCs, STs, OBCs and women. Elections to these bodies were held in early 1987. This new framework has the potential to reduce the power of patronage in the hands of ministers. If the Mandal Panchayats and Zilla Panchayats are allowed to function without excessive interference from the State Government, it is possible that some restructuring of the political relationship will occur. The possibility insists that there will be more effective participation by the backward classes. The Janata party can use this as an opportunity to widen its support base especially since the Congress has lost, at least for the moment, its organisational gains.

Finally, four years of Janata governance have slowly led to a feeling of distrust, now being articulated audibly that Hegde lacks the kind of political will which alone can transform a society.

NOTES

1. The following works make important contributions: Duskin (1974), Hetine (1978), Manor (1977), Chandrashekar (1985). Interesting materiel is available in Kannada especially in the memoirs of former civil servants.
2. This point regarding the congruence of concentration of minority OBCs was made by S. Bheemappa, President, Karnataka Backward Classes Federation in an interview on 19 May, 1987.

27

Karnataka Land Reforms

Political-Administrative Dynamics and Economic Change

S.V. DESHPANDE

An attempt is made in this paper to assess Karnataka land reforms in terms of two inter-related issues: Firstly, (a) to look into the underlying political-administrative process involved in the policy implementation; and (b) to analyse the economic change brought about by land reforms policy intervention. These two are inter-linked components, since any economic change which has been effected as a result of policy intervention is partly influenced by macro political-administrative dynamics and *vice versa*.

Conceptually, land reforms should not be identified with the term agrarian reforms. The former has specific contextual reference while the latter has broader connotation. The agrarian reforms may be defined as an integrated programme of measures designed to eliminate obstacles to economic and social development arising out of defects in the agrarian structure.[1] On the other hand, land reforms refer to public programmes that seek to restructure land relationship in such a way that more equitable distribution of income of agrarian wealth takes place.[2] Basically, land reforms is related to questions of land redistribution and tenancy reforms. It involves policy measures such as providing security of tenure, fixation of fair rents and ceiling on ownership of agricultural holding so that surplus land is distributed to landless and marginal farmers. Land reforms involve implementation of two principles: land to the tiller and land to the landless.

Karnataka Land Reforms: Retrospect

In the post-independence era, land reforms in Karnataka may be situated in terms of three historical phases. The first phase consisted of initiation of measures towards abolition of intermediaries implemented in the early and late fifties. The second phase is characterised as steps taken in tenancy reforms: security of tenure, fixation of fair rents and conferment of ownership rights to the eligible tenants. This was initiated in later part of sixties. The third phase corresponds to demands a social justice front which implied activating measures such as complete abolition of tenancy and lowering of land ceiling limits. This was started in the early seventies and continued till the late eighties.

Let us elaborate on each of these:

(A) Abolition of Inams

In Karnataka, inam lands were created during the British colonial rule and those who held such lands were called inamdars. They were intermediary persons. They use to collect land revenue or other levies from cultivators on behalf of the government and paid fixed amounts to the government. There were various classes of such inams: Inams held for personal benefit; inams for religious (Devadaya) and charitable (Dharmadaya) purposes and inams for various services such as irrigation, tank maintenance, village service, artisan service and miscellaneous services.

Such inam lands were predominantly cultivated by tenants and sub-tenants. In some cases, the layers between actual cultivator and owner constituted a long chain. In course of time, there developed a tendency among inam land holders to get settled in nearby cities and their lands were supervised and cultivated by permanent tenants agreed by them. This form of cultivation is called absentee landlordism.

The pleas for abolition of intermediaries and absentee landlordism was made long before Indian independence. However, it gained momentum only in the post-independence period. In Karnataka the legislation to abolish inams was brought about in the mid-fifties. The delay was attributed to the then administrative resistance to abolish inam.[3]

The 1954 legislation abolished various types of inams like personal inams, inam villages known as Kayamgutta villages, inams known as Kodagi and miscellaneous services of inams. In the subsequent year (1955) another act was passed to abolish inams granted to religious and charitable institutions. This was known as Mysore (Religious and Charitable) Inam Abolition Act of 1955.

Among all land reform measures implemented in Karnataka, inam abolition was most successful. This was mainly for two reasons. Firstly, most of the inam holders were absentee landlords and thus their overall position in the rural setting was weak compared to resident proprietors. Secondly, a majority of the inam holders belonged to a social group which was numerically small and many of their tenants were part of dominant castes who were powerful in the then state ruling regimes.

The 1961 Land Reform Act

There were significant political-administrative changes in the latter part of sixties. States of the Indian union were demarcated and the state of Karnataka (then called New Mysore) was constituted comprising five Kannada-speaking areas of Bombay Karnataka, Hyderabad Karnataka, Old Mysore, Coorg and Madras Karnataka. In such a changed context, it was necessity to enact comprehensive land reform legislation. In May, 1957, the State Government appointed a committee under the Chairmanship of B.D. Jatti called the Mysore Tenancy and Agricultural Land Laws Committee. This committee presented its report in September 1957. The Bill was passed in 1961 after the report was examined by a Joint Select Committee of both the Houses. It received the assent of the President of India and became law on 5th March, 1962. However, its operation was delayed till 2nd October, 1965.

Thus there was a long gap of eight years between the presentation of the report and the operation of the land reform legislation: 3 years in the hands of Joint Select Committee and later 3½ years while waiting for the President's assent. The unusual delay was due to "legal and constitutional complexity and bureaucratic foot-dragging at the Central Government level".[4] Firstly, the State Government took time to get certain amendments passed which were put forward by the Central Government. Secondly, the delay was due to the Supreme Court judgement which pronounced soon after the President's assent was accorded. This compelled the state to wait till the centre carried out the constitutional amendment. In the intervening period, the state had thought of a few changes which were put into the detailed legislation. Finally the Act came into force only on 2nd October, 1965.

There were some positive provisions in the 1961 Land Reforms Act. It was first time that an act recommended banning the leases. It declared all non-resumable land to be vested in the government and to be handed over to the tenants who were cultivating those lands. The law determined that rent payable under leases would be 25 per cent in case of assured irrigation and 20 per cent for non-irrigated lands. Thus, rents were regulated. For the first time, ceiling was imposed on the ownership of agricultural holding. The ceiling for each family was 27 standard acres. The term standard acre referred to one acre of first class irrigated land. The family was defined by kinship relationships among its members and included the spouse and dependent children and grand children. Each standard acre was made equivalent to 8 acres of dry land. The dry land was defined as land which received rainfall less than 25" per year.

However, these positive aspects were considerably diluted in the actual implementation process mainly due to the serious loopholes which were in-built in the legislation itself. For instance, though the act banned leases, it allowed exemptions to numerous categories. The exemptions for Defence Forces and Merchant Navy were justified to some extent but exemptions for legal minors (persons less than 18 years old), widows, unmarried women, persons suffering from physical and mental disability and small holders gave ample scope for manipulations. They could still resort to leasing in the name of exempted categories. This is what actually happened in the implementation of the 1961 Act.

Similarly, the law allowed resumption (the withdrawal of land given on lease) of tenanted land in case of landlords willing to resort for personal cultivation. Thus, the law distinguished two types of tenanted lands: resumable and non-resumable. The former permitted landlords to take lands for personal cultivation and the latter entitled tenants to claim ownership rights. The tribunal appointed for the purpose had to first decide the provision for resumable land and the remaining non-resumable had to be handed over to the concerned tenants. This was a highly complicated procedure. The tribunal received nearly 1 lakh resumable applications from the land owners and it became unmanageable to them to dispose off those applications.[5]

Another outcome of such a provision was that large scale evictions resorted to by the landowners. The growth of agricultural labourers during this time in Karnataka was mainly due to many tenants becoming agricultural labourers.[6]

Finally, the ceiling on agricultural holding was extraordinarily liberal. For instance, a family of five persons could own as much as 216 acres of dry land and a family of ten could own 432 acres. The 27 standard acres in case of assured irrigation was also on a higher side. In most cases whatever surplus land thus became available could not be distributed as it was trapped in litigation. Ceiling exemptions allowed for plantations and sugar factories made ceiling legislations almost ineffective. To illustrate, it may be mentioned that in 1971 one sugar factory was permitted to retain 25,000 acres of sugarcane land on the basis that its total requirement was one and half lakh acres.[7]

The failure of the 1961 Act may be also attributed to the nature of the state ruling regime during that time. The state power structure was dominated by dominant castes who predominantly shared landed interests. Though there was occupational differentiation within these castes, many who held political positions belonged to the landed elite. Those who did not hold political positions acted as pressure groups both in law-making and implementation activities. The exercise of their influence is reflected in some of the provisions of the 1951 Act, namely, the resumptions allowed on tenanted land, exemption granted to various categories and more importantly extraordinary higher ceiling limits. These loopholes in a way primarily contributed for the ineffectiveness of the 1961 Act in Karnataka.

The Changed Political Context

The early seventies marked some important change both at the national level and in Karnataka. At national level, there was shift in the development strategy from the perspective of growth combined with distributive justice. This was mainly due to the increasing trend of poverty levels both in urban and rural areas. The growth benefits did not percolate to bottomline in improving the living standards of the bulk of the Indian masses. The World Bank also pointed out that issues like poverty need separate attention. It could no longer be tackled as part of achieving growth perspective.

This macro level shift in the development approach influenced state policy processes and Karnataka was not an exception. Besides, political processes in Karnataka underwent marked changes. The non-dominant under-privileged social groups came to be represented in larger numbers in Karnataka state politics; and as a result the dominance of dominant castes was to some extent mitigated. Devaraj Urs (then Chief Minister of Karnataka) was instrumental in bringing about this political change. He cutting across caste and class lines and mobilised weaker sections through raising issues connected with social justice.

It was against this backdrop of change in the perspective in development strategy and changed political situation that the 1961 Karnataka Land Reforms Act was taken for revision. The national guidelines which were formulated at the Centre also provided impetus for such a revision.

The 1961 Act was drastically amended leading to initiation of a new Act, namely, Land Reforms Amendment Act of 1974. This Act makes a radical departure from the original Act and its effects on the agrarian structure was so persuasive that the 1974 Act constituted virtually a new law.[8]

The 1974 Land Reforms Amendment Act

The fundamental change brought about by the 1974 Act was that no one except soldiers and seamen could lease out land. The earlier resumption allowed to certain categories was cancelled. The law also gave no scope to appropriate the yield without doing any personal cultivation. Abolition was complete and made no concession.

The act corrected some of the loopholes inherent in the 1961 Act. For instance, it defined the term personal cultivation in clear terms to refer to cultivation of land by one's own labour or by the labour of any member of one's own family or by servants or hired labour. Though it permitted hired labour, the payment of wages had to be in cash or kind but not in crop share. The right of resumption was completely eliminated and not merely restricted as in the previous law.

The ceiling provisions were clear and not bogged down by ambiguity. It substantiated earlier concept of standard acre by the term unit. One unit was, one acre of land of the highest value. The ceiling limit was 10 units to each family. There were differential ceiling limits imposed on various categories of land; the differentiation was mainly in terms of type of crops grown (paddy or other crops) and source of irrigation. In case of dry land, a family could own maximum of 54 acres of land.

The 1974 Act constituted land tribunals in each taluk of the state which had been empowered with final authority to implement land reforms provisions. The tenants who had leased-in land (as on March 1974) had to apply before the land tribunals for the conferment of ownership rights. Those landowners who owned land above the ceiling limit were required to file declarations before the land tribunal. The tribunal was supposed to decide the surplus land (if any) that existed in the declaration filed by the landowners. The land tribunal consisted of four non-official members and a chairman who was official equivalent to the rank of Assistant Commissioner of the sub-division in the district. The four non-official members were expected to have on-spot knowledge about the kind of land relationships that existed in the given area. The Chairman's main function was to regulate the proceedings within the framework of the rules as embodied in the Act. Thus the imposition of land tribunals embodied the principle of official and non-official participation in the administrative decision-making process.

The land tribunal was a kind of quasi-judicial body and decisions were arrived at by cross-examination of the parties concerned and verification of written records. The tribunal decisions were final; it could be challenged only in the High Court and later by District Appellate Authority appointed for that purpose. The District Appellate Authority was constituted at a later stage as to facilitate the aggrieved parties to file petitions at the district level instead of at the state.

Implementation Review

Land tribunals all over the state received some 7,55,000 tenancy applications. All except 1,000 applications and more were disposed by the tribunals. The maximum number of applications were received in Dakshina Kannada district (1 lakh 76 thousand), followed by Uttara Kannada (98,976), Kodagu (3,760), and Chitradurga (7,452) received the lowest number of applications. This was due to the fact that in the pre-reforms period the magnitude of tenancy was highest in the coastal area of Karnataka and lowest in the old Mysore regions (Table 27.1).

Table 27.1: Incidence of Tenancy in Karnataka

Region	*Total holding*		*Total tenanted holding*		*Percentage of tenanted holding*	
Southern Region						
Bangalore	240708	448679	12184	12642	05.1	02.8
Bellary	127834	553151	7504	23861	05.9	04.3
Chikmagalur	91967	248781	7515	10382	08.2	04.2
Chitradurga	177348	705808	2620	6715	01.5	01.0
Kodagu	36786	136258	530	891	01.4	00.6
Hassan	166658	359933	5769	5052	03.5	01.4
Kolar	209342	394044	14078	10510	06.2	02.7
Mandya	215805	294636	4218	3829	02.0	01.3
Mysore	271912	513801	9720	10102	03.6	02.0
Tumkur	285330	613522	4769	7070	01.7	01.2
Northern Region						
Belgaum	198345	971532	47511	114066	15.9	11.8
Bidar	87644	479356	2446	9089	02.8	01.9
Bijapur	247440	1454578	24353	118802	09.8	08.2
Dharwad	268577	1128661	49021	162093	18.2	14.4
Gulbarga	212682	1263243	22592	110533	10.6	08.7
Malnad Region						
Uttara Kannada	106217	147785	72456	64057	68.2	43.3
Shimoga	147234	326614	31688	43727	21.5	13.4
Dakshina Kannada	129881	205915	70591	89794	54.4	43.6
Total	**3551230**	**11367825**	**397642**	**835109**	**11.2**	**07.3**

It may be seen that 43.3 and 43.6 percentage of area was tenanted in Uttara Kannada and Dakshina Kannada respectively. The extent of tenanted area coming under northern Karnataka comes in the middle and thus tenancy applications received in this region were in between these two extremes. Pertinent question would be: how many tenants were granted ownership rights among total applications disposed off by the tribunals (i.e., successful applications). Table 27.2 indicates the details about successful tenant applications. Some 60 per cent tenants were granted ownership rights in the state.

Table 27.2: Proportion of Successful Applicants to Total Disposals

	No. of applications received	*No. of applications disposed*	*No. of successful applications*	*Proportion of successful applications*
Southern Region				
Bangalore	7452	7389	2544	34.42
Bellary	18066	17914	6618	36.94
Chikmagalur	50626	50586	21781	43.05
Chitradurga	36692	36439	20767	56.82
Kodagu	14309	13904	5532	39.78
Hassan	14833	14822	8263	55.74
Kolar	19533	19483	11132	57.13
Mandya	24669	24669	12776	51.78
Mysore	29326	29326	13882	47.33
Tumkur	3760	3748	1052	28.06
Northern Region				
Belgaum	41597	41597	24291	58.42
Bidar	21754	21754	4796	22.04
Bijapur	61265	61265	10933	17.84
Dharwad	70300	70300	51042	72.60
Gulbarga	6091	6083	1647	27.07
Malnad Region				
Uttara Kannada	176237	176115	136881	77.72
Shimoga	98976	98944	80975	81.70
Dakshina Kannada	59568	59568	33149	49.75
Total	**755054**	**753882**	**448061**	**59.43**

The highest number of successful tenant applications were found in Uttara Kannada (81.8) followed by Dakshina Kannada (77.7). Gulbarga (18 per cent) and Raichur (22 per cent) had the lowest number of successful tenants' applications. Thus, the coastal region recorded highest number of successful tenant applications, while northern part of Karnataka recorded the lowest number. There have been three underlying reasons responsible for each differential performances in these two regions. Firstly, the maintenance of record of rights (which served the basis for arriving at decisions on tenant applicants) was not satisfactory in northern part while this was relatively better in the coastal regions.

Secondly, the functioning of tribunals was facilitated in the coastal, while the same could not hold true in the northern region. Finally, the coastal part was characterised by existence of tenant organisations while it was almost absent in the northern part of Karnataka.

Ceiling Implementation

Table 27.3 details about the implementation of ceiling legislation.

Table 27.3: Ceiling Implementation

1.	Total number of declarations received	142,400
2.	Average extent per declaration (in acres)	50
3.	Number of surplus holders	9,362
4.	Area covered under surplus land (in acres)	202,078
5.	Percentage of surplus cases to total declarants	6.5

Some, 1,42,400 landowners filed ceiling declarations. The extent of average area per declarant yielded 50 acres. Only 9,362 landowners were declared as surplus holders yielding 2,82,078 surplus land. This means that only 6.5 per cent were declared as surplus holders to the total declarations filed. The extent of surplus land yielded was marginal to the total extent of area covered by total declarations filed.

Thus, ceiling legislation made little impact on changing the skewed land ownership pattern, prevalent especially in the northern part. Benams transfers, partition of lands, ineffective maintenance of record of rights and collusion of landowners with the concerned authorities were cited as the main reasons.

Land Reforms *vis-a-vis* Economic Change

The first visible change that has been brought about by land reforms is with respect to change in the form of cultivation. Tenancy was practised as the predominant form of cultivation. It was exploitative in nature as those who actually cultivated the land could not secure due share of their labour in the production process. There was also the problem of insecurity and tenure as many of the inferior tenants used to get evicted from the land they cultivated.

Land reforms by abolishing tenancy has changed land relationships. Tenancy was replaced by what may be referred to as self-proprietorship—the owners either themselves cultivating their own land or their family members participating in the cultivation process; sometimes they employed some hired labour on cash/kind basis.

In the pre-land reforms situation tenants were categorised as superior and inferior tenants depending upon their socio-economic situation prevailing in the countryside. Who among these have been benefited as a result of land reforms implementation? Narender Pani has argued that superior tenants who earlier owned some portion of land have been benefited.[9] However, this is applicable only to some parts of northern Karnataka. In contrast, in the coastal part of Karnataka (where the largest number of tenants were granted ownership rights) were conferred small plots of land averaging 1 acre of land. This included homestead lands as well. In the old Mysore region tenancy was not the predominant form of cultivation and those who were granted ownership rights acquired land ranging from 2-5 acres.

This is one dimension of change that has been brought about as a result of land reform implementation. The other dimension is to look into the actual economic change that can be seen in the livelihood of tenant beneficiaries and surplus land allottees. The author has studied this issue in the context of selected districts: Dakshina Kannada and Gulbarga: tenant beneficiaries in the former district and surplus land allottees in the latter.[10]

Tenant Owners: Below 2 Acres

In the pre-land reforms period, those who tenanted 2 acres of land were below subsistence farmers. Because, they had to part with the agricultural produce as rent to the landlord which alienated more than half of their produce. In addition they were required to pay tributes in the form of coconuts or vegetable, etc. But more importantly, they were required to provide free labour to the landlords for specified man-days in a year. The homestead dwellings where they lived belonged to the landlords and at any time they could be evicted.

All this was changed in the post-land reforms period. They became owners of the tenanted land. They had been liberated from payment of rent besides providing unpaid labour. More importantly they became owners of the homestead sites. All these conditions raised them to the status of subsistence farmers from below subsistence level. However, they still continued to maintain themselves at the level of subsistence because what the land could produce for them was meagre. It could sustain the family for a period of five to six months. For the rest of the period they had to maintain themselves either by working as casual or agricultural labour or some members working in other occupations like beedi-rolling or construction workers.

Tenanting 2-5 Acres

Peasants, tenanting 2-5 acres of land earlier, could be described as poor peasants. They were poor because these peasants not only cultivated their tenanted land but more than half of their income depended upon agricultural labour. They were also sharing half of the produce as rent to their landlords besides providing unpaid labour to their landlords for specified man-days.

In the post-land reforms period, they become middle peasants. Because, these peasants improved the condition of their land and they produced more than one crop. It has been observed that some peasants even acquired irrigation facility by which they are grew commercial crops like cotton, sugarcane, cashewnuts and arecanuts, etc. It is because of these changes that these peasants have ceased to work as agricultural labourers any more and cultivate land with their own family members.

Tenanting 5 Acres and Above

As to the tenant beneficiaries belonging to 5 acres and above the improvement is more than the size class (2-5). This was in respect of a small surplus available for market, better education for children, more diversified pursuit of occupation within the family (secondary and territory sectors) and markedly better housing conditions. Though not quite, they may perhaps be described as rich peasants.

Ceiling legislation did not fundamentally alter the economic status of surplus land allottees. The present author interviewed some of the surplus land allottees in the selected district

(Gulbarga). He found out that there had been some marginal change in raising the economic status of the allottees. They have been elevated from the status of landless to the status of marginal and in some cases small farmers. However, their main problem is to meet the cost of cultivation of land which they acquired. They said that the government had not taken any follow up measures like providing institutional credit and land development packages so that land may become viable for cultivation.

Summing Up

Among all land reform measures implemented in Karnataka, inam abolition was most successful. This was mainly because of the favourable regime responsiveness to implement inam abolition. There is differential achievement with reference to tenancy implementation. In coastal Karnataka tenants acquired small plots of land and many of them became at least subsistence and poor peasants. On the average they obtained 1 acre of land. In northern part of Karnataka, many of the tenants were superior tenants; they were also landlords and as a result of tenancy implementation they acquired additional land. Most of the peasants in southern part of Karnataka were peasant proprietors; thus tenancy legislation had little impact in the region.

The ceiling implementation did not bring any substantive change in the pattern of skewed distribution. Hardly, 6 per cent were declared as surplus holders to the total land declarations filed by the landowners.

In a comparative perspective, Karnataka land reforms achievement is in between the most successful achievement state like West Bengal and the most failure land reform states like Uttara Pradesh and Bihar. It is characterised as moderate performance achievement state. Atul Kohli sums up the post-land reforms situation[11] as (1) reform policies in Karnataka were not aimed at securing the redistribution of surplus land; (2) given the size of the tenancy problem, the achievement is not so significant; (3) those who lost land were not well entrenched land owners; and (4) the beneficiaries of reforms were not always and not even the rural poor.

NOTES

1. Inayatullah, (Ed.), *Land Reforms: Some Asian Experiences,* APDAC, Kaulaumpur, 1980.
2. *Ibid.*, p. 4.
3. Thimmaiah and Abdul Aziz are of the opinion that "there was evidence to say that large numbers of inam holders, who had migrated to towns and cities had taken up jobs in the service sectors". Hence, there was bureaucratic resistance to implement inam abolition.
   Thimmaiah and Abdul Aziz, *Political Economy of Land Reforms,* New Delhi, Ashish Publishing House, 1984, p. 51.
4. Rajan, M.A.S., *Land Reforms in Karnataka: An Account by a Participant Observer,* New Delhi, Hindustan Publishing House, 1986, p. 20.
5. *Ibid.*, p. 23.
6. Narender Pani, *Reforms to Preempt Change: Land Legislation in Karnataka,* New Delhi, Concept Publishing House, 1983, p. 2.
7. Rajan, M.A.S., op. cit., p. 20.
8. Narender Pani says that the 1974 Amendment Act is radical in nature. However, this should be understood in the relative context. The radical nature of the amendment act must be seen in relation to earlier original 1961 land reform legislation. The 1961 did not abolish tenancy altogether, but its amendment act did it. Besides, the ceiling limits on agricultural holding was considerably lowered in amendment act which was not the case in original legislation.
9. Narender Pani, op. cit.
10. The analysis relating to land reforms *vis-a-vis* economic change is taken from author's doctoral dissertation entitled, *Administering Land Reforms in Karnataka: A Case Study of Two Districts.* As part of this work, two district case studies: Gulbarga and Dakshina Kannada have been selected on the basis of contrasting differential land reforms performances.
11. Atul Kohli, *State and Poverty in India,* Cambridge, Cambridge University Press, 1986, p. 2.

28

The Press and State Politics

K.V. NAGARAJ

Before independence, the nationalist press in Kannada-speaking areas had focussed only on one issue, i.e., political freedom. The pre-independence obsession with politics continued to be the hallmark of Karnataka press till the end of the twentieth century. Because, journalism was considered one of the means to achieve political goals. Besides, many politicians were journalists before independence and many journalists became politicians.

True, the political struggle of almost a century brought independence and transition of power from the British to the Indians was smooth. The Indian-owned English press and the Indian language press gloated over their role and achievement in the struggle for national freedom. Yet the country had to complete the real task of unification as many states remained outside the Indian Union.

For instance, the princely states like Travancore, Mysore, and Hyderabad continued to be ruled by their Maharajas and the press in these states still had the mission of supporting the political struggle for their unification with the Indian Union. The Kannada press in particular found that its struggle was incomplete since the Mysore state had not opted for a popular government yet and the Maharaja continued to administer the state under the guidance of the then Dewan, Arcot Ramaswamy Mudaliyar. As the Maharaja did not show even a semblance of inclination for a negotiated settlement of the issue, the Mysore State Congress announced its decision to launch a mass movement to achieve its avowed objective and the entire

Kannada press, both inside the Mysore state and outside, offered an unqualified support to the struggle.

As was its usual wont, the state administration resorted to repressive measures to curb the press as well as the Congress movement. Pre-censorship was imposed by the promulgation of the Press Emergency Act of August 31, 1947. Some prominent citizens mediated between the press and the Maharaja and as a result, newspapers in the state generally agreed to spare the Maharaja and his family from criticism, though a few of them including the **Samyukta Karnataka**, the **Deshabandhu** and the **Pouravani** voiced their dissent. As a sequel, both the **Samyukta Karnataka** and the **Pouravani** were banned. Many journalists who had backed the popular movement found out a technique of publishing irregular newspapers under different titles to evade the ban and succeeded in disseminating the news of the struggle to the reading public, much to the chagrin of the government.

P. Sheshappa was one such daring journalist. He and his band of scribes published such an irregular venture, the Dhikkara which carried a joint declaration thus:

> Whereas the government of Mysore as a part of its repressive measures to put down the People's Movement for the establishment of responsible Government struck the first blow on the freedom of the PRESS, by imposing pre-censorship on certain newspapers in Bangalore and whereas, to further gag all independent expression of public opinion, the same government responsible to none but itself, promulgated—as from 1-9-47—an obnoxious Act called the Mysore Newspapers (Emergency) Act, 1947. Whereby a ban is imposed on the publication of any newspaper other than those prepared to bolster the present irresponsible regime.
>
> Now, therefore, in vindication of the Freedom of Press and in vindication of the People's Demand for the overthrow of the present irresponsible and autocratic government and for the establishment of a government of the People, by the People, for the People—We, the undersigned journalists of Mysore, do hereby make a public affirmation that we are, jointly and severally, the editors of the "DHIKKARA", that we are jointly and severally, publishers of same "DHIKKARA".

We further declare that our sole object in so doing is to defy the provisions of the obnoxious Mysore Newspapers (Emergency) Act, 1947 and hereby:

1. To vindicate the Freedom of the Press and the Freedom of the opinion, and
2. To uphold the people's demand for the establishment of a popular and Responsible Government.

In witness whereof, we have, each one of us, set our hand hereto on this twenty-second day of September, Nineteen hundred and Forty-seven.

P. Sheshappa, M.A. Sham Iyengar, R.S. Narayan, M.S. Chintamani.

In order to escape the ban, the **Pouravani** of H.S. Doreswamy shifted the publication to Hindupur, and the publication appeared there on September 19, 1947, under a different title, the **Pouraveeravani**. The paper returned to Bangalore when the Maharaja accepted the popular demand. The **Kesari** of R.S. Narayan and the **Janatha** of A. Keshav were similar publications from Bangalore supporting the popular cause.

The Newsprint Control (No. 3) Order, 1947, was another step to curb the press. Most of the journalists considered it a blatant transgression of their freedom and as such anathema to a free society, for it prescribed that journalists and newsprint sellers should submit statistics of stock and disbursement of newsprint to the Controller of Newsprint. The order evoked strong protests resulting in the ban of several newspapers. Authorities had to bow to the pressure of public opinion following a satyagraha by the scribes, which ended on October 15, 1947, when the government assured them to rescind the harsh provisions of the order. Subsequently, in tune with the assurance given, a revised order was issued on November 4.

The popular agitation for a responsible government became vociferous and ultimately, the Maharaja had to concede the demand and make way for the establishment of a representative and democratic government. The **Mysoorina Mahakranthi** was one such publication that fought for the cause of popular government. Mention must also be made of the **Jagriti**, a political weekly published by Kamala Devi Chattopadhyaya in Mumbai in 1947 for the Karnataka Newspapers and Publications Limited. The weekly supported the movement as an organ of the Socialist Party. The first editor, Sasahitlu Venkata Rao after two months of its launch was succeeded by Khadri Shamanna. It was shifted from Dharwad to Bangalore, where its writings incurred the displeasure of the government of the day. Unable to pay a security deposit of Rs. 2,000/-, the **Jagriti** went into wilderness. As a matter of fact, it was one of the few newspapers to oppose the Congress party and support the socialist group under the leadership of Ram Manohar Lohia and Jayaprakash Narayan who differed with the economic and foreign policies of the then Prime Minister, Pandit Jawaharlal Nehru.

New Ventures

With the dawn of independence, and the establishment of a responsible government, the journalistic scene in Mysore in particular and Karnataka in general turned conducive for the growth of daily newspapers. The nationalistic outlook of journalists metamorphosed into commercial benefits with the arrival of a new band of proprietors who considered newspapers both an industry and a business. The emergence of new monopoly houses in journalism was on cards. In the Mysore state the first signs of change were visible when the then Dewan Arcot Ramaswamy Mudaliyar persuaded two excise contractors, K.N. Guruswamy and K. Venkataswamy to start a tabloid English daily, the **Deccan Herald** in 1947 at Bangalore with the versatile Pothan Joseph as its editor. There was no good daily newspaper in Kannada in the state except the **Tainadu**, these business magnates realised the need for a Kannada daily that could reach the vast masses of readers. As a result, the **Prajavani** was launched in October 1948, borrowing the name of a weekly that existed in Mysore in 1940 under the Editorship of G.S. Krishna Rao. The new daily was a great success as it catered to the changing taste of readers.

The initial euphoria of achieving the long cherished goal of political freedom gradually gave way to the realism of national reconstruction. No longer did the reader look for political stories of the type of yesteryears. The new political and economic institutions demanded a new type of journalism and the old stalwarts had either to adjust and adopt themselves to the new environ or get relegated to the background. Several newspapers of such type were rejected outright by the readers following the entrance of the **Prajavani** on the scene. The **Vishwa Karnataka,** the **Desha Bandhu** and others folded and the **Tainadu** was affected.

The responsible government which came into being had its own skirmish with the press. K.C. Reddy, the first Chief Minister of Mysore, ran into difficulties. The press by all accounts played the role of a constructive opposition. Never did it play to the gallery of the Congressmen. The establishment of the **Prajavani** created many landmarks in Kannada journalism. The attractive emoluments offered by its proprietors lured the cream of the talent available in the profession. It directly launched the trend of improvement in the pay structure for journalists who had not dreamt of getting a good salary earlier. Surely, the motive of a comfortable life ushered in a new trend in Kannada journalism, both in terms of profit and professionalism.

The litmus test for its professionalism came to **Prajavani** when two of its editors, Khadri Shamanna and C.G.K. Reddy participated in the HAL strike and were arrested. These two firebrand journalists were also committed socialists. The newspapers sought their resignations since professional rules expected them not to take active part in trade union activities. Upon their exit, the mantle fell on the then news editor, T.S. Ramachandra Rao. Affectionately called TSR by his fellow professionals, he wrote a popular column, Chhoobana. Known for its wit, humour and satire, the column poked fun at both politics and politicians for almost three decades.

In Karnataka, political developments were not dissimilar from what were happening in the country. Newspapers slowly started exposing the mistakes of the Congress government. For a long time to come, the **Prajavani** remained the torchbearer of dissent.

In north Karnataka, the **Samyukta Karnataka** consolidated its position and continued to support the policies and programmes of the Congress government. Naturally, the Congress government counted on the backing of the press and the initial honeymoon was soon to make for a critical press.

Bickering within the Mysore Congress surfaced when Mudaliyar's tenure as Dewan came to an end in 1949.

K. Hanumanthaiah emerged a strong prospect to replace K.C. Reddy as the Chief Minister. He succeeded in his efforts and became the Chief Minister in March 1952. During his days as Chief Minister the relations between the government and the press were on collision course.

Kengal attempted to clip the influence of various lobbies on the state administration. However, the **Prajavani** group vociferously opposed the policies and programmes of the Chief Minister. The very construction of Vidhana Soudha became a fodder for the rumour mill. On one count, the entire Kannada press was united. That was the unification of Kannada-speaking areas and the formation of united state of Karnataka.

Even other Chief Ministers like B.D. Jatti and S.R. Kanthi every now and then had the press breathing on their neck. Yet another Chief Minister who had a running feud especially with the **Prajavani** group was S. Nijalingappa. The paper did not like Nijalingappa entering into the legislative assembly through by-elections, as he could not win, not even once, in the general elections. His policies were considered retrograde, conservative and against the interests of the state. His prohibition policy also elicited the ire of the excise contractors. The campaign ceased only with his exit.

The national trend of monopoly houses owning newspapers percolated into Karnataka also. The big press in Karnataka was essentially a capitalist press reflecting the character of national newspapers. In a way the nexus between politicians and the industrialists was responsible for it. The stint of Kadidal Manjappa as Chief Minister was too brief and after three months, S. Nijalingappa replaced him. Political compulsions forced him out of office in May, 1958. He returned to power in 1962 and once again the local press was up-in-arms against him. Nijalingappa sought the help of Ramanath Goenka and as a result, the Bangalore edition of the **Indian Express** commenced its publication in 1967. The hold of dominant newspapers was challenged in 1967 with the arrival of **Kannada Prabha,** a publication of the Express group. The battle of wits among newspapers of the state raged with the Bangalore edition of **Samyukta Karnataka** trying to have its portion of the cake.

The split in the Congress party at the historic Bangalore session and the socialist leanings of Mrs. Gandhi divided the press, but still the mainstream press was sceptical of intentions. The political defections and the unceremonious removal of Virendra Patil raised many ethical questions. The mid-term elections forced by Mrs. Gandhi also raised debates on countervailing issues.

The Chief Ministership of Devaraj Urs saw the press softening its stand on the government. The 1970s also saw the issue of the press being controlled by the upper castes. This was raised in both political and social circles. This was the period of arrival of political scandal sheets. The worst period of Karnataka journalism was the period of emergency. Except for a few underground publications, most major newspapers exhibited a lackadaisical attitude towards the suspension of civil liberties and fundamental rights and also the imposition of censorship, a blot on the history of journalism in the country. When political liberty was restored in 1977, a few of them turned extremely hostile to the Congress dispensation. The publications that led such papers were the **Indian Express** and the **Kannada Prabha**. The other publications opted for the middle path of an issue based on support or criticism. The installation of the Janata government at the Centre and the Congress State government created a plethora of issues to the delight of the press. The resurrection of Mrs. Gandhi from Chikmagalur, her return to power, the ouster of Devaraj Urs from Chief Ministership and also the subsequent events brought a clear division in the press as anti- and pro-Congress. The Chief Ministership of R. Gundu Rao saw the press-government relation reach a new low. The attack on two leading newspapers houses, the **Deccan Herald** and the **Indian Express**, culminated in becoming a national issue. The installation of the first non-Congress government under the Chief Ministership of Ramakrishna Hegde mitigated the anti-establishment sentiments of the press. His close association with several journalists and their advisory role in state politics and politics brought a new dimension to the press-politician relationship. The legislative council also saw journalists becoming its members.

The campaign against Hegde in the famous Revajeethu case by a section of the press resulted in his resignation. Thereafter, though the love-hate relationship between the press and politicians continued, the influence of journalists on state politics became blatantly visible. Image-building through the press became an obsession for many a politician. Politicians belonging all types of dispensations do their utmost to cultivate the press. Favours are also distributed to those who are pliable.

To the credit of the press in Karnataka, it must be accepted that it played quite often the role of a responsible opposition to the powers-that-be. Investigative stories, crusades and biting editorials and columns made the ruling class cautions. However, the obsession with politics has not dwindled despite developments in the other fields. Still it occupies a larger chunk of newspaper space. A slight change first appeared during the period of emergency (1975-77) in the contents as far as political news was censored. The second event of change appeared in 1990s with the introduction of economic reforms. Contents pertaining to technology, sports, economics and fashion have also become prominent. Yet elections, ministry-making and political party affairs get precedence over others.

The Fourth Estate is slowly making inroads into the political structure of the polity thus redefining the principle of separation of powers. The arrival of electronic media especially the private television channels has changed the scenario. More than the press, the electronic media have become attractive to politicians. On an overall assessment, it appears that the Karnataka press has lost its spirit to crusade and to keep politicians in check, a sad comment indeed !

Index

1857 War of Liberation 2
20-Point Programme 113
73rd and Constitutional Amendment Acts 172–75, 193

Abbey Falls 389
Abolition of Inams 415
Abolition of Intermediaries 415
Adjournment Motion 83
Administrative Reforms Commission 225
Administrative Reforms Division 147, 156
Administrative Research 15
Advani, L.K. 391
Agricultural Extension Officer 12
Agricultural Marketing Department 255
Agricultural Policy of Karnataka 324
AIDs
Prevention of 117
Private Member Bill on Prevention of 116
Akhand Karnataka Rajya Nirman Parishat 37
Alexandar, P.C. 156
All India Anna Dravida Munnetra Kazhagam (AIADMK) 241, 340
All India Services 9
All Karnataka State Formation Conference 37
Ambedkar, Dr. 299
Andhra Pradesh Panchyat Raj Act 193
Anti-Social Elements 351
Appiko Chalavali 316
Arabian Sea 22
Arcot Ramaswamy Mudaliyar 428
Arms Act of India 380
Arthasastra 94–95
Arunachal Pradesh Panchyat Raj Ordinance 194
Ashok Mehta Committee 193
Assam Panchyat Raj Act 194

Baba Buden Giri Hills 357
Backward Class Commission 238, 389
Backward Special Group 401
Badagarakeri Cross 385
Bahujan Samaj 260
Bajranga Dal 356
Baliga, B. Vaikunt 73, 77, 79, 90–91
Balwant Rai Mehta Committee 193
Banakar, B.G. 84
Bangalore Challo 391
Bangalore City Corporation 210
Bangalore Development Authority 210
Bangarappa, S. 239, 253, 263, 338
Bannary Amman Factory 317
Basavalingappa, B. 5
Bayaluseema Development Board 215
Bharatiya Janata Party 240, 256, 341
Bidari Kavli Land Struggle 319
Bihar Panchyat Raj Act 193
Bimaru States 225
Block Development Officer 12
Bombay Districts Municipal Act 163
Bombay Municipal Boroughs Act 163
Bombay Presidency 34
Bombay Village Panchayats 194
Bommai, S.R. 45, 62, 238, 253, 265, 339
Border Disputes 54, 116
Bose, Subhas 161
Brass, Paul R. 365
Brecher, Michael 259

British
 Discriminatory 381
 East India Company 206
 Indian Territory 34
 Provincial 55
 Raj in India 207, 312
Buddhism 23
Building Bye-Laws 171

C.H. Hanumanth Rao Committee 193
Calling Attention Notice 81
Cause Courts Act 104
Cauvery
 Agitation 346
 Basin River Projects 299
 Water Dispute 41, 51, 116
Ceiling
 Exemptions 418
 Legislation 425
Central Board of Secondary Education (CBSE) 50
Chaluvali Movement 345
Chamber of Commerce and Industry 242, 296
Changalaraya, K. 62
Chatterji, Sri Bankim Chandra 300
Chief Justice of India 137
Chipko Movement 316
Choudhari, Gen. J.N. 363
Christianity 23
Circuit Courts 95
Citizen-Administration Relations 19
City Improvement Boards 165
City Municipal Corporations 164, 196
City Municipalities Act 162
Civil Disobedience 313
Civil Service Officers 96
Code of Civil Procedure 103
Collective Responsibility, Principle of 4
Commercial Tax Laws 209
Common Civil Code 359–60
Common Intellectual Property 325
Commonwealth Parliamentary Association 79
Communal Issues 349
Communist Party of India 343
Community Development
 Block 12, 209
 Movement 220
 Programme 15, 219
Comptroller & Auditor General of India 120
Confidence-Building Exercise 360
Congress Culture 46
Congress Movement 2, 35
Constitution of India 69, 97, 146, 165, 352
 Obligations 70
Consultative Functions 126
Contempt of Courts 99
Co-operation Law 209
Co-operative Movement 380
Coorg Agricultural Society 382
Coorg National Council 390, 395
Council for Planning 18
Court of Sessions 105
Cow Slaughter 352
Criminal Courts, Powers of 106
Criminal Jurisdiction 95
Criminal Procedure Code 11, 97, 102, 104–06
Cubbon, Mark 379–80
Culture of Constitutionalism 56
Customary Law 94

Dakshina Kannada 23, 316
Dakshina Kannada Jilla Parisaraskti Okkuta 316
Dalit
 Movement 314, 318, 320
 Sangharsh Samiti 242
 Bandaya 318
Das, C.R. 161
Dastur-Ul-Amal 163
Decentralisation and Participation 177
Decentralised Planning 292
Decentralization 192
Delhi Challo 391
Demand for Separate State 361
Department of
 Collegiate Education 218

Personnel and Administrative Reforms 15
Desai, Morarji 46, 62
Desert Development Programme 220
Development Commissioner 8, 147
Dhar Commission 35
Dharmasutras 94
Dharna in Vidhana Soudha 321
Directive Principles of State Policy 165, 352
Disraeli, Benjamin 110
District Administration 10
District Appellate Authority 420
District Development Council 18, 220
District Planning
Approach 291
Committees 18
District Rural Development Societies 220
Districts of Bellary and South Kanara 2
Divisional Commissioner 10
Diwani to Fauzdari 207
Domination of Dominant Community 234
Dominion Government 55
Draft Cabinet Note (DCN) 151
Dry Land Development 221
Dunkel Draft Treaty 322–24
Dvaita, Philosophies of 23

East India Company 162
Ecology Movement 314
Education Guarantee Scheme 301
E-Governance Measures 255
Ekikarana (Unification) Movement 38, 334
Election Commission 121, 260
Electoral Politics, Impact of Language on 342
Electronic City (Bangalore) 28
Emergency 110
Employment
Exchanges 135
Fund 265
Guarantee Scheme 294–95
English Common 98
Environment Action Group 318
Environment Support Group 318
Eve Teasing 355
Expenditure Commission 299
Exploration of Oil and Gas 27

Farmer's Movement 321
Fazal Ali Commission 246
Finance Commission 286
Five Year Plan 11, 17, 296, 300–01
Flag Satyagraha 335
Forest Movement, Enter the 328
Forest Satyagraha 313
Free and Fair Elections 120
Freedom Movement 381
Fundamental Rights 352

G.V.K. Rao Committee 193
Gaddigouda Committee 209
Gandhi, Indira 46, 62, 235, 237, 262, 337–38, 434
Gandhi, Rajiv 46, 62, 166 239, 263
Gandhi, Sanjay 237
Gandhi, Sonia 58
Gandhiji 3, 32, 218
Garibi Hatao (Abolish Poverty) 400
GATT 322, 325
Gav Bhandi to Jal Samadhi 314
Gender Related Development Index 29
Geneva 322
Geography of Karnataka 22
Ghataprabha Right Bank Canal 117
Goenka, Ramanath 433
Gokak Agitation 340, 346
Gokhale 161
Gomal Lands 319
Gopala Gowda 75
Gota Court 95
Government of India Act 162
Government-Controlled Industrial Unit 16
Gowda, D.B. Chandre 83–84
Gowda, G. Vankatai 76
Gowda, H.D. Deve 45, 62, 254, 265
Gowda, H.N. Nanje 80
Gram Panchayats 196

Gram Raj 218
Gram Sabha 174, 176, 179–80, 190
    Working of 185
Gram Swarajya, Idea of 193
Gramasahayaks 13
Gramsevakas 12
Guardians and Wards Act 104
Guddagadu Abhivraddi Samiti 315
Gujarat Panchyat Raj Act 193
Gundappa, D.V. 382
Gutka, Banning of 117

Harial Singh Kharra Committee 193
Harihar Polyfibre Company 315
Harmon Doctrine 54
Harold Macmillan 118
Havanur Commission 401
Havanur, L.G. 236, 400
Hegde, Ramakrishna 19, 48, 62, 252, 264–65, 341, 402
Helsinki Doctrine 54
Herbert Morrison 70
Himachal Pradesh Panchyat Raj Act 194
Hindu Jagruti Manch 356
HIV Prevention Bill 116
Horata, Kasunur 315
Horticulture 218
House of Commons 90
Human Rights of Farmers, Violation of 323
Hundekar Committee 209
Hyderabad Freedom Struggle 363
Hyderabad Karnataka Development Agitation (HKAHS) 375
Hyderabad Karnataka Development Board (HKABD) 367
Hydro-Electric Projects 4
Hydro-Power Plants 27

Idgah Ground Conflict 263, 357
IMF 322
Imperialist Jurisprudence 323
Indian Administrative Service 148, 214, 220
Indian Constitution 4, 7, 14, 72, 397
Indian Lunacy Act 104
Indian National Congress 35–36, 334, 343
Indian National Movement 193
Indian Penal Code 106
Indicator of Development 30
Indo-Gulf Fertiliszer Ltd. 316
Industrial Policy 283
Integrated Rural Development Programme 220, 224
Inter-Group Conflicts 31
Internal Financial Advisor (IFA) 152
International Neem Campaign 325
Inter-Religious Marriage 358
Inter-State Dispute Resolution 51
Inter-State Water Dispute 114
Intra-Party Factionalism 6
Introduction of Economic Reforms 435
IRDP 187, 283
Irrigation Investment Management 290
Irrigation Projects 4
Islam 23

Jail Bharo Agitation 321
Jail Manual 209
Jainism 23
Jaipur Congress Session 36
Janata Government 17
Janata Kranti Ranga 341
Janata Paksha 246
Janata Party Government 18
Jatti, B.D. 5, 62, 234, 416
Jennings, Sir Ivor 70
Jha, L.K. 156
Judicial Magistrate Courts 106
JVP Committee 36

Kalpavriksha 318
Kannada Chaluvali Movements 346
Kannada Chaluvali Vathal Paksha 260, 267, 340–41
Kannada Computer Software 217
Kannada Kranti Ranga 338
Kannada Sahitya
    Parishad 241
    Sammelan 364

Kannada Watchdog Committee 48
Kannada-Speaking
  Areas 44
  Farming Community 52
  People 47, 208
Kantakasodhana Courts 95
Kanthi, R.D. 5
Kanthi, S.R. 5, 73, 76, 90, 234, 249
Karnatak Vidyavardhak Sangh 241
Karnataka Administrative Reforms Commission 225
Karnataka Administrative Service 9–10, 148, 214
Karnataka Backward Classes Commission 236, 400, 402
Karnataka Civil Courts 102
Karnataka Congress Party 246, 254, 260
Karnataka Development Board 215
Karnataka Education Act 155
Karnataka Education Bill 84
Karnataka Ekikarana Movement 2, 233, 336
Karnataka Electricity Board 282
Karnataka Government Secretariat Service 148
Karnataka Kranti Ranga 246
Karnataka Land Reforms 414
Karnataka Legislative
  Assembly Rules 69, 89
  Council 110
  Salaries 111
Karnataka Municipalities Act 164, 165
Karnataka Panchyat Raj Act 193
Karnataka Politics, Impact of Language on 345
Karnataka Power Corporation 282
Karnataka Pradesh Congress Committee (KPCC) 37, 334
Karnataka Public Service Commission 14, 119
Karnataka Rajya Raitha Sangha 260, 321
Karnataka Right of Information Act 302
Karnataka Sarvodaya Mandal 315
Karnataka Slum Clearance Board 165
Karnataka State Housing Board 165
Karnataka Unification 2–3
Karnataka Vidyavardhak Sangh 233
Karnataka Water Supply and Sewerage Board 165
Kashappanavar, S.R. 88
Kazis 96
Keladi Nayaka Royal Family 378
Kengal Hanumanthaiah 63
Kerala Panchyat Raj Act 194
Khalander, Baba Hayat 357
Khariff Crops 26
Kisan Mazdoor Praja Party 343
Kodagu Area 164
Kodagu Rajya Mukti Morcha 390
Kohli, Athul 240
Kondajji Basappa Committee Report 180
Kothavale, S.D. 73, 79
Koujalagi, V.S. 86
Krishna Water Dispute 116
Krishna, S.M. 46, 56, 60, 62, 73, 86, 239, 255, 339, 395
Krisi Marata Vahini 255
Kudremukh National Park 318
Kumar, G. Narayan 345
Kumar, Raj 56
Kumar, Ramesh 86
Kunzru, Pandit H. 37

Land Grab Struggle 320
Land Gram Movement 330
Land Reform Act 12, 416, 419
Land Struggles 319, 329
Language-Policy Evolution 48
Lanudy, Philip 71
Law of Procedure 94
Laxmi Mal Singhvi Committee 193
Leader of Opposition 109–10
Legislative Council 66
Liberation Warriors of Kodagu 390
Lingappa, M. 75
Lingayat
  Community 233
  Ideologues 39
Linguistic Provinces Committee 36

Liquor Bottling Case 252
Local Cess 163
Lohia, Ram Manohar 431
Lok Sevak Sangh 240
Lokayukta Office 20
London Mission 370
Long March 321
Lord Dalhousie 83
Lower Division Clerk 13

Madhya Pradesh Panchyat Raj Act 194
Madras District Municipalities Act 163
Madras Presidency 54, 163
Madras Town Improvement Act 163
Maharaja of Mysore 74
Maharashtra Ekikaran Samiti 241, 340
Maharashtra-Mysore Border Problem 343
Maidan Development Board 292
Malappa, K. 383
Mallamma, Belavadi 2
Mallikarjunaiah, S. 240
Malnad Area Development Board 215, 292
Mandal Panchayats 180, 220
Mangalore City Corporation 169, 172
Manipur Panchyat Raj Act 194
Manjappa, Hardekar 232
Manjappa, Kadidal 5 234
Mannu Rakshanan Koota 315
Manor, James 336
Marginal Farmer and Agricultural Labourer Development 220
Mass Rapid Transit System 298
Mega Industries, Agitation against 316
Mehta, Ferozeshah 161
Menon, V.P. 364
Merton, Robert K. 157
Miller Committee 398
Miller, Leslie 50
Mining, Agitation against 317
Minor Irrigation 221
Moily, Veerappa 62, 253, 263
Movement
against Eco-Development Programme 327
for Social Forestry 314
for Statehood 377
for Unification 233
Mukerjee, Hiren 70
Mukhyasevikas 12
Multi-Party System, Emergence of 254
Municipal Laws 209
Municipalities Act 164
Murthy, U.R. Anantha 48
Muslim Personal Law 359
Mussoorie Academy of Administration 14
Muthanna, I.M. 384
Muttige, Dehali 324
Mysore (Religious and Charitable) Inam Abolition Act 416
Mysore Backward Classes Committee 399
Mysore Chief Court Regulation 96
Mysore Legislative Assembly 343
Mysore Newspapers (Emergency) Act 430
Mysore Public Service Commission 14
Mysore Representative Assembly 213, 215
Mysore Tenancy and Agricultural Land Laws Committe 416
Mysoreans 44

NABARD 385
Nachappa, N.U. 390
Nagan Gowda Committee 230, 399
Nagar Division 312
Nagaraj, Vatal 81, 345
Nagaratnamma, K.S. 81
Nagarika Seva Samiti 316
Nagpur Session 35
Nandy, Ashis 261
Nanjundappa, D.M. 376
Narayan, Jayaprakash 174, 237, 431
Narsimhaiah, H. 48
National Front Government 167

National Human Rights Commission 115
National Movement 231
National Parks 25, 328
National Rural Employment Programme 220
Nauroji, Dadabhoy 161
Nehru Rozgar Yojana 220
Nehru, Jawaharlal 2, 63, 68, 161–62, 431
Netravati Valley 23
New Social Movements 313
Nijalingappa, S. 5, 51, 62, 234, 247
Nirmal Karnataka Project 265
Nizam's Territory 2
Non-Co-operation 313
Non-Tax Agitation 321
Non-Zero-Sum Games 56
Notified Area Committees 164
NSS Data 294

One-Party-Dominant Period 247, 249, 251, 253, 263
Orissa Gram Panchayats 194

P.K. Thungan Committee 193
Page Committee 82
Pakistan Matches 356
Palmer, Norman D. 259
Palya, Munireddy 351
Panchayat Raj
- Acts 193
- Institutions (PRIs) 191, 298, 174, 190, 284, 292, 301
- Women in 194

Panini, M.N. 336
Pannikar, K.M. 37
Paramountcy Doctrine 208
Patel, J.H. 45, 46, 62
Patel, Sardar Vallabhbhai 3, 363
Patel, Vithalbhai 68, 78
Patil, H.K. 110
Patil, K.H. 6, 80
Patil, Veerendra 5–6, 48, 62, 234, 253, 262, 339
Patil, Virendra 434
Peasant Struggle 312
Pensions and Allowances Act 111
People's Global Action 326
Physical Quality of Life Index Based 286
Planning Commission 285
Police Academy 14
Police Laws 209
Political Mobilization 231
Political Sub-System, Emergence of 33
Politics of Federation of Backward Castes 235
Poonacha, C.M. 382, 390
Positive Discrimination, Nature of 397
Post-Colonial Period 312
Post-Land Reforms Period 424
Poverty Alleviation Measures 220, 283
Praja Samyukta Paksha 335
Praja Socialist Party 240
Prajamitra Mandali 50
Prasad, Rajendra 36
Prayer Call 355
Pre-Censorship 429
Presidency Towns 105
Press and State Politics 428
Press Emergency Act 429
Pre-University Education 370
Prevention of Land Alienation Act 319
Private Member 116
Privileges Committee 115
Public Interest Litigation 101
Public Policy Decisions, Implication of 256
Public Service Commission 9, 121, 132–34, 136, 140
Public Service, Functions of 119
Public Works Department 385
Punjab Panchyat Raj Act 194
Puttappa, K.V. 48

Quasi-Federal System 39
Quota System 14

R. Tottenham Committee 156

Radial Railway System 297
Radical Land Reforms Act 236
Rail and Rasta Roko Agitation 321
Raj Kumar Fans Association 241
Rajasthan Panchyat Raj Act 194
Ramaswamy, Dr. Harish 277
Rangacharlu, Dewan 64–65
Ranganath, K.H. 82, 239
Rao, Alur Venkat 39, 246
Rao, Gundu 5–6, 62
Rao, K. Raghavendra 336
Rao, P.V. Narasimha 193, 253, 264
Rao, R. Gundu 237
Razakar Movement 362
Recruitment
    Committees 131
    Process 122–23
    Rules 124
Reddy, C.R. 50
Reddy, K.C. 5, 62, 233 433
Regional Development Policy 291
Regulatory Departments 221
Religious Places
    Conflict over 356
    Procession 350
Representative Assembly 66
Republic Party (Gavi Group) 250
Reservation Policy, Implementation of 201
Reservoir at Kannambadi 54
Resurrection of Powerful Communities 237
Right to Information 304
Road Block Agitation 321
Role of Kannada in Unification 334
Roy, Prannoy 261
Royal Commission 163
Rudrappa, H.S. 73, 75, 90
Rural Development 283
Rural Electrification 26–27, 221
Rural Housing Scheme 295
Rural Industries 221
Rural Information Development Fund (RIDF) 385
Rural Landless Labourer Employment Guarantee Programme 220
SAARC 178
Sadar Court 96
Sangolli Rayanna 2
Secretariat Administration 8
Self-Financing System 296
Sericulture 218
Several Welfare Measures 237
Shadow Cabinet 109
Sharath System 312
Sharavati Projects 4
Shastri, Sandeep 277
Shaw Lefevre 89
Sheshappa, P. 429
Shettageri, T. 385
Shetty, A. Krishna 77
Shetty, K. Jayaram 87
Shivakumar, D.K. 88
Siddaiah, H. 73, 75 90
Siddalingaiah, T. 74
Sidlipur Land Struggle 319
Singh, Dharam 255
Singh, K.P. 167
Singh, V.P. 46, 62
Sivappa, S. 78
Small Farmer Development Agency 220
Social Moral System in Society 299
Socio-Economic Philosophy 262
Speaker
    and Parliamentary Democracy 67
    Election of 68
    Powers and Functions of 71
Special District Commissioner 11
Special Judicial Magistrates 105
Special Marriage Act 104
Srinivas, M.N. 336
Sriramulu, Potti 36
State Legislature 6
States Reorganisation Act 3, 22, 97, 229
States Reorganisation Commission 36, 383
Statutory Moral Order 299
Struggle
    against Eviction 329
    against Rape 320

against Untouchability 320
for Student Hostels 320
Subbaiah, A.K. 340
Subordinate Courts of Criminal Nature 104
Supreme Court 50, 138, 153, 302, 327, 400
Swadhyaya Movements 117
Swamy Ramananda Tirtha 363

Taluka Development Board 12, 220
Taluka Land Tribunals 236
Taluka Panchayats 194
Tamil Nadu Panchyat Raj Act 194
Telugu-Speaking People 34
Tenant Owners 424
Third World Countries 226
Tilak, Lokamanya 44, 161
Timma, L.H. 74
Town Municipal Council 165, 196
Town Panchayats 196
Town Planning Authorities 165
Tribal Struggles 327
Tripura Panchyat Raj Act 194
Two-Tier Panchayat Raj System 220

Unification Movement 2
Uniform Revenue 209
Union Constitution Committees 35
Union-State Relations 18
United Front Government 82
United Kingdom 79
United Opposition 82
United Provinces 207
Upper Krishna Projects 366
Urban Development Policy 297
Urban Local Bodies, Women in 196
Urban Mass Rapid Transit System 297

Urs, Devaraj 3, 5–6, 45, 51, 58, 62, 235, 249, 267, 419
Uttar Pradesh Panchayat (Amendment) Act 194
Uttara Kannada Ulisi Andolana (UKUA) 316

Vadeyaraj, G.P. 82
Vajpayee, A.B. 62, 356
Vankatappa, M.V. 73, 88, 90
Venkappaiah, C.S. 382
Venkat Swamy Commission 238
Venkatappa, V. 73–74, 90
Venkataswami, T. 402
Vibrant Kannada Literature, Emergence of 233
Vidhana Soudha 63
Vigilance Commission 9
Vijayanagar Administration 95
Vijayangar Empire 43
Village
Accountant 13
Panchayat 175
Vishvesariah, M. 4, 16–17, 50
Vishwa Hindu Parishad 356
Vokkaliga Dominance 400

Waldo, L.D. Wight 146
Warabandi System 26
Warranto, Quo 100
Welfare Department 218
West Bengal Panchayat (Amendment) Act 194
WHO 284
Wild Life Sanctuaries 25
Wilding, Norman 71
Wodeyar, Chamarajendra 64
Women Education 372
World Bank 322, 328
World Farmers Campaign 325
WTO 326

Yelahanka Thermal Power Stations 27
Yellow Cards 265
Youth Services and Sports 221

Zero Hour 81, 112
Zero Sum Approach 52
Zilla Panchayat 176, 187–88, 190, 196, 221, 223–24, 227, 413
Zilla Parishads 221, 237, 390